D1438717

Educational and Developmental Aspects of Deafness

Educational
and
Developmental Aspects
of
Deafness

Donald F. Moores
Kathryn P. Meadow-Orlans

Editors

Gallaudet University Press
Washington, D.C.

Gallaudet University Press, Washington, DC 20002
© 1990 by Gallaudet University. All rights reserved
Published 1990
Printed in the United States of America

Library of Congress Cataloging-in Publication Data
Educational and developmental aspects of deafness / Donald F. Moores, Kathryn P. Meadow-Orlans, editors.
    p.   cm.
    Includes bibliographical references and indexes.
    ISBN 0-930323-52-1
    1. Deaf—United States—Education.   2. Children, Deaf—Psychology.
I. Moores, Donald F.   II. Meadow-Orlans, Kathryn P.
HV2430.E383   1990
371.91'2—dc20   90-14014
                                                     CIP

Contents

Contributors

LYNNE BLENNERHASSETT, Ph.D., is associate professor of psychology at Gallaudet University. She is a former school psychologist at the Kendall Demonstration Elementary School for the Deaf.

BRIAN CERNEY, M.A., is a research associate at the Center for Studies in Education and Human Development at Gallaudet University. He is a former instructor in the Gallaudet University English Department.

DAVID DEYO is a certified audiologist and research associate at the Center for Studies in Education and Human Development at Gallaudet University. He is a former audiologist at the Kendall Demonstration Elementary School.

BIRGIT DYSSEGAARD, Ph.D., is director of special education, County of Copenhagen, Denmark. From 1981 to 1983 she was a visiting scholar in the Gallaudet Research Institute, where she collaborated on a comparative study of deaf children in Denmark and the United States.

CAROL ERTING, Ph.D., is a professor in the Gallaudet University Department of Linguistics and Interpreting. She is a former research scientist with the Center for Studies in Education and Human Development and now is director of the Culture and Communication Studies Program in the Gallaudet Research Institute.

CAROLYN EWOLDT, Ed.D., is Graduate Program Director of the Faculty of Education at York University. She is a former research scientist with the Center for Studies in Education and Human Development at Gallaudet University.

MILO GARCIA, B.A., is a research technician at the Center for Studies in Education and Human Development at Gallaudet University. He is currently a graduate student in the University of the District of Columbia Department of Psychology.

MARK T. GREENBERG, Ph.D., is a professor in the Department of Psychology at the University of Washington. He has written extensively about deaf children and their families and has developed the PATHS (Providing Alternative Thinking Strategies) curriculum.

NATALIE GRINDSTAFF, B.A., is a research assistant at the Center for Studies in Education and Human Development at Gallaudet University. She is currently a graduate student in the Gallaudet University Department of Linguistics and Interpreting.

MARY K. GUTFREUND, Ph.D., is a research associate with the Educational Research Unit at the University of Bristol (England). She is coauthor, with Gordon Wells, of the Bristol Language Scales Manual. She was a visiting scholar at the Center for Studies in Education and Human Development at Gallaudet University, where she collaborated on studies of mother-infant dialogue.

LEONARD P. KELLY, Ph.D., is a research scientist at the Center for Studies in Education and Human Development at Gallaudet University. He is a former evaluator in the Instructional Development and Evaluation Center at Gallaudet University.

THOMAS N. KLUWIN, Ph.D., is a senior research scientist at the Center for Studies in Education and Human Development and professor in the Department of Educational Foundations and Research at Gallaudet University.

LYNNE SANFORD KOESTER, Ph.D., is a research scientist at the Center for Studies in Education and Human Development at Gallaudet University. From 1983 to 1987 she was a visiting research fellow at the Max-Planck Institute for Psychology (Munich, West Germany). She is a former associate professor in the Department of Child Development and Family Relations at the University of North Carolina, Greensboro.

ROBERT H. MACTURK, Ph.D., is a research scientist at the Center for Studies in Education and Human Development at Gallaudet University. He is former head of the Early Development Unit of the Child and Family Research Section at the National Institute of Child Health and Human Development.

SUSAN M. MATHER, M.A., is a research associate at the Center for Studies in Education and Human Development at Gallaudet University. She is currently a doctoral student in the Applied Linguistics Department at Georgetown University.

KATHRYN P. MEADOW-ORLANS, Ph.D., is leader of the infancy group in the Center for Studies in Education and Human Development and professor in the Department of Educational Foundations and Research at Gallaudet University. She is former adjunct professor of sociology at the University of California, San Francisco.

DONNA M. MERTENS, Ph.D., is associate professor in the Department of Educational Foundations and Research at Gallaudet University. She has conducted research studies on the educational evaluation of special populations.

DONALD F. MOORES, Ph.D., is director of the Center for Studies in Education and Human Development and professor in the Department of Educational Foundations and Research at Gallaudet University. He is currently the editor of the *American Annals of the Deaf*. He is former professor of psychoeducational studies at the University of Minnesota and former head of the Department of Special Education and Communication Disorders at Pennsylvania State University.

HAROLD ORLANS, Ph.D., has conducted policy research in a variety of areas and settings, including the Brookings Institution and the National Academy of Public Administration.

TIMOTHY REAGAN, Ph.D., is associate professor of education at Central Connecticut State University. He is a former assistant professor in the Department of Educational Foundations and Research at Gallaudet University.

PATRICIA E. SPENCER, Ph.D., is a research scientist at the Center for Studies in Education and Human Development at Gallaudet University. She is former coordinator of the Gallaudet Pre-College National Assessment Center.

CATHERINE A. SWEET, M.A., is coordinator of the Winston Salem (NC) Center for the Hearing Impaired. She is a former research associate at the Center for Studies in Education and Human Development at Gallaudet University.

ABRAHAM ZWIEBEL, Ph.D., is head of the Special Education Program at Bar-Ilan University in Ramat-Gan, Israel. From 1983 to 1985 he was a visiting scholar at Gallaudet University, where he translated the Meadow-Kendall Social Emotional Assessment Inventories into Hebrew.

Acknowledgments

In addition to her contribution as one of the authors of chapter 7, Cathy Sweet shouldered the administrative responsibility for the organization of the text and served as liaison with the authors of the various chapters. Her assistance was invaluable.

We would like to express our appreciation to several colleagues who are not listed as chapter authors, but who have made significant contributions over the years to the success of the Center for Studies in Education and Human Development. Karen Saulnier has been a research scientist with CSEHD since its inception in 1981 and has been involved with research on Signed English, early literacy, and factors predictive of literacy in deaf adolescents. Karen Kautz, as administrative secretary, has been responsible for the day-to-day functioning of the Center and we owe her a debt of gratitude. Linda Stamper was one of the Center's first research assistants and has contributed to several studies. Victoria Patterson was the Center's word processing specialist for many years and her work was always efficient and prompt. In 1989 she was ably replaced by Betty Lee.

Dr. Carol Erting and Carlene Prezioso (now director and research associate, respectively, of the Gallaudet Culture and Communication Studies Program) made significant contributions to the work of the Infancy Research group, as did Victoria Trimm, when she joined the Center in 1988.

Finally, through the decade of the 1980s the Center was fortunate enough to employ more than 100 research assistants and part-time undergraduate and graduate assistants. We hope the experience has been as beneficial for them as it has been for us.

Introduction

DONALD F. MOORES, KATHRYN P. MEADOW-ORLANS

In the past twenty years, there has been enormous progress in educational, social, and vocational opportunities for deaf children and adults. There has been a virtual revolution during this time, culminating, perhaps, in the selection of the first Deaf president of Gallaudet University in 1988. Some of the changes that both caused and reflect these positive changes include:

1. Earlier intervention for young deaf children.
2. Increased numbers and kinds of opportunities for advanced education.
3. Increased interest in sign language and manual communication.
4. Increased availability of sign interpreters.
5. Technological advances leading to closed captioning of television programs, new telephone communication possibilities, computer communication, etc.
6. Changing attitudes and growing acceptance of deafness as a social condition, not a pathology.

The authors have had the opportunity to be both participants in and observers of this revolution. We first met at a tumultuous session at an annual meeting of the Alexander Graham Bell Association in 1968, where the possible use of manual communication had been vigorously discussed and opposed by a majority of those in attendance. We had recently completed our Ph.D. dissertations—Meadow-Orlans at Berkeley and Moores at Illinois—and found common cause as part of a small minority in support of signing with deaf children. Meadow-Orlans' training in sociology, and Moores' experience as a teacher of the deaf and training in educational psychology, provided complementary perspectives on the needs of deaf individuals and their families.

We continued to interact for more than a decade through exchanges of preprints and joint presentations before such audiences as the American Speech and Hearing Association, the Council for Exceptional Children, and the Society for Research in Child Development, as well as at Gallaudet. Throughout this period we shared common interests, goals, and philosophies. Our individual research efforts encompassed the life span from birth to old age as our studies were conducted in various settings in the home, the school, and the work place.

The opportunity for closer research interaction came in 1980 when Moores joined Meadow-Orlans at Gallaudet and we helped organize the Center for Studies in Education and Human Development (CSEHD), which was established in 1981. Since that time, we have had the opportunity to continue major lines of research, establish new initiatives, and interact with a stimulating group of colleagues within the Center, throughout the University, and with collaborators across the United States and abroad.

AGENTS OF CHANGE

Many of the developments in the past generation have been facilitated by federal legislation enacted because of perceived needs articulated by a range of advocates. The increase in opportunities for both undergraduate and graduate education in recent years is one of the most striking changes. Not too long ago, Gallaudet University was almost the only place where deaf persons might obtain postsecondary training. The creation of the National Technical Institute for the Deaf (NTID); the Leadership Training Program at California State University, Northridge; and the program at Seattle Community College are important additions. The most recent edition of *College and Career Programs for Deaf Students* (Rawlings 1988), published by Gallaudet University and NTID, lists almost 150 postsecondary opportunities.

As professionals who came to Gallaudet after establishing major programs of research elsewhere, we are perhaps more aware of the impact of the University than those who have spent their entire careers at the school. A great deal of legislation and many programs on behalf of deaf persons have been advanced through Gallaudet channels. Sign language training programs have provided a growing number of interpreters, thus giving many deaf persons broader access to many services and activities. Gallaudet itself is a microcosm of changes in attitudes about and opportunities for deaf persons. For example, in the late 1800s, Alexander Graham Bell testified before the U.S. Senate against establishing a teacher training program for students with normal hearing at Gallaudet College on the grounds that the college would also accept deaf students into the program (Moores 1987). Although this reasoning is so anachronistic as to seem laughable today, one of the authors (Moores) received an M.A. from Gallaudet in 1959, a time when deaf students were not allowed into the graduate school. Gallaudet did not accept deaf students into the graduate school until the 1960s, only twenty-five years before a deaf person was chosen to be president of the institution.

Enmeshed with the positive visibility provided by many Deaf community leaders has been the increasing visibility of sign language in the United States. Today there is hardly a junior college or adult education program that does not offer at least one course in sign language. Some high schools include sign language in the curriculum. Presidential candidate Jimmy Carter used a Sign interpreter during his nationally televised acceptance speech at the Democratic national convention in 1976, and interpreters frequently have been used in national campaigns since. A number of universities accept sign language proficiency to fulfill a foreign language requirement for the Ph.D. Many television stations employ sign language interpreters for locally produced TV programs.

The work of the National Theatre of the Deaf (NTD) should be mentioned. Its use of American Sign Language (ASL) is seen as an art form, not only in the Deaf community but by hearing theatergoers as well. The NTD was funded by the federal government, through the creative leadership of one energetic and sympathetic friend of deaf people, Mary Switzer.

Another development contributing to change was the passage by Congress of Section 504 of the Rehabilitation Act of 1973, requiring equal access to public buildings and functions for all handicapped groups, which was interpreted successfully by Deaf people to mean that interpreters must be provided for them. Organizations of Deaf people joined together with representatives of other handicapped groups to form a large and powerful lobby to effect this law.

Thus, many interlocking strands lead to social change. These strands include increased opportunities for education, growing leadership by Deaf people, lobbying for legislative progress, and a spiral of achievement leading to more achievement. Of major importance are the ability and the willingness of Deaf people to lead the fight for themselves, and also their willingness to accept the support of hearing parents and friends in their struggle for more participation in social and community life.

CONTRIBUTIONS OF RESEARCH

It should be pointed out that there have been significant contributions by research to the field of deafness. The impact of research over the past generation on attitudes and practices has not received the attention it deserves. A very limited list of contributions would include work in demographics, ASL, postsecondary education, early intervention programs, and child development. Although each of these will be considered in detail later, it is instructive to look at these areas briefly in order to develop an appreciation of the impact of research.

Demographics

Deafness is the only field in special education with comprehensive demographic data. The Center for Assessment and Demographic Studies (formerly the Office of Demographic Studies) at Gallaudet University has gathered data since 1967 on a nationwide basis, and this information has contributed immeasurably to an understanding of the characteristics of deaf children, of their families, and of the programs serving them. These statistics have served to further many policy changes at the national, state, and local levels. More recently, researchers in this group have contributed to the development and norming of achievement tests that have helped to improve the educational standards and expectations for deaf children.

Child Development

One overriding outcome of recent research in development of deaf children has been the emphasis on the essential normality of the growing deaf child. Although a deaf individual faces a considerable number of difficulties during childhood and in adult life, there has been a change in attitudes, with emphasis moving from the deficiency model toward the facilitation of optimal functioning.

Postsecondary Education

The need for a wider range of postsecondary programs for deaf students was identified by research in the mid-1960s. Following the establishment of programs, further research documented the benefits and cost effectiveness of the models that had been developed. The efficacy of educating deaf students in vocational technical programs designed for hearing students, with the addition of interpreters, note-takers, and special counseling, was established.

American Sign Language

American Sign Language has been accepted as a full-fledged language in every sense. It is agreed that ASL contains all the richness, expressivity, and power of a spoken language. Before 1960, many observers considered ASL to be a concrete system of gestures with a limited vocabulary and primitive grammar, incapable of expressing abstract ideas. Research by William Stokoe and his colleagues, beginning about 1960, lent to ASL a scientific respectability that previously it had been denied.

Early Intervention Programs

Researchers first identified the lack of impact of traditional early intervention programs for the deaf in the 1960s and suggested new techniques and emphases. Other researchers later documented the effectiveness of programs employing modifications such as use of manual communication, increased home visitation, and greater academic emphasis.

Invented Sign Systems

The work of Harry Bornstein, Gerilee Gustason, and others in creating pedagogical English-based sign systems helped overcome the resistance of hearing parents and educators to the use of sign language with younger children. Again, research on the use of sign language with various populations was a factor contributing to increased acceptance, as was the political activity of hearing parents who wanted Sign as an option for their children.

THE CENTER FOR STUDIES IN EDUCATION AND HUMAN DEVELOPMENT

The Center for Studies in Education and Human Development was established in 1981 with the mission of conducting pragmatic and programmatic research of benefit to deaf individuals and their families. The Center was constituted from smaller existing units in child development, psychology, mental health, and educational research. Multidisciplinary teams have been organized around programmatic themes of research, including literacy, child development, family dynamics, educational placement, and academic achievement.

The term "program research" itself refers to the relating of many discrete research activities to a common well-defined goal or problem area within the context of a single theme. This program provides the investigators with the flexibility to shift gears to follow up new leads or drop approaches found to be nonproductive. A programmatic research activity differs from a research center in that the support is generally used to answer a broad particular question with a multifaceted approach, while a research center might involve one or more areas of programmatic research and/or several discrete research projects.

By definition, program research involves interdisciplinary cooperation. A sharing of knowledge and an integration of skills is mandatory. When conducted effectively, the whole of program research is definitely greater than the sum of its parts. Program research, then, is both longitudinal and interdisciplinary in nature. It has a focus that is developed and accepted by a team. The results must be beneficial to all concerned. Peer review, monitoring, and feedback are necessary. Mechanisms for incorporating new disciplines and strategies for phasing out activities must be established.

Special Considerations of Research Methodology in the Study of Deaf Persons

A major consideration for research involving deaf persons is the heterogeneous nature of any random group. When this is combined with low incidence (only one child per thousand has an early, severe to profound hearing loss), wide geographical dispersion, and widespread use of sign language, the difficulties of conducting research are sometimes overwhelming.

The diversity of groups of deaf children stems from the wide range of demographic and diagnostic characteristics that influence educational and developmental variables usually of interest to social or behavioral scientists. For example, a child who is profoundly deaf is quite different from one with a great deal of residual hearing. Sometimes even apparently slight differences in hearing can mean a great deal in terms of defining the variety of experience for the two children. The use and comfort of hearing aids is important, plus the description of hearing loss when a hearing aid is being used. The nature of the hearing loss (that is, the sound frequencies at which children hear) may influence the child's ability to benefit from speech training, and to process speech sounds.

The child's age at the time of onset of deafness has major significance. For many years, the tradition has been to divide "prelingually deaf" research subjects from those who are "postlingually deaf." At first glance, this might seem a simple matter. However, the complexities begin to be apparent when we point out that the cut-off point customarily used twenty years ago was age three. Then the accepted dividing line shifted to eighteen months, then to twelve months. As more is learned about the process of language acquisition, more importance has been attached to an infant's receptive language skills, which develop long before expressive language.

The presence or absence of handicaps in addition to deafness is an important variable in differentiating between individuals in a group of deaf children. It is estimated that one-third of all deaf children have additional handicaps of a physical, cognitive, or emotional nature. Depending on the research problem to be addressed, this may be an important characteristic in a research population. (Etiology of deafness is sometimes investigated for possible clues to problems related to disorders of the central nervous system.)

The age at which children are exposed to sign language can be an important control variable for some kinds of research. Often, the hearing status of the child's parents is used as a shorthand determination of this characteristic. For some studies, it may be important to know the variety of Sign used by the child's parents and/or teachers, and the Sign proficiency of others in the child's environment.

All of these demographic and linguistic factors can have an important effect on the child's performance on a series of tests or research procedures, or can influence the child's developmental course. They can contribute more to the outcome being investigated than do the experimental procedures applied by the research investigator. Thus, it is of the utmost importance that a researcher understand which factors are important for a particular study and control for them either through subject selection or by statistical means after the data collection has been completed.

One of the important aspects of The Education for All Handicapped Children Act of 1975 (PL 94-142) was the inclusion of a clause prescribing that all instruments used in deciding the school placement of handicapped children be normed for children with their particular handicap. In many cases, these specialized instruments did not exist. This example illustrates the importance of making sure that a research instrument is appropriate for the groups of deaf children being studied. Often, the language of an instrument previously utilized with hearing children may be inappropriate for deaf children. Sometimes an instrument must be translated to Sign, and skilled interpreters must be trained in the standardized presentation of the material. In any case, the researcher must address this issue.

Another problem of research methodology is the small numbers of deaf children distributed through the population. This means that subjects who fit research criteria may be difficult to find. The research process may thus take much longer than it would if the subjects were to come from a different population. A good example of this problem can be seen in some of the research of the Center's Infancy Research Group. In 1984, the group began to recruit deaf and hearing infants with hearing and deaf parents who could be videotaped during their first year of life. In a three-year period, only four deaf infants with deaf parents were located in the Washington, D.C., area, plus ten hearing infants with deaf parents, and three deaf infants with hearing parents. As a result of this experience, a grant proposal was submitted to a federal agency, allowing the recruitment of infants in four other metropolitan areas in the United States. The research design prescribed that infants were to be studied first at the age of six months. After nine months of an intensive recruitment effort, only three six-month-old deaf babies with hearing parents had been located. For this group, the problem not only is one of low incidence, but also includes the difficulty of early diagnosis.

DEAF CHILDREN AND THEIR FAMILIES

We have been concerned throughout our careers with the lack of attention that has been devoted to the families of deaf children. It is almost as if deaf children have been thought of as living in a vacuum outside the educational setting. This is especially worrisome because most deaf children are born into families with hearing parents who have had no prior exposure to deaf individuals and who have no idea of the linguistic, psychological, social, and educational implications of early childhood deafness. Thus the paucity of family-oriented research is even more disturbing.

Perhaps the most significant aspect of research with families of deaf children is its historical absence prior to the late 1960s. In fact, educators have taken over for parents, either at the parents' implicit or explicit request, or because there seemed to be no educational alternatives. It is relatively recently that residential schools stopped accepting three-year-old deaf children as live-in students. Most researchers interested in deafness focused on students' academic achievement or on their performance on standardized tests of one kind or another. The place where most research with deaf children took place was on the campus of residential schools for the deaf.

One of the first research studies with deaf children that included work with parents in their homes was completed in the late 1960s (Meadow 1967, 1969).

Interviews with both deaf and hearing parents of deaf children were completed. This work set the stage for later studies, but research studies involving the families of deaf children remain few in number.

SUMMARY

This book is designed to present the state of the art in several areas of research on education and human development in the area of deafness. It is written by individuals with training in a variety of disciplines, including anthropology, education, linguistics, psychology, and sociology. All the contributors have participated in program research with deaf individuals in the areas under consideration. The emphasis will be both programmatic and pragmatic; that is, research is not seen as an end in itself but rather as an instrument to foster better understanding of the needs and characteristics of deaf individuals and of the programs designed to serve them. For each area, we will try to explicate in terms of research not only where we have been and where we are at present, but also what the practical implications of the work might be and where they may lead us.

Although this volume covers a wide range of topics, it cannot be considered a complete and comprehensive overview of research in the field. Rather, it represents the efforts of an identifiable group of experts who, we believe, have made significant and far-reaching contributions to the field.

From our experience, it is absolutely clear that there are no major sources dealing with applied research in educational and developmental aspects of deafness. There are, of course, some excellent texts in education, human development, and psychology that are addressed to professional trainers and that utilize research in the field. Those texts, by the nature of their audience, are practitioner oriented. We believe that there is also a need for a research-based text that can serve as a reference point for researchers and research consumers. In this volume we have taken the perspectives and experiences of our careers and attempted to mold them with a presentation of major activities conducted by members and affiliates of the Center for Studies in Education and Human Development, perhaps the largest identifiable group of researchers currently engaged in developmental and educational research in deafness.

REFERENCES

Meadow, K. 1967. The effect of early manual communication and family climate on the deaf child's development. Ph.D. diss. University of California, Berkeley.

———. 1969. Self-image, family climate on deafness. *Social Forces* 47(5): 428–438.

Moores, D. 1987. *Educating the deaf: Psychology, principles and practices.* 3d ed. Boston: Houghton Mifflin.

Rawlings, B. 1988. *A guide to college/career programs for deaf students.* Washington, DC: Gallaudet University.

PART ONE

The Deaf Child at School

1

Research in Educational Aspects of Deafness

DONALD F. MOORES

In addition to the usual issues facing education in general, education of the deaf has been embroiled for over two centuries in three distinct but overlapping controversies. Very simply, they may be expressed in three questions:

1. How should deaf students communicate?
2. Where should they be taught?
3. What should they be taught?

The first question, of course, refers to the "methods" controversy, which has been debated with consuming passion since the middle of the eighteenth century (Moores 1987) and which today swirls around the classroom use of speech, residual hearing, signs, and fingerspelling.

Many readers may not be aware that the question of placement also has a long history of conflict and predates the recent "mainstream" movements in the United States. Gordon (1885) has documented what may be considered mainstreaming movements in Great Britain, France, Bavaria, and Prussia as early as 1815. The question of school placement has implications not only for the provision of educational services but also for the quality and quantity of family relationships. All these issues increase in importance as larger numbers of deaf children attend school daily rather than residentially.

The question of curriculum, of what we should teach deaf children, is of paramount importance but has received little attention. Historically, the priorities of education of the deaf have concentrated on the mastery of grammar and on production and understanding of speech. Teacher training programs have emphasized these areas at the expense of content subjects such as math, science, literature, social studies, and history. In a typical school day, deaf children spend less time on academic subject matter than hearing children. Since the beginning of the 1980s, education in general has placed greater and greater emphasis on academic achievement and has mandated higher standards for promotion and graduation. Education of the deaf is not immune from such a powerful societal force and must respond. The issue of trade-offs will raise complex questions that research is helping to answer.

The essential consideration is time on task. Everything else being equal, the more time a child spends on an activity, the higher the level of mastery. Given the demands of visual attending, it is unreasonable to expect deaf children to have a longer school day. Because deaf students have special needs, educators frequently are faced with a Hobson's choice of cutting back on special training or on academic content. In the past the choice—usually implicit—has been to cut back in academic content. The situation may be changing with the increased emphasis on achievement. A responsibility of educational researchers in deafness now is to make the special training techniques as efficient as possible while improving the teaching of academic content.

Certain readily identifiable themes appeared in several sources as appeals were made for higher standards and a commitment to excellence. Recommendations from various sources included such remedies as longer school days and school years, competency testing for teachers, merit pay, additional academic coursework for promotion and graduation, restructuring of teacher training, and improved classroom discipline.

Howe (1984) raised the question of what educators might do to respond to this flood of interest, this "barrage of criticism and free advice." Simply put, he asked if American education has a knowledge base from which to react to this free advice and from which to generate appropriate changes. Is there any evidence, for example, that increasing the school day by one hour or the school year by one month will have a positive impact on school achievement? Can we predict the effect of testing or merit pay for teachers on student learning? Are teachers trained at the graduate level demonstrably superior to those trained as undergraduates?

Although American education has undergone continuous, often critical, examination since its inception in the seventeenth century, it was exposed to an unparalleled intensity of attention in the early part of the 1980s. This attention culminated in a spate of reports and studies demanding inquiry and action. The consensus of opinion, supported in part by data, was that levels of academic achievement had declined over a period of twenty-five years and that schools were not preparing students for the complex demands of our increasingly technological society.

EQUITY AND EXCELLENCE

As will be seen in following chapters in this section, researchers have approached the three questions in a variety of ways. As should become quickly apparent, the three simple questions are also somewhat simplistic. In real life the situation is far more complex and cannot be resolved by either-or, yes-no solutions. There are too many individual and situational differences. However, the ultimate goal of educational research is to document the achievement and progress of students and to demonstrate ways in which achievement can be optimized.

It must be acknowledged, in dealing with questions of education, that the gap between the ideal and the real is always great. Educators have an ideal of total optimalization, i.e., the ultimate, unobtainable, goal is complete self-actualization and the realization of human potential in all areas. Any average child, hearing or deaf, has a potential for excellence, and the success of any program should be measured in terms of the extent to which it helps children reach their social, intellectual, and physical potentials.

The concept of *excellence* used in this context, i.e., the idea that the average child has an untapped potential for outstanding achievement, is somewhat at variance with the way the term has been used in some considerations of education, and a discussion of the concepts of *equity* and *education* is called for at this point. To some extent the themes of *equity* and *excellence* have been incompatible throughout American education. The support for equity is drawn from the strongly held belief that there should be equality of opportunity for all. There is similarly strong support for the belief that outstanding achievement, or excellence, should be highly rewarded.

In the United States the trend has been to make education more encompassing and more available to all elements of the population. With the enactment of Public Law 94-142, the Education for All Handicapped Children Act of 1975 (PL 94-142), the right to a free appropriate public education was extended to all children regardless of handicapping conditions. In fact, then, equity of access to education is guaranteed to all American children. The case for excellence, traditionally and currently, is more difficult to trace. To a large degree, it has referred to an elite, either social or intellectual, that has received special benefits in education. Private colleges and private preparatory schools dating back to colonial times have educated a social elite and in more recent times an intellectual elite. In the public schools, excellence traditionally has been pursued through systems of tracking and of special junior and senior high schools to separate out and educate children with high academic potential. In addition to such long standing public schools as Boston Latin School (established in 1636) and the Bronx High School of Science, there are special academic schools in most large city and metropolitan areas, as well as some state-wide programs.

To a large extent, advocates of equity have addressed access to educational services and not necessarily the quality of the services per se. From 1960 to 1985 they were quite successful in opening up access to public education on a "zero-reject" basis. Critics have argued that the access has come at the expense of quality and has accounted, to some extent, for the measurable decline in achievement of school leavers during that period. As a result, there has been a growing emphasis since the early 1980s on academic achievement.

Over the next generation, it remains to be seen whether educators can agree to interpret the terms *equity* and *excellence* so that excellence is the goal for all students and not only for a small proportion of the school population.

It is my position that excellence is achievable by most students, hearing and deaf, and that excellence and equity are mutually achievable. Given the basic premise that deaf children are essentially normal, it follows that much of the research conducted on hearing students can be generalized to deaf students, once allowances are made for different life experiences and modes of communication.

THE TWO SIGMA PROBLEM

In the field of education, the gap between the real and the ideal has been characterized as the "two sigma problem" (Bloom 1984). By this Bloom means that an average student under ideal tutoring conditions achieves two standard deviations above the average student under typical classroom conditions. Put another way, the average tutored student achieves above 98% of children placed in traditional classroom environments. Ideally all children should have individual tutors. Realistically, this will not happen. One goal of pragmatic research is to develop small-group and large-group methods of instruction that will approach the effectiveness of individual tutoring.

In developing the concept of the two sigma problem, Bloom relied heavily on the research of Walberg (1984), who synthesized the results of thousands of research studies to identify the most important factors influencing learning. Walberg concluded that there are nine powerful factors, which he placed under three categories.

Student Aptitude Factors

1. Ability or prior achievement
2. Development
3. Motivation or self-concept

Instructional Factors

4. Amount of time engaged in learning
5. Quality of instruction

Environmental Factors

6. The home
7. The classroom social group
8. Peer groups outside of school
9. Use of out-of-school time

Walberg and his colleagues (Walberg 1984; Walberg and Shanahan 1983) have concentrated on the extent to which each factor is alterable to improve achievement. As might be expected, student aptitude factors are the least alterable, and environmental factors are the most alterable. Walberg (1984) concluded that the largest alterable effects were:

1. Graded homework. Homework that is graded or commented on has three times the effect of homework that is merely assigned.
2. Class morale.
3. Home interventions in the form of school-parent program to improve academic conditions in the home.

In a somewhat different emphasis, Bloom (1980) studied six classes of alterable variables: quality of teaching, use of time, cognitive and affective characteristics of students, formative testing, rate of learning, and home environment. In 1984 Bloom reported impressive effects on ten very powerful variables.

1. Tutorial instruction
2. Reinforcement
3. Mastery learning
4. Cues and explanations
5. Student classroom participation
6. Student time on task
7. Improved reading/study skills
8. Cooperative learning
9. Graded homework
10. Classroom morale

The most striking finding was that the average student under tutoring was two standard deviations (two sigmas) above the average student in conventional instruction. The difficulty resulting from Bloom's (1984) two sigma problem is that we can't afford tutors for each of the fifty million American school children. As Bloom phrased the question: "Can researchers and teachers devise teaching-learning conditions that will enable the majority of students under *group* instruction to attain levels of achievement that at present can be reached only under good tutoring conditions?" (pp. 4–5).

Much of what is needed to improve achievement, then, is already known. The issue is the implementation of changes. Moores (1987) has identified a number of variables from general research and from special education research that can be applied immediately to improve education of the deaf. He groups these under instructor variables, program variables and home variables, with some straightforward suggestions.

Instructor Variables

Here, the teacher is the key. In addition to knowledge of subject matter and skill in communicating with deaf children, the following instructional variables enhance the teaching/learning process.

1. *Reinforcement.* The teacher should provide appropriate reinforcement and positive feedback.

2. *Mastery learning*. The addition of teaching and feedback procedures to conventional instruction enhances learning.
3. *Graded homework*. Meaningful homework that is assigned, graded, and responded to will result in increased learning.
4. *Time on task*. There is a positive correlation between the time spent on a subject and the amount learned. This may seem a simplistic statement, but many teachers, particularly teachers of the deaf in academic content areas, spend surprisingly little time on task.
5. *Class morale*. Teachers should strive to maintain cohesiveness, satisfaction, and goal direction in the classroom.

Program Variables

Program variables are instruction variables that are under the domain of a program rather than an individual teacher. In addition to fostering the teacher's individual efforts, programs should concentrate on the following components, found by research to be desirable:

1. *Reading training*. Over and above conventional reading instruction, there should be a special program to train deaf students in adjusting reading strategies for various purposes.
2. *Special programs*. Deaf students with high potential should be identified and should receive accelerated training.
3. *Tutoring*. Although the ideal one-to-one situation cannot be attained, with careful planning, the low student/teacher ratio in programs for the deaf can lead to significant one-to-one and small-group instruction.
4. *Cooperative parent programs*. The alterable curriculum of the home can be manipulated to foster school achievement.

Home Variables

The idea behind use of the alterable home curriculum is not to place the responsibility for teaching on parents, but to encourage academic achievement. The results have been excellent. Basic things that parents are asked to do include

1. Keeping television viewing to twelve hours a week or less.
2. Monitoring homework to see that it is completed.
3. Encouraging leisure reading.
4. Discussing school with the child.
5. Expressing interest in the child's progress.

Moores argues that, with guidance and support from the schools, most parents can substantially improve the academic environment of the home by following a few relatively simple procedures. The same principles can easily apply for students at residential schools contingent upon open communication between teaching and dormitory personnel. In chapter 2, Mertens provides a more comprehensive model of school achievement for deaf students.

RESEARCH TO APPLICATION

Although American educational research has made significant contributions to our understanding of principles of teaching and learning, it is readily apparent that the main thrusts of traditional educational research have not addressed the areas that the public identifies as most important.

In a very broad sense, the classical research to application model has been of limited utility in American education and, by extension, in the field of deafness. In the classic model, several discrete segmented stages can be identified. At the first stage, the concentration is on "basic" or "pure" research. In some cases, this may involve close observation, and in others, systematic manipulation of treatment variables. As the base of knowledge is strengthened and expanded, the orientation moves more toward an emphasis on development activities. These typically are limited in scope and are quite tentative (i.e., they are subject to major revision on the basis of experimental findings). The third stage moves into demonstration of effective techniques. Then the efficacy of techniques that are theoretically sound and have stood the test of empirical investigation in clinical and experimental settings are adapted and studied in more natural environments. The final step is adoption into the educational process.

THE ACQUISITION OF KNOWLEDGE AND THE APPLICATION OF KNOWLEDGE

Although there are several ways of categorizing the research to application continuum, it is beneficial to bear in mind a distinction between the research process—the acquisition of knowledge—and the application of knowledge (Garner 1971). The interrelationships of research and application must be carefully explicated; isolation of one from the other is destructive. It must be emphasized that interaction is mutually beneficial to both theory and practice. It is a little-known fact that most theoretical scientific work has been influenced by applied problems.

For education in general in the United States, as well as for special education, there has been a gulf between representatives of scientific (research) and service (educational) disciplines. McKenna (1973) notes that

> In the past, a great deal of educational and psychological research has been done in academic isolation as a partial requirement for a degree or by scholars in their spare time from teaching, with or without funds. Such projects derived from an individual's interest in a special problem or from the availability of subjects for

research. As a result, little work was done on broad issues with practical implications requiring investigations for protracted periods of time by members of
different professions. This often had the effect of reinforcing inertia and insuring
a kind of built-in conservatism with regard to innovation in educational establishments. (p. 24)

The process by which the discovery of new knowledge is accomplished and
eventually translated into educational innovation is a complex one that may be
viewed as extending over a series of identifiable stages. Gallagher (1968) (Table
1.1) incorporates five phases—research, development, demonstration, implementation, and adoption—into an ongoing educational operation. Each phase requires a different emphasis, concentration of professional skills, and organizational support.

The ultimate criterion of successful educational research must be the initiation of changes in the educational system that are of demonstrable benefit to children. Anything less than this should be unacceptable. A major component of any
educational research must be careful consideration of the means by which results
can be used to ameliorate the condition of children.

The present time lag in American education between the initiation of research activities and the adoption of changes can be attributed to a number of
factors. A basic obstacle is presented by the fact that the research and adoption
ends of the continuum have been perceived as the separate domains of colleges
and public schools respectively, two types of organizations that currently address
themselves to different orders of priorities. At the college level the priorities and
reinforcements have been arranged in such a way as to encourage behavior that
tends to concentrate on research activities to the exclusion of other stages. Systems
that rely exclusively on project-by-project funding reinforce this behavior. The
outcome has been a closed system in which research is frequently conducted for
the benefit of other researchers. An individual might conceive of a problem, develop a design, run an experiment, and then report the results in esoteric jargon
incomprehensible to the educational practitioner. Researchers can succeed in their
goal of causing useful change only when effective communication is established
with educational practitioners.

Two inevitable outcomes of the present system have been that (1) Much
educational research has been conducted that is clearly irrelevant to education; and
(2) Much clearly relevant research that has been conducted has not been of educational benefit because of the lack of mechanisms for translating knowledge into
behavior. Figure 1.1 illustrates the situation that exists when researchers and practitioners do not interact and where the translation of knowledge to action is
blocked by misunderstanding and lack of cooperation between the two systems.

It is clear that the breakdown occurs at the point where college and school
cooperation should be at the maximum level, that is, at the demonstration stage,
which, in Gallagher's terms, involves an effective conjunction of organized knowledge and the child. For any such conjunction to be believable, it must be accom-

Table 1.1
Classical Research to Application Model

Developmental Phase	Purpose	Supporting Organizations
Research	The discovery of new knowledge about handicapped children or about those intellectual and personality processes that can be applied in these children.	These are usually research centers and institutions, often found in universities, which can provide organizational support for long range attacks on difficult research problems.
Development	Knowledge, to be educationally useful, must be organized or packaged into sequences of activities or curricula that fit the needs of particular groups of children.	Sometimes done through research and development centers that concentrate on sequencing of existing knowledge; basic setting is still the university.
Demonstration	There must be an effective conjunction of organized knowledge and the child. This conjunction must be demonstrated in a school setting to be believable.	A combination of university or government and school cooperation required. Usually, the elementary or secondary school is the physical setting, and additional resources are supplied by the other agency.
Implementation	Local school systems with local needs usually want to try out, on a pilot basis, the effective demonstration they have observed elsewhere to establish its viability in a local setting.	Additional funds for retraining personnel and for establishing a new program locally are needed. Some type of university, state, or federal support is often needed as the catalyst to bring about this additional stage.
Adoption	To establish the new program as part of the educational operation. Without acceptance of the new program at the policy level, demonstration and implementation operations can atrophy.	Organized attempts need to be made to involve policy decision makers (i.e., school board members, superintendents, etc.) in the developmental stages so far. Items like cost effectiveness need to be developed to help make decisions.

Source: J. J. Gallagher, "Organization and Special Education," *Exceptional Children* 34 (1968): 485–491.

plished in a school setting. Without an effective bridge, there is little confluence of knowledge and practice.

For the schools to progress, they must be open to input from a number of sources, with the colleges providing a significant impetus for innovation. If researchers are to exert a major influence, they must to a greater degree adopt a learner's role and be more sensitive to the needs of children and to the realities of the classroom. For an idea to be accepted, it must stand the test of empirical verification in the field.

Ideally, the schools and colleges should function as partners in all phases of

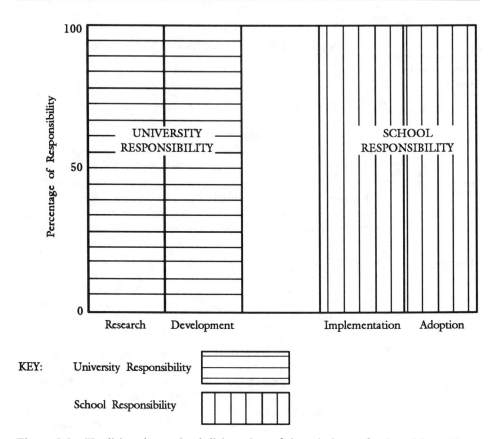

Figure 1.1 Traditional perceived disjunction of the missions of universities and schools.

Source: D.F. Moores, "Moving Research Across the Continuum." In *American Psychological Association Symposium Papers,* ed. J. E. Turnure. (University of Minnesota Research, Development and Demonstration Center in Education of Handicapped Children, Occasional Paper #24, 1973): 54.

the research to adoption continuum. Although the colleges should assume the major responsibility for the first stages, the schools must be able to influence the type of research activities undertaken. At the other end, the colleges should contribute their unique skills to the evaluation and modification of programs that have been adopted into the ongoing educational operation. Figure 1.2 presents an ideal university–school symbiotic relationship.

The classic research to application model has many important factors. Primarily, it is knowledge based and theory based. As a stage model, each stage is dependent on work successfully accomplished at preceding levels. The process may be characterized as slow, meticulous, and incremental, developing out of an accretion of knowledge ranging from the basic to the applied.

If such a model were used consistently, American education would be built upon data-based, consistent, and theoretically sound principles. However, it is clear that the research to application process occurs relatively infrequently and that

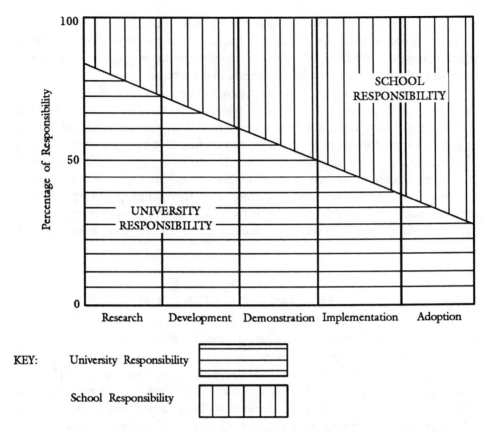

Figure 1.2 Ideal university/school sharing of responsibility.

Source: D. F. Moores, "Moving Research Across the Continuum." In *American Psychological Association Symposium Papers*, ed. J. E. Turnure. (University of Minnesota Research, Development and Demonstration Center in Education of Handicapped Children, Occasional Paper #24, 1973): 51.

much educational practice is neither theory based nor data based. The situation may be explained in part by large-scale societal forces that mandate changes on the basis of political, economic, and social developments. Educators face realities of life dictated or heavily influenced by outside forces ranging from changes in the American family, to the impact of immigration policy, to differing interpretations of the principle of separation of church and state.

In addition to perceived disjunctions between schools and institutions of higher education in the research to application process, many of the problems may be attributed to inadequate communication within colleges and across teaching and research faculty. The distinction between research and teaching is perhaps greater in schools of education than in any other field. In fact, in many places, educational research may be conducted for the most part by faculty in disciplines such as psychology, sociology, and linguistics. University training programs may interact with the schools, and university research programs may interact with the schools, but typically they do not interact with each other. The detrimental effects on research and practice are obvious, detracting from the quality of educational research and delaying the application of relevant new knowledge from preservice training to the training of teachers currently in the schools.

The applied researcher, then, must play three roles. One involves a commitment to basic long-term examination of fundamental principles. For those of us concerned with the education of deaf individuals, this includes work in the fields of anthropology, sociology, psychology, and human development, among others. The second role is more difficult. It involves identifying areas in which well-formulated research may have a positive influence on practice. While realistically taking outside forces into account, we must keep them in proper perspective and resist a tendency to be overwhelmed by them. The third role is to interact in mutually beneficial ways with teacher trainers at the university level as well as with educators in the schools.

PROGRAMMATIC RESEARCH

We are faced with a situation in which research activities have had undeniably important impacts upon the field of deafness and have significantly altered perceptions and practices. This influence, however, has been uneven and the application of results has been unsystematic. McKenna's (1973) comments that much educational research has been done in isolation to fulfill degree requirements or by scholars in their spare time has particular relevance in the area of deafness today, especially in view of the complex issues that are being identified. Our traditional reliance on doctoral dissertations and short-term research projects cannot provide the necessary knowledge base upon which to build programs of research that will benefit deaf individuals.

In his series of reviews on the application of child development research to exceptional children, Gallagher (1975) constantly reiterated the tremendous difficulty inherent in attempting to master several fields. Given the complexities of the problems we face, it is unrealistic to expect investigators to have competence in more than one discipline. Clearly, the major issues facing us cannot be addressed solely by individuals working in isolation on short-term projects. The weakness of such a system has long been acknowledged, and there have been efforts to remedy it, with relatively little success. For example, in 1968, Mueller discussed federal patterns of support for research in special education as follows:

> In the past, support related to the education of the handicapped was largely limited to individual project grants. Those were, generally speaking, of relatively short duration and were designed to answer fairly specific research questions. The present trend is toward support of research programs, although not to the exclusion of support for specific projects. This pattern is more efficient, allows for better integration, provides for program continuity, and institutionalizes

major research efforts. . . . Integration of individual projects bearing on a given problem which may cut across various areas of disabilities and various research disciplines is another advantage of this pattern of funding. From the point of view of the researcher, the continuity provided by program support is a particular advantage. Support is for a longer period, and lapses of funding are avoided. (p. 525)

Unfortunately, Mueller's predictions of more program research have not come to pass.

The term "program research" itself refers to the relating of many discrete research activities to a common well-defined goal or problem area within the context of a single theme. This program provides the investigators with the flexibility to shift gears and follow up new leads or drop approaches found to be nonproductive. A programmatic research activity differs from a research center in that the support is generally used to answer a broad, particular question with a multifaceted approach, while a research center might involve one or more areas of programmatic research and/or several discrete research projects.

By definition, program research involves interdisciplinary cooperation. A sharing of knowledge and an integration of skills is mandatory. When conducted effectively, the whole of program research is definitely greater than the sum of its parts. Program research, then, is both longitudinal and interdisciplinary in nature. It has a focus that is developed and accepted by a team. The results must be beneficial to all concerned. Peer review, monitoring, and feedback are necessary. Mechanisms for incorporating new disciplines and phasing out activities must be established. Programmatic research might or might not be conducted within the context of a center or of a particular institution. In fact, several effective programs of cooperative research are currently underway involving investigators based in a university but working with several school systems.

REFERENCES

Bloom, B. 1980. The new direction in educational research. *Phi Delta Kappan* 61(6): 382–385.

——. 1984. The 2 sigma problem: The search for methods of group instruction as effective as one-to-one tutoring. *Educational Researcher* 13(6): 4–16.

Gallagher, J. J. 1968. Organization and special education. *Exceptional Children* 34: 485–491.

——. 1975. *The application of child development research to exceptional children*. Reston, VA: Council for Exceptional Children.

Garner, W. R. 1971. The acquisition and application of knowledge: A symbolic review. *American Psychologist* 27: 941–946.

Gordon, J. 1885. Deaf mutes and the public schools from 1815 to the present day. *American Annals of the Deaf* 30(2): 121–143.

Howe, H. 1984. Introduction: Symposium on the year of the reports. *Harvard Educational Review* 54(1): 1–3.

McKenna, J. 1973. Introduction. In *The present situation and trends of research in special education*, 11–66. Paris: UNESCO.

Moores, D. 1973. Moving research across the continuum. In *American Psychological Association symposium papers*, ed. J. Turnure. Occasional Paper #24. University of Minnesota Research, Development and Demonstration Center in Education of Handicapped Children.

———. 1987. *Educating the deaf: Psychology, principles and practices.* 3d. ed. Boston: Houghton Mifflin.

Mueller, M. W. 1968. Trends in support of educational research of the handicapped. *Exceptional Children* 34: 523–527.

Walberg, H. 1984. Improving the productivity of America's schools. *Educational Leadership* 41(8): 19–30.

Walberg, H. and T. Shanahan. 1983. High school effects on individual studies. *Educational Researcher* 12(7): 49.

2

A Conceptual Model for
Academic Achievement:
Deaf Student Outcomes

DONNA M. MERTENS

The purpose of this chapter is to present a conceptual model that will help explain who gets mainstreamed and what variables influence the academic achievement and social-emotional development of deaf students. The model is based on one for general school effectiveness (Bloom 1984; Centra and Potter 1980; Glasman and Biniaminov 1981; Walberg 1984) that has been modified to take into account variables that are uniquely associated with education of deaf students.

METHODOLOGY

To obtain an overview of variables that are related to general school effectiveness, several secondary sources were examined (Bloom 1984; Centra and Potter 1980; Glasman and Biniaminov 1981; Walberg 1984). Computer and manual searches were then conducted of the ERIC database and the Exceptional Children Education Resources database. The descriptors that were used included various combinations of the words *mainstreaming, deaf, academic achievement, reading comprehension, mathematics, social development, emotional development,* and *prediction.* Relevant articles from these searches were located, and their bibliographies provided another source of studies.

In addition to the primary sources obtained through the database searches, the following steps were taken:

1. Current issues of the *American Annals of the Deaf, Volta Review,* and *Directions* were reviewed;
2. Staff members were contacted at two of Gallaudet University's research centers—Center for Assessment and Demographic Studies and Center for Studies in Education and Human Development—to obtain relevant research reports;

3. Two major bibliographies on mainstreaming were reviewed (Clarkson 1982; Hein and Bishop 1978); and
4. The *Handbook of Research on Teaching* (Wittrock 1986) was reviewed.

The purpose of looking at general school effectiveness literature was to provide a basis for determining research needs with deaf subjects and to provide guidance in the planning of the needed research. Therefore, secondary reports of school effectiveness with normally hearing subjects were deemed appropriate for inclusion. Because a review of this nature was not previously available for research with deaf subjects, the author sought primary reports of research that established an empirical relationship between predictor variables and student placement or outcomes. It is recognized that not every study that addresses placement and outcomes for deaf students was located. However, the studies that were included represent a wide range of research, and consistent trends do appear in the identified research. Consequently, readers must judge for themselves whether the major conclusions of the present study would be changed by the addition of any inadvertently omitted studies.

MODELS OF SCHOOL EFFECTIVENESS

Numerous models of school effectiveness have been proposed (Averch et al. 1974; Bridge, Judd, and Moock 1979; Centra and Potter 1980; Dunkin and Biddle 1974; Glasman and Biniaminov 1981; Shulman 1986; Walberg, 1981). Most authors have proposed fairly similar categories of variables for inclusion in their models.

An investigation of the Centra and Potter model and the Glasman and Biniaminov model formed the starting point for the present conceptual framework because the components that are common to both are also shared by most other models of school effectiveness, the importance of interrelationships among variables in educational modeling cannot be overemphasized, and current research (Bloom 1984; Walberg 1984) suggests that the interactions between teacher and students are the most potent and manipulable factors in effecting student achievement.

Centra and Potter (1980) presented a structural model of the many variables that contribute to variation in student learning. They based their model on research literature dealing with school effects and with the relationship between teacher behavior and student growth. They did not intend to present an intensive review and critique of the literature dealing with any single factor in their model. Rather, they intended to explore the heuristic and synthetic value of such a model. Consequently, they focused on particular factors at the expense of others and were selective rather than inclusive in their coverage of the literature in each area. Centra and Potter included the following variables: (1) school or school district conditions, (2) within-school conditions, (3) teacher characteristics, (4) teaching performance, (5) student characteristics, (6) student behavior, and (7) student learning outcomes.

Glasman and Biniaminov (1981) also presented a structural model of school input and output variables. They contrasted their model with that of Centra and Potter by saying that their own was "much more focused and comprehensive. The justifications for most of the components of the model suggested here are data based" (p. 509). They also did not include studies that deal with characteristics of ongoing teacher–student and student–student interactions, nor did they try to address longitudinal aspects of effects of school inputs on school outputs. Glasman and Biniaminov included the following variables: (1) school conditions, (2) school-related student characteristics, (3) instructional personnel, (4) student background characteristics, (5) student attitudes, and (6) outputs (cognitive and noncognitive). Essentially, Glasman and Biniaminov hypothesize more interrelationships among the groups of variables, and they do not emphasize the roles of teacher characteristics and student behavior as much as Centra and Potter do.

Figure 2.1 shows a model of school effectiveness as it relates to variables uniquely associated with deafness. Based on the integration of the Centra and Potter model and the Glasman and Biniaminov model and variables uniquely associated with education of the deaf student, the major categories of variables include

1. Student background characteristics (family background and student background characteristics).
2. School and/or school district conditions (school facilities, expenditures, and staff).
3. Within-school conditions (sociodemographic characteristics of the student population, attendance, quantity of schooling, administrative organization).
4. Instructional personnel (teacher background and personal characteristics, teacher assignments, teacher attitude).
5. Student attitudes (internal/external control, self-concept).
6. Student placement (mainstream, self-contained).
7. Instructional personnel performance (use of reinforcement, communication mode).
8. Family support (involvement in school activities, expectations).
9. Student mediation processes (attentive, task-oriented).
10. Student outcomes (cognitive, noncognitive).

The variables within each category resulted from the integration of the two models, except as follows: (1) Bloom's (1984) and Walberg's (1984) work on methods of group instruction that will improve the productivity of schools was used for the instructional personnel performance and family support variables; (2) Bodner-Johnson (1983) provided additional information concerning family support variables; and (3) McKinney, Mason, Perkerson, and Clifford's (1975) and Wittrock's (1986) work was used to identify student mediation processes.

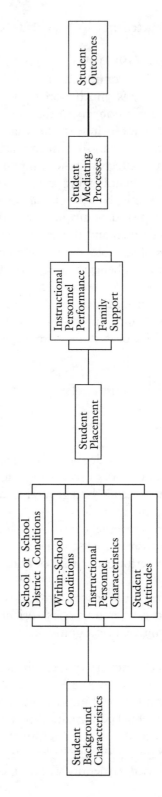

Figure 2.1 A conceptual model of school placement and outcomes for the deaf student.

While the model of school effectiveness is based on the process-product model of teaching and learning, the present chapter should not be viewed as advocating the process-product approach to research on teaching. Shulman (1986) identified the process-product model as the most vigorous and productive model of the last decade; however, it is now losing vigor in the research community because of its atheoretical nature and because of problems with the definition of the dependent variable and unit of analysis.

Research based on the process-product model has concentrated on specific variables of teaching styles and methods and has identified hundreds of variables among the different teaching styles (Shulman 1986). From the hundreds of variables, especially those significantly related to achievement, investigators synthesized a style or pattern of teaching (i.e., a composite) that seems to be associated with desirable student outcomes. Process-product research (while based on naturally occurring conditions) defined effective teaching through an act of synthesis, with little evidence that any observed teacher had ever performed in the classroom according to the collective pattern of the composite. Then, when field experiments were conducted, teachers who had been trained using the composite typically produced higher achievement gains among their students. However, it was also found that the teachers in the experimental treatment did not always engage in the desired behaviors and not all the trained behaviors continued to correlate with achievement. Therefore, investigators concluded that all the elements in the composite were not needed for effective performance. Why the particular combination of behaviors led to gains and others did not was left unanswered by the process-product model because of its atheoretical nature. Shulman suggested that the solution to this problem might be in the mediators (cognitive processes) between teaching and learning.

Shulman (1986) also noted problems with the definition of the dependent variable and the unit of analysis in the process-product model. Typically, process-product research has relied on standardized tests as dependent variables. However, standardized tests lack sensitivity to the specific classroom under investigation. Consequently, there is a high probability of a mismatch between the text and the test. In terms of the unit of analysis, process-product research assumes that teaching can be reduced to the frequency of occurrence of behavior without concern for the sequences of presentation that are carefully planned and sensitively conducted.

Shulman (1986) discussed the emergence of alternatives to the process-product approach, including the study of cognitive (mediating) processes of teachers', students' ethnographic and linguistic backgrounds, and teachers' knowledge of the subject matter. While Shulman believed that these alternatives have potential for avoiding the weaknesses of the process-product approach, he warned that researchers must not lose sight of the larger context in which teaching and learning occur. Therefore, the conceptual model presented here provides a framework for directing further research in a cognitive mode.

Student Background Characteristics

The student background characteristics (SBC) refer to those variables that are established prior to the student's school experience. SBCs are divided into two categories—family background and student characteristics. Research that examined the effect of these variables is summarized in Table 2.1 for general school effectiveness variables and in Table 2.2 for variables associated with education of the deaf student.

Research on a normally hearing population indicates consistent trends for the family background characteristics. When parents have more children, a lower income, a lower occupational status, fewer home possessions, and less education, their children tend to fare less well in school. Similar trends are evident in the research that was done with deaf subjects, although fewer (or no) studies have used such variables as family size, occupational status, possessions, and parental education. Except for the Bodner-Johnson (1983) study, the results for family income parallel those of the hearing population. Bodner-Johnson reported that the inclusion of socioeconomic status (SES) in the data set did not contribute any additional discriminating power when family environment and communication mode used in the home were included in the analysis. A fuller description of family environment is included under the section on family support below.

Two family background variables are uniquely associated with research with a deaf group—the hearing status of the parents and the communication mode used in the home. Six of seven studies support the academic superiority of deaf children of deaf parents over deaf children of hearing parents. Bodner-Johnson (1983) reports that parental hearing status has little effect on reading level when parenting practices are controlled. Her results are consistent with the position that parental hearing status is a proxy for differential communication and parenting experiences (Sisco and Anderson 1980). The Karchmer and Trybus (1977) finding that deaf children of deaf parents are less likely to be mainstreamed may also reflect differences in preferred communication mode or in speech intelligibility.

The findings of Jensema and Trybus (1978) and Bodner-Johnson (1983) differed in regard to the effect of the communication mode used in the home. This conflict resulted from the definitions that the researchers used for this variable. Jensema and Trybus performed separate partial correlation analyses for high–low use of speech and high–low use of sign. They concluded that the effect of communication (i.e., high vs. low speech use and high vs. low sign use) on academic achievement was trivial. Bodner-Johnson (1983), on the other hand, defined communication mode used in the home as either oral (the child primarily receives input through speechreading and amplification of sound, and expresses himself or herself through speech) or simultaneous (input and expression are through oral communication plus manual signs, fingerspelling, or gestures). Using a multivariate statistical analysis, Bodner-Johnson found that the use of simultaneous communication in the home was associated with higher reading and math scores.

The student characteristics in the general school effectiveness models included sex, race, age, kindergarten attendance, and prior ability (Table 2.1). For the normally hearing group, females tend to have more positive school outcomes than males, except in the areas of mathematics and verbal achievement. Findings for the deaf samples were similar in that females generally had more positive outcomes, although no sex differences were found in math for this group.

The generally negative achievement record for normally hearing minorities was repeated in the deaf group. For the deaf group, it was also found generally that minorities were less likely to be mainstreamed. The one study that found a higher percentage of mainstreamed minorities attributed this to an artifact of their sampling strategy (Allen and Osborn 1984).

Age tends to be a negative factor in the research with hearing subjects and a positive factor in the research with deaf subjects. This difference is a result of the definition of the variable. In the hearing sample studies, age is defined as being over age for the grade, and these people tend to have lower test scores. In the deaf samples, older subjects had higher reading scores (Wolk and Allen 1984) and were more likely to be mainstreamed (Wolk, Karchmer, and Schildroth 1982; Allen and Osborn 1984). In other words, less mainstreaming occurs in the early elementary years than in high school.

Kindergarten attendance was found to have a positive effect on later school achievement in research with hearing subjects. The effect of this variable has not been included in school effectiveness research with a deaf sample. This may be an important variable to consider in light of the emphasis on early detection and intervention for deaf people.

The effects of prior ability level on school achievement has been examined in research with both hearing and deaf samples. The results are consistent for both groups in that persons with higher prior ability also tend to achieve higher in their later academic experiences.

Student characteristics that are uniquely associated with education of the deaf include the age of onset of hearing loss, the cause of the loss, communication skills, degree of loss, hearing aid usage, and the presence of additional handicaps (Table 2.2).

Prelingual loss of hearing and degree of hearing loss are negatively associated with being mainstreamed, probably because of the interrelationship of these two variables with speech ability. No relationship was reported between age of loss and presence of emotional problems.

The effect of the cause of deafness on school achievement was not important in a comparison of rubella as the cause of deafness vs. other causes (Allen and Karchmer 1981). However, when the cause of deafness was divided into heredity, mumps, and otitis media vs. other noninherited causes, poorer school performance was associated with the other noninherited causes. Jensema (1975) suggested that some noninherited causes of deafness were more often associated with the presence of additional handicaps. The presence of additional handicaps is

Table 2.1
Student Background Characteristics

	Research with Hearing Students				Research with Deaf Students			
Group of Variables	Independent Variable	Dependent Variable	Direction of Effect	Level and Source	Dependent Variable	Direction of Effect	Level	Source
				General School Effectiveness Variables				
Family Background	Family size (number of people)	Verbal	Negative	Elementary & secondary (Glasman & Biniaminov, 1981)	Reading	Negative	Age 10 to 12	Bodner-Johnson, 1983
		Reading	Negative		Math	Negative		
		Math	Negative					
		Student attitudes	Negative					
	Family income	Verbal	Positive	Elementary & secondary (Glasman & Biniaminov, 1981)	Mainstream	Positive	Elementary & secondary	Karchmer & Trybus, 1977; Rawlings and Jensema, 1977 Bodner-Johnson, 1983
		Reading	Positive		Math	Positive		
		IQ	Positive		Reading	Positive		
		Composite achievement	Positive		Reading	Little effect when parenting practices were controlled	Age 10 to 12	
		Dropouts	Negative					
	Family occupational status	Verbal	Positive	Elementary & secondary (Glasman & Biniaminov, 1981)				
		Reading	Positive					
		Math	Positive					
		Composite achievement	Positive					
		General academic achievement	Positive					
		Nonverbal	Positive					
		General information	Positive					
		Aspirations	Positive					

Variables Associated with Education of Deaf Students

Independent Variable	Dependent Variable	Relationship	Grade Level / Setting	Study
Mainstream	High school completion	Positive	Elementary and secondary	Karchmer and Trybus, 1977
	Continuation in higher education	Positive		
Family Possessions	Verbal	Positive	Elementary & secondary	Glasman & Biniaminov, 1981
	Reading	Positive		
	Math	Positive		
	Academic ability	Positive		
Parental Education	Verbal	Positive	Elementary and secondary	Glasman & Biniaminov, 1981
	Reading	Positive		
	Math	Positive		
	Academic ability	Positive		
	General information	Positive		
	Abstract reasoning	Positive		
	Student attitudes	Positive		
	Continuation in higher education	Positive		
	Attendance at a 4-year college	Positive		
Hearing status of parents (1 = deaf parents)		Positive	10 to 18.11 years	Brasel and Quigley, 1977
		Positive	8 to 18 years	
		Positive		

Table 2.1 (continued)

Group of Variables	Research with Hearing Students				Research with Deaf Students			
	Independent Variable	Dependent Variable	Direction of Effect	Level and Source	Dependent Variable	Direction of Effect	Level	Source
0 = hearing parents)					Language Reading Math		Elementary and secondary	Jensema and Trybus, 1978; Meadow, 1967; Vernon & Koh, 1970
					Mainstream	Negative	Elementary and secondary	Karchmer and Trybus, 1977
					SAT-HI	Positive	Age 13–19	Convey and Koelle, 1981
					Reading	Little effect when parenting practices are controlled	Age 10–12	Bodner-Johnson, 1983
Communication mode used in the home					Reading	Positive for use of simultaneous communication	Age 10–12	Bodner-Johnson, 1983
							Elementary and secondary	Jensema, 1975 Karchmer et al., 1979; Meadow, 1967; Vernon & Koh, 1970
					School achievement	No effect of speech vs. sign use	Elementary and secondary	Jensema and Trybus, 1978

General School Effectiveness Variables

Student Characteristics	Variable	Relationship	Reference (context)	Variable	Relationship	Grade Level / Sample	Reference
Sex (1 = Female, 0 = Male)	Verbal	Negative	Elementary and secondary (Glasman & Biniaminov, 1981)	Reading	Positive	Age 15–16	Allen and Karchmer, 1981
	Reading	Positive		Mainstream	Positive		
	Math	Negative		SAT-HI Non-math	Positive	Age 13–19	Convey & Koelle, 1981
	Nonverbal	Negative		SAT-HI Math	No difference		
	General information	Negative		Behavioral problems	Negative	Elementary and secondary	Jensema and Trybus, 1978
	Composite achievement	Positive		Reading	Positive	Elementary and secondary	Trybus and Karchmer, 1977; Wolk and Allen, 1984; Babbini and Quigley, 1970
	Spelling	Positive		Overall academic performance	Positive	4.4 to 5.7 years	Fiedler, 1969
	Student attitudes	Positive					
	High school completion	Positive					
	Continuation in higher education	Positive					
Race (1 = Minority status, 0 = Caucasian)	IQ	Negative	Elementary and secondary (Shuey, 1966)	Achievement	Negative	Elementary and secondary	Jensema, 1975
	Achievement	Negative		Mainstreaming	Negative	Age 15–16	Allen and Karchmer, 1981
				Achievement	Negative	Elementary and secondary	Jensema, 1975

Table 2.1 (*continued*)

Group of Variables	Research with Hearing Students				Research with Deaf Students			
	Independent Variable	Dependent Variable	Direction of Effect	Level and Source	Dependent Variable	Direction of Effect	Level	Source
	Achievement		Negative	Elementary and secondary (Jones, 1984)	Mainstream	Negative	Elementary and secondary	Karchmer & Trybus, 1977;
					Reading	Negative	Elementary	Karchmer et al., 1979; Trybus and Karchmer, 1977
					Math			
					Reading	Negative	Elementary and secondary	Wolk and Allen, 1984
					Mainstream	Negative	Elementary and secondary	Wolk, Karchmer, & Schildroth, 1982; Gregory, Shanahan, and Walberg, 1984
					Mainstream	Positive		Allen and Osborn, 1984
Age	Reading		Negative[a]	Elementary and secondary (Glasman & Biniaminov, 1981)	Reading	Positive	Elementary	Wolk and Allen, 1984
	Math		Negative[a]					
	Nonverbal		Negative[a]					
	General information		Negative[a]		Mainstream	Positive	Elementary and secondary	Wolk, Karchmer, and Schildroth, 1982; Allen and Osborn, 1984

Variable	Measure	Direction	Sample / Grade	Study
Kindergarten attendance	Reading	Positive		
	Math	Positive		
	Grade aspirations	Positive		
Ability level, IQ, or prior achievement	Cognitive outcomes	Positive	Elementary	(Glasman & Biniaminov, 1981)
			Elementary and secondary	(Centra and Potter, 1980)
	College GPA	Positive	Postsecondary	Long and Cogiola, 1980
	Reading	Positive	8–15	Pollard and Oakland, 1982
	Math	Positive	Age 15–16	Allen and Karchmer, 1981
	Reading	Positive, may be spurious[b]		
	Academic achievement	Positive	Grade 10 to 12	Joiner et al., 1969
	Reading	Positive	8–14 years	Serwatka, 1979
	Reading	Positive	8–13 years	Savage, Evans, and Savage, 1981
	Reading	Positive	15–16½ years	Conrad, 1977; 1979

[a]Students who are over age for their grade tend to have lower scores.
[b]May be due to minority status.

Table 2.2
Student Background Variables Associated with Education of Deaf Children

Independent Variable	Dependent Variable	Direction of Effect	Level	Source
Age of loss (1 = prelingual, 0 = postlingual)	Mainstream	Negative	Elementary and secondary	Allen and Osborn, 1984; Trybus and Karchmer, 1977
	Emotional problems	No relationship	Elementary and secondary	Jensema and Trybus, 1975
Cause of hearing loss	Achievement	No relationship[a] (1 = Rubella, 0 = Other)	15–16 years	Allen and Karchmer, 1981
	Vocabulary Reading Math	Positive[b] Positive[b] Positive[b]	Elementary and secondary	Jensema, 1975
Communication skills	Mainstream	Positive (degree of speech intelligibility)	Elementary and secondary	Jensema, Karchmer, and Trybus, 1978; Karchmer and Trybus, 1977
	Mainstream	Positive (speechreading skills)	Secondary	Kindred, 1980
	College GPA	Positive (written language skills)	Postsecondary	Long and Coggiola, 1980
	Academic achievement	Positive (communicative attitudes, speech, and speech-reading)	Elementary and secondary	Pflaster, 1981
	Reading	Positive (speech discrimination)	8–14 years	Serwatka, 1979
Degree of hearing loss (greater loss)	Mainstream	Negative	15–16 years	Allen and Karchmer, 1981
	Reading Math	Negative No effect		
	Mainstream	Negative	Elementary and secondary	Allen and Osborn, 1984; Wolk, Karchmer, and Schildroth, 1982; Libbey and Pronovost, 1980; Karchmer and Trybus, 1977

Table 2.2 (*continued*)

Independent Variable	Dependent Variable	Direction of Effect	Level	Source
	Academic achievement	Negative	Elementary and secondary	Jensema, 1975
	Speech intelligibility	Negative	Elementary and secondary	Jensema, Karchmer, and Trybus, 1978
	Emotional problems	No effects	Elementary and secondary	Jensema and Trybus, 1975
	Use of speech	Negative		
	Reading	Negative	Elementary and secondary	Karchmer et al., 1979
	Math	Mixed		
	Reading	Negative	Elementary and secondary	Wolk and Allen, 1984
	Reading	Negative	8–14 years	Serwatka, 1979
Hearing aid usage	Use of speech	Positive	Elementary and secondary	Jensema and Trybus, 1978
	Reading	No effect (of age of initial use)	8–14 years	Serwatka, 1979
Presence of additional handicaps	Mainstream	Negative	Elementary and secondary	Allen and Osborn, 1984
	Reading	Negative	15–16 year olds	Allen and Karchmer, 1981
	Math	Negative		
	Academic achievement	Negative	Elementary and secondary	Jensema, 1975
	Emotional problems	Positive	Elementary and secondary	Jensema and Trybus, 1978
	Speech use	Negative	Elementary and secondary	Jensema and Trybus, 1978
	Reading	Negative	Elementary and secondary	Karchmer et al., 1979
	Achievement	Negative	Elementary and secondary	Trybus and Karchmer, 1977
	Reading	Negative	Elementary and secondary	Wolk and Allen, 1984

[a]The effects of rubella-caused deafness can be accounted for by its significant negative correlation with minority status.

[b]Positive for hereditary, mumps, and otitis media as compared to other causes.

consistently associated with poorer school achievement and more emotional problems.

The effect of communication skills has focused on speechreading, speech intelligibility, written language skills, and attitude toward communicating with others. All these variables are associated with more positive student outcomes. The school system appears to be more effective with the deaf student who has good expressive and receptive speech skills. (This is also supported by the consistent finding that the greater the loss of hearing, the lower the school achievement.) No research has addressed the influence of the students' signing abilities, nor ways the schools can be more responsive to the "more deaf" student. Hearing aid usage was found to be positively related to the use of speech, but not to reading ability (Jensema and Trybus 1978).

School-Level Variables

The present study adopted Centra and Potter's (1980) division of school-level effects into school or school district conditions and within-school conditions. The school or school district variables characterize differences between schools or school districts, and the within-school conditions describe conditions within an individual school. For example, the former include facilities and expenditures, and the latter include sociodemographic characteristics of the students and administrative organization.

The effects of school or school district conditions are classified as facilities, expenditures, staff, and other variables associated with education of the deaf (Table 2.3). Many diverse effects of school conditions or school district conditions have been documented in research with hearing students. Consequently, research on school effectiveness should include such variables. However, these variables are not commonly addressed in research on school effectiveness with deaf students.

With regard to the need for materials and supplies, Kindred (1980) stated that special education materials need to be partially rewritten or adapted for the mainstreamed deaf student. However logical this appears, no empirical relationship has been documented between expenditures for materials adaptation and student outcomes.

Nelson (1982) studied the relationship between schools' fiscal characteristics and their expenditures for special education (not specific to education of the deaf). He did not study the effect of special education expenditures on student outcomes directly, yet his findings suggest something about that relationship for the deaf student. He reported that increases in expenditures were associated with an increase in the identification of low-cost handicapped children (e.g., learning disabled, educable mentally retarded), and not with providing more expensive services per pupil. Thus, deaf students may not be the beneficiaries of increased expenditures because they do not fall into the category of low-cost handicapping condition. Nelson went on to make the point that small school districts do not benefit from the economies of scale. This is especially true with the deaf student, because a full-time interpreter or a teacher of the deaf would be needed even if a school had only one deaf student.

Numerous professionals were recommended to serve in an educational program for the deaf (DeSalle and Ptasnik 1976; Rawlings and Trybus 1978). No study examined the relationship between the presence of these specialists and stu-

Table 2.3
School or School District Conditions as a Factor in Research with Normally Hearing Samples and Variables Associated with Education of Deaf Children

Group Variables	Independent Variables	Dependent Variables	Direction of Effect	Level
		General School Effectiveness Variables		
Facilities	Science lab (1 = yes, 0 = no)	Verbal	Positive	Secondary
	Age of building	Verbal	Negative	Elementary and secondary
		Nonverbal	Negative	
		Reading	Mixed	
		Math	Negative	
		Dropouts	Negative	
	Size of school site	Verbal	Positive	Elementary
		Math	Positive	
	Size of school enrollment	Verbal	Negative	Elementary and secondary
		Reading	Negative	
		Math	Negative	
		Composite achievement	Negative	
		Dropouts	Positive	
		Continuation in higher education	Positive	
	Number of books in library per student	Verbal	Positive	Elementary and secondary
		Reading	Positive	
		Math	Mixed	
		Abstract reasoning	Positive	
		Composite achievement	Negative	
		Variable Associated with Education of Deaf Children		
	Size of deaf student enrollment[a]			
		General School Effectiveness Variables		
Expenditures	Library	Composite achievement	Negative	Elementary and secondary
		Dropouts	Negative	
	Materials and supplies	Dropouts	Negative	Secondary
	Administrative expenditures	Composite achievement	Positive	Elementary and secondary
	Instructional expenditures	Composite achievement	Positive	Secondary
	Extracurricular expenditures	Verbal	Positive	Secondary
	Teacher salaries	Student attitudes	Negative	Elementary and secondary
		Verbal	Positive	
		Reading	Mixed	
		Math	Positive	

Table 2.3 (*continued*)

Group Variables	Independent Variables	Dependent Variables	Direction of Effect	Level
	Total expenditures	Composite achievement	Positive	Secondary
		G.P.A.	Positive	
		Dropouts	Negative	
		Interest in school	Positive	
		Verbal	Positive	
		Abstract reasoning	Positive	
		Reading	Positive	
		Math	Positive	

Variables Associated with Education of Deaf Children
Special education expenditures
Expenditures for hearing impaired programs[a]

General School Effectiveness Variables

Group Variables	Independent Variables	Dependent Variables	Direction of Effect	Level
Staff	Administrative personnel	Verbal	Positive	Secondary
		Reading	Negative	
		Math	Negative	
	Auxiliary personnel	Verbal	Negative	Secondary
		Self-concept	Negative	
	Teacher turnover	Verbal	Mixed	Elementary and secondary
		Nonverbal	Positive	
		Reading	Positive	
		Math	Negative	
		Educational aspirations	Negative	
		Student attitudes	Negative	

Variables Associated with Education of Deaf Children
Special education personnel[a]
Other Variables Associated with Deaf Children

Services
Planning
School support[a]

Source: N. S. Glasman and I. Biniaminov, "Input-output Analysis of Schools," *Review of Educational Research* 51(4)(1981): 509–539.
[a]No data are available for these variables.

dent outcomes. The recommended personnel included such positions as an administrator of the deaf education program who is at the same level as the principal, teachers of the deaf, liaison teachers, media specialists, counselors, speech therapists, notetakers, teacher aides, nurses, physicians, and audiologists. Rawlings and Trybus (1978) further recommended that schools provide the following services for their deaf students: health exams, routine vision exams, genetic counseling, sex education, parent training, audiometric tests, and hearing aid services.

In a study of predictors and outcomes of mainstreaming severely handicapped students, Brinker and Thorpe (1984) discussed numerous planning activities at the state and local level that would facilitate the process. While their study did not focus specifically on deafness, they did suggest several variables that should be tested in future research with deaf samples. Brinker and Thorpe noted that state-level planning was necessary before implementing a mainstreaming program that included teacher training programs, funding, defining the categories of exceptionality, establishing procedures for hearings on least restrictive environment, certification requirements, providing state consultants, placement options, funded demonstration programs, and in-service training in special education. At the local level, Brinker and Thorpe identified the following variables as predictors of the degree of integration: whether the local school served as a demonstration site, total district enrollment, availability of support staff, and preparation of non-handicapped students. It is not yet known whether these state- and local-level planning variables influence the placement and subsequent academic success of deaf students.

The within-school conditions category includes three groups of variables: sociodemographic characteristics of the student population, student attendance, and administrative organization (Table 2.4). The study of the effect of sociodemographic characteristics of the student population yielded fairly consistent results for the racial and socioeconomic composition of the school. Schools with a higher percentage of minority students and a higher percentage of low-income students were associated with poorer student outcomes. While larger class size was generally associated with poorer student outcomes, conflicting findings were reported for composite achievement and for different sizes of different types of classes. Centra and Potter (1980) suggest that contradictory findings for class size can be explained by the threshold effect for class size (Glass and Smith 1978) and by the poor design of many class size studies. The threshold effect indicates that dramatic gains can be achieved when class size is reduced to fifteen or below, and very few research studies of class size included classes under fifteen.

Research has not yet been conducted with a deaf sample on the effect of sociodemographic characteristics of the student population. Nor has research been conducted on the effect of class size for the deaf student in a mainstreamed or a self-contained classroom. Kindred (1980) recommended that one teacher of the deaf was needed to assist a regular classroom teacher if more than one deaf student was in a class. No empirical relationship was established between this recommendation and student outcomes. As self-contained classrooms tend to have very small classes, there may not be enough variability to warrant conducting such research. Student attendance variables included student turnover, days present, quantity of schooling, unexcused absences, and lateness. While the effects of these variables have only been reported at the elementary level, the results were all consistent with what would logically be expected (i.e., the more days that students actually attend school, the better their performance). Again, no research with deaf subjects has examined the effect of these variables.

Table 2.4
Within-School Conditions

Group Variables	Independent Variables	Dependent Variables	Direction of Effect	Level	Source
		General School Effectiveness Variables			
Sociodemographic characteristics of the student population	Racial composition (percentage of minority students)	Math	Negative	Elementary & secondary	Glasman and Biniaminov, 1981
		General academic ability	Negative		
		Verbal	Negative		
		Reading	Negative		
		General information	Negative		
		Nonverbal	Negative		
		Composite achievement	Negative		
		Continuation to higher education	Negative		
	Socioeconomic composition	Verbal	Positive	Secondary	Glasman and Biniaminov, 1981
		Reading	Positive		
		Abstract reasoning	Positive		
	Class size	Composite achievement	Positive	Elementary & secondary	Glasman and Biniaminov, 1981
		Verbal	Negative		
		Nonverbal	Negative		
		Reading	Negative		
		Math	Negative		
		General information	Negative		
		Educational aspirations	Negative		
	Size of type of class (e.g., average class size in science)	Reading	Mixed	Elementary & secondary	Glasman and Biniaminov, 1981
		Spelling	Negative		
		Math	Mixed		
		General academic ability	Negative		
		Abstract reasoning	Positive		
		Composite achievement	Positive		
		Variables Associated with Education of Deaf Children			
	Deaf student-teacher ratio				

Table 2.4 (*continued*)

Group Variables	Independent Variables	Dependent Variables	Direction of Effect	Level	Source
		General School Effectiveness Variables			
Student attendance	Student turnover	Reading	Negative	Elementary	Glasman and Biniaminov, 1981
	Days present	Math	Positive	Elementary	Glasman and Biniaminov, 1981
	Quality of schooling	Verbal Reading Math	Positive Positive Positive	Elementary	Glasman and Biniaminov, 1981
	Student unexcused absences and lateness	Composite achievement	Negative	Elementary	Glasman and Biniaminov, 1981
		General School Effectiveness Variables			
Administrative organization	Degree of control, authority Environment/ ambiance[a]	Math	Negative	Elementary	McDonald, 1976b
	Variables associated with education of the hearing-impaired[a]				
	Administrator's attitude toward deaf children[a]				
	Administrator's attitude toward mainstreaming deaf children[a]				
	Process of decision-making for deaf student placement[a]				

[a]No data are available for these variables.

Glasman and Biniaminov (1981) reported that no studies investigated the effects of administrative tasks or styles, and that studies that used school principals' characteristics yielded insignificant results. Centra and Potter (1980) included administrative organization and environment or ambience in their list of within-school variables. They suggested that the administrative organization of the school may have some influence on student learning through its effect on teachers and teaching practices. McDonald (1976b) found that greater centralization of decision making was associated with less independent pupil seatwork and more teaching the class as a whole. In turn, teaching the class as a whole was a negative predictor of pupil learning in second-grade mathematics.

The effect of administrative organization is not a closed issue for researchers who use normally hearing subjects, and it represents unexplored territory for those who conduct research with the deaf. Nelson (1982) examined the effect of centralized administrative control in special education (not specific to the deaf), and he did not attempt to examine the effect of that control on student outcomes. He did find that as the strength of centralized control decreased, evaluation procedures, staffing patterns, and programming strategies showed greater variability because school officials were able to exercise greater discretion over policies and procedures of identification and classification.

The principal's attitude toward deaf students and mainstreaming deaf students is a variable that has not yet been related to student outcomes. DeSalle and Ptasnik (1976) reported that the attitude of the building principal greatly influenced the attitudes of regular classroom teachers toward their deaf mainstreamed students. Kindred (1980) suggested that full administrative support is needed for successful mainstreaming. Only administrators can permit flexible scheduling and allow time for staff orientations early in the fall, and only administrators can authorize substitutes so that teachers can attend eligibility conferences. Brinker and Thorpe (1984) reported that the degree of principal support was a significant predictor of the amount of integration of severely handicapped students (not specifically deaf students).

Instructional Personnel

The instructional personnel category includes general school effectiveness variables related to the teacher's background and personal characteristics, assignment, and attitudes (Table 2.5). Very little research has been conducted with these variables using a deaf sample, and no research was located that addressed the relationship between these variables and outcomes for deaf students.

The research on general school effectiveness suggests that teacher background characteristics are related to student outcomes. The level of education, years of teaching experience, time in major, and verbal ability are positively associated with student outcomes. The relationship between a teacher's race and student outcomes is dependent upon the predominant race of the student body. In a predominantly black school, being a black teacher is associated with higher student outcomes, while the reverse of this is true in predominantly white schools. Being male was associated with more positive student outcomes in elementary-level reading and math. However, being female was associated with higher levels of abstract reasoning abilities at the secondary level. Increased teacher load is negatively associated with student outcomes, and teacher job satisfaction is positively associated with student outcomes.

Several instructional personnel characteristic variables are uniquely associated with education of the deaf, including ability to work as a team member, orientation and support, signing ability, role of the teacher of the deaf, skill in IEP development, and years of working with deaf students. No research was located

Table 2.5
Characteristics of Instructional Personnel Who Work with
Normally Hearing Subjects

Group Variables	Independent Variables	Dependent Variables	Direction of Effect	Level	Source
Teacher background and personal characteristics					
	Education degree	Reading	Positive	Elementary and second-ary	Glasman and Biniaminov, 1981
		Math	Mixed		
		General academic ability	Positive		
		High school completion	Positive		
	Undergrad-uate educa-tion degree	Verbal	Positive	Elementary and second-ary	Glasman and Biniaminov, 1981
		Reading	Positive		
		Composite achievement	Positive		
	Years of teaching experience	Verbal	Positive	Elementary and second-ary	Glasman and Biniaminov, 1981
		Nonverbal	Positive		
		Reading	Positive		
		Math	Positive		
		Composite achievement	Positive		
		General infor-mation	Positive		
		High school completion	Positive		
		Continuation in higher education	Positive		
	Verbal achievement	Verbal	Positive	Elementary and second-ary	Glasman and Biniaminov, 1981
		Nonverbal	Positive		
		Reading	Positive		
		Math	Positive		
		General infor-mation	Positive		
	Race (1 = Black, 0 = Other)	Reading	Positive	Elementary (black)	Glasman and Biniaminov, 1981
		Math	Positive	Elementary (black)	
		Verbal	Negative	Elementary (white)	
		Math	Negative	Elementary (white)	
	Sex (1 = male, 0 = female)	Reading	Positive	Elementary (black)	Glasman and Biniaminov, 1981
		Math	Positive	Elementary (black)	

Table 2.5 (*continued*)

Group Variables	Independent Variables	Dependent Variables	Direction of Effect	Level	Source
		Abstract reasoning	Negative	Secondary	
	Teacher time in discipline	Reading	Negative	Elementary	Glasman and Biniaminov, 1981
	Teacher time in major	Verbal	Positive	Secondary	Glasman and Biniaminov, 1981
		Abstract reasoning	Positive		
		Composite score	Positive		
Teacher assignment					
	Teacher load	Verbal	Negative	Secondary	Glasman and Biniaminov, 1981
		Math	Negative		
		Interest in school	Negative		
		Self-concept	Negative	Elementary	
		Reading	Negative		
Teacher attitudes					
	Job satisfaction	Verbal	Positive	Elementary and secondary	Glasman and Biniaminov, 1981
		Reading	Positive		
		Math	Positive		
		Grade aspirations	Positive		
		Interest in school	Positive		
Variables associated with education of deaf children					

Ability to work as a team
Orientation and support
Signing ability
Role of the teacher of the deaf
IEP development
Interpreter's role
Years of working with deaf students

that directly addressed the relationship between these variables and student outcomes.

Kindred (1980) discussed the process of developing an Individualized Education Plan (IEP) for deaf students. She reported that IEP development requires thinking through the meaning of the least restrictive environment for each student and carefully assessing the student's test scores, academic grades, and psychological evaluations. One or more sessions with the student and the parent(s) may be required. No research is available on the relationship between student outcomes and the IEP development process. The advantages or disadvantages have not yet been documented on the effect of involving the general classroom teacher in the IEP development process for a mainstreamed deaf student.

Kindred further suggested that the ability to work as part of a team is important for successfully mainstreaming deaf students and that the team should include the principal, the administrator of deaf education, the liaison teacher, and the regular teacher. In an earlier study, Kindred (1976) recommended an orientation session and ongoing support for the regular teacher who teaches deaf students.

The role of the teacher of the deaf was described as that of a public relations agent who must sell the regular teachers on the idea of accepting deaf students in their classes (DeSalle and Ptasnik, 1976). The teachers of the deaf must work for good rapport with all school personnel, parents, and the community. DeSalle and Ptasnik suggested that mainstreaming is more successful if the regular teacher knows sign language and can use total communication. They did not present evidence that linked such variables with improved student outcomes.

Interpreters play a very important role in the mainstream program for deaf students. However, no research could be located that linked their characteristics, assignments, or attitudes with student outcomes.

Student Attitudes

Student attitudes can be viewed as both inputs and outputs in a school effectiveness model. At this point in the model, the only consideration is that of input (i.e., what is the effect of student attitude on student outcomes, including academic achievement?). The student attitude variables in the general school effectiveness model include internal control, self-concept, academic aspirations, study habits, and motivation (Table 2.6).

Studies using hearing samples reported a positive correlation between each of the variables and various measures of achievement. A similar trend is evident in research with deaf subjects for internal control and self-concept. No research could be located that specifically addressed the relationship between academic aspirations, study habits, and motivation, and student outcomes with deaf subjects. Kindred (1980) noted that the successful mainstream deaf student must have good study skills and be highly motivated. Gregory et al. (1984) noted that deaf students tend to spend less time studying than hearing students.

Student attitude is particularly important in the education of deaf students. Several researchers have reported that deaf students tend to be more impulsive than hearing students (Levine 1956; Meadow 1980), and Harris (1975) reported a strong positive relationship between impulse control and academic achievement. Pflaster (1981) found that the best predictor of academic achievement for the mainstreamed deaf student was the student's communicative attitude (i.e., the willingness to communicate using spoken language).

The influence of hearing students' attitudes toward deaf students, as well as

Table 2.6
Student Attitudes

	Research with Hearing Students			Research with Deaf Students			
Independent Variable	Dependent Variable	Direction of Effect	Level and Source	Dependent Variable	Direction of Effect	Level	Source
Variables Associated with the General School Effectiveness Model							
Internal control	Verbal Math Nonverbal Reading General information	Positive Positive Positive Positive Positive	Secondary and elementary (Glasman and Biniaminov, 1981)	SAT-HI	Positive	Age 13–19	Convey and Koelle, 1981
Self-concept	Verbal	Positive	Secondary (Glasman and Biniaminov, 1981)	SAT-HI Academic achievement	Positive Positive	Age 13–19 Grades 10 to 12	Convey and Koelle, 1981 Joiner, et al., 1969; Meadow, 1967
Academic aspirations	Verbal Math	Positive Positive	Secondary and elementary (Glasman and Biniaminov, 1981)				

Variables Associated with Education of Deaf Children

Study habits	Academic achievement	Positive	Elementary and secondary (Walberg, 1984)	
Motivation	Academic achievement	Positive	Elementary and secondary (Walberg, 1984)	
Impulsivity	Academic achievement	Negative		Harris, 1975
Deaf students' attitudes toward communication	Academic achievement	Positive	Elementary and secondary	Pflaster, 1981
Hearing students' attitudes toward deaf students[a]				
Deaf students' attitudes toward hearing students[a]				

[a]No data are available for these variables.

deaf students' attitudes toward hearing students, on other student outcomes has not yet been investigated. This is an important area, considering the problems that deaf students encounter in mainstream classrooms. Deaf adolescents cited among their biggest problems making friends, communicating with hearing people, feeling comfortable talking with hearing teachers and students, being accepted, being made fun of, and feeling uneasy with teachers and students (Libbey and Pronovost 1982; Mertens 1986).

Student Placement

The effect of participation in a mainstreamed setting is a central concern in the present research. However, this issue must be examined carefully because the basic premise of this research is that numerous variables influence both student placement and student outcomes. Whether a student is placed in a mainstreamed setting depends upon the student's background characteristics, school or school district conditions, within-school conditions, instructional personnel characteristics, and student attitudes. The outcomes of student placement are influenced not only by these variables, but also by instructional personnel performance, family support, and student behavior. Consequently, answers to the question "What are the effects of mainstreaming deaf students?" must begin with "It depends. . . ." It depends on who is being mainstreamed, where mainstreaming occurs, and what happens in the school and classroom.

As Wolk, Karchmer, and Schildroth (1982) pointed out, it also depends on the way mainstreaming is defined. It is important to distinguish between academic integration (i.e., instructional classes, math, reading, and science) and nonacademic integration (i.e., shared school settings such as recess, lunch, physical education, or art class). Libbey and Pronovost (1980) reported that participation in mainstream situations is greatest in nonacademic areas.

Numerous studies document the effects of student placement on social and academic outcomes (Table 2.7). One of the espoused goals of mainstreaming is to improve the attitude of hearing students toward deaf students. Generally, research tends to support the conclusion that interaction between the two groups leads to more positive attitudes on the part of the hearing students toward the deaf students (Board of Education of the City of New York 1956; Jacobs 1976; Kennedy et al. 1976).

Antia's (1982) research suggests that simply placing deaf students in a regular classroom will not lead to increased interaction between hearing students and deaf students. She examined the amount and type of interaction in mainstream and self-contained elementary classrooms among hearing and deaf children and their teachers. The hearing students had more interaction with their peers and less with their teachers than did the deaf students. The frequency of interaction between deaf students and their peers was the same in mainstreamed classrooms and self-contained classrooms. Antia concluded that physical proximity is a necessary

Table 2.7
Student Placement

Independent Variable	Dependent Variable	Direction of Effect	Level	Source
Mainstream (1 = main-streamed, 0 = self-contained classroom)	Academic achievement	Spurious	Age 15 to 16	Allen and Karchmer, 1981
	SAT-HI Reading	Positive	Elementary and	Allen and Osborn
	SAT-HI Math	Positive	secondary	1984
	Interaction with peers	No difference	Elementary	Antia, 1982
	Interaction with teacher	Negative		
	Hearing students' attitude toward deaf students	Positive	4th grade	Board of Education of the City of New York, 1956
		Positive	Postsecondary	Jacobs, 1976
	Academic achievement	Positive	Elementary	Connor, 1975
	Reading	Positive	Elementary	Dale, 1984
	Social adjustment	Positive	Elementary	
	Self-esteem	Negative	Age 10 to 15	Farrugia and Austin, 1980
	Social adjustment	Negative	5 to 16	Fisher, 1966
	Peer acceptance	Positive	Elementary	Kennedy, et al., 1976
	Math achievement	Positive	Secondary	Kluwin and Moores, 1985
	Social adjustment	Positive	Secondary	Ladd, Munson, and Miller, 1984
	Reading[a]	Positive	Elementary	Reich, Hambleton,
	Self-concept	No difference	Elementary	and Houldin,
	Social adjustment	Positive	Elementary	1977
	Language	Positive	Secondary	
	Self-concept	Mixed	Secondary	
	Reading	No difference	Secondary	
	Social adjustment	No difference	Secondary	
	Self-concept	No difference	Grades 4 to 9	Risley, 1977
	Achievement	Positive	Elementary	Rister, 1975
	Achievement	Negative	Elementary	O'Connor and Connor, 1961

Table 2.7 (*continued*)

Independent Variable	Dependent Variable	Direction of Effect	Level	Source
Day School	Self-concept	Negative	9.5 to 12 years	Craig, 1965
	Accurary of self-concept	Negative		
	Self-concept	Negative[b]	Age 6 to 18	Schlesinger and Meadow, 1972
		No difference[c]		
Curriculum taken[d]				

[a]Itinerant group (i.e., deaf students who were fully integrated into regular classes with periodic visits from an itinerant teacher of the deaf) had higher self-concepts than the fully integrated group (i.e., fully integrated without any support services).

[b]Deaf children of hearing parents attending a public day school compared to deaf children of deaf parents attending a residential school.

[c]Deaf children of hearing parents at a day school compared to deaf children of hearing parents at a residential school.

[d]No data are available for this variable.

but not sufficient condition for promoting interaction between hearing and deaf children. Carefully planned situations are needed to encourage and increase such social interaction.

Social Development

Conflicting results have been reported concerning the effect of school placement on students' social development. The differences in the findings result from (1) the type of placements that were compared, (2) the grade levels, and (3) the differences among the programs that the students experienced.

Schlesinger and Meadow (1972) reported that deaf children of deaf parents in residential schools had more positive self-concepts than deaf children of hearing parents in public day schools. This comparison confounds parental hearing status and school placement and, therefore, cannot be used to support the argument that attendance at residential schools is related to a more positive self-concept. When Schlesinger and Meadow compared deaf children of hearing parents at residential schools with those at public day schools, they found no difference in self-concept. Thus, the more positive self-concept of the deaf children of deaf parents may be more the result of parental hearing status (and the implied communication practices and parental acceptance of deafness) than of the school placement.

Craig (1965) also compared deaf students at a residential school with those at a public day school. The deaf students in the residential group rated themselves significantly higher in terms of general self-acceptance than did the day school group. Craig points out that the high ratings of the residential group "may be more a function of the protective institutional environment" (p. 470). In addition, deaf day students who must travel long distances have more limited opportunities for social interaction because they cannot socialize with their classmates after school hours.

Farrugia and Austin (1980) also reported that the self-esteem and social adjustment ratings were lower for deaf students in public day schools than for those in residential schools. However, the researchers did not obtain an accuracy measure of the self-concepts of these students. Therefore, a question remains concerning the influence of the residential setting on social development. Does the sheltered environment of the residential school overprotect deaf students so that they develop an overinflated self-concept? Does the regular school placement give the deaf student an "overdose of reality" and thus destroy the fragile self-concept of the deaf student? Does the deaf student in the regular classroom experience such social isolation that social development is impaired?

Reich, Hambleton, and Houldin (1977) compared four types of placements at both the elementary and the secondary levels: (1) full integration with no support services; (2) an itinerant program (full integration, with a teacher of the deaf who visits periodically); (3) partial integration (students are integrated in subjects in which they have competence); and (4) partial segregation (a self-contained classroom of deaf students in a regular school and perhaps some nonacademic integration). At the elementary level, they reported no differences in self-concept and social adjustment among the four groups. At the secondary level, the itinerant group had a higher self-concept rating than the fully integrated group. However, when the data were analyzed longitudinally, the itinerant group became somewhat less socially adjusted the longer they received such help, and the fully integrated students' self-concepts declined with time. Providing support services seems to encourage development of a more positive self-concept. However, despite such services, a negative trend in self-concept is still evident.

Ladd, Munson, and Miller (1984) added another dimension to the influence of school placement on the deaf students' social development. They reported an increased number of social interactions over a two-year period in a mainstreamed occupational education program. Occupational education is the type of setting in which interactions can be encouraged (as alluded to by Antia [1982]). As a result of this increased interaction, peer ratings for the deaf were much the same as for the hearing. In addition, ratings of the deaf students' considerateness increased in the second year, and disruptiveness ratings decreased. Ninety-four percent of the deaf students said they had hearing friends.

Given the documented behavioral problems of deaf children (Fisher 1966; Hess 1960; Levine 1956; Meadow 1980), it is not surprising that development of a healthy self-concept presents such a challenge to educators, no matter what the school placement. The documentation of positive self-concepts for residential students does not automatically lead to the conclusion that life in a mainstreamed classroom is detrimental to the deaf student's social development. If the environment in the residential setting is overprotective, it may lead to an overinflated sense of self. Thus, the deaf person is not prepared to cope with the hearing world upon graduation.

However, if the regular classroom environment leaves the deaf student socially isolated (Antia 1982), then it does not foster healthy social development. Social development is dependent upon the amount of interaction, and the amount of interaction is dependent upon the structuring of activities that promote such interaction. To wit, in the Ladd et al. (1984) study, the occupational education setting fosters interaction and, consequently, social development. In addition, other variables that influence positive social development include parenting practices (Schlesinger and Meadow 1972), provision of supportive services (Reich, Hambleton, and Houldin 1977), and opportunity for after-school socializing (Craig 1965).

In a carefully documented longitudinal field study, Dale (1984) reported the results of a mainstreaming program that combined carefully structured activities, involvement of parents, and provision of support services. This study of London school children extended from 1972 through 1977. At the end of that period, Dale concluded that the mainstreamed children became more socially mature at a more normal rate and that all of the deaf children had hearing friends. Consequently, mainstreaming done improperly may inhibit the deaf child's social development. However, when mainstreaming is done properly, the deaf child stands to gain in the social arena.

Mertens (1989) attempted to isolate the factors that contributed to a positive or negative experience for deaf high school students. After interviewing students in residental school and mainstream settings, she found that all but one of the deaf students in residential schools described their experiences as positive. (The one student who reported a negative experience had transferred into the residential school in her senior year.) The residential school graduates attributed their positive experiences to their teachers' ability to sign and to the opportunity to socialize with friends and participate in after-school activities.

Half of the deaf students in mainstream settings described their experiences as positive, while the other half described theirs as negative. Those who reported having negative experiences described their high school years as a time of social confusion and isolation, without supportive services and without the opportunity to participate in after-school activities. The deaf students who had positive experiences characterized their high school setting as being supportive. They had access to classes and activities through interpreters, their parents were involved in the program, the school provided structured interactive activities and opportunities to participate in sports, and teachers and peers took an active interest in learning to sign and improving deaf awareness in the school. These students also had better reading skills and many of them used their voices and speechread.

One cautionary note, however: A more positive feeling about high school experiences must not be confused with social maturity. Although, the factors that contribute to the more positive feelings might easily exist in a setting that encourages social development.

Academic Achievement

Generally, positive results have been reported regarding the relationship between mainstreaming and academic achievement. In an early study, O'Connor and Connor (1961) reported that half of the twenty-one students who had been mainstreamed into public schools from the Lexington School for the Deaf were academically unsuccessful. However, 35% of the children received *no* extra help once they had enrolled in an ordinary school, and the other 65% received only occasional visits from a speech therapist or hearing therapist. Guidance personnel, psychologists, and remedial teachers were only minimally involved. In a later study of transfers from the Lexington School (Connor 1975), a much higher success rate was reported. Between 1968 and 1975, a total of 124 prelingually deaf children had been transferred to regular school programs. Only two of those students had to be returned to the residential school as "unsuccessful." Connor attributed the success to improved administrative dedication, teacher-of-the-deaf support, and parental cooperation.

Two studies that used the *Annual Survey of Hearing-Impaired Children and Youth* reported that mainstreamed deaf students exhibited higher achievement than their nonmainstreamed peers (Allen and Karchmer 1981; Allen and Osborn 1984). In both studies, statistical techniques were used to control for differences in prior experience and background variables between the two groups. When these variables were controlled, the effect of mainstreaming appeared to be negligible. More potent predictors of achievement appeared to be prior achievement, degree of hearing loss, sex, age, race, and additional handicapping conditions.

It would be erroneous to conclude from this that differences in the type of students who are mainstreamed totally accounts for the positive effects on academic achievement that other researchers have reported (Connor 1975; Dale 1984; Reich, Hambleton, and Houldin 1977; Rister 1975). Of course, it is important to control for background differences when trying to explain program effects. This is the strength of the work of Allen and Karchmer (1981) and Allen and Osborn (1984). However, because these studies aggregated data for all mainstream programs in the national survey, their results obscure the effects of truly effective mainstreaming programs.

In a carefully designed study, Kluwin and Moores (1985) controlled for differences in background variables. In addition, they were able to compare mainstreaming vs. self-contained programs and identify the differences that contributed to the academic success of the mainstreamed deaf students. Kluwin and Moores identified deaf students in high school who had been mainstreamed into mathematics classes. Using the criteria of prior math performance, degree of hearing loss, and social adjustment, they selected a control group who could have been mainstreamed (based on application of these criteria) but who were not. In addition, they controlled statistically for age, sex, ethnicity, and socioeconomic status.

The results indicated that the students in the mainstreamed math course achieved significantly higher than those in the self-contained classes. Kluwin and Moores discussed the following explanatory factors:

1. Regular classroom teachers had higher expectations for the integrated students.
2. The mainstreamed students were exposed to a larger quantity of demanding content.
3. The regular classroom teachers were trained in teaching mathematics, while the teachers in the self-contained classrooms were trained in deaf education (i.e., speech, language, communication skills).
4. More academic support was provided to the integrated students in terms of monitoring of progress and use of interpreters, tutors, and resource room teachers. Individual attention was greater for the integrated students.

Mertens and Kluwin (1986) conducted a follow-up study in eighteen secondary-level mathematics classrooms to determine support for Kluwin and Moores' (1985) findings. The actual content taught in mainstream and self-contained mathematics classrooms was compared on a scale of 1 to 12, with 12 indicating the most difficult type of problem. The average difficulty in mainstream classrooms was 4.81, while the average difficulty in self-contained classrooms was 1.0. In addition, the majority of the teachers in the mainstream classrooms were trained and certified to teach mathematics, while none of the teachers in self-contained classrooms were so certified.

No research was found that examined the relationship between actual courses taken and student outcomes for deaf persons. Gregory, Shanahan, and Walberg (1984) did report that deaf high school students take fewer traditional academic courses than their hearing peers.

Instructional Personnel Performance

Numerous researchers have reported specific instructional process variables that explain student achievement (Airasian, Kellaghan, and Madaus 1979; Bloom 1976, 1984; Brimer et al. 1977; Brophy and Good 1986; Cazden 1971; Centra and Potter 1980; Kamii 1971; Karweit 1984; Haertel, Walberg, and Weinstein 1983; McDonald 1976b; Madaus, Kellaghan, and Rakow 1975; Shulman 1986; Smith 1976; Stodolsky 1972; Walberg 1984). The search for instructional processes that improve student outcome has been aided by the application of meta-analytic techniques to the problem.

Bloom (1984) presented a list of empirically valid variables that synthesizes much of the research in this area. Bloom adapted Walberg's (1984) meta-analysis results and reported that the following variables were associated with increased achievement.

1. Tutorial instruction.
2. Reinforcement.
3. Corrective feedback (i.e., a mastery learning approach in which formative tests are given for feedback followed by corrective procedures and parallel

summative tests to determine the extent to which the students mastered the subject area).

4. Cues and explanations (i.e., teachers, peers, or printed materials available to help students with items they missed).
5. Student classroom participation.
6. Student time on task.
7. Improved reading/study skills.
8. Cooperative learning (i.e., help students develop a support system in which groups of two or three students study together, help each other when they encounter difficulties, and review for tests).
9. Graded homework.
10. Classroom morale.
11. Enhanced initial cognitive prerequisites (i.e., develop an initial test of the prerequisites for the course [such as the final exam from a prior course], then help students learn the specific prerequisites they lack using corrective-feedback procedures).
12. Home-environment intervention (discussed further in the section on family support).
13. Peer and cross-age remedial tutoring.
14. Assigned homework.
15. Use of higher order questions.
16. New science and math curriculum.
17. Teacher expectancy.

No parallel research could be located that used a deaf sample. Sass-Lehrer (1984) identified a number of competencies that instructional supervisors thought were important for elementary teachers in schools for the deaf. However, she did not validate these competencies in terms of their effects on student outcomes.

Larrivee and Algina (1983) observed 118 elementary school teachers who had mainstreamed students in their classes. The majority (93) of the students were learning disabled and only one was deaf. The researchers validated the effects of thirty-three teaching behaviors in terms of students' reading achievement, self-perception, and peer acceptance using a series of partial correlation analyses. Controlling for grade placement, sex, length of time mainstreamed, hours of special services provided, and prereading achievement, they reported that the following variables predicted postreading achievement.

1. Giving positive feedback (+)
2. Responding supportively to low ability students (+)
3. Maintaining a positive relationship with the students (+)
4. Efficient use of classroom time (+)
5. Student transition time (+)
6. Need for discipline (−)

7. Off-task behavior (−)
8. Incidence of intervention (−)

Three variables were significant correlates of peer acceptance: (1) giving sustaining feedback (i.e., asking subsequent clarifying questions to students making incorrect responses) (+); (2) criticizing incorrect student responses (−); and (3) teacher transition time (−). None of the behaviors correlated significantly with self-perception.

A correspondence clearly exists between Bloom's list based on general school effectiveness and Larrivee and Algina's list based on mainstreamed classrooms. Thus, future research using these variables with a deaf sample is strongly recommended. In addition, research is needed to determine those variables that affect noncognitive outcomes.

The mode of communication used in the classroom is one instructional personnel performance variable that is uniquely associated with the education of deaf students. Bodner-Johnson (1983) reported that adolescent deaf students achieved higher reading levels in classrooms in which total communication was used. Delaney, Stuckless, and Walter (1984) confirmed these findings for an adolescent group of deaf students. They found that the total communication group scored higher than a group with previous experience in an oral/aural program on such measures as reading comprehension, mathematics, and overall academic achievement.

Moores (1985) reported that use of an intensive, coordinated program of auditory training, speech, and manual communication from the start was predictive of success in preschool and early elementary school deaf children. The results indicated that use of manual communication at an early age has no effect on oral reception and expressive skills, but it does facilitate academic achievement and the development of English skills.

Interaction patterns in mainstream classrooms are also affected by variables uniquely associated with the presence of deaf students in the class, as well as by the medium of communication that is used. Hemwall (1984) conducted an ethnographic study of interactional patterns in junior high and high school mainstream classrooms where the deaf students communicated with their teachers through an interpreter. She found that the teachers' who reported feeling uncomfortable with deaf students treated those students inconsistently, especially regarding disciplinary actions. Communication was difficult (even with interpreters) because (1) the teachers were stressed by the unusual sound of the deaf students' voices, (2) they were frustrated by having to use the interpreter as an intermediary, and (3) they were discouraged that students could not easily understand them. The deaf students came to depend on their interpreters for everything, which diminished both their sense of independence and self-reliance. Clearly, research on instructional personnel performance in mainstream classrooms must consider many unique variables.

Johnson and Griffith (1986) compared interactional behaviors in two fourth-grade spelling classes—a self-contained class for deaf students and a mainstream class. Interactions in the mainstream class were characterized by rapid conversational shifts and complex academic task structures, as well as complex language usage. Interactions in the self-contained class were characterized by routinized tasks and simple language structure. It can be hypothesized that students moving between classes with similar communication patterns will experience fewer adjustment difficulties than students moving between classes with dissimilar patterns. Study of such interactional patterns may provide insight into why mainstreamed deaf students have difficulty adjusting to their new instructional setting.

Other variables that are uniquely associated with education of deaf students also require additional research. The teacher's behavior toward the mainstreamed student, the teacher's involvement in writing IEP objectives, and the student's ease of speechreading have not yet been empirically linked to student outcomes. The interpreter's role in the classroom is another important area in need of empirical research (Zawolkow and DeFiore 1986).

Family Support

Measures of environmental processes and interactions in the home are more powerful predictors of performance on standardized achievement tests than are measures of home and parent status (Airasian, Kellaghan, and Madaus 1979; Bloom 1964, 1984; Dave 1963; Linnan and Airasian 1974; Walberg and Marjoribanks 1976; Wolf 1964). Correlations between such indices as parents' SES, education and occupation, and measures of achievement tend to be about .4, while correlations of .7 and above have been found between achievement and such home process variables as parents' strategies of learning reinforcement, mother's language model, and enforced sense of time and space in the home (Airasian, Kellaghan, and Madaus 1979; Bloom 1984; Fraser 1959).

Two major studies have addressed the family environment factors that are related to achievement: Bloom (1984) reported results for normally hearing students and Bodner-Johnson (1983) reported results for a sample of deaf students. Bloom reported that the following home processes influence achievement:

1. Work habits of the family (i.e., the degree of routine in the home management, the emphasis on regularity in the use of space and time, and the priority given to schoolwork over more pleasurable activities).
2. Academic guidance and support (i.e., the availability and quality of the help and encouragement parents give the child for his or her schoolwork and the conditions they provide to support the child's schoolwork).
3. Stimulation in the home (i.e., the opportunity provided in the home to explore ideas, events, and the larger environment).
4. Language development (i.e., opportunities in the home for the development of correct and effective language usage).

5. Academic aspirations and expectations (i.e., the parents' aspirations for the child, the standards they set for the child's school achievement, and their interests in and knowledge of the child's school experiences).

Bloom cited a recent study in Thailand (Janhom 1983) that revealed the extent to which home environments could be altered and the effect of that alteration on the child's school achievement. The most effective home intervention was found to be a meeting between a parent educator and a group of parents for about two hours twice a month for six months. The parent educator made an initial presentation on one of the home environment processes, and then the parents discussed what they did and what they hoped to do to improve their children's learning. Janhom reported an increase of one standard deviation in reading and arithmetic for children of parents who attended the meetings.

Bodner-Johnson (1983) investigated differences in background characteristics and family environment between deaf students who were successful readers and those who were not. The criteria for selecting the family included a child whose hearing level was no better than 70 dB in the speech range in the better ear; age at onset was no later than two years; the child had no additional handicaps; and the child was ten to twelve years old. When Bodner-Johnson controlled for IQ, family SES, gender, race, commuter vs. residential status, parent hearing status, and social-emotional development, she found that the communication mode used in the home (i.e., simultaneous communication) was positively associated with reading level. In addition, she reported the following seven factorially derived scores of family environment that were significantly related to reading achievement.

1. Adaptation to deafness (i.e., the extent of parents' participation in deaf communication; degree of their belief that deafness is an integral, personal characteristic of the child; and the extent of their activities in sign language).
2. Family involvement/interaction (i.e., the extent and content of educational and recreational activities that parent and child do together; the parents' discussion about the child's speech, school, and overall communication program; and the extent the parents read to the child at an early age).
3. Expectations and reinforcement (i.e., level of the parents' expectations and aspirations for the child's education and occupation; the extent the child reads books independently; and the level of standards for the child's school grades).
4. Press for independence (i.e., the age at which parents expect or allow the child to sleep at a friend's home overnight, stay home alone in the evening for a few hours, or babysit at someone else's home).
5. Knowledge of education/communication (i.e., the extent parents work for and encourage the child's correct and effective language usage; the extent of the parents' knowledge of the nature of the child's hearing loss, hearing aid, grades and progress in school; the number of times the parents meet the teacher to discuss the child's progress in communication and speech).

6. Child-rearing orientation (i.e., the parents' belief regarding the need for establishing special behavior rules for deaf children, any special discipline techniques).
7. Parent-child recreation (i.e., the extent of recent and planned future outings and extent parents monitor and discuss child's TV viewing).

Meadow (1972) reported that restrictive child-rearing practices also negatively influenced a deaf child's development of social maturity. Deaf children of hearing parents are rated significantly lower than deaf children of deaf parents on social maturity scales. The hearing parents were more reluctant than the deaf parents to grant neighborhood independence to their deaf child (Meadow 1967).

Student Mediation Processes

Centra and Potter (1980) reported that very little research had been conducted on the student behaviors that are related to student outcomes. McKinney, Mason, Perkerson, and Clifford (1975) described the academically successful students as attentive, independent, and task-oriented in their interactions with peers. Students who are distractible, dependent, and passive in peer group activities are less likely to succeed.

Wittrock (1986) reviewed research on students' thought processes that included the effects of teachers' instructional methods on students' perceptions, expectations, attentional processes, motivations, attributions, memories, understanding, beliefs, attitudes, learning strategies, and metacognitive processes that mediate achievement. In contrast to process-product research, which studies how teachers or instructional processes directly contribute to student achievement, research on students' thought processes examines how teaching or teachers influence what students think, believe, feel, say, or do and how that affects their achievement. Thus, many of the problems of the process-product model of teaching are addressed by the cognitive model of mediated learning.

Student achievement is also enhanced by teacher expectations, if an individual student perceives the teacher's expectations as high (Wittrock 1986). Some students in a classroom will show changes in thinking while others will not, resulting in a teacher expectancy effect only for some students, a finding commonly reported in the literature.

Student-reported attention correlated with success on mathematics problems more highly than did classroom observers' reports of time-off-task (Peterson and Swing 1982). With ability differences controlled, reports of understanding the lesson also correlated positively with achievement, as did students' reported use of learning strategies, such as relating the problems to experience. Students' ability to determine why and what they understood also correlated with achievement. Achievement was better for students who used specific cognitive strategies, such as relating information to prior knowledge. In addition, motivational self-thoughts correlated positively with attitudes toward achievement.

Wittrock (1986) also reported that achievement was improved as a result of training programs that focused on attention, internal control, and use of such learning strategies and mnemonics as associations, visualization, imaging, and organization. Wittrock concluded that the study of student mediating processes provides a useful way (1) to ask new questions about teaching and (2) to develop and test hypotheses that explain, as well as predict, some of the effects of teaching. At this time, studies on student mediation processes with deaf subjects are rare to nonexistent.

Kindred (1980) described the successfully mainstreamed deaf student as flexible, initiating, and independent. She did not empirically validate the relationship between these behaviors and achievement.

Student Outcomes

The general school effectiveness variables include both cognitive and noncognitive areas. The cognitive variables include verbal, math, reading, general academic ability, abstract reasoning, composite achievement, general information, high school completion, and continuation in higher education. The noncognitive variables include social skills, social emotional development, educational aspirations, and attitudes toward school, peers, and the teacher.

Three other variables are uniquely associated with education of the deaf: normally hearing students' attitudes toward deaf students, deaf students' attitudes toward hearing students, and attainment of IEP objectives.

Cognitive variables have been studied extensively within a general school effectiveness model. Substantial research supports the influence on hearing students of student background characteristics, school or school district conditions, within-school conditions, and instructional personnel characteristics on such skill areas as verbal, reading, math, general academic ability, and abstract reasoning, and on high school completion and continuation in higher education. Research with deaf subjects has primarily focused on the effect of student background characteristics on reading, math, mainstreaming, and general achievement. A small number of studies have examined the effect of student placement and attitudes, but no studies have examined the effects of school or school district conditions, within-school conditions, instructional personnel characteristics, instructional personnel performance, or student mediating processes. One significant study examined family support effects, but this was limited to reading achievement in ten- to twelve-year-old deaf children (Bodner-Johnson 1983).

Fewer general school effectiveness studies with normally hearing subjects examined the full range of independent variables with noncognitive dependent variables. Student attitudes have been examined in relation to student background characteristics, school or school district conditions, and instructional personnel characteristics. Research with deaf students on variables that influence noncognitive areas considered some student background characteristics. The influence of student placement has been studied with regard to hearing students' attitudes toward deaf students. The relationships between student outcomes and other categories of independent variables have not yet been studied.

CONCLUSION

A summary of areas in need of research is presented in Table 2.8. As previously noted, research with deaf subjects tends to take some student background characteristics into account. However, there are a few such characteristics that have not yet been studied with a deaf sample. These include the effects of parental occupational status, family possessions, parental education level, and kindergarten attendance.

No research was found that investigated the relationship between general school effectiveness and school-level variables with student outcomes for deaf samples. In addition, no research was located that addressed school-level variables that are uniquely associated with education of the deaf. Outstanding questions include the effect of school facilities, expenditures, staffing patterns, administrative organization, sociodemographic characteristics of the student population, or student attendance on student outcomes for deaf students. More specifically, what are the effects of the deaf student enrollment, special education expenditures for deaf programs, special education personnel, planning efforts, school support, administrators' attitudes toward deaf students and mainstreaming deaf students, and the deaf student-teacher ratio? Finally, what are the processes that are used to place deaf students, and what are the effects of using those processes?

A gap exists in present knowledge regarding the effect of instructional personnel characteristics on deaf student outcomes. No studies addressed the effects of teacher background characteristics, assignments, or attitudes. In addition, no information is available on the effects of the following variables that are associated with education of the deaf: ability of instructional personnel to work as a team, orientation and support, signing ability, role of the teacher of the deaf, interpreter's characteristics and roles, and IEP development.

The influence of student attitudes on other student outcomes was studied in terms of both internal control, impulsivity, deaf students' attitudes toward communication, and self-concept. However, no studies addressed the effects of academic aspirations, study habits, motivation, hearing students' attitudes toward deaf students, or deaf students' attitudes toward hearing students.

Student placement has been studied in terms of student background characteristics. Important questions remain unanswered concerning the effect of student placement on school-level characteristics, instructional personnel characteristics and practices, student attitudes, family support, and student behaviors. Questions that need further research include: What are the effects of the decision-making process used for student placement? What are the effects of the specific classes taken by the deaf student? What are the instructional processes that are effective in the mainstreamed classroom?

Table 2.8
Summary of School Effectiveness Research Conducted with Hearing
and Deaf Subjects

Category of Variables		Availability of Research	
		Hearing Subjects	Deaf Subjects
Student background	GSE[a]	Yes	Yes
characteristics	HI[b]		Yes
School or school	GSE	Yes	No
district conditions	HI		No
Within-school conditions	GSE	Yes	No
	HI		No
Instructional	GSE	Yes	No
personnel	HI		No
Student attitudes	GSE	Yes	A little
	HI		A little
Placement	HI		A little
Instructional	GSE	Yes	No
personnel	HI		No
performance			
Family support	GSE	Yes	A little
	HI		Yes
Student behavior	GSE	A little	No
	HI		No

[a]GSE = General school effectiveness variables (i.e., variables generally associated with school effectiveness).

[b]HI = Hearing-impaired variables (i.e., variables uniquely associated with education of deaf students).

This leads to the question of instructional personnel performance. The work of Bloom (1984) and Larrivee and Algina (1983) provides an excellent basis for studying the instructional process variables that are related to deaf student outcomes. In addition to a need to study the effect of Bloom's and Larrivee and Algina's variables, important questions remain concerning the instructional personnel performance variables that are unique to education of the deaf. These questions include: What is the effect of the teachers' attitudes toward deaf students? What is the effect of the teacher's involvement in developing the IEP? What is the effect of the communication mode used in the classroom? What is the role of the interpreter?

Bodner-Johnson (1983) has provided an excellent framework for studying the effects of family support, but her study is limited to reading achievement for deaf students aged ten to twelve. The results of this study need to be replicated with other age groups and student outcome measures. Additional research is also needed in the area of student behaviors for both hearing and deaf samples.

According to Shulman (1986) and Wittrock (1986), this line of inquiry holds great promise for understanding the teaching–learning process. Shulman's and Wittrock's comments pertained to future trends for research on teaching in general; they did not specifically refer to deaf students. It seems fitting that lessons learned from research with hearing students should inform research with deaf students. The model identified in this chapter should be viewed as an attempt to identify those variables that must be considered in the conduct of research on teaching, no matter which model of teaching and methodological approaches are used.

REFERENCES

Airasian, P. W., T. Kellaghan, and G. F. Madaus. 1979. *Concepts of school effectiveness as derived from research strategies: Differences in findings.* Boston: Boston College. (ERIC Document Reproduction Service No. 192 456)

Allen, T. E., and M. A. Karchmer. 1981. Influences on academic achievement of hearing-impaired students born during the 1963–65 rubella epidemic. *Directions* 2(3): 40–54.

Allen, T. E., and T. I. Osborn. 1984. Academic integration of hearing-impaired students: Demographic, handicapping, and achievement factors. *American Annals of the Deaf* 129: 100–113.

Antia, S. D. 1982. Social interaction of partially mainstreamed hearing-impaired children. *American Annals of the Deaf* 127: 18–25.

Averch, H. A., S. J. Carroll, T. S. Donaldson, H. J. Kiesling, and J. Pineus. 1974. *How effective is schooling?* Englewood Cliffs, NJ: Educational Technology Publications.

Babbini, B. E., and S. P. Quigley. 1970. *A study of the growth patterns in language, communication, and educational achievement in six residential schools for deaf students.* Urbana, IL: Illinois University, Institute for Research on Exceptional Children.

Bloom, B. S. 1964. *Stability and change in human characteristics.* New York: John Wiley and Sons.

———. 1976. *Human characteristics and school learning.* New York: McGraw-Hill.

———. 1984. The two sigma problem: The search for methods of group instruction as effective as one-to-one tutoring. *Educational Researcher* 13(6): 4–16.

Board of Education of the City of New York. 1956. *The integration of deaf children in a hearing class.* Publication No. 36. New York Bureau of Educational Research.

Bodner-Johnson, B. 1983. *A study of families and their learning environments for deaf children.* Final report under U.S. Office of Education Grant No. G008102720. Washington, DC: U.S. Office of Education.

Brasel, K. E., and S. P. Quigley. 1977. Influence of certain language and communication environments in early childhood on the development of language in deaf individuals. *Journal of Speech and Hearing Research* 20: 81–94.

Bridge, R. G., C. M. Judd, and P. R. Moock. 1979. *The determinants of educational outcomes.* Cambridge, MA: Ballinger Publishing Company.

Brimer, A., et al. 1977. *A study of the sensitivity of measures of school effectiveness in England.* Report submitted to the Carnegie Corporation of New York.

Brinker, R., and M. E. Thorpe. 1984. *Evaluation of the integration of severely handicapped students in regular education or community settings.* Report No. RR-84-11. Princeton, NJ: Educational Testing Service.

Brophy, J. E., and T. L. Good. 1986. Teacher behavior and student achievement. In *Handbook of research on teaching,* ed. M. C. Wittrock, 328–375. New York: Macmillan.

Cazden, C. B. 1971. Evaluation of learning in preschool education. In *Handbook on formative and summative evaluation of student learning,* ed. B. S. Bloom, J. T. Hastings, and G. F. Madaus, 345–398. New York: McGraw-Hill.

Centra, J. A., and D. A. Potter. 1980. School and teacher effects: An interrelational model. *Review of Educational Research* 50(2): 273–291.

Clarkson, M. C. 1982. Mainstreaming the exceptional child: A bibliography. San Antonio, TX: Trinity University Press.

Connor, L. E. 1975. Mainstreaming the special school. *Proceedings of the International Congress on Education of the Deaf,* August. Tokyo, Japan.

Conrad, R. 1977. The reading ability of deaf school-leavers. *British Journal of Educational Psychology* 47: 138–148.

———. 1979. *The deaf school child.* London: Harper and Row.

Convey, J. J., and W. H. Koelle. 1981. Improving the prediction of achievement of deaf adolescents by modifying a locus of control and self-concept instrument. Paper presented at the annual meeting of the Eastern Educational Research Association, Philadelphia, Pennsylvania. (ERIC Document Reproduction Service No. 210 875)

Craig, H. B. 1965. A sociometric investigation of the self-concept of the deaf child. *American Annals of the Deaf* 110: 456–474.

Dale, D. M. C. 1984. *Individualized integration: Studies of deaf and partially-hearing children and students in ordinary schools and colleges.* Springfield, IL: Charles C. Thomas.

Dave, R. H. 1963. *The identification and measurement of environmental process variables that are related to educational achievement.* Ph.D. diss. University of Chicago.

Delaney, M., E. R. Stuckless, and G. G. Walter. 1984. Total communication effects: A longitudinal study of a school for the deaf in transition. *American Annals of the Deaf* 129: 481–486.

DeSalle, J. M., and J. Ptasnik. 1976. Some problems and solutions: High school mainstreaming of the hearing impaired. *American Annals of the Deaf* 121: 533–536.

Dunkin, M. J., and B. J. Biddle. 1974. *The study of teaching.* New York: Holt, Rinehart, and Winston.

Farrugia, D., and G. F. Austin. 1980. A study of social emotional adjustment patterns of hearing impaired students in different educational settings. *American Annals of the Deaf* 125: 535–541.

Fiedler, M. F. 1969. Developmental studies of deaf children. *ASHA Monograph* (No. 13).

Fisher, B. 1966. The social and emotional adjustment of children with impaired hearing attending ordinary classes. *British Journal of Educational Psychology* 36: 319–321.

Fraser, E. 1959. *Home environment and the school.* London: University of London Press.

Glasman, N. S., and I. Biniaminov. 1981. Input-output analysis of schools. *Review of Educational Research* 51(4): 509–539.

Glass, G. V., and M. L. Smith. 1978. *Meta-analysis of research on the relationship of class size and achievement.* Boulder, CO: Laboratory of Educational Research, University of Colorado.

Gregory, J. F., T. Shanahan, and H. J. Walberg. 1984. Mainstreamed hearing-impaired high school seniors: A re-analysis of a national survey. *American Annals of the Deaf* 129: 11–16.

Haertel, G. D., H. J. Walberg, and T. Weinstein. 1983. Psychological models of educational performance: A theoretical synthesis of constructs. *Review of Educational Research* 53(1): 75–91.

Harris, R. I. 1975. *Impulse control and parent hearing status in deaf children.* Paper presented at the 7th Congress of the World Federation of the Deaf, August. Washington, DC.

Hein, R. D., and M. E. Bishop. 1978. *Bibliography on mainstreaming.* Springfield, VA: National Technical Information Service.

Hemwall, M. K. 1984. Ethnography as evaluation: Hearing impaired students in the mainstream. In *Ethnography in educational evaluation,* ed. D. M. Fetterman. Beverly Hills, CA: Sage Publications.

Hess, W. 1960. *Personality adjustment in deaf children.* Ph.D. diss., University of Rochester.

Jacobs, L. R. 1976. Attitudes of normal-hearing college students toward their hearing-impaired classmates. In *Selected readings in the integration of deaf students at CSUN,* Series No. 1. Northridge, CA: Center on Deafness.

Janhom, S. 1983. *Educating parents to educate their children.* Ph.D. diss., University of Chicago.

Jensema, C. J. 1975. *The relationship between academic achievement and the demographic characteristics of hearing impaired children and youth.* Series R, No. 2. Washington, DC: Gallaudet University, Office of Demographic Studies.

Jensema, C. J., M. A. Karchmer, and R. J. Trybus. 1978. *The rated speech intelligibility of hearing impaired children: Basic relationships and a detailed analysis.* (Series R, Number 6). Washington, DC: Gallaudet University.

Jensema, C. J., and R. J. Trybus. 1975. *Reported emotional/behavioral problems among hearing-impaired children in special education programs: United States, 1972–1973* (Series, R, Number 1). Washington, DC: Gallaudet University.

———. 1978. *Communication patterns and educational achievement of hearing impaired students.* (Series T, No. 2). Washington, DC: Gallaudet University, Office of Demographic Studies.

Johnson, H. A., and P. L. Griffith. 1986. The instructional patterns of two fourth-grade spelling classes: A mainstreaming issue. *American Annals of the Deaf* 131: 331–338.

Joiner, L. M., E. L. Erickson, V. B. Crittendon, and V. M. Stevenson. 1969. Predicting the academic achievement of the acoustically-impaired using intelligence and self-concept of academic ability. *The Journal of Special Education* 3: 425–431.

Kamii, C. K. 1971. Evaluation of learning in preschool education: Socio-emotional, perceptual-motor, and cognitive development. In *Handbook on formative and summative evaluation of student learning,* ed. B. S. Bloom, J. T. Hastings, and G. F. Madaus. New York: McGraw-Hill.

Karchmer, M., B. W. Rawlings, R. J. Trybus, S. Wolk, and M. N. Milone. 1979. *Educationally significant characteristics of hearing impaired students in Texas, 1977–78* (Series C, Number 4). Washington, DC: Gallaudet University.

Karchmer, M. A., and R. Trybus. 1977. *Who are the deaf children in "mainstream" programs?* Series R, No. 4. Washington, DC: Gallaudet University, Office of Demographic Studies.

Karweit, N. 1983. *Time-on-task: A research review.* Report No. 332. Baltimore: Center for Social Organization on Schools, Johns Hopkins University.

Kennedy, P., W. H. Northcott, R. W. McCauley, and S. M. Williams. 1976. Longitudinal sociometric and cross-sectional data on mainstreaming hearing impaired children: Implications for preschool programming. *Volta Review* 78: 71–81.

Kindred, E. M. 1976. Integration at the secondary school level. *Volta Review* 78(1): 35–43.

———. 1980. Mainstream teenagers with care. *American Annals of the Deaf* 125: 1053–1056.

Kluwin, T., and D. Moores. 1985. The effects of integration on the mathematics achievement of hearing-impaired adolescents. *Exceptional Children* 52(2): 153–160.

Ladd, G. W., H. L. Munson, and J. K. Miller. 1984. Social integration of deaf adolescents in secondary level mainstreaming programs. *Exceptional Children* 50(5): 420–429.

Larrivee, B., and J. Algina. 1983. *Identification of teaching behaviors which predict success for mainstreamed students.* Paper presented at the annual meeting of the American Educational Research Association, Montreal, Quebec.

Levine, E. S. 1956. *Youth in a soundless world, search for personality.* New York: New York University Press.

Libbey, S. S., and W. Pronovost. 1980. Communication patterns of mainstreamed hearing impaired adolescents. *Volta Review* 82: 197–219.

Linnan, R., and P. W. Airasian. 1974. *Ethnic comparisons of environmental predictors of three cognitive abilities.* Paper presented at the annual meeting of the American Educational Research Association, Chicago, Illinois.

Long, G. L., and D. Coggiola. 1980. Prediction of academic performance and student classification using five cognitive skills measures. Paper presented at the annual meeting of the American Educational Research Association, Boston, Massachusetts (ERIC Document Reproduction Service No. ED 191 238).

Madaus, G. F., T. Kellaghan, and E. Rakow. 1975. *A study of the sensitivity of measures of school effectiveness.* Report submitted to the Carnegie Corporation of New York. Educational Research Centre, St. Patrick's College, Dublin; and Boston College.

Madden, N. A., and R. E. Slavin. 1983. Mainstreaming students with mild handicaps: Academic and social outcomes. *Review of Educational Research* 53(4): 519–569.

McDonald, F. J. (1976a). *Summary report: Beginning teacher evaluation study, Phase II.* Princeton, NJ: Educational Testing Service.

———. 1976b. *Teachers do make a difference.* Princeton, NJ: Educational Testing Service.

McKinney, J. D., J. Mason, K. Perkerson, and M. Clifford. 1975. Relationship between classroom behavior and academic achievement. *Journal of Educational Psychology* 67: 198–203.

Meadow, K. P. 1967. *The effect of early manual communication and family climate on the deaf child's development.* Ph. D. diss., University of California, Berkeley.

———. 1972. Sociolinguistics, sign language, and the deaf subculture. In *Psycholinguistics and total communication: The state of the art,* ed. T. J. O'Rourke, 19–33. Washington, DC: American Annals of the Deaf.

——— 1980. *Deafness and child development.* Berkeley, CA: University of California Press.

Mertens, D. M. 1986. Social development for hearing impaired high school youth. Paper presented at the Annual Meeting of the American Educational Research Association, San Francisco, California.

————. 1989. Social experiences of hearing impaired high school youth. *American Annals of the Deaf* 134: 15–19.

Mertens, D. M., and T. N. Kluwin. 1986. Academic and social interaction for hearing impaired high school students. Paper presented at the Annual Meeting of the American Educational Research Association, San Francisco, California.

Moores, D. F. 1985. Early intervention programs for hearing impaired children: A longitudinal assessment. In *Children's language,* vol. 5, 159–196, ed. K. Nelson. Hillsdale, NJ: Lawrence Erlbaum Associates.

Nelson, F. H. 1982. A simultaneous equation model of the provision of services to handicapped children at the school district level. *American Educational Research Journal* 19(4): 579–597.

O'Connor, C. D., and L. E. Connor. 1961. Deaf children in regular classrooms. *Exceptional Children* 27: 483–486.

Peterson, P. L., and S. R. Swing. 1982. Beyond time on task: Students' reports of their thought processes during direct instruction. *Elementary School Journal* 82: 481–491.

Pflaster, G. 1981. A second analysis of factors related to the academic performance of hearing-impaired children in the mainstream. *Volta Review* 83(2): 71–81.

Pollard, G., and T. Oakland. 1982. Variables associated with the educational development of residential deaf children. Paper presented at the Annual Meeting of the American Psychological Association, Washington, DC.

Rawlings, B. W., and C. J. Jensema. 1977. *Two studies of the families of hearing impaired children.* Washington, DC: Gallaudet University.

Rawlings, B. W., and R. J. Trybus. 1978. Personnel, facilities, and services available in schools and classes for hearing impaired children in the United States. *American Annals of the Deaf* 123: 99–114.

Reich, C., D. Hambleton, and B. K. Houldin. 1977. The integration of hearing-impaired children in regular classrooms. *American Annals of the Deaf* 122: 534–543.

Risley, G. W. 1977. *The effects of mainstreaming and self-contained education for hearing impaired students.* Los Altos, CA: Los Altos School District. (ERIC Document Reproduction Service No. ED 150 762)

Rister, A. 1975. Deaf children in mainstream education. *Volta Review* 77(5): 279–290.

Sass-Lehrer, M. 1984. *Instructional supervisors' perceptions of critical competencies for teaching.* Paper presented at the Annual Meeting of the American Educational Research Association, New Orleans, Louisiana.

Savage, R. D., L. Evans, and J. F. Savage. 1981. *Psychology and communication in deaf children.* New York: Grune and Stratton.

Schleslinger, H. S., and K. P. Meadow. 1972. *Sound and sign: Childhood deafness and mental health.* Berkeley: University of California Press.

Serwatka, T. S. 1979. Nonverbal production of reading achievement in hearing impaired children. Ph.D. diss., Kent State University.

Shulman, L. S. 1986. Paradigms and research programs in the study of teaching. In *Handbook of research on teaching,* ed. M. C. Wittrock, 3–36. New York: Macmillan.

Sisco, F. H., and R. V. Anderson. 1980. Deaf children's performance on the WISC-R relative to hearing status of parents and child rearing practices. *American Annals of the Deaf* 125: 923–930.

Smith, M. 1976. Evaluation of educational programs. In *The evaluation of social programs,* ed. C. Abt, 430–434. Beverly Hills, CA: Sage Publications.

Stodolsky, S. S. 1972. Defining treatment and outcome in early childhood education. In *Rethinking urban education,* ed. H. T. Walberg and A. T. Kopan. San Francisco: Jossey-Bass.

Trybus, R., and M. Karchmer. 1977. School achievement scores of hearing impaired children: National data on achievement status and growth patterns. *American Annals of the Deaf* 122: 62–69.

Vernon, M., and S. D. Koh. 1970. Early manual communication and deaf children's achievement. *American Annals of the Deaf* 115: 527–536.

Walberg, H. J. 1981. A psychological theory of educational productivity. In *Psychology and education: The state of the union,* ed. F. H. Farley and N. Gordon. Berkeley, CA: McCutchan.

Walberg, H. J. 1984. Improving the productivity of American schools. *Educational Leadership* 41(8): 19–27.

Walberg, H. J., and K. Marjoribanks. 1976. Family environment and cognitive development: Two analytic models. *Review of Educational Research* 46(4): 527–551.

Wittrock, M. C. 1986. Students' thought processes. In *Handbook of research on teaching,* ed. M. C. Wittrock, 297–314. New York: Macmillan.

Wolf, R. 1964. *The identification and measurement of environmental process variables related to intelligence.* Ph.D. diss., University of Chicago.

Wolk, S., and T. E. Allen. 1984. A five year follow-up of reading comprehension achievement in a national sample of hearing impaired students in special education programs. *The Journal of Special Education* 18(2): 161–176.

Wolk, S., M. A. Karchmer, and A. Schildroth. 1982. *Patterns of academic and nonacademic integration among hearing impaired students in special education.* Washington, DC: Gallaudet University, Center for Assessment and Demographic Studies.

Zawolkow, E. G., and S. DeFiore. 1986. Educational interpreting for elementary- and secondary-level hearing impaired students. *American Annals of the Deaf* 131(1): 26–28.

3

Cultural Considerations in the Education of Deaf Children

TIMOTHY REAGAN

Although the education of deaf children has been marked by intense, and often divisive, internal debate through most of its history in this country, educators of the deaf—manualists and oralists alike—have generally shared a number of important assumptions about the nature of deafness and about the goals and objectives that are most appropriate for teaching deaf children (Reagan 1988b). As I have argued in considerable detail elsewhere (Reagan 1989),

> manualism and oralism have tended to operate from a series of similar, if not always identical, assumptions about the pathological nature of deafness, the need for deaf children to fit into and function in the hearing world, the importance of acquiring English (generally as their vernacular language), and the need and desirability for hearing people to make educational and social decisions on behalf of the deaf. (p. 45)

In this chapter, an alternative model of deafness and of the function of deaf education will be suggested. Rather than focusing on deafness as a pathological medical condition, we will consider the education of the deaf as a dominated cultural and linguistic minority in American society. Such an approach to deaf education, while still far from widely accepted, has been gaining credibility and support since the 1970s (Erting 1978; Padden 1980; Reagan 1986; Stokoe 1980; Wilcox 1987; Woodward 1982). The goal of this approach, in essence, has been to "depathologize" deafness. As Woodward (1982, p. 7) has cogently put it, what is being attempted is "to describe Deaf people from the point of view of Deaf cultural values [so that] differences between Deaf and Hearing people can be seen as cultural differences, not as deviations from a Hearing norm."

THE DEAF CULTURE

In order to understand deaf people as they understand themselves, a familiarity with both the traditional perspective assumed by hearing people about deaf people and the distinctive nature and characteristics of the Deaf culture is necessary. As Padden and Humphries (1988) noted in the introduction to their book, *Deaf in America: Voices from a Culture,*

> The traditional way of writing about Deaf people is to focus on the fact of their condition—that they do not hear—and to interpret all other aspects of their lives as consequences of this fact . . . In contrast to the long history of writings that treat them as medical cases, or as people with "disabilities," who "compensate" for their deafness by using sign language, we want to portray the lives they live, their art and performances, their everyday talk, their shared myths, and the lessons they teach one another. We have always felt that the attention given to the physical condition of not hearing has obscured far more interesting facets of Deaf people's lives. (p. 1)

This passage provides a valuable clue to the difference between hearing and Deaf views of deafness. The hearing view of deafness is concerned almost exclusively with the audiological features of deafness and, as a result, emphasizes what the deaf person cannot do (or cannot do as a hearing person would do). In short, it assumes what might be termed a "handicapped" or "pathological" model of deafness. The Deaf view of deafness, on the other hand, is concerned with social, linguistic, anthropological, and cultural aspects of the deaf experience. Indeed, given some hearing loss, the actual degree of hearing loss is not particularly important or significant within the Deaf culture. As Padden (1980) has noted,

> Being Deaf usually means the person has some degree of hearing loss. However, the type or degree of hearing loss is not a criterion for being Deaf. Rather, the criterion is whether a person identifies with other Deaf people, and behaves as a Deaf person. (p. 95)

This suggests that the meaning of "being Deaf" is actually a socially determined construct and that the criteria (or conditions) for an individual to count as "Deaf" will be radically different for the hearing and Deaf worlds. Deafness in a sociocultural sense entails a number of significant components that serve both to identify the Deaf community and to establish the parameters which delimit that community. Among the more important aspects of deafness conceived in this manner by various authors in the United States (Erting 1978; Reagan 1985) and Great Britain (Deucher 1984; Kyle and Woll 1985; Woll, Kyle, and Deucher 1981) are

1. Linguistic differentiation
2. Attitudinal deafness

3. Behavioral norms
4. Endogamous marital patterns
5. Historical awareness
6. Voluntary organizational networks

Each of these aspects of the Deaf culture in the United States will now be discussed.

Linguistic Differentiation

Language generally plays a key role in cultural and ethnic identification (Fishman 1966), and this is especially true in the case of Deaf people (Baker and Cokely 1980; Erting 1978; Markowicz and Woodward 1982; Padden 1980). Erting (1980), for example, has argued that "the most effective signal of membership in the deaf ethnic group . . . is language." Specifically, membership in the Deaf community is contingent upon communicative competency in American Sign Language (ASL) (Markowicz and Woodward 1982), which thus performs a dual function as the community's vernacular language and as its principal identifying characteristic.

While individual Deaf people demonstrate a wide range of language competence in ASL and English, the Deaf community in the United States can, nevertheless, be accurately described as bilingual in nature, with language usage falling along two overlapping linguistic continua ranging from pure ASL to English. The result in day-to-day practice is a fascinating instance of diglossia, in which signing that is closest to English tends to function as the "H" (high status) variety, while signing that is closer to ASL functions as the "L" (low status) variety (Deucher 1977; Markowicz and Woodward 1982). However, ASL also serves as a remarkably effective barrier to hearing people's access to the Deaf culture and community, marking them clearly as outsiders (Erting 1980). In short, there is a kind of ambivalence about ASL and language use present in some segments of the American Deaf community. As Meadow (1975) has commented about language in general,

> It [a language] can serve as a cohesive, defining source of pride and positive
> identification and simultaneously as a focus for stigma and ridicule from mem-
> bers of the majority culture. (p. 17)

Further, it is not at all uncommon for some members of a language community whose language is stigmatized by the dominant cultural and linguistic group to accept the dominant group's judgment about their language, and this, too, sometimes takes place within the Deaf community.

Attitudinal Deafness

Attitudinal deafness refers to the view held by members of the Deaf culture that they are in fact *culturally* and *socially* Deaf. Attitudinal deafness is distinct from the recognition that one is audiologically deaf; the former requires a positive affective commitment to the Deaf culture and community, while the latter simply means that one's hearing is impaired. This is an important distinction that helps to explain why many deaf people would not be accepted as Deaf—a feature of the Deaf culture that is no doubt quite puzzling to many hearing people not familiar with the world of the deaf. Again, it is important to stress that Deafness in its cultural sense is not contingent on the degree of hearing loss. As Padden (1980) has commented,

> there is one name for all members of the cultural group, regardless of the degree of hearing loss: Deaf. In fact, the sign DEAF can be used in an ASL sentence to mean "my friends," which conveys the cultural meaning of "Deaf." (p. 100)

Behavioral Norms

The Deaf are culturally distinct from their hearing compatriots not only in terms of their language and their self-identification, but also in terms of the behavioral norms that govern their social and interpersonal interactions. Among the more obvious examples of variations in behavioral norms between Deaf and hearing people would be eye contact patterns, rules governing physical contact and touching, the use of facial expressions, gesturing, and so on. Such variations in what would constitute socially acceptable behavior can, and often do, result in misunderstandings and even resentment between hearing people and Deaf people (Padden and Markowicz 1976).

Endogamous Marital Patterns

The maintenance of endogamous marital patterns is often seen by cultural and ethnic groups to be a key to their survival. In the case of Deaf people, in-group marriage appears to be by far the most typical pattern (Erting 1978; Meadow 1975). Estimates of the percentage of endogamous marriages within the Deaf community range from 86 percent to well over 90 percent (Rainer, Altshuler, and Kallman 1963; Schein and Delk 1974). The range is small enough to be of little concern; the important point is that few contemporary American ethnic and cultural groups are as endogamous as is the Deaf community. This is especially impressive, incidentally, when one takes into account the historical resistance of many leading educators of the deaf who were opposed to in-group marriages among the deaf out of misguided fears about the hereditary nature of deafness (Neisser 1983; Reagan 1989).

Historical Awareness

The Deaf community has a strong historical awareness, but this awareness has, until recently, been inaccessible to nonsigners, since the history of the Deaf from a

Deaf perspective was entirely an "oral" (i.e., a signed) history. The publication of Jack Gannon's *Deaf Heritage: A Narrative History of Deaf America* in 1981, however, helped to change this, making much of the oral history of the Deaf community available to the general public. Further, a number of books have provided us with additional detailed insights into various aspects of the history of the deaf. Most notable in this regard have been Harlan Lane's *When the Mind Hears: A History of the Deaf* (1984b), *The Deaf Experience: Classics in Language and Education* (1984a), and Nora Ellen Groce's *Everyone Here Spoke Sign Language: Hereditary Deafness on Martha's Vineyard* (1985). Perhaps most encouraging in this regard has been the development of curricular materials for teaching deaf children about the heritage of the Deaf community (Val 1985). However, despite the recent spate of publications concerned with the history and historical background of the American Deaf community, it is clear that the historical awareness of the community is still transmitted primarily through sign and that only through the medium of sign can one really come to grips with the Deaf understanding of Deaf history.

Voluntary Organizational Networks

The network of voluntary social and community organizations, of virtually all sorts, that serve the Deaf community are comparable to those serving any other ethnic or cultural group in contemporary American society. In addition to the National Association of the Deaf (NAD) and the various state organizations, there are social clubs, sports associations, the World Games for the Deaf (or Deaf Olympics, as they are more commonly known), the National Theatre of the Deaf, and a host of others (Erting 1978; Meadow 1975). Such organizations and activities are especially significant given Padden's (1980) assertion that "Deaf people consider social activities an important way of maintaining contact with other Deaf people" (p. 97). In short, the organizational network that serves the Deaf community helps both to maintain the cohesiveness of the group and to provide for the companionship needs of group members.

DEAF CULTURE OR DEAF ETHNICITY?

It is clear, then, that Deaf people in the United States constitute a distinct cultural and linguistic group in our society. While one might have reservations about whether the label *ethnic group* is appropriate, given the normal emphasis on kinship patterns as a necessary component of ethnicity, it is nonetheless beyond question that the Deaf community must be dealt with as a socially, linguistically, and culturally different and distinct group. At this point, we can turn to a brief discussion of the role of the residential school in the maintenance and transmission of this Deaf culture.

The Role of the Residential School

The importance of the residential schools for the deaf in the maintenance and transmission of Deaf culture cannot be overstated. It is clear that such institutions have historically played a pivotal role in recruiting new members for the Deaf community, and the centrality of residential schools in Deaf life has been widely discussed (Meadow 1972; Neisser 1983). With the implementation of Public Law 94-142 and the advent of widespread mainstreaming of deaf youngsters, however, the traditional education of deaf children has undergone a major transformation. More and more deaf children are now attending public schools, both in special classrooms for the deaf and in regular classrooms. As a result, the experience of the residential school is not a part of many of these students' lives, and their identification both with ASL as the language of the Deaf community and with the Deaf community per se may be weaker than that found in students attending residential schools.

If the trend away from the general use of residential schools in the education of the deaf continues, it is quite possible that recruiting new members for the Deaf community will become increasingly difficult. Since the Deaf community, unlike most other cultural and ethnic groups, depends on voluntary identification later in life as its primary means of continuity, this lack of exposure to the formative experience of the residential school may result in major changes and realignments within the Deaf community. With such an outcome possible, it is easy to see mainstreaming, at least in the case of deaf children, as a way of encouraging assimilation and/or amalgamation into the dominant hearing society in much the same way that other ethnolinguistic minorities were assimilated into Anglo-American culture (Appleton 1983). We may also find that there are differences in the degree to which a child identifies with Deaf culture and the Deaf community, based at least in part on the amount of time spent, and the degree of interaction, with hearing children in public school programs.

At this point, we can turn to a discussion of some of the complexities surrounding the acceptance of the Deaf community as a dominated culture group in American society, focusing first on the culture of deafness and then on the challenge of the Deaf ethnic.

THE CULTURE OF DEAFNESS

Thus far, we have discussed the evidence for accepting the existence of a distinctive Deaf culture in contemporary American society. However, there is another aspect of this discussion to which we have only alluded up to this point—the problem of those individuals who are audiologically but not socioculturally deaf. These individuals, taken together, constitute a unique intermediary group between the world of the Deaf and that of the hearing. Members of this group share many of the frustrations and life experiences of the socioculturally Deaf and often utilize

much of the same technology in coping with their deafness. However, these individuals identify with the hearing population rather than with the Deaf community
and are generally rejected by Deaf people. In fact, there is even a sign in ASL used
to describe a person who is deaf, but who thinks like a hearing person.

Included in this intermediary group would be deaf people who have been
educated in oral programs (and have never learned to sign or learned to sign later
in life), individuals who have lost their hearing after they had already mastered
spoken English, and individuals with enough residual hearing to function effectively in the hearing world. It is important to remember, though, that many members of the Deaf community might also fit into one of these categories. Without
making any attempt to evaluate or to make value judgments about these individuals and the lives that they lead, it is nevertheless important for us to (1) be cogni-
zant of the characteristics and problems they face in common with Deaf people
and (2) recognize that although they will generally identify with the hearing
world, they are in fact culturally somewhere between the hearing and Deaf worlds.
As we design educational programs and curricular materials to meet the social and
cultural needs of deaf students, it is essential that we take into account not only
the Deaf community, but also this shared culture of deafness.

Ethnicity and Deafness

An issue of growing concern and importance in deaf education in the United
States is the child who is both a member of a dominated minority group (other
than that of the Deaf) and also is deaf (Delgado 1984; Hairston and Smith 1983).
Educational models and discussions of such children generally tend to place emphasis on the child's membership in the non-Deaf minority group (black, Hispanic, etc.), rather than on the child's deafness. The child who is both deaf and a
member of an additional minority group is indeed faced with a social and educational "double whammy" (Hairston and Smith, 1983), and current educational
practices and approaches, no matter how well-intentioned, are not adequate for
addressing the needs of such children. As the percentage of children in this category increases, as it will continue to do for at least the immediate future (Delgado
1984), we will be faced with a growing challenge to develop innovative and effective techniques for meeting the social, cultural, and linguistic needs of children
who are caught not in a bilingual and bicultural matrix, but rather in a multilin-
gual and multicultural one.

The challenge of multiculturalism in deaf education is not limited to deaf
children from socially and economically oppressed backgrounds. There are also,
of course, deaf children who are members of an ethnic (or hyphenated ethnic)
group that is not currently a dominated group in Anglo-American society (e.g.,
Polish-American, Greek-American, Irish-American, and so on). The home culture
for such a child may, to various degrees, differ from that of the dominant hearing
culture as well as from the mainstream of the Deaf culture. Ethnic differences in
such cases, while not necessarily reflective of social or economic discrimination or

oppression, may nonetheless have significant social and educational implications
for the child that need to be taken into account by the school and the teacher. An
additional challenge for educators with respect to multiculturalism and education,
though one that is beyond the limits of this chapter, is that of incorporating information about deafness and the Deaf culture into the curricula to which hearing
children are exposed (Reagan 1988a).

"Mapping" Cultural Group Membership

The central problem that has emerged so far in this chapter is that of diversity that
exists within and outside the boundaries of the Deaf community. Not only is there
a range of biculturalism and bilingualism (as well as diglossia) found among members of the Deaf community, but the situation is complicated by the presence of
audiologically deaf individuals who share the culture of deafness with the Deaf
community but who do not participate in the Deaf community and by the growing number of ethnic Deaf individuals who maintain identification both with the
Deaf community and with other cultural communities. Further, there is the possibility that being black and Deaf, for instance, entails (in cultural terms) membership in multiple cultural communities—black, Deaf, *and* black Deaf (not to men-
tion membership, which may be marginal depending on the individual, in the
dominant hearing culture).

A useful way to envision the diversity that so strongly affects any meaningful
discussion of culture and ethnicity in the context of deaf education is to "map" an
individual's cultural group membership(s). (I am grateful to Professor Orlando
Taylor of Howard University for suggesting this representative model.) Consider,
for instance, the individual who is a member of the Deaf community, but who
lives in and interacts with the surrounding, dominant hearing culture on a daily
basis with a fair degree of success. This individual's cultural identification is represented in the Venn diagram in Figure 3.1. Note that this person is, in essence, a
member of three different cultural groups: (1) the Deaf culture; (2) the dominant
hearing culture; and (3) the bicultural community that straddles both (1) and (2).
This third community consists of those individuals who are able to move between
the first two communities with a reasonable degree of ease (though they need
identify themselves as members of only one of the two communities).

The situation, and hence the map, will become more complicated as we try
to represent the cultural identification(s) of a person who is Deaf and a member
of an additional cultural group, and who also functions successfully in the dominant hearing society. For such an individual, our map would look like Figure 3.2.

We see, then, that this person is actually a member of at least seven different
cultural groups, each of which would have distinct attributes and characteristics.
Of course, even this is a gross oversimplification, since it fails to take into account
such variables as age, gender, and social class (as well as what some have termed
"ethclass") (Appleton 1983). Each of these variables would, of course, enlarge the
map that we have created here—to the point where a two-dimensional represen-

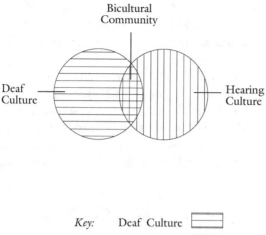

Key: Deaf Culture ▭
Hearing Culture ▭
Bicultural Community ▦

Figure 3.1 Theoretical cultural memberships of a Deaf individual who interacts with hearing culture.

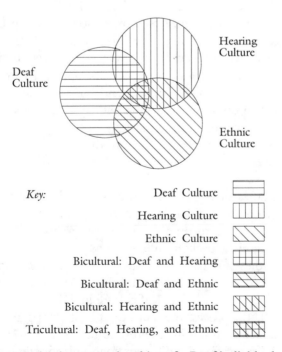

Key:

Deaf Culture ▭
Hearing Culture ▭
Ethnic Culture ◺
Bicultural: Deaf and Hearing ▦
Bicultural: Deaf and Ethnic ◹
Bicultural: Hearing and Ethnic ◹
Tricultural: Deaf, Hearing, and Ethnic ◹

Figure 3.2 Theoretical culture memberships of a Deaf individual who interacts with hearing culture and an ethnic culture.

tation becomes virtually impossible. Further, we could easily imagine the case of the deaf child who is black and Hispanic (and, for that matter, also Jewish), with each variable making significant differences in the child's cultural identification. Another important consideration here is that an individual may choose to identify to a greater or lesser extent with the different cultural groups to which he or she is connected. The point of such mapping is really quite simple: The reality facing the teacher is an immensely complex, complicated, and diverse one, and questions of culture and cultural diversity are not amenable to simple or easy resolution. Although this would be true of any target population in contemporary American society, it is especially true—and especially complex—in the case of deaf people.

FUTURE DIRECTIONS IN RESEARCH

The research and knowledge base that currently exists with regard to the relationship between culture and the education of deaf children is, by virtually all accounts, somewhat sparse. Little empirical research has been conducted, and that which has been done, while generally of fairly high quality, is simply not adequate as it now stands, either to further our understanding of the role of culture in the education of the deaf or to help us establish policy guidelines to direct and improve pedagogical practice concerned with issues of culture and cultural diversity in deaf education. A number of possible explanations for the paucity of research studies on the role of culture and cultural variation in deaf education can be offered, including the incredible complexity of the situation, the difficulty in designing and carrying out research studies in the area, and, perhaps most of all, the presence of cultural and linguistic barriers and biases. Despite these problems, however, it is clear that questions of culture and cultural diversity are likely to be of continuing, and in fact growing, significance in the education of deaf children, and such questions must be addressed. Toward this end, a few possible directions in which future research might usefully proceed are:

1. Comparative studies of competence in and attitudes toward both ASL and English in students from different types of educational programs (e.g., residential schools, mainstreamed public school programs), and in students from different ethnolinguistic backgrounds.
2. Comparative studies of the degree of identification with or knowledge of Deaf culture based on educational background and on ethnolinguistic background.
3. Studies of acculturation into the Deaf culture in different types of educational programs (e.g., Is the process the same, or at least comparable? Is one kind of program more likely to result in acculturation than another?)
4. The effect of identification with different nondominant ethnolinguistic groups on the degree of identification with the Deaf culture.
5. The effects of teacher attitudes toward (a) ethnic differences among deaf stu-

dents and (b) Deaf culture, on both student achievement and student cultural identification.

These are just a few of the many possible kinds of questions and issues that researchers might begin to address. Which questions are chosen at this point in our studies of the relationship between culture and the education of deaf children is probably not the most important factor; what *is* important is that such studies be undertaken, and that they be taken seriously by teachers of the deaf and by educational policy-makers.

CONCLUSION

Where, then, does all this leave us? It most certainly leaves us without any answers. We are not particularly adept yet at dealing with cultural and linguistic diversity in the hearing population, and we have invested considerable time, effort, and expense in attempting to understand and appreciate our differences. Cultural diversity is in many ways a relatively new topic in deaf education, so perhaps we should not be too hard on ourselves for the distance we have yet to go. However, we do need to beware of the easy answers, for these are the answers that are most likely to involve new sorts of oppression and domination. Calls for cultural and linguistic assimilation are easy to make, but solutions too easily arrived at are likely to be painful and unproductive in practice.

REFERENCES

Appleton, N. 1983. *Cultural pluralism in education: Theoretical foundations.* New York: Longman.

Baker, C., and D. Cokely. 1980. *American Sign Language: A teacher's resource text on grammar and culture.* Silver Spring, MD: T. J. Publishers.

Delgado, G., ed. 1984. *The Hispanic deaf: Issues and challenges for bilingual special education.* Washington, DC: Gallaudet University Press.

Deucher, M. 1977. Sign language diglossia in a British deaf community. *Sign Language Studies* 17: 347–356.

———. 1984. *British sign language.* London: Routledge and Kegan Paul.

Erting, C. 1978. Language policy and deaf ethnicity in the United States. *Sign Language Studies* 19: 139–152.

Fishman, J. 1966. *Language loyalty in the United States.* The Hague: Mouton.

Gannon, J. R. 1981. *Deaf heritage: A narrative history of deaf America.* Silver Spring, MD: National Association of the Deaf.

Groce, N. 1985. *Everyone here spoke sign language.* Cambridge: Harvard University Press.

Hairston, E., and L. Smith. 1983. *Black and deaf in America.* Silver Spring, MD: T. J. Publishers.

Kyle, J. G., and B. Woll. 1985. *Sign language: The study of deaf people and their language.* Cambridge: Cambridge University Press.

Lane, H. 1984a. *The deaf experience: Classics in language and education.* Cambridge, MA: Harvard University Press.

―――. 1984b. *When the mind hears: A history of the deaf.* New York: Random House.

Markowicz, H., and J. Woodward. 1982. Language and the maintenance of ethnic boundaries in the United States. In *How you gonna get to heaven if you can't talk with Jesus: On depathologizing deafness,* ed. J. Woodward. Silver Spring, MD: T. J. Publishers.

Meadow, K. P. 1972. Sociolinguistics, sign language and the deaf subculture. In *Psycholinguistics and total communication: The state of the art,* ed. T. J. O'Rourke, 19–33. Washington, DC: American Annals of the Deaf.

―――. 1975. The Deaf subculture. *Hearing and Speech Action* 43: 17.

Neisser, A. 1983. *The other side of silence: Sign language and the deaf community in America.* New York: Alfred A. Knopf.

Padden, C. 1980. The deaf community and the culture of deaf people. In *Sign language and the deaf community: Essays in honor of William C. Stokoe,* ed. C. Baker and D. Cokely, 89–103. Silver Spring, MD: National Association of the Deaf.

Padden, C., and T. Humphries. 1988. *Deaf in America: Voices from a culture.* Cambridge, MA: Harvard University Press.

Padden, C., and H. Markowicz. 1976. Cultural conflicts between hearing and deaf communities. In *7th Congress of the World Federation of the Deaf,* 407–411. Silver Spring, MD: National Association of the Deaf.

Rainer, J., K. Altshuler, and F. Kallman, eds. 1963. *Family and mental health problems in a deaf population.* New York: New York State Psychiatric Institute.

Reagan, T. 1985. The deaf as a linguistic minority: Educational considerations. *Harvard Educational Review* 55: 265–277.

―――. 1986. American Sign Language and contemporary deaf studies in the United States. *Language Problems and Language Planning* 10: 282–289.

―――. 1988a. Multiculturalism and the deaf: An educational manifesto. *Journal of Research and Development in Education* 22: 1–6.

―――. 1988b. The oral-manual debate in deaf education: Language policies in conflict. *Journal of the Midwest History of American Society* 16: 19–33.

―――. 1989. Nineteenth-century conceptions of deafness: Implications for contemporary educational practice. *Educational Theory* 39: 39–46.

Schein, J., and M. Delk. 1974. *The deaf population of the U.S.* Washington, DC: Gallaudet University Press.

Stokoe, W. C., ed. 1980. *Sign and culture: A reader for students of American Sign Language.* Silver Spring, MD: Linstok Press.

Val, S. 1985. *None so deaf.* Washington, DC: Pre-College Outreach, Gallaudet University.

Wilcox, S. 1987. Breaking through the culture of silence. *Sign Language Studies* 55: 163–174.

Woodward, J., ed. 1982. *How you gonna get to heaven if you can't talk with Jesus: On depathologizing deafness.* Silver Spring, MD: T. J. Publishers.

Woll, B., J. Kyle, and M. Deucher, eds. 1981. *Perspectives on British Sign Language and deafness.* London: Cacom Helm.

The Early Literacy Development of Deaf Children

CAROLYN EWOLDT

The work presented in this chapter is part of an ongoing program of research that began with my doctoral dissertation, "A Psycholinguistic Description of Selected Deaf Children Reading in Sign Language" (Ewoldt 1977). Drawing heavily on the work and philosophy of Kenneth and Yetta Goodman, who had discovered through their research the importance of context in reading and the detrimental effects of phonics instruction, I did a miscue analysis and a cloze analysis of four deaf students (ages six to sixteen), reading a variety of materials and retelling them in Sign. From that study I came to appreciate the strengths of deaf readers. I became convinced that their problems with literacy had been exaggerated in the literature and that changes in literacy instruction for deaf children were needed.

My research was enormously facilitated when I became part of the research faculty at Gallaudet University in 1977. The support, both financial and collegial, as well as the opportunity to learn about deafness firsthand and to interact with deaf people on a daily basis, allowed me to continue to investigate the questions, beliefs, and theories that arose from my first study.

Further impetus for the work described in this chapter came from graduate students who challenged my belief that deaf children could learn to read and write easily and naturally if they were allowed to experiment rather than being taught by traditional methods. It was my opinion that instruction of deaf preschool children in the United States had very little foundation in research and theory. Tradition and eclecticism seemed to be the guiding principles in many programs. Teachers looked for step-by-step instructions for teaching deaf children, and few programs truly strived to build on children's existing store of knowledge about the world and about print.

Thus, I undertook to show that deaf children could learn to read and write without direct instruction. The naturalistic observational data that came out of my

The author is deeply indebted to Ms. Janice Welborn for her contributions to this portion of the paper.

study of preschool children engaged in learning to read and write have been documented elsewhere (Manson 1982; Ewoldt 1985). In this chapter I present the findings from the more structured component of our research, in which the same children engaged in specific literacy-related tasks on a yearly basis.

The developing literacy of the young deaf child has received very little research attention. Because the deaf child is often viewed as a *tabula rasa* by teachers, instruction may proceed under the presumption that the child has no information about print and no strategies for developing the ability to produce it. However, the deaf child has access to print through vision, and in our society there is abundant information to be gained through television, billboards, books, magazines, and other sources.

This chapter reports on two studies of the early writing attempts of four deaf children of hearing parents. The first study provided the impetus for a second, more formal, research effort investigating the literacy development of ten deaf children, nine of whom had deaf parents and one of whom had hearing parents. Both studies addressed the following questions: What concepts about literacy do deaf children demonstrate in their early attempts? How is their literacy behavior similar to that of hearing children? What information can be gained about influences on literacy development in general and on literacy development for the deaf specifically?

PILOT STUDY

A preschool class in the Kendall Demonstration Elementary School on the campus of Gallaudet University in Washington, D.C., was selected for the study. All the children in the class had hearing parents and lived at home. The children ranged from three years, three months to four years, 0 months at the beginning of the study, and data were gathered over a six-month period. In addition to the normal exposure to print in their environment, the children were read to by the teacher at least three times a week. The teacher used simultaneous speech and signs when reading, as in all communication with the children. Books were available in the classroom, and the children had a free period each morning to choose books they wanted the teacher to read to them. No formal reading or writing instruction was given.

The teacher was asked to allow approximately ten minutes per day for "writing" sessions. Lined and unlined paper were provided, and the children were encouraged to write or draw anything they wanted with primary, colored, or regular pencils; crayons; or nonpermanent markers. They also had access to a chalkboard and to colored and white chalk.

Samples of each child's writing were collected periodically from October through April. The teacher dated each sample and recorded anything the child told her about it. Other information about the children was obtained from home visits.

Case #1: Robert

Robert was three years, three months old at the time of the first writing sample. Few books and magazines were available in his home. His parents stated that they did not read to him but made a practice of pointing out to him printed signs in his environment. Robert's parents felt that his writing ability was extremely limited, and they apparently did not encourage Robert to write at home.

Before a sample was taken in October, Robert's writing consisted of uncontrolled and controlled scribbling. Some of his early scribbling was done with two pencils in one hand or with his palm guiding the top of the pencil, as defined by Platt (1977):

> Scribbling begins when a child realizes that a tool, be it pencil, stick, or crayon, will leave a mark on a surface. After grasping the connection between the motions of the hand and the scribbled results, the child begins to derive pleasure from producing and repeating lines. At first, these lines have no meaning and correspond to a baby's first cooings. (p. 263)

Robert demonstrated his print awareness through signing. When playing with a ruler, he noticed a Coca-Cola logo imprinted on it and excitedly pointed to the ruler and made a sign which can be glossed *soda pop*. Even out of its usual context the printed symbol and its meaning were recognized, and Robert was able to produce an appropriate sign.

Case #2: Eugene

Eugene was three years, ten months old at the time of the first writing sample. Eugene's home had many books, of which he identified a substantial number as his own. His family was Spanish-speaking and knew very little Sign by which to read to him. However, Eugene was familiar with the contents of his books, as indicated by his use of meaningful gestures to describe objects and scenes in the pictures. He would also point to real objects in his environment that were illustrated in his books. His parents gave no information about Eugene's having done any writing at home.

In a sample collected in November, Eugene drew a large oval shape with a line down one side. He told his teacher that this was Robert. It was not clear whether Eugene meant the boy or the boy's name. The oval shape is sometimes used to represent a human figure (Platt 1977), but the shape could also be an attempted lowercase *e*.

On the following day Eugene produced similar shapes and announced that this was his name. His use of the word *name* indicates clearly his understanding of the sign concept. Clay (1975), in her study of hearing children's writing, found that "when he has mastered the initial letter . . . it has the quality of a monogram—that letter equals him. To adults who understand the principle of abbreviation, the letter stands for his name, but to the child it *is* his name" (p. 46).

Eugene also formed the same letter (an *e*) in various positions, demonstrating his lack of concern for the conventional placement of the *e*. Clay (1975) determined that

> Left to experiment with letter forms children will create a variety of new symbols by re-positioning or decorating the standard forms. In this way they explore the limits within which each letter may vary and still retain its identity. Many 'errors' in children's early writing must be regarded as indicators of flexibility. (p. 43)

This flexibility was evident in Eugene's writing attempts throughout the rest of the study.

Case #3: Danny

Danny was three years, nine months old at the start of data gathering. He had an older sister and brother, both of whom read and did homework around Danny. His brother particularly enjoyed writing but did not teach Danny to write. Danny did not have many books of his own. Danny's mother was the only parent of the four children in the study who signed well, and she always used Sign when communicating with him.

In one sample Danny made three shapes. He signed *second* when making the second shape. He then pointed to the three shapes and signed *same*. Danny clearly intended to draw three rectangles but lacked the motor control to produce them consistently. As with Eugene's writing samples, the recurring principle seemed to be operating: Children tend to repeat as a way of rehearsing movements, language, or concepts.

When Danny produced another sample that resembled *D*s, an *n*, and a *y*, the teacher asked, "What is that?" Danny responded *my*, a further demonstration of the sign concept. "An early linking of sign and meaning is often the child's own name, although at first it will be thought of as 'my sign' rather than letters or words" (Clay 1975, 48). In producing a similar sample, Danny pointed to a paper with his name on it and then to his own writing and signed *same*. Some of the marks in this sample resembled letters also, and this time they appeared in a linear progression on the page.

One month later Danny was making more well-defined letters with a great deal of repetition. On one occasion he made a shape like a *D* with an extended line. Danny may have been testing the limits of *D* (flexibility) or he may have been studying the differences between *D*s and *P*s (contrast).

Case #4: Delbert

Delbert was four years old at the beginning of the study. His mother often read to him, primarily from a collection of Signed English books. She read the same books repeatedly, and Delbert's father looked at books with him but did not read to him. Delbert was free to write at home. His parents often helped him trace his name and other letters of the alphabet.

In November, Delbert was producing linear mock writing (Clay 1975), a scribble that resembles cursive writing and is written in a line across the paper. Over the next four months his writing showed a progression toward conventional letters and the message concept (Clay 1975). In January, Delbert identified his markings as "a letter to Eugene," demonstrating this concept.

In February, his teacher asked, "What is this?", pointing to an *E* on Delbert's paper. Delbert signed the name sign for Eugene and then signed *sick*, indicating that Eugene was sick at home. The letters in this sample were clearly formed, showing a dramatic change from the previous month and also showing that a specific message was intended.

Summary

The children in this study, who had received no formal writing instruction in school, demonstrated their awareness that markings on paper can be representative of real objects. Several principles and concepts identified by Clay (1975) in her study of hearing children were also identified in the writing of the deaf children—namely the sign concept, the message concept, the flexibility principle, the recurring principle, and the contrastive principle. (The "sign" concept Clay refers to concerns the relationship between print and an object, not to a manual sign in American Sign Language.)

Harste, Burke, and Woodward (1983) speak of the "demonstrations" of literacy concepts provided by significant others, sometimes directly and sometimes inadvertently. Variations in the demonstrations provided by home environments were reflected in the strengths exhibited by these children. Robert, whose parents focused his attention on environmental print, recognized the Coca-Cola logo. Eugene, who had many books at home, was able to relate pictures to real objects. Danny, whose mother signed consistently to him, demonstrated linguistic sophistication in his labeling of objects as "second" and "same." Delbert, who perhaps had had access to more literacy demonstrations at home than the other children, was generating messages in print and producing some conventional letters by the end of the school year.

One instructional implication derived from this study is that deaf children need the opportunity to experiment with pencil and paper at an early age. Much of the language play that is so beneficial to hearing children can be done by deaf children through writing. Parents and teachers of deaf children can learn a great deal about their children's language abilities and print awareness by observing the children in a daily free-writing activity.

LONGITUDINAL STUDY

As a result of this pilot, it was determined that a more detailed long-range study was needed. Deaf children of deaf parents, with one exception, were chosen as subjects for the follow-up study because it was assumed that they would have a better developed language base and their progress would therefore be more rapid, making it possible to trace the children's language development over a shorter period of time.

In this study, ten young children from the Kendall Demonstration Elementary School were followed over a three-year period. Nine children had deaf parents. One additional child, a deaf child of hearing parents, was also included, primarily to avoid excluding him from the research activities in which his classmates participated. At the beginning of the study, the age range was from four years, two months to five years, five months. One child's parents moved out of the area in the second year of the study. Thus, data presented for the second and third years come from nine children.

All the children had severe to profound hearing losses. Prior preschool experience varied considerably, ranging from one month to four years, but none of the children had had any classroom instruction in reading or writing. All the children had parents who used sign in their home communication. For those with deaf parents there was some variation. In some of their homes ASL predominated, and in others there was greater reliance on Manual English. In five of nine cases, voice was also used. For the child with hearing parents, Mike, voice and oral English were employed.

During the first year, almost no formal literacy instruction occurred (Manson 1982). The children were observed frequently, and samples of their writing were collected (Ewoldt 1985).

In addition to writing, the study also investigated reading, art, and through-the-air story production. The thrust of this study is a description of the videotaped literacy tasks performed by the children every spring for three years. In the first year the children were four and five years old, and in the third year they were six and seven. Different tasks adapted from a study by Harste, Burke, and Woodward (1984) were analyzed in the study.

1. Write a letter
2. Write a story
3. Read the written story (on the same day)
4. Read a book
5. Retell the book (in years 2 and 3)
6. Dictate a story
7. Read the dictated story (on the same day and one day later)

The tasks were socially negotiated contracts that each child had to agree to perform. The percentage of children who readily agreed to each task was computed and averaged for each task.

In the first year, there was immediate agreement to perform the task in an average of 70 percent of the cases. This percentage increased slightly in the second year to 75 percent and increased dramatically in the third year to 97 percent. Outright refusal to participate occurred in 16 percent of the tasks in the first year and 3 percent in the second year. There were no refusals in the third year.

Delays in task performance started at 14 percent, peaked at 22 percent in the second year, and declined to 3 percent in the third year. It did not appear to be reading or writing itself, but the nature of the reading or writing task, that discouraged risk-taking. Reading a book came to be perceived as safe. Reading a dictated story was more threatening. Writing a story was relatively safe, but writing a letter became threatening in the second year. A further look at the children's performance of these tasks might provide some explanation for the children's reactions.

Writing a Letter

Each child was given paper, writing utensils, and an envelope and was asked to write a letter to Mother. Although several of the children were not yet composing conventional messages, we wanted to see whether they demonstrated any knowledge of the format or components of a letter.

With regard to format, none of the children's attempts in the first year had the shape of a letter. In the second year, three of the children wrote letters that looked like letters. Six letters written in the third year had letter formats.

All but two children wrote a salutation at least once in the three years. The most popular salutation was *Dear,* followed by *Mom* and/or *Dad* six times and by the parent's first name three times. The salutations *Dear Parents* (used by two children) and *To Parents* (used by one child) all appeared in the second year.

All the children except Matt used a closing in at least one letter. The closing most often used was *From* (seven times); *Love* was used five times; and Bobby wrote *From Your Son* in the third year.

All the children included a signature at least once in the three letters. The first name alone was used twelve times; the first and last names, three times.

On the envelopes, the parents' names (usually *Mom* or *Dad*) appeared most often (twenty-one times), followed by the child's name (ten times) and the address of the child (three times). Only two of the children used the parents' last names. None of the children wrote the address in close proximity to the parents' names.

There was not as much growth in the children's awareness of the components of an envelope as of the components of a letter. By the third year, five had included all three parts of a letter, but none had included all the parts of an envelope. Only Jill included two of the four parts in the third year.

Apparently the children had had much more experience with writing letters than with addressing envelopes. Perhaps their teachers or parents usually took the responsibility for envelopes because of their concern that the letters actually reach their destinations.

Since the children were directed only to write a letter to their mothers, they were free to write anything they wished. In fact, Becky reacted to the lack of purpose for the letter in the third year by asking "Why?" when we asked her to write it. Nevertheless, the children did respond by writing sentences in 61 percent of the cases and single words in 21 percent. The contents of the letters (in order of frequency) were love messages (29%), information about school (13%), lists of names (10%), plans (6%), niceties (6%), questions (6%), requests (6%), apologies (3%), suggestions (3%), information about home (3%), reprimands (3%), comments about others (3%), symbols such as happy faces (3%), and stories (3%).

With the exception of the lists and the story, all the other topics are appropriate contents of letters. Even Mike's drawing in the first year was somewhat appropriate: he drew a picture of a mail carrier with a letter.

The children's experimentation with punctuation is of interest. Garth and Bobby were perhaps overgeneralizing from the comma after *Love* when they used a comma after *from* (i.e., *from, your son, Bobby*). Jill and Becky each misplaced the colon in their salutations (i.e., *Dear: Parent*). Three of the children used exclamation marks. Susie used two exclamation marks. Matt covered himself by using two forms of end punctuation (*I hope I will have fun.?*). Becky used a possessive apostrophe but misplaced it (*Susies' house*). All these efforts demonstrated a growing attention to the conventions of writing during year 3.

Writing a Story

The most interesting observation to be made about the story-writing task is that the children voluntarily edited their writing, both during the writing process itself and later in reading back their stories. Harste, Burke, and Woodward (1983) refer to this editing as "fine-tuning."

The following text of Susie's story, written at six years of age, is marked to show the extent of her fine-tuning while she was in the process of writing the story.

A WOMAN WHO IS RICH TOLD HER CILDREN THAT SHE HAVE TO GO TO

THE STORE THE CILDREN SAID WHAT CAN WE DO? OH PLAY

OUTSIDE YEP THEN BOY DID IN WANT TO GO WITH

HIS SISTER THE HE SAW HIS MOTHER COMMING BACK FROM

THE STORE HELLO!" YIKES WHEW SHE SAID YOU

SCARED ME SHE SAID OH SORRY MOM MY IS

COMMING!" HE SAID HELLO! SHE SAID AS

SHE WAVE HER ARM" YIKES YOU SCARE ME"

OH SORRY" SHE SAID MOM SAID I HAVE

TO SLEEP OH NO OK?"" THEN SHE WENT TO BED

THEN THEY THOUGHT FOR A MINUTE HEY!!

WHY DON'T WE ASK MOM TO GO TO THE

FAIR SHE ALWAYSE SAID OK YEAH LETS GO" THEY SAID

TO EACH OTHER THEY ASKED THEIR MOTHER TH SHE SAID

THAT SHE SAID OK BUT HE HAVE TO GO TO THE STORE FIRST!!

THE END

The numbers indicate the order in which the particular changes were made. Of special interest is Susie's fine-tuning of the first two sentences. The first change occurs after the word *do*. Susie added a set of quotation marks to the end of that question, then added them at the beginning of the question. Next she put quotation marks at the end of *store* in the previous sentence, but she was then faced with a dilemma, as the original sentence was an indirect quote, rather than a direct one. Susie paused for several seconds and then added the *I* to change the sentence to a direct quote (Ewoldt 1988).

Arrows indicate other points in the text where Susie changed items. For example, after writing *did in* in line 3, she moved back into the word to add an apostrophe.

Susie continued to edit her story during reading. Some of the more interesting changes are as follows:

A woman who is rich told her children that she "I have to go to the store"

Note that in reading her story Suzie deleted the *I* in the sentence that had presented a problem for her in composing. Clearly she still wanted an indirect quote in that part of the text.

"Yikes Whew" she said "You scare me to death"
Mom said that I have to sleep now"

The following is an example of Becky's fine-tuning during reading:

my cat   spots
I love a cats my cats name is Stopsy because he have a black and white
                and body.
on her face

These examples illustrate that the children perceived story writing as a process rather than a finished product. The children were not asked to fine-tune their stories; they did so voluntarily. The examples also serve to demonstrate that writing requires attention to many different levels. Changes were made in lexical items, letter formations, punctuation, sentence structures, and content.

Several of the children used their writing as a tool of social interaction. Maggie wrote *fiish* (finish) at the bottom of her story, as deaf children her age tend to do. She then turned the paper around to the researcher and pointed to the word *fiish* as a way of signalling the end of the interaction.

After writing about riding in a rocket in the second year, Garth wrote *NO* and then explained to the researcher, "Me, afraid me leave of earth."

In the third year Garth drew a grid with many squares. He put circles and letters inside some of the squares. He then used this picture as his source of inspiration for a story, stopping to consult the picture from time to time. The first sentence of his story was *This is field of war an S stand for spy.*

Garth used the abbreviation principle when he deliberately wrote one letter (*S*) and intended it to signify a full word. Clay (1975) noted that evidence of this principle occurs only rarely in children's writing. Perhaps it is more common in deaf children, who frequently use initials in their name signs.

Evidence for de Beaugrande's intertextual tying (1980) was noted. Bobby wrote a story about Woody Woodpecker on the left side of his paper and a story about Bugs Bunny on the right. He then divided the stories by drawing a vertical line down the middle of the page. He numbered the parts of each story, illustrating each part. Not only had Bobby tied to his writing his prior experiences with the texts of cartoons, but he had also linked his writing to his experiences with the format of expository prose.

Growth in awareness of punctuation demonstrated in the third year of the letter-writing task was also apparent in the story writing. No punctuation was attempted in the stories of year 1. Only two children attempted punctuation in year 2. By year 3, six of the children were attempting some form of punctuation. Susie used the most types of punctuation, which included quotation marks, a question mark, an apostrophe in a contraction, and exclamation points. Mike used a comma to separate numbers; Bobby and Matt used periods at the ends of sentences. Garth used a cartoon bubble for dialogue. Although not a conventional punctuation mark, the bubble shows an awareness that dialogue is separated from the rest of the text.

The children's reluctance to write stories in year 1 could have been due to an early awareness of the task demands in story writing. This point will be discussed in a later section.

Reading Own Written Stories

Half the children refused or delayed the reading of their own written stories in year 1. Six of the children had produced pictures, unidentified shapes, or scribbles for their "story" in year 1. Over the two years all six children who delayed performing this task had produced scribbles or pictures. They were then asked to "read" their "stories."

The primary reason for their reluctance seems to be a reaction to the instructions. They did not associate reading with pictures, shapes, or scribbles, and they therefore found it difficult to respond. Their eventual responses usually took the form of connected messages, however, rather than labels. Thus, the delays seem to be evidence of an awareness that print is involved in reading.

A Comparison of Story Writing and Letter Writing

In both story writing and letter writing, the graphic form of the message followed a clear sequential path. However, the steps differed somewhat:

Story Writing	Letter Writing
Scribbles	Scribbles, letters, words
Unidentified shapes	Words
Picture	Picture
Invented message (must be interpreted by child)	Picture + words
Picture + name	Picture + sentence(s)
Picture + words	Sentences only
Picture + sentence	
Sentences only	

Although the children skipped some steps (to be expected, given the lapse of a year between testing sessions), the order of the steps was the same for all nine children.

The interesting differences between the steps of the story and the steps of the letter are that letters and words came into the letter writing earlier than into the story writing, and that no invented messages were noted in the letters. For six children the graphic form of the letter was more sophisticated than that of the story in year 1. In year 2, only the graphic form of Matt's story was more sophisticated than the letter. In year 3, the letters and stories were about equal in graphic form, with the exception of Mike's letter, which reverted to drawing.

The greater sophistication of the graphic form used in the letters suggests that the children perceived letters to be both more formal than stories and written to be shared beyond the immediate context of situation. The examples of social interaction described earlier suggest that the stories were perceived to be available for sharing immediately, and therefore the reader could depend in part on the context of this situation to guide his or her interpretation.

Some support for this view comes from the instances of invented (nonconventional) spellings, which occurred more frequently in the stories (twenty-five instances) than in the letters (seventeen instances) over the three years. Additionally, the children tended to fine-tune their stories much more than their letters, indicating that the letters were perceived more as finished products. Thus, the somewhat larger number of children who showed greater reluctance to produce letters than stories in years 2 and 3 may have been due in part to their perception that the letter-writing task was product-oriented, to be shared with a distant audience rather than in an immediate context.

The children progressed toward the format of a story over the three years. In year 1, Susie was the only child who produced a story that looked like a story (with spacing, margins, and linear writing). In year 2, four additional children produced the format of a story, and in year 3, all the children produced the format of a story. The format of the letter followed a similar progression (with the exception of Garth, who produced a letter-like format in the second year but not in the third). However, the progression was slower, with only six of the children producing letter formats by year 3.

Reading a Book

The children were also asked to read a book, *Little Gorilla* (Bornstein 1976), each year. *Little Gorilla* is a large picture book with one or two lines of print on 78 percent of the pages. The other pages have pictures but no print. In year 1, all ten children looked at the book from front to back, demonstrating some knowledge of book handling. Susie was the only child whose eye gaze and attention consistently progressed from left to right across the pages. Matt attended from left to right 62 percent of the time, and Jill, 50 percent of the time. All the other children predominantly perused the pages from right to left.

Also in year 1, Jill responded to a larger percentage of pages without print (83%) than to those with print (73%), as did Becky—50 percent and 32 percent respectively. Daniel, Mike, and Tommy each responded to half the pages without print.

Matt responded to only one of the pictures and did so by critiquing the author's choice of colors:

> *What that? Snake? No! Not snake.*
> *Should snake should have . . . green.*
> *Snake have green, yes! But red? Red?*
> *Not red! No!*

He also objected to the fact that there were only animals and no people in the book. This lack of acceptance and appreciation is quite likely to be related more to a lack of prior experience with fanciful text than to any developmental stage.

Susie refused to read the book in year 1, signing *Won't tell. Me don't know what word say.* As with the letter writing, this reluctance could have been due to increasing awareness of the task demands. Although several different questions were used in an attempt to get the children started when they refused to read initially, none were very successful. Those who knew they didn't know could not be persuaded otherwise.

Biemiller (1970) identified among young hearing readers a nonresponse stage at which time the children omitted many words rather than substitute a graphically dissimilar word as they had done earlier in the year. Following the nonresponse stage, these hearing children began to read with higher graphic similarity to the text.

This nonresponse stage seems to correspond to the deaf children's refusals and delays in performing the literacy tasks over the three years. When children recognize that a reading task requires some use of the print information, they may begin to omit any words for which they are not able to produce a match. They may refuse or delay the reading.

They may also begin to fingerspell excessively to assure that the match is made. Sometime in the second or third year, the children in this study discovered fingerspelling (FS) as an alternate strategy. Fingerspelling was most frequently used by Mike in reading the book in year 3 (32%), e.g.,

FS FS FS   FS   FS
Lion roared his loudest roar for him.

A Comparison of Reading a Book and Reading Own Written Stories

In addition to fingerspelling and nonresponses, three other strategies were employed by the children in reading their own stories and in reading a book. One strategy was to pretend to read by describing pictures or signing a message that did not graphically match the text, as in the first stage in Biemiller's study. Another was to name objects—either signing one word in the text or giving a label for a picture—rather than signing connected text. An additional strategy was to read the text with a high degree of graphic match between the print and the child's response—Biemiller's third stage.

In reading a book in year 1, 79 percent of the pages Daniel read had no graphic match with the text. In year 2, he recognized the task demands and refused to read. In year 3, he produced a high graphic match on every page. These strategies are exemplified by the following excerpt from the book:

TEXT: *Giraffe, walking tall through the forest, was there when Little Gorilla needed him.*

Year 1: (Gesture—move, bite)
Year 2: ———   FS
Year 3: *Giraffe walk tall through the forest was there when Gorla needed him.*

Retelling the Book

The position taken here is that reading and writing involve construction. Reading is viewed as a process of making predictions about the printed material based on one's prior knowledge (Goodman 1967). Because each reader's knowledge base is different, no two readers construct exactly the same meaning for a text—just as two writers will not construct exactly the same text. Thus, the memory of text information will vary from child to child and by one child from year to year as the child's background knowledge changes and grows.

Retelling scores were obtained for years 2 and 3. These were derived by assigning points to each of the propositions in the original text and matching them to the propositions in each child's retelling (Table 4.1). All but one of the children's retelling scores improved over the two years, with Susie making the greatest gain.

Some of the information in the retellings was probably obtained from the pictures rather than the print. For example, in year 1 Susie said, "The giraffe tried to get the gorilla with his long neck." The text says, *Giraffe, walking tall through the forest, was there when Little Gorilla needed him.* This was the only time that Susie retold information exclusively from the pictures. All the children retold information from the pictures at least once.

Jill and Becky used pictures more than any of the other children in year 2. In year 3, each of them listed some of the characters in the story as part of their retelling, and this information may have also come from the pictures. Information exclusively derived from the pictures was not included in the retelling scores.

Four of the children made inferences about the story in year 2, with Bobby making three. Inferences as used here are defined as any statements the child makes that are not specifically given in the text but are plausible in the story. In year 3, two children made inferences. These inferences all seemed to be based primarily on information from the pictures. For example, Bobby (year 2) said, "First, gorilla go to tree, then sit." One page shows the little gorilla sitting in a tree. Bobby filled in the action prior to the time that the gorilla is shown.

However, the inference "Then get up, help, know walk, walk to giraffe," may have also been influenced by the printed text. The picture shows Little Gorilla holding on to a branch with one hand and looking to the giraffe for help. The text says, *Giraffe, walking tall through the forest, was there when Little Gorilla needed him.* Thus, some of the information may have come from the written text.

Bobby's one misconception in year 2 also came from the picture. He said, "Then other animal run away." On one page all the animals are running. In the next picture the animals seem to be watching from a distance. Bobby may have assumed that they ran away and then turned to watch.

Dictating a Story

Each child was given a bagful of toys and other small objects and asked to select three to use in telling a story. These dictated stories were recorded by a deaf re-

Table 4.1
Book Retelling Score Gains

Student	Year 2	Year 3	Gain in Points
Maggie	59	77	18
Matt	19	35	16
Bobby	26	97	71
Becky	21	89	68
Jill	17	11	−6
Garth	0	14	14
Susie	62	197	135
Daniel	37	83	46
Mike	7	67	60

search assistant. The child was asked to read back the story immediately and was asked to read it again the following day.

The children were relatively cooperative in performing the dictation task. In year 2, Daniel insisted on doing his own writing, and some of the children tried to negotiate for an additional toy from the bag, but there were no refusals, and all the children maintained the contract, although some occasionally needed prompting.

The children changed their mode of presentation over the three years. In the first year, three children manipulated the objects rather than use language to tell the story. In the second year, five of the children used language in conjunction with the manipulation of objects. In the third year, six of the children put the objects on the table and did not move them again, telling their story exclusively through oral and/or sign language.

In every instance where the child did not comply immediately, the child was at the stage of manipulating objects rather than using language. In all but one instance, the children who immediately complied with the task used language exclusively or in conjunction with the manipulation of objects. Thus, the difficulty of telling a story linguistically accounts for the delays in performing the task in the first two years.

Several instances of intertextual tying were related to the story dictation task. Bobby's story in year 3 was a loose version of "The Night Before Christmas." He had chosen a Santa (which probably suggested that theme), a horse, and a noise-maker, which was a large round shape on a stick. This he converted symbolically into a Christmas tree.

Mike told a story about an elephant that grew bigger and bigger, five days after reading *The Little Gorilla,* in which the gorilla grew bigger and bigger.

Becky used the same character in her story in year 1 that the researcher had used in giving her an example of a story.

All the children's stories in the first two years were closely constrained by the objects they had chosen. In year 3, only the stories by Garth and Jill were still constrained by the objects that had been selected. One example of this tie between the story and the object occurred when Maggie chose a male doll with a suction cup on the bottom of its feet in year 2. In her story a soldier became stuck to a wall.

The length of the children's stories increased an average of nineteen propositions over the three years. In year 3, the percentage of propositions that were cohesive with the other story propositions was never less than 75 percent (scored by Jill) and ranged up to 100 percent (Garth, Daniel). This percentage ranged from 40 percent (Becky) to 100 percent (Garth, Tommy) in year 1. Thus, as shown in Table 4.2, some of the children were producing cohesive texts from year 1, and all were producing largely cohesive texts by year 3.

Reading Dictated Stories

With the exception of Susie, Tommy, and Maggie, all the children refused to read their dictated story in year 1, either on the day it was dictated or on the following day.

Tommy attempted to invalidate the contract in the following ways:

T: (Stares at toys) *Me not know* (Looks away) *Not know* (Looks at Research Assistant [RA], looks away) *Not know* (Looks at RA)

RA: *What's happening?*

T: *No know* (Moves back; tries to hide face; looks down) *No know.* (Looks at paper) *Not know.*

RA: *What that say?* (Points to paper)

T: (Looks at toys, at RA, at toys)

Tommy finally attempted to read the story, but it was clear that he did not expect to be successful, and in fact he was not successful, with only 14 percent of his dictated sentences being syntactically and semantically acceptable when he read them back. He was very dependent on graphic information, as exemplified by the following anecdote: The research assistant had written *dogs* for Tommy several times, and twice she had not closed the *d* completely, so that it looked like *clogs*. Tommy fingerspelled the word as *clogs* and *cogs,* even though he used the appropriate sign for *dogs* every other time it appeared in the story.

In years 1 and 2, some of the children predicted exclusively on the basis of meaning rather than print. This emphasis on meaning served them well when the dictated material was fresh, but the memory decayed by the second day. In year 3, some of the children relied solely on meaning for the first day and attended to print on the second day, demonstrating a recognition that meaning can be more easily constructed when print cues are also used. In 33 percent of the cases, the children used different strategies on the two days. This phenomenon demonstrates

Table 4.2
**Number of Propositions in Story Dictations and Percentages of
Cohesive Propositions within Stories: Years 1, 2, and 3**

	Year 1		Year 2		Year 3	
Student	Number of Propositions	Percent of Cohesive Propositions	Number of Propositions	Percent of Cohesive Propositions	Number of Propositions	Percent of Cohesive Propositions
Garth	2	100	6	100	18	100
Jill	1	—	10	30	8	75
Matt	16	63	4	100	43	93
Bobby	12	58	20	90	13	87
Daniel	10	77	5	100	13	100
Susie	7	71	5	100	35	97
Becky	5	40	6	100	28	93
Tommy	16	100	6	67	45	87
Maggie	4	100	13	77	41	88

that strategies can be influenced by the task given the child and this demonstration was consistent with a case reported by Ewoldt (1977). In this case, a deaf six-year-old exhibited an integrated use of syntax and semantics while reading a predictable story, but changed to a strategy of no graphic match combined with omissions and fingerspelling within the same text when reading a difficult story.

The children's reluctance to read their dictated stories in the first two years may have been due in part to the fact that some children were merely manipulating objects, while the research assistant was trying to produce a linguistic equivalence to the manipulation that was not a good match with the children's original intent. It is the opinion of the investigator that the children were producing more sophisticated stories through the air than they were able to produce on paper in year 1.

Comparing Written and Dictated Stories: Progression of Concept of Story

The story production of four children was of special interest. Jill remained low in both tasks for all three years, succeeding finally in producing only a series of propositions related by character. Jill had had the least time in the instructional setting of any of the children. She had been in the program only one month at the beginning of the study, as compared to Susie, who had been in the program for three and a half years. Jill was also one of the two youngest children in the study.

Susie produced the most sophisticated written "story" of the group in year 1, and one of the more sophisticated dictated stories. In year 2, Susie's written story was again the most sophisticated of the group, but her dictated story was much less story-like than those of most of the other children. In year 3, Susie's written story was again among the most sophisticated, as was her dictated story.

Daniel's stories in year 1 were very primitive, but they were among the most sophisticated in year 2. In year 3, Daniel's written story was well ahead of his dictated story. Maggie followed a similar pattern, with both stories high in year 1 and low in year 2. Year 3 saw a surge of written story competence for Maggie that was not matched by the dictated story.

For Susie, Daniel, and Maggie, there was a period when their written stories surpassed their dictated stories. Should continued emphasis in the school be on producing written stories, one would expect that trend to continue or to reestablish itself for the other children.

Eight children were able to produce a one-episode story by year 3 by writing, dictating, or both. Five children included a beginning, an attempt, and an outcome (terminology used by Mandler and Johnson 1977). Three children used an ending emphasis, and there was one instance each of goal and ending.

Maggie's story from Year 1 was:

Beginning	*The baby cry.*
Attempt	*And baby's mother carry the baby.*
Outcome	*The baby stop crying.*
Ending	*The baby happy.*
Emphasis	*Finish.*

Comparison of Reading Book and Reading Dictated Story

In this study the children read the same book and their own dictated stories each year. Therefore, the strategies they exhibited seemed to result more from a developmental progression than from the influence of materials. This progression took the form of three sets of strategies.

1. No match with print and naming (labeling words or pictures)
2. Fingerspelling and omissions
   or refusal to perform task
3. Syntactic acceptability of sentences
   Semantic acceptability of sentences
   and fewer fingerspelling + omissions than at previous level

The one exception to the developmental progression occurred in year 2 when Garth reverted to naming and no graphic matches for 41 percent of the pages but also read some pages with semantic and syntactic acceptability.

Thus, it appears that the children initially approached the reading task using a strategy that was driven by meaning, supported by context, and heedless of the graphic information. Somewhere around the second or third year, their attention became drawn to the print, their perception of the task changed, and they temporarily adopted a bottom-up model—fingerspelling, omitting, or refusing the task.

According to Smith (1971), this bottom-up processing occurs because the beginning reader must deduce meaning from surface structure, which requires a maximum of visual information. "Since there is no prediction of what surface structure will be, the novice reader is forced to analyze all the constituents of the surface representation. . . ." (pp. 221–222)

Having gone through this period, some children returned to a meaning-based strategy. However, the strategy would never again be so completely reliant on meaning alone, because the child would always be aware that print also carries information.

If these children are to become proficient readers, they will continue to use print, but it will be primarily a source of confirming information rather than the basis for prediction. If they become stuck at the nonresponse or bottom-up stage (usually because of instructional focus), they may never become proficient readers.

DISCUSSION

Although more information is clearly needed, the studies reported here support the hypothesis that deaf children and hearing children demonstrate similar behaviors and take similar paths toward literacy. Table 4.3 presents the information provided by these studies, as well as information from a study (not included here) of children's emerging art concepts.

It might seem incongruous to include reading and writing behaviors as influences on literacy development. However, these behaviors are as much facilitators of the process as they are products of it. As an example, a child's attention to environmental print is not only evidence of developing literacy but also the stimulus for additional graphic–semantic associations.

Motor coordination begins to play a central role at the stage of scribbling. The first scribble form, identified by Kellogg and O'Dell (1967), is a collection of dots on paper, resulting from an uncontrolled arm-banging motion. As children develop better coordination of arm and hand movements, they progress through eighteen other scribble forms to well-formed circles drawn with a controlled motion, with straight lines tending to appear before curved lines (Dileo 1970; Eng 1931). Motor coordination and other factors converge at a point when the child is able to make conventional letters, first in manuscript (print) and later in cursive script. Smith (1971) has stated that sufficient visual acuity for reading is reached when the child has the eye-hand coordination necessary to pick up a pin. Beyond that point, additional development of motor control and visual acuity appears to be unnecessary for composing or reading.

The scribbles produced by children demonstrate the beginnings of spatial concepts, one of the first of these being that drawing/writing utensils must be confined to a space (e.g., the writing tablet or a wall) to produce satisfactory results.

In conjunction with this spatial concept comes the child's first affective experience with writing—the pleasure of making arm movements and at the same

Table 4.3
Developmental and Contextual Influences on Literacy

Motor Coordination	Writing/Drawing Behavior	Reading Behavior	Language Behavior	Cognitive Factors	Affective Factors	Personality Factors	Literacy Concepts	Literacy Environment
Arm-banging motions	Uncontrolled scribbling	Environmental print awareness		Spatial concept-writing confined to a space	Satisfaction with arm movements and results; Use and enjoyment of places, products associated with environmental print		Organization; Intentionality; Function	Print in environment; Child's own marks on paper
Increased motor control	Controlled scribbling; Fortuitous realism (drawing)			Symbolism				
Eye-hand coordination	Mock letters; Repetition; Contrast	Describes pictures in books		Construction		Flexibility	Sign concept; Generativeness	Access to alphabet; Access to books; Access to models of reading and writing
	Linear mock writing; Shapes	Interprets own written message		Spatial concept-linear	Closeness of parent and child during book sharing		Intentionality; message concept; Organization; Schema for letters	Child names and makes letters; Parent reads to child

Pragmatic interpretation	Labels, captions for pictures	Recognizes fantasy	Appreciation of fantasy	Risk-taking	Organization—awareness of task demands	Input from teacher/parents
						Framework for establishing and working toward goals
				Relinquishing risk	Story cohesion	Learning climate that encourages risk-taking or relinquishing risk
					Spelling	
	Story-telling through manipulation of objects	Spatial concepts—spaces between words			Book read from front to back	
		Perspective	Desire to be accepted		Storytelling	
					Writing as socially acceptable behavior	
No graphic match with text						
Describes pictures as reading strategy						
Names objects in picture or words in text						

Greater attention to graphic information	Storytelling through object manipulation and language	Intertextual tying	Enjoyment of social interaction		Message carried primarily by print	Intertextual tying (by parents and teachers)
Fingerspelling					Writing as social interaction	Experiences with variety of texts
Nonresponse to text						

Conventional letters
Fortuitous realism (writing)

Pictures
Names
Words
Sentences
Inventory
Invented spelling
Unanalyzed wholes
Generic to specific
Print as substitute for drawing
Language play through art

Story format
Letter format
Components of social letter
Contents of letter

Table 4.3 *(continued)*

Motor Coordination	Writing/ Drawing Behavior	Reading Behavior	Language Behavior	Cognitive Factors	Affective Factors	Personality Factors	Literacy Concepts	Literacy Environment
							Organization— punctuation Social letters Book read from left to right Different language and formats for different functions	
Folding letters for envelopes	Components of envelope Complex sentence patterns Draws figure in profile with action	Reading while writing, re-reading after writing Graphic information used primarily for sampling and confirming Greater semantic and syntactic acceptability	Storytelling through language alone	Inferencing Summarizing			Fine-tuning Abbreviation principle Organization— language patterns Envelopes Sequence Episodes	

time creating something on paper. This affective element, in turn, stimulates more writing behavior.

The child's scribbles become part of his or her literacy environment as the child sees the marks and determines to make more of the same, and as the child interprets the marks symbolically (fortuitous realism). For example, the child may make a scribble and see that it resembles a duck. Thereafter, that scribble *is* a duck.

Scribbling and attending to environmental print may occur simultaneously, as was the case with the child who recognized the Coca-Cola logo on a ruler. Because children have access to a great deal of environmental print, they are able to develop concepts important to further literacy growth. One of these is the concept of organization (Harste, Burke, and Woodward 1983). The child begins to recognize that print information is organized in specific ways and begins to make generalizations about these organizational schemes (e.g., pragmatic, semantic, syntactic, and graphic).

The child also begins to develop the concept of function and its relation to print, a concept that is usually well established by this period in the hearing child's expressive language (Halliday 1973). Signs in the environment signal some function for the deaf child as well—*McDonald's* signals eating, for example.

An additional concept developing at this time with regard to reading is intentionality (Harste, Burke, and Woodward 1984). The child begins to realize that because environmental signs are associated with function, they are planned, rather than haphazardly placed in the environment.

With the appearance of mock letters in the child's early writing come repetition and contrast, as well as evidence of flexibility in the placement and formation of letters. With the strategies of contrast and repetition, and with flexibility, come awareness of the generative principle (Clay 1975). The child begins to understand that the same components can be reorganized to form new wholes. Thus, a variety of letter combinations are made possible by rearranging the letters of one's own name.

Because construction is strongly tied to the generative principle, it is listed here, although it probably occurs from birth. Construction can be defined as the process of making links between old and new information to construct new meanings and solve new problems. Children construct meanings for pictures, and they construct written messages in this phase.

Children also recognize that they each have a sign, a symbol on paper, that stands for themselves. This growth in understanding of symbolism affects their experiences with books, and they are able to see the relationship between pictures and real objects. With linear mock writing the child demonstrates the linear spatial concept. Linear mock writing, which resembles adult cursive writing, also demonstrates that the child has observed elders in the act of writing and has begun to develop an organizational scheme for the features of writing. This development is accompanied by the formation of shapes. The developmental order that has been identified in the drawing of geometric shapes by hearing children progresses from crosses to squares, to triangles, to diamonds (Gessell and Ames 1946).

From shapes and mock writing, the child usually progresses to conventional letters. The context in which this occurs for some children is one of direct teaching by the parents. However, access to and interaction with print in the environment appear to be sufficient for this development to occur (Ewoldt 1985).

It is important to an understanding of the paradigm to recognize that earlier behaviors, concepts, and environmental influences may still be ongoing and important in each new phase of literacy development. One example is intentionality, which may be signalled by fortuitous realism in writing. The child may intend to make a specific letter or number, but if he or she is unsuccessful and the marks on paper resemble a different symbol, the child will accept the new symbol rather than viewing it as a badly formed example of the originally intended symbol. Intentionality is clearly demonstrated when the child interprets his or her written "message" for others, and intentionality continues to guide all further literacy growth.

With conventional letters and pictures, the child's written messages become less "inventive" and more open to interpretation by others. At approximately the same period, the child begins to refine old strategies and develop new strategies for interpreting the writing of others. Expanding on the base strategy of associating environmental print with function, the child may begin to make pragmatic interpretations of pictures and print (e.g., *That picture looks like a bread box, but you can't bake in a bread box, so it must be an oven*).

Expanding on the base strategy of describing pictures in books, the child may begin to use naming as a reading strategy—labeling an object in a picture or recognizing one word out of all the words on a page. At this point there is often very little graphic match between the text and the child's interpretation of it.

If children are being read to, they will undoubtedly encounter fantasy or fanciful elements in stories, and they will begin to recognize them as being different from reality. A child may not be accepting of fantasy if he or she has not had prior experience with it, but children who have had earlier experiences with fantasy will usually accept and enjoy it.

Children who have been read to will also begin formulating their own "stories," which may not be well-formed as yet but will begin to contain cohesive propositions (i.e., all the sentences will be about the same topic and will logically follow each other).

If writing, reading, and story-telling are part of children's literacy environment, either at home or at school, they will begin to demonstrate awareness that these activities are socially acceptable behaviors, and they will want to participate because of their desire to be accepted.

If the child's literacy environment has been one in which he or she was not corrected or censured, the child will also want to participate in literacy activities because of the enjoyment of communicating with others through these modes. This enjoyment is fostered by the security of knowing that one is free to take risks (with regard to spelling, for example) without being criticized and also of knowing that one is free to relinquish the risk whenever it becomes too uncomfortable (e.g., the child might ask an adult scribe to finish writing a dictated story instead of writing the whole story alone).

Children may also begin to show some perspective in their drawing at this time. They may, for example, draw an object that looks far away or show that one object is behind another.

As children progress along the continuum of literacy development, their prior experiences with literacy become increasingly facilitative. If they have not had these experiences, the next phase will be slow in developing, or development may be arrested altogether.

Clearly, for a child to know about social letters, he or she must have received them and written them. Similarly, a child who reads, who is read to, and who writes stories will demonstrate awareness that stories are spaced a particular way on paper (format), that different language and different formats are necessary for different functions, and that books are read from left to right. The child will also become aware of the uses of punctuation.

If children have had many experiences with a variety of texts—informational, realistic, fanciful, functional, social—they will make associations between formats and contents of previously experienced texts and the currently experienced text, and these ties are essential for learning. Parents and teachers can help children make these connections by calling to their attention the similarities between a prior experience and the current experience, the prior text and the current text.

At this time the child may show a greater awareness of the role of print in reading. Up to this time, the child may have "read" a well-known or predictable text by telling the story without awareness of or concern for the lack of graphic match. Now the child may enter a nonresponse stage—refusing to read, skipping, or fingerspelling all unknown words.

From this phase the child should move to a phase in which the graphic aspect of text achieves a more balanced perspective and the child's reading will again be guided by a strategy in which meaning is predicted first (from prior experiences) and print is used as confirmation rather than being the focus, as in the attempted template-matching strategy of the prior phase.

Inferencing, which is always present in reading and writing, becomes more evident as the child begins again to take risks with printed messages after the phase of greater attention to print. At this time the child will usually use reading as a strategy for composing and will reread his or her writing as a confirmation and reminder of the message that is being produced.

With this reading and rereading of the child's own text comes fine-tuning (also called editing). The child, both while writing and while reading, will fine-tune the text by adding, subtracting, or rearranging elements of the text. This fine-tuning becomes increasingly necessary as the child attempts more complexities in writing and begins to summarize large chunks of information while writing or reading. At this time children also begin to turn their drawings of figures sideways, allowing them to depict action.

A final word of caution is necessary in the interpretation of the paradigm. The children in this study exhibited some diverse strategies, but because of the structured tasks the children were required to perform, more homogeneity was demonstrated in this aspect of the study than was evidenced from the observation of their free-writing activities, where the children's individual goals and learning strategies exerted a strong influence, and their attention to one component of written language occasionally caused a regression in another.

Therefore, the developmental steps outlined here should not be accepted unquestioningly. A lack of knowledge concerning the relative contributions of all the factors influencing literacy development makes it difficult to determine whether the behaviors described here resulted from specific factors within the home or school environments or from the research tasks themselves, or even if any of these behaviors have a long-term effect on literacy development.

It appeared that these concerns could best be addressed through additional research that was longitudinal, qualitative, and contextually based. Thus, we initiated another research project that is still in progress at this writing. Principal investigators for this project are Carolyn Ewoldt and Karen Saulnier.

Building on the earlier work described in this chapter and the questions it engendered, the current study began with deaf children who were three years old. Much has already occurred in the literacy careers of three-year-olds that is of interest to the study of ultimate literacy success, and we hoped to capture more of that development by beginning with younger children than previous studies by Ewoldt had addressed.

The project is longitudinal because we hope to be able to determine whether early demonstrations of literacy success are in any way predictive of later school success in literacy. Thus, we have followed the same children for four years. We are primarily interested in children with hearing parents, since the previous study described in this chapter addressed children with deaf parents.

A qualitative approach was taken for the project because of a strong belief in the power of qualitative research methods to uncover phenomena often left concealed by predetermined hypotheses.

The large number of research participants (twenty-eight in the Gallaudet study as well as data contributed by a network of researchers around the United States) required that the project be more tightly structured than is typical for a qualitative study. However, due to the fact that this project was part of an ongoing program of study, more was known about the questions at the outset than is usually the case. For this reason we felt it legitimate to use some existing tasks, selected and adapted from the research literature, rather than relying exclusively on naturalistic data.

Despite these deviations, this research falls within the qualitative tradition in the following ways:

1. Underlying the project is the assumption that individuals (children, parents, and teachers) have meaning structures that determine much of their behavior.

Thus, to the extent possible, the perceptions of the participants were taken into consideration.

2. There are no strong research hypotheses, only questions that were proven in the prior research to be of interest to the intentions of this project, that is, to investigate factors that contribute to literacy success for deaf children and to describe the literacy messages that deaf children are receiving. By literacy messages we mean subtle clues as well as overt demonstrations about the relative importance of the available cue systems in reading and writing. For example, a parent who relates a story to the child's prior experiences is demonstrating that interpretation of text is based on prior knowledge; a teacher who gives children phonics worksheets is conveying the message that reading is a process of articulating sounds. In this case the child would be receiving conflicting messages at home and at school.

3. Context is an important consideration in interpretation of the data. The contexts in which the current study was conducted were the school, and the home, and surrounding community.

4. While numerical results are also presented, the final report is primarily of a descriptive nature.

5. The findings are analyzed using accepted inductive analysis procedures.

Data sources were the home, school, and the children.

Home

The data came from parent interviews, videotapes of parents reading to their children, and community observations.

Parent interviews in the home and videotapes of parents reading to their children were important sources of participant input. Although there is an abundance of research literature that describes parent–child book sharing between hearing parents and hearing children, we were aware of only two studies that described such events with deaf children (Maxwell 1980; Musselman, Lindsay, and Wilson, 1985). Since the beginning of our study, Andrews and Taylor (1987) have written about the interactions between a deaf child and a deaf parent that were videotaped as part of the current project, and Truax, Prendeville, and Whitesell (1988) have analyzed similar booksharing events and contributed a great deal to our understanding of our own data. Analysis of the remaining taped interactions is under way.

This component of the project provides previously undocumented information about booksharing practices that occur in homes with deaf children, as well as informing us about the kinds of literacy messages these children are receiving at home. It will be recalled that the pilot study described at the beginning of this chapter pointed to a strong relationship between literacy messages received at home and literacy-related behavior in school. We wanted to explore that relationship more fully, particularly because the research on literacy with hearing families shows a strong relationship between parent–child booksharing and literacy success in school (Mason and Blanton 1971; Teale 1981; Snow and Ninio 1986).

School

Data for this segment came from school observations, interviews with principals, examination of curriculum guides, teacher questionnaires and interviews, classroom observations, and videotapes of teachers reading to their class.

Classroom observations, teacher questionnaires and interviews, and videotapes of teachers reading to their class were also important sources of participant input. We were unaware of any literature related to teacher booksharing with hearing-impaired children. Using data collected as part of this project, Mather (1987, 1988) has described booksharing events between a deaf teacher and her class and a hearing teacher and her class. Analysis of additional taped interactions is also under way. These will give us information from the school that is similar to that provided by the videotapes of home booksharing and, again, a better sense of the types of literacy messages being given to the children.

Children

The data on the children included observation of children engaged in drawing/writing activities, videotapes of children "reading" books, environment print task, book handling task, and children's "writing" of letters and stories.

These tasks and naturalistic observations will help us understand the relationship between early success in such endeavors and later school success, as well as the relationship between the children's behavior and the literacy messages they are receiving. Here we relied more heavily on prior research where it was available. For instance, we modified an environmental print task that had been used with hearing children (Goodman and Altwerger 1981) because the observational data from the study reported in this chapter, as well as the pilot study, had presented scanty, but provocative, evidence that young deaf children do attend to functional print in their environment, such as McDonald's signs and stop signs.

We adapted a book handling task (Goodman and Altwerger 1981) as well, because we had demonstrations from the study described in this chapter of young children holding a book upright and looking at the pages from left to right. We wanted to know how early that awareness of appropriate book handling occurred, and we wanted to trace the development of knowledge about print and books for these children.

Videotapes of the children "reading" books were also made from the first year of the study. Following Sulzby (1985), we traced the development of each child's concept of what reading was about by asking that each child read the book that the teacher had previously read to the class. Having identified three sets of strategies in the reading of the children in the prior study, we wanted to see whether the strategy sets would be maintained for a larger group of children, most of whom did not have deaf parents, as the children had in the previous study. We will also use this task to help us see the relationship between the literacy messages given to the child and the child's perception of strategies involved in reading.

Other sources of data were school files, a play scale (Saracho 1984) and a language scale (Ski-Hi 1979).

We believe that the current study, building on the work described in this chapter, will provide a much clearer picture of the early literacy development of deaf children and will enable educators to take full advantage of these critical early years to become better facilitators of literacy.

REFERENCES

Andrews, J., and N. Taylor 1987. From sign to print: A case study of picture book "reading" between mother and child. *Sign Language Studies* 56: 261–274.

Biemiller, A. 1970. The development and use of graphic and contextual information. *Reading Research Quarterly* 6: 76–96.

Bornstein, R. 1976. *Little gorilla.* New York: Seabury.

Clay, M. 1975. *What did I write?* Aukland, New Zealand: Heinemann Books.

deBeaugrande, R. 1980. *Text, discourse, and process: Toward a multi-disciplinary science of texts.* Norwood, NJ: Ablex Publishing.

Dileo, J. 1970. *Young children and their drawings.* New York: Brunner/Mazel, Inc.

Eng, H. 1931. *The psychology of children's drawings.* London: Harcourt Brace.

Ewoldt, C. 1977. A psycholinguistic description of selected deaf children reading in sign language. Ph.D. diss. Wayne State University, Detroit, Michigan.

———. 1985. A descriptive study of the developing literacy of young hearing-impaired children. In *Learning to write and writing to learn,* ed. R. Kretchmer, 109–126. Washington, DC: The Alexander Graham Bell Association for the Deaf.

———. 1988. Emerging literacy in three- to-seven year old deaf children. In Proceedings of Lehman College 1987 National Conference: *Removing the writing barrier: A dream?* New York: Lehman College.

Gesell, A., and L. Ames. 1946. The development of directionality in drawing. *Journal of Genetic Psychology* 68: 45–61.

Goodman, K. 1967. Reading: A psycholinguistic guessing game. *Journal of the Reading Specialist* 4: 126–135.

Goodman, Y., and B. Altwerger. 1981. Print awareness in pre-school children. Working paper. Tucson: Program in Language and Literacy, Arizona Center for Research and Development, University of Arizona.

Halliday, M. 1973. *Explorations in the functions of language.* London: Edward Arnold.

Harste, J., C. Burke, and V. Woodward. 1984. *Language stories and literacy lessons.* Portsmouth, NH: Heinemann Educational Books.

Kellogg, R., and S. O'Dell. 1967. *The psychology of children's art.* Del Mar, CA: CRM Associates for Random House.

Mandler, J., and N. Johnson. 1977. Remembrance of things parsed: Story structure and recall. *Cognitive Psychology* 9: 111–151.

Manson, G., and W. Blanton. 1971. Story content for beginning reading instruction. *Elementary English* 48: 793–796.

Manson, M. 1982. Explorations in language arts for preschoolers (who happen to be deaf). *Language Arts* 59: 33–39.

Mather, S. 1987. Eye gaze and communication in a deaf classroom. *Sign Language Studies,* 54: 11–30.

———. 1989. Visually oriented teaching strategies with preschool deaf children. *The sociolinguistics of the deaf community,* ed. Ceil Lucas. San Diego: Academic Press.

Maxwell, M. 1980. Language acquisition in a deaf child: The interaction of sign variations, speech and print variations. Ph.D. diss. University of Arizona.

Musselman, C., P. Lindsay, and A. Wilson. 1985. Linguistic and social development in preschool deaf children. Toronto: The Ontario Institute for Studies in Education.

Platt, P. 1977. Grapho-linguistics: Children's drawings in relation to reading and writing skills. *The Reading Teacher* 31: 262–268.

Saracho, O. N. 1984. Construction and validation of the play rating scale. *Early Child Development and Care,* October.

Ski-Hi language development scale: Assessment of language skills for hearing-impaired children from infancy to five years of age. 1979. Logan, UT: Ski-Hi Outreach, Utah State University.

Smith, F. 1971. *Understanding reading.* New York: Holt, Rinehart and Winston.

Snow, C., and A. Ninio. 1986. The contribution of reading books with children to their linguistic and cognitive development. In *Emergent literacy: Writing and reading,* ed. W. Teale and E. Sulzby. Norwood, NJ: Ablex Publishing.

Sulzby, E. 1985. Children's emergent reading of favorite storybooks: A developmental study. *Reading Research Quarterly* XX (4).

Teale, W. 1981. Parents reading to their children: What we know and need to know. *Language Arts* 58: 902–912.

Truax, R., J. Prendeville, and K. Whitesell. 1988. Parents interacting with their hearing impaired children: Going from learning the ropes to taking the ropes. Paper presented at International Reading Association, Toronto.

5

School Placement and Least Restrictive Environment

Donald F. Moores, Brian Cerney, Milo Garcia

Since the establishment of schools for deaf children in the United States, controversies have raged over what, how, and where to teach them. To date there have been no definitive resolutions. Answers have varied as the United States has grown from an agrarian confederation of approximately four million inhabitants of thirteen eastern states to a postindustrial continental nation of 250 million citizens.

Uncertainty over school placement and other aspects of the education of deaf children is understandable in light of the fact that deaf education is a relatively recent phenomenon. Deafness was mentioned in Egyptian papyri as early as the seventeenth century BC, and Socrates dealt in detail with the sign language of the deaf in ancient Greece (Moores 1987). However, there is no record of any attempt to educate deaf children until the sixteenth century, when the Spanish monk Pedro Ponce de León successfully taught a number of deaf children of the Spanish aristocracy, which, because of generations of inbreeding and the presence of recessive genes for deafness, had produced an unusually large number of deaf offspring (Chaves and Solar 1974). It was not until two centuries later that the first real school for the deaf was established in Paris in 1755 by the Abbé Charles Michel de l'Épée (Moores 1987). Thus, the idea that deaf children could benefit from an education and could achieve literacy is a recent one.

EARLY PATTERNS OF PLACEMENT

The first school for the deaf in the United States, the Connecticut Asylum for the Education and Instruction of Deaf and Dumb Persons, in Hartford, was established in 1817. Its curriculum and its system of communication were based on the model of the Paris school. In fact, the first teacher of the deaf in America, Laurent Clerc, graduated from the Paris school and taught there before he was recruited to come to the United States. He modified the instructional sign system used in

Preparation of this chapter was supported by the National Institute on Disability and Rehabilitation Research (Grant NIDRR 87-01-28).

France to reflect English, and he based his instruction on the French curriculum (Stedt and Moores 1990).

The issue of school placement (i.e., the question of what constitutes the most appropriate environment in which to educate children with severe to profound hearing losses) is complicated by the fact that early childhood deafness is a rare condition that calls for very special instructional techniques. Thus, the low incidence of profound early childhood deafness, estimated by Ries (1986) as occurring in one child per 1,000, and the special communication and educational needs of deaf children, have been a force for the establishment of separate schools and facilities. A counteracting force has been the natural desire of parents to keep their children—especially young children—at home and have them educated in local settings.

School placement was not immediately seen as a problem at the Connecticut Asylum, primarily because students typically did not begin school until after age ten. Based on previous attempts to conduct censuses of the deaf population, the numbers of deaf individuals in the country were seriously underestimated, and it was assumed that one residential facility in Hartford could provide education and vocational training for all the deaf in the republic. The identification of significant numbers of deaf individuals in small towns and in cities quickly dispelled this assumption (Moores 1987).

The first three schools for the deaf were established in metropolitan areas: Hartford, New York, and Philadelphia. The schools in New York and Philadelphia were originally established as day schools but quickly evolved into residential schools serving students from wide geographic areas. From the establishment of the Connecticut Asylum (now the American School for the Deaf) until the Civil War, education of the deaf was driven by three primary motivations: (1) to provide deaf individuals with religious and moral training, (2) to provide them with vocational skills, and (3) to teach them to read and write.

The curriculum used in the first schools was based on that developed in Paris, as modified at the American School, with the addition of moral training and a religious emphasis different from that encountered in French schools for the deaf, which were established and run by the Roman Catholic clergy. In the United States, the predominant religious orientation was Protestant, and schools for the deaf reflected the ethos of early nineteenth-century New England—a deeply religious society in the first stages of industrialization. In common with schools for the hearing at that time and place, emphasis was on the five Rs: reading, 'riting, 'rithmetic, religion, and rules of conduct (Soltow and Stevens 1981). The practical nature of training for deaf students is illustrated by the fact that, in 1822, the American School instituted one of the first industrial training programs in the United States.

Although the emphasis was the same for deaf and hearing students, the education of deaf children was conducted in separate settings. From the founding of the American School until after the Civil War, deaf children were educated almost exclusively in residential institutions. There is no evidence of any deaf children attending school with hearing children before 1867, with the exception of Alice Cogswell, who attended a private girls' school in Hartford prior to her enrollment at the American School for the Deaf. In the fifty-year period 1817–1867, twenty-four residential schools for the deaf came into existence. The schools in Hartford, New York, and Philadelphia were in operation by 1820. During the next two decades, only four schools were added. From 1844 to 1860, seventeen schools for the deaf, or an average of one school per year, opened their doors. The geographic location of the later schools may reflect a change during the nineteenth century in public perceptions both of deafness (and other disabilities) and of the potential benefits of education for handicapped populations. Where the first schools were in metropolitan areas such as Philadelphia, New York, and Hartford, state legislatures later placed schools in communities such as Danville, Kentucky; Fulton, Missouri; Staunton, Virginia; and Delevan, Wisconsin. Many states also placed schools for the blind and/or for the retarded in the same town. Often schools for the blind and schools for the deaf were under the same administration in combined or adjacent facilities (Jones 1918).

The first successful day schools for the deaf, in which children commuted to special schools on a daily basis, were not established until 1867, when the Pittsburgh Day School and the Boston Day School came into existence. Because of a small population base, the Pittsburgh school later evolved into the predominantly residential Western Pennsylvania School for the Deaf, but the Boston school, now known as the Horace Mann School, has continued to the present as a day school.

The trend toward isolation and segregation of deaf children that lasted throughout the nineteenth century occurred, of course, within a cultural context, and educators of mentally retarded and other handicapped populations have written about similar developments (Dworkin 1976; Kauffman 1980). These movements were small parts of even greater changes as American society and the demographic composition of the population were undergoing fundamental alterations.

Programs for the handicapped (i.e., the blind, the retarded, and the deaf) that were developed in the early and middle nineteenth century essentially reflected an optimistic view of the potential benefits of education and training. They were humane and had educational orientations. The goal was to prepare handicapped individuals to function in society at large (Kanner 1967; Kauffman 1980). The outstanding early educators of the handicapped—such as Thomas Hopkins Gallaudet, Laurent Clerc, Samuel Gridley Howe, and Edouard Seguin—were firm believers in educability. Seguin, who came to the United States after the French Revolution of 1848, was especially effective in popularizing this philosophy.

Different attitudes were apparent by the later part of the nineteenth century. First, evidence began accumulating that not all handicapped individuals could be educated to take their place in society, especially a technical society. Second, the expansion of schools and institutions was seen more and more as a drain on the treasuries of the various states. Third, the conviction grew that many handicapped individuals, especially the retarded, constituted a threat to society. Residential institutions became less educational and more custodial in nature, with the expectation that many individuals would stay in them for their entire lives. This trend was accompanied by the previously noted tendency to build facilities away from population centers.

Segregation of handicapped individuals into isolated institutions tended to reduce the perceived threat to civilization but brought them into closer contact with each other in adult life. Influenced by the impact of the eugenics movement, Americans developed a willingness not only to segregate but also to sterilize large numbers of individuals judged "unfit." Laws restricting marriage and calling for sterilization were passed in many states.

The situation was never as grim for the deaf population as it was for those with other conditions, but schools for the deaf increasingly were established away from large cities. At times, restrictions on marriage and on procreation of deaf adults were seriously considered.

The complex patterns of placement and segregation were further compounded by a brutal system of racial segregation and the establishment of so-called separate but equal programs for black handicapped children. These programs were poorly funded and inadequately staffed, and they provided substandard housing. In Washington, D.C., the Kendall School for the Deaf served only white children. Black deaf children from the District of Columbia had to go to an all-black program in Maryland to receive an education. This situation existed until the 1950s. Throughout the South, separate residential schools for black deaf children were established, sometimes in the same community as schools for white deaf children and sometimes in physical contiguity.

In some cases there even existed four segregated residential schools under one administration—schools for the black deaf, the white deaf, the black blind, and the white blind (Jones 1918). In each case, the administrator was a hearing, seeing, white man.

It is a fact of life, then, that for most of the history of the United States, education of black deaf children either was nonexistent or took place in racially segregated schools with inadequate physical plants and poorly trained teachers. In 1949, there were separate residential schools for black deaf children in thirteen states. As late as 1963, eight states maintained separate schools for black and white deaf students (Babbidge 1965).

NINETEENTH-CENTURY ATTEMPTS AT INTEGRATION

In Europe, unlike the United States, there were several national movements to integrate deaf children in the public schools. Such integration was advocated in the early part of the nineteenth century in England by Arrowsmith (1819), and the practice was widespread for a time in Germany, especially Prussia (Gordon 1885a). In the middle of the nineteenth century, the integration movement was so strong in France that it was predicted that all residential schools for the deaf would be closed (Moores 1987).

In every case, the national integration movements of the nineteenth century disappeared without a trace, and the efforts were written off as failures. From today's perspective, it is relatively easy to identify the reasons for the failure of the first mainstreaming attempts. In essence, it was assumed that the very act of placing deaf children in physical contiguity in school with hearing children would have a beneficial effect on the development of speech, behavior, and academic skills by deaf children. It was believed that, by functioning in a hearing environment, deaf children would absorb the language of the larger community more easily than if they were segregated in residential institutions with other deaf children and used manual languages of communication. This simply did not happen. It was a classic example of fitting the child into the environment and expecting the child to adapt instead of altering the environment to facilitate development. In these movements there were no serious efforts to modify curricula or to provide special instructional support to deaf children. It was sink or swim, and most deaf children sank.

For little-understood reasons, the United States experienced no widespread integration movement in the nineteenth century. There were some attempts at integration, mostly with younger children, but they did not follow the European model of placing one deaf child in a class of hearing children. The best, and most successful, example of such programs was a "family school" established by Bartlett, who accepted both hearing children and deaf children in his school (Bartlett 1852). He followed a natural language approach, and all modes of communication were used by both deaf and hearing children. He believed that the use of the manual alphabet improved spelling and that signs improved ease and expressiveness in hearing children. Thus, Bartlett's program was different from European attempts in that deaf children were not in the minority and hearing children communicated by manual as well as oral means. According to Gordon (1885b), Bartlett's program was a success, but it did not survive its founder.

The single most influential proponent of integrated programs for deaf children in the United States was Alexander Graham Bell, who based his opposition to residential schools for the deaf primarily on genetic, not educational, grounds. Among his numerous interests, Bell was a firm advocate of eugenics and was a leader in the American eugenics movement, carrying out breeding experiments with sheep (Moores 1987). Like many other eugenicists of that time in Germany, Great Britain, and the United States, Bell was concerned with the proliferation of "undesirable" traits in the human species. Given his interest in education of the deaf, Bell had a special concern for the inheritance of deafness.

Bell initiated a study of the occurrence of deafness in families within and across generations, with special attention to Martha's Vineyard, an island off the coast of Massachusetts, which throughout most of the nineteenth century had an unusually large number of deaf inhabitants for its small population. The island at that time had a homogeneous population of English, mostly Kentish, stock, with the exception of a small Indian town (Groce 1980). The presence of recessive genes for deafness combined with the inbreeding of the population to produce a large number of deaf individuals.

Bell discerned that migration from the island to Maine and Massachusetts and then to other parts of New England was accompanied by increases in the incidence of deafness in newly settled areas. Bell was alarmed at the possibility of a tremendous increase of the incidence of deafness in the United States.

In a memorable work entitled *Memoir on the Formation of a Deaf Variety of the Human Race* (1883), which was followed by an article called "Fallacies Concerning the Deaf" (1884), Bell raised the alarm over what he considered the dangerous marriage patterns of deaf Americans. Bell acknowledged that deaf Americans were better educated and more successful than their European counterparts but argued that this success, in itself, was a problem in that it brought deaf people together, and they would then tend to marry other deaf people. Bell feared that the outcome could be the establishment of a new variety of the human race. Realizing the difficulty of enacting legislation to restrict marriages of deaf Americans, he proposed measures that would isolate deaf people from each other on the grounds that "the production of a defective race of human beings would be a tragedy" and that "intermarriages have been promoted by our methods of instruction" (1884, p. 41). The primary changes that Bell called for were (1) elimination of educational segregation of the deaf, (2) elimination of the "gesture language," which Bell believed caused the deaf to associate with and among each other, and (3) elimination of the use of deaf teachers.

Bell's efforts met with some success in restricting the use of signs in classrooms and in limiting employment of deaf teachers to vocational education and instruction of older children. He realized only limited success in his efforts against residential schools and separate day schools for the deaf. Except for an extensive day class movement in the state of Wisconsin, education of the deaf remained primarily in the hands of residential schools or separate day schools in large metropolitan areas.

FROM 1900 TO WORLD WAR II

At the beginning of the twentieth century, a system of school placements for deaf children existed that would continue with only minor modification through the first two-thirds of the twentieth century. In essence, there were three discrete subsystems: public residential schools (including separate schools for black children in many states), public day schools, and private residential schools. Some background information is necessary to have a clear picture of the form and function of each kind of school.

The term *public residential school* covered a wide variety of school types in the early twentieth century (Day, Fusfeld, and Pintner 1928). Many such schools had private governing boards, and some owned their land separately. These types of schools were especially common in the eastern part of the country. Typically, they had been established as private schools and over the years had become so dependent on state support that they evolved into de facto state schools. The term *public residential school* also included schools throughout the country that had been established by state legislatures and were operated under the jurisdiction of a state department of education and welfare.

Public day schools, without exception, had been situated in large urban areas and, as part of the public school system, were under the control of local boards of education. As such, they were much more closely attuned to public school curricula and to local communities.

Private residential schools, although few in number, had a disproportionate influence on the education of deaf children in relation to their size. These schools served a national—even international—constituency and had not come under the control of state systems of education. Like the public day schools, their mode of instruction was always oral-only. Unlike the public day schools and public residential schools, their student populations were drawn from relatively affluent and highly educated segments of the population. The private schools provided most of the leadership in the development of speech curricula and English-language curricula for the deaf and in advances in the use of residual hearing. Along with Gallaudet, they were the only sources of research on deafness during most of the twentieth century. The Clarke School for the Deaf in Northampton, Massachusetts, was noted for its tradition of research in genetics and deafness, and the Central Institute for the Deaf in St. Louis, Missouri, was noted for its research on audiology. Gallaudet College research was somewhat more educational in nature, as illustrated by the national survey in 1924–1925.

A National Survey

In what has been called the largest and most comprehensive in situ study of programs for the deaf in history, Day, Fusfeld, and Pintner (1928) analyzed the governance structure, physical facilities, teacher background, student characteristics, and student achievement scores of twenty-nine public residential schools for the deaf and thirteen public day schools for the deaf in a national survey covering the 1924–1925 academic year. No private residential schools were involved. The differences found between the day schools and the residential schools were fascinating and appeared across all the variables studied.

In the public residential schools, approximately 84 percent of the academic teachers were hearing and 84 percent were female. In the industrial programs, 58 percent of the teachers were deaf and 40 percent were male. In the public day schools, the teaching staff consisted "practically entirely of women and there were no deaf teachers" (Day et al., p. 122).

The residential schools obviously functioned more in loco parentis. For example, all twenty-nine had courses in moral training, and twenty-six had Sunday school classes taught by teachers, usually male. Only four of the day schools had moral or ethical training courses, and children were expected to attend religious services with their families.

The overwhelmingly oral mode of instruction in day schools was used with 97 percent of the children, with manual communication permitted in only one school. For the residential schools, there was great variability, with many schools using two or more of four options—oral-only, auricular, manual-only, or combined. The auricular option, which concentrated on the use of residual hearing, was available in schools with a substantial number of children identified as hard of hearing. The combined mode of instruction, as the name implies, combined oral and manual communication in instruction. Generally, children would start off with oral instruction. Those children who were classified as "oral failures" would be reassigned to either manual-only or combined classes, depending on the philosophy of the school. Overall, 62 percent of children in residential schools were taught through oral-only means as compared to 97 percent in day schools.

Differences also existed in child characteristics. On the average, children in public day schools had more moderate hearing losses. Day, Pintner, and Fusfeld reported average hearing losses of 65–70 percent for day school students and 75–80 percent for residential school students. Day school students also tended to have a later age of onset of deafness. For 74 percent of the residential students, deafness was either congenital or present by age two. This was true for only 57 percent of the day school students. Day school students began school at earlier ages, and their intelligence scores were higher. As might be expected, measured school achievement also was higher.

The data on family variables also reflected fascinating differences, with the day school children representative of immigrant settlement in the large cities. Only 30 percent of the day school children had both parents born in the United States; in 57 percent of the cases, *both* parents were foreign born. For 68 percent of the residential students, both parents were native born. A language other than English was spoken in one-third of the homes of the day school students, with Yiddish (12.4%) and Italian (12.1%) most common. In the residential schools, another language was spoken in less than 17 percent of the homes, with Italian (5.3%) and Yiddish (2.9%) accounting for almost half the cases.

In summary, day schools for the deaf in the 1920s were taught almost exclusively by hearing women using oral-only modes of communication. The residential schools had greater representations of deaf teachers and male teachers and used a variety of modes of communication. Students in day schools tended to have less severe hearing losses, later onset of deafness, earlier entry into school, higher intelligence, and higher academic achievement. The majority of children in day school programs were children of foreign-born parents, and a language other than English was spoken in 33 percent of the homes, usually Yiddish or Italian.

The pattern of placement continued to follow the tripartite breakdown of public residential school, public day school, and private residential school up to

World War II, with a slight trend toward increased public day school placement. This was offset in some states during the Depression years of the 1930s, when there was a noticeable increase in residential school enrollment, perhaps related to an inability of families to provide for their children.

DEVELOPMENTS FROM WORLD WAR II TO 1975

The patterns of school placement for deaf children, influenced by a number of demographic variables, became much more complex after World War II. The trend for deaf children to attend school on a day basis continued, but, for the first time, significant numbers of day classes for the deaf were established. Unlike the completely separate urban day schools, one or more classes for the deaf would be located within an elementary or secondary school serving a predominantly hearing school population. Such classes might be established in urban, suburban, or even rural areas. In the early years the classes were usually self-contained (i.e., deaf children were taught in separate classes by trained teachers of the deaf). Integration, such as it was, occurred in the lunchroom or playground and tended to be minimal. In some cases, however, high-achieving deaf children might attend one or more of the hearing classes, usually for mathematics. Such children tended to be hard of hearing, possessing good expressive and receptive oral skills (Day, Fusfeld, and Pintner 1928).

From 1945 to 1975, as in other periods, trends in placement of deaf students were influenced by developments in general and special education and by societal forces. The most obvious developments after 1945 were the urbanization and suburbanization of the country, accompanied by a tremendous population increase. Because of an extended baby boom, extensive immigration, and increases in life expectancy, the U.S. population during this period became approximately double that of prewar years. There are more people now, and they are more highly concentrated in metropolitan areas. At a time when the baby boom was ending in the early 1960s, education of deaf children was faced with the results of the largest known worldwide rubella epidemic, which greatly increased the number of deaf children (Moores and Kluwin 1986).

The appearance of this unusually large number of deaf children in the middle of the 1960s presented unique problems to the field of education of the deaf. As in American society in general, the numbers of deaf children in the U.S. population and in U.S. schools had been increasing for more than a generation. However, beginning in 1965, the general preschool and elementary school-age population was declining at the same time education of the deaf was faced with the problem of moving an unusually large block of children through the educational system. One important outcome was that the presence of such numbers speeded up the process of public school placement, which may be seen as the result of three interacting factors:

1. A postwar increase in the American school-age population up to 1965;
2. Urbanization and suburbanization of the population, accompanied by efficient metropolitan highway systems; and
3. The rubella-related increase in deaf children in 1964 and 1965 concurrent with a decline in births in the general population.

With the appearance of children deafened by the rubella epidemic, some implicit decisions were made immediately by state legislatures. Of primary importance was the fact that the existing residential schools did not have the resources to handle such an influx of students at one age level, especially a younger age. In most residential schools, preschool programs themselves were relatively recent phenomena, and few teachers of the deaf were trained to work at the preschool level. Also, many children deafened by rubella had secondary handicaps, and not all schools were equipped to deal with this type of student. Except for a few states, state legislatures gave little or no consideration to the construction of additional residential facilities. The children were seen as a one-time-only educational problem, and states were reluctant to invest in construction that would be underused after this group left.

The third factor, the contemporary birth rate decline, was at least of equal importance. For the first time, schools built to accommodate a burgeoning population had empty classrooms. The presence of children deafened by the rubella epidemic coincided with the appearance, for the first time since the Depression, of unused classroom space.

Public Law 94-142

Beginning in the 1960s, some special educators began to question the efficacy of residential or special class placement of handicapped children (Dunn 1968). It was at this time that the term *mainstreaming* came into popular use. Several court cases regarding educational treatment and placement of handicapped individuals established precedents. The best-known of these were *Pennsylvania Association for Retarded Citizens (PARC) v. Commonwealth of Pennsylvania* (1972) and *Mills v. Board of Education of the District of Columbia* (1972). In both cases it was ruled that exclusion of retarded individuals from a free public education was illegal. In both cases, regular classroom placement was judged to be preferable to special class placement, which in turn was preferable to placement in a residential school or institution. The implication was that, to be acceptable, placement in a residential school or institution should be demonstrably superior to placement in a special class or a regular class for a particular child. The burden of proof was on the educator to justify enrollment of a child in a residential program.

In the fall of 1975, President Ford signed into law U.S. Public Law 94-142—The Education for All Handicapped Children Act. This legislation represented a shift toward direct federal involvement in special education and fundamentally altered the relationship between the federal government and the state and local agencies educating handicapped children. The basic thrust of the law was a mandate for a free appropriate public education for all handicapped children in the least restrictive environment (LRE) appropriate to an individual child's needs (Harvey and Siantz 1979). The law calls for nondiscriminatory testing and for an individualized education plan (IEP) to be developed for every child. This plan must be reviewed as least annually in consultation with parents. The IEP should describe a child's present level of performance, educational objectives, and the procedures for evaluating progress.

The law stipulates that handicapped children should be educated with non-handicapped children to the greatest appropriate degree. Because many of the key terms in the law—including *least restrictive environment* and *free appropriate public education*—have not been operationally defined, there has been controversy regarding federal regulations written to implement PL 94-142. The process has followed a three-step sequence that is common in the implementation of major laws, namely, legislation—regulation—litigation. It appears that the mandate for least restrictive environment is subsumed under that of appropriate public education. This is interpreted as meaning that placement cannot be limited to one type of setting; alternatives may include instruction in regular classes, resource rooms, self-contained classes, and special schools and institutions.

In the education of deaf children, the best-known case to date regarding PL 94-142 involved the provision of support services in the form of an interpreter for a deaf girl, Amy Rowley, who was integrated into a regular elementary school class. The differences between the 1982 U.S. Supreme Court ruling and the 1979 decision of a lower court highlight the great diversity in interpreting the law. The deaf parents of a deaf child had requested that a sign language interpreter be provided to facilitate their daughter's ability to function in public school at the level of her academic and intellectual capacity. The school district refused, arguing that the child was achieving at grade level and therefore was receiving adequate support. The conflict rested in the parents' argument that the child should receive support to enable her to function at maximum levels. The school district responded that PL 94-142 mandates the provision of adequate, not necessarily optimal, services. At the district court level (*Rowley v. the Hendrick Hudson Board of Education and the Commissioner of Education of the State of New York,* 1979), the ruling was in favor of the child, and the plaintiffs were upheld on the grounds that the educational needs of the child in question could best be met through the services of an interpreter in the regular classroom.

The school district and the state of New York appealed the decision. The U.S. Supreme Court overturned the district court judgment and ruled that the school did not have to provide an interpreter. The particular decision itself is of less importance than the rationale (Rehnquist 1982). The U.S. Supreme Court decided that, in the enactment of PL 94-142, the U.S. Congress did not impose on the states any greater substantive educational standard than would be necessary to make access to education meaningful, declaring that "the intent of the Act was more to open the door of public education to handicapped children on appropriate terms than to guarantee any particular level of education once inside" (p. 14). The U.S. Supreme Court further declared that PL 94-142 imposes no clear obligation upon recipient states beyond the requirement that handicapped children receive some form of specialized education because "to require . . . the furnishing of every specialized service necessary to maximize each handicapped child's potential is, we think, further than Congress intended to go" (p. 22).

The U.S. Supreme Court interpreted PL 94-142 as offering only a "floor of opportunity" for handicapped children, as opposed to maximizing the potential achievement of each handicapped child. The implication is that the legal mandate for extensive special services is limited.

There are indications that a report of the Commission on Education of the Deaf (1988) may facilitate placement of some deaf children in residential settings. The Commission was established by Congress to assess the condition of education of deaf children and to make recommendations for improvement. A major claim of the report was the position that placement of some deaf children in a mainstream or regular class setting can severely restrict their opportunity for an appropriate free public education. The report stressed that the least restrictive environment for many deaf children was placement in central schools with sufficient numbers of deaf children at specific ages and grade levels to allow for appropriate class placement. In a case in which parents disagreed with a school district's plan to educate a deaf child locally and demanded placement in a school for the deaf, *Austin v. Beauregard Parish School System* (1988), a consent decree was developed in which both parties agreed to place the child at the Louisiana School for the Deaf. The basis for the decision was reference to the opinion of the Commission on Education of the Deaf concerning least restrictive environment.

CHANGES IN SCHOOL PLACEMENT: 1975 TO PRESENT

A significant increase in the placement options for deaf students has occurred in recent years, and there is a resultant confusion of terminology, with different school districts using different terms. Moores (1987) identified five basic classifications, with as many as twelve modifications in any one state.

1. *Residential schools.* In residential school programs, there are facilities to house students as well as to educate them. In areas accessible to large populations, substantial numbers of children live at home and commute daily. Children living within commuting distance generally attend on a day basis, and those living farther away stay at school, at least during weekdays. In recent years, approximately 40 percent of students in residential schools for the deaf have attended on a day basis.
2. *Day schools.* In larger metropolitan areas, programs may be established in separate day schools for the deaf. Children commute to them daily, and hearing children are not enrolled.

3. *Day classes*. Day class programs are classes for the deaf and hearing impaired established in a public school building in which the majority of children have normal hearing. Instruction may be in completely self-contained classes, or children may spend part or most of their time in regular classrooms.
4. *Resource rooms*. Most resource rooms are planned so that children spend most of their day in regular classes, returning to the special class for additional attention, usually in English and in particular academic areas. Whereas day class programs tend to have several classes in one school, with homogeneous grouping of children, in a resource room the teacher is generally expected to provide individualized services to students varying in age, hearing loss, and academic achievement.
5. *Itinerant programs*. In itinerant programs, children attend regular classes full time and receive support services from an "itinerant" teacher who may work with children from several different schools. The support services vary from daily to weekly lessons, depending on a child's individual needs. (p. 18)

Many school districts now centralize their programs in order to consolidate resources and support services. It is not uncommon for school districts to provide services in day classes, in resource rooms, and with itinerant teachers all in one building with a majority of hearing students. Given the requirements of an annual IEP and the possibility that a child will require different types of placement over a period of years, the concentration of programs in one area reduces the chance of frequent school changes.

In the past, only the children with the most residual hearing and the best oral communication skills were placed in resource-room and itinerant-program settings. The use of sign language interpreters in regular classrooms has led to an increase in the past several years in the number of children with profound hearing losses attending regular classes for at least some academic subjects (Moores, Kluwin, and Mertens 1985).

One way to understand the impact of PL 94-142 on placement is to compare enrollment data for Fall 1974 (the year before PL 94-142 was passed) with data for Fall 1986. The 1975 edition of *American Annals of the Deaf* (Craig and Craig 1975) has enrollment data for October 1974, and the 1987 directory (Craig and Craig 1987) has similar data for 1986.

As shown in Table 5.1, there was an overall decline in enrollment for the twelve-year period of 10.9 percent. This is consistent with a decline in the general public school enrollment over the same decade. From 1974 to 1986, public residential school enrollment declined by 6,945 students, while public day class enrollment increased by 8,163. Of the eight types of programs listed in Table 5.1, all but public day classes experienced a decline in enrollment of 35 percent or more over the twelve years.

Although enrollment dropped over a twelve-year period, public residential schools still enrolled approximately one-fourth of all deaf school children in the United States. An interesting feature of the residential school population is that

Table 5.1
Enrollments of Deaf Students 1974–1986

Schools and Classes	1974[a]			1986[b]			Enrollment Change 1974–1986	
	Number of Programs	Student Enrollment	Percentage of Total Enrollment	Number of Programs	Student Enrollment	Percentage of Total Enrollment	Students	Percentage
Public residential schools	63	19,063	36.0	64	12,118	25.7	−6,945	−36.4
Private residential schools	16	1,501	2.8	8	409	0.9	−1,092	−73.8
Public day schools	68	7,269	13.7	33	3,271	6.9	−3,998	−55.0
Private day schools	21	806	1.5	13	524	1.1	−289	−35.0
Public day classes	489	21,446	40.5	640	29,609	62.7	+8,163	+29.8
Private day classes	45	810	1.5	10	186	0.4	−624	−70.0
Other handicapped facilities	84	2,114	4.0	64	1,124	2.4	−990	−47.2
Total	786	53,009	100%	824	47,241	100%	−5,768	−10.9%

[a]Adapted from W. Craig and H. Craig, eds., "Directory of Services for the Deaf," *American Annals of the Deaf*, 120 (1975).
[b]Adapted from W. Craig and H. Craig, eds., "Directory of Services for the Deaf," *American Annals of the Deaf*, 132 (1987).

4,616, or almost 40 percent, were day students who commuted to school from home (Craig and Craig 1987, p. 124). The sizable enrollment in residential schools so many years after the enactment of PL 94-142 suggests that large numbers of deaf children will be educated in these facilities for the foreseeable future.

Table 5.1 shows that PL 94-142 and societal trends in general have had more impact on private programs and public day schools than on public residential schools. Enrollment in public day schools declined more than 50 percent, falling from 7,269 in 1974 to 3,271 in 1986. This drop reflects the tendency in large metropolitan areas to move from separate day schools for the deaf to day classes for the deaf within schools in which the student body is predominantly hearing.

The most startling changes have been associated with the decline in private residential schools and private day classes (Table 5.1). Only ten private day classes, with a total enrollment of 186, were identified in 1986, a decline of 70 percent from 1974. The drop in private residential school enrollment is as dramatic. Enrollment in 1986 (409) was about one-fourth of that in 1974 (1,501). By 1986, fewer than 1 percent of deaf children attended private residential schools.

Several private residential schools historically served a national and even international constituency, drawing students from many geographic areas. The data indicate that the remaining private residential schools now serve students on a regional basis. Approximately 40 percent of the students at private residential schools in 1984 were day students (Craig and Craig 1987, p. 132), a percentage similar to that of day students in public residential schools.

The precipitous declines in enrollment in private residential schools, combined with the erosion of private day classes, suggest that the free appropriate public education stipulations of PL 94-142 have had an enormous impact on private programs. In 1974, almost 6 percent of deaf children were educated in private schools and classes. By 1986, private enrollment had declined to 1.5 percent of the total: enrollment in private schools and classes is now negligible.

The evidence suggests that, by 1986, education of the deaf had become almost exclusively a public school responsibility, probably largely because of the free appropriate public education requirements of PL 94-142. There was also a movement away from residential school placement and toward enrollment in day classes. To some extent this was probably an effect of the least restrictive environment requirements of PL 94-142. Substantial numbers of deaf students, however, continue to attend residential schools, which enroll approximately one-fourth of the deaf students in the United States. One significant change from the past is that approximately 40 percent of residential school students attend school on a day basis, that is, they commute to school from home.

In summary, patterns of educational placement of deaf children have undergone significant changes from the beginnings of education of the deaf in America in 1817. Over the past several generations, the trend has been toward educating deaf children in public school programs on a commuting basis, a trend that was accelerated by the rubella epidemic of the mid-1960s and by the passage of Public Law 94-142. At present more than 60 percent of deaf children are educated in public school day class programs, with opportunities for academic integration on a class-by-class basis. A little more than 25 percent of students are educated in public residential schools, meaning that almost 90 percent of deaf children are in one of two settings—public day classes or public residential schools. The only other significant enrollment is in separate public day schools, which enroll almost 7 percent of deaf students. Enrollment in private day schools and residential programs has declined significantly and now constitutes a negligible part of the deaf school-age population.

A MODEL FOR LEAST RESTRICTIVE ENVIRONMENTS

This section reports on the development phase of a three-year study, still in progress, funded by the National Institute on Disability and Rehabilitation Research. No data currently are available and no conclusions have been reached. What follows is an overview of the structure and aims of the research.

Program Narrative

This program of research has been designed to address the issue of providing effective educational services to deaf children within least restrictive environments. The activities of this project encompass four interrelated elements.

1. Identify exemplary components of service provision in various educational programs, with emphasis on six factors:
   a. Academic achievement
   b. Student postsecondary success
   c. Parental involvement
   d. School climate
   e. Student social adjustment
   f. Degree of special placement.
2. Develop strategies and guidelines for replication of successful program components.
3. Conduct a validation study in three states while providing technical assistance for the replication of the successful procedures and while assisting in the development of a network of cooperative programs.
4. Disseminate the final guidelines and networking strategies on a national basis.

Overall Plan

The activities are being conducted in two eighteen-month phases involving programs for deaf children across the United States, including the complete range of placements from full integration to residential, self-contained classrooms. During the first stage of the study, we are gathering and analyzing a large body of data related to program effectiveness and least restrictive environment. The goal during this phase is to identify, not exemplary programs per se, but exemplary program *components* that are effective. From previous experience, we expect that a program that is exemplary in one component may not necessarily be exemplary in others.

Because we perceive schooling as a complex interactive process including a number of variables, we are using all six of the measures of effectiveness listed above.

Based on the identification of successful program components, a set of guidelines will be developed for implementation on a statewide basis. The guidelines will be designed to foster academic achievement, postsecondary success, parental involvement, school climate, and appropriate social adjustment within the context of least restrictive environments involving cross-program cooperation. Implementation of the guidelines on a pilot basis in three states, and evaluation of the process with final recommendations for dissemination of the model, will constitute the second phase of the study.

The final result, then, will be

1. Identification of factors necessary for school effectiveness;
2. A model for creation of least restrictive environments; and
3. Interaction of state or regional networks.

Phase I consists of two sets of activities: (1) compiling available data in order to identify exemplary programs, and (2) identifying elements in programs that make them exemplary.

Identification of exemplary program components is taking place in two stages: (1) empirical identification using school-wide regressed means for the six measured areas of effectiveness, and (2) identification of program features that contribute to effectiveness in those six areas. The same procedure will be used for each of the measures of school effectiveness; that is, all the dependent measures will be adjusted for local school population differences. The dependent measures will be achievement, student social adjustment, student career success, parental satisfaction and involvement, staff morale, and academic placement.

Regressed dependent measure means will be used to identify exemplary programs for each of the six measures. An exemplary program on any measure is defined as a program in which the average regressed score is one-half standard deviation or more above the overall mean.

While the exemplary programs for each outcome category were being identified, questionnaires on school process and structure were distributed in order to establish the characteristics of the effective programs. The data collection process has been to

1. Secure available data from the Center for Assessment and Demographic Studies at Gallaudet University;
2. Schedule and conduct student and parent data collections; and

3. Collect staff background, school climate, and school organization information.

For each variable in which categorical data are collected, means, standard deviations, or cross-tabulations will be computed for school, sex, ethnic status, academic placement, and degree of hearing loss. In addition, as a regular part of the process of data collection, reliability figures will be computed for every paper and pencil instrument. Intercorrelation matrices will be computed for all variables across subjects for the different groups: students, parents, teachers, administrators, and school or program.

The purpose of Phase II of the project will be to disseminate the guidelines developed in Phase I, to create small model informational networks, and to evaluate the feasibility of cooperation among different school systems.

The second goal of this phase is to create information exchange networks as a way of promoting cooperation among the various programs. It is reasonable to expect that some of the problems that programs for the deaf encounter can be ameliorated by the rapid exchange of information among programs within a reasonably sized service area. For example, curriculum development and the availability of instructional materials is a chronic problem in the education of deaf children because of the constant need to revise materials for the reading ability and interest levels of deaf students.

The third goal of this phase is to evaluate the feasibility of cooperation among different school systems. Two activities typify this objective of Phase II. First, we will identify local organizations that can be used to enhance cooperation among programs. Second, we will perform a formative evaluation of the success of our process of encouraging cooperation.

Participating Programs

The goal is to obtain the cooperation of both residential schools and public school day programs, with representation from different geographic regions of the United States. The areas have been designated as Northeast, Southeast, Midwest, Southwest, and West. A target of 25 participating programs was established in the approved proposal. Later, on the advice of a National Advisory Committee, an effort was made to include a substantial number of "smaller" public school programs. The reason for this was that, because of cost factors, relatively little research has been conducted with small programs, and it is important for a comprehensive study to investigate such programs. Because of this, also, we are planning to have one of the three states in the final phase represent a sparsely populated rural area.

As shown in Table 5.2, 55 programs were contacted, and 33 are participating in the study, slightly better than a 60 percent participation rate. This was higher than the 50 percent rate we had anticipated. All 9 of the residential schools and separate day school programs that were contacted agreed to participate, as com-

Table 5.2
Numbers of Programs Contacted and Participating

Category	Number Contacted	Number Participating
Residential school for the deaf	8	7
Separate day school for the deaf	2	2
Local or county public school program for the deaf	<u>45</u>	<u>24</u>
Total	55	33

pared to 24 of 45 local or county programs. For logistical reasons, one of the residential schools did not participate.

The reasons for not participating varied greatly. In some cases, it was felt that too much information was being requested and that it would put a strain on the system. In other cases, the procedures for obtaining permission were so involved that it would require up to one academic year to obtain complete approval. Another reason given for nonparticipation was involvement in other studies.

In general, the turn-down rate was highest for the small public school programs enrolling fewer than 35 deaf students. Less than half of such programs are involved in the study. It was the judgment of the investigators that, at least to some degree, many such programs had little or no previous experience with research and did not have procedures or policies in place to take part in the study.

Table 5.3 lists the participants in the study. As may be seen from the table, enrollment in the residential schools ranges from 104 to 455, with a mean of 272 students. Enrollment at the 2 separate day schools are quite disparate, 156 and 410. The local and county school programs represent a much wider range of enrollments, from 16 to 341. There is roughly a tripartite breakdown, with 9 programs enrolling fewer than 35 students, 8 with 35 to 100 students and 7 with 142 or more students.

SUMMARY

The issue of what constitutes appropriate educational placement continues to be highly emotional and controversial. Throughout the twentieth century, the trend has been to educate more and more deaf children in public school settings to which they can commute from home. This trend has been facilitated by diverse factors such as the general population increase, the rubella epidemic of the 1960s, and federal legislation, especially PL 94-142. With the emphasis now on individualized instruction, research should not be concerned with identifying some "best" placement for all deaf children, but with procedures for identifying the proper match of program and child at a particular time in the child's development.

Table 5.3
Participating Programs
June 1988

Type of Program	Enrollment
Residential Schools	
1. New York School for the Deaf, Rome	135
2. Model Secondary School for the Deaf, District of Columbia	389
3. New Mexico School for the Deaf	104
4. Florida School for the Deaf	455
5. California School for the Deaf, Riverside	322
6. Maryland School for the Deaf	108
7. Indiana School for the Deaf	390
Subtotal	1,903
Separate Day Schools	
8. Horace Mann School, Boston, Massachusetts	156
9. Atlanta, Georgia, Day School for the Deaf	410
Subtotal	566
Local and County Public School Programs	
10. Bergen County, New Jersey	70
11. Philadelphia Public Schools, Pennsylvania	341
12. Hinsdale Public Schools, Illinois	53
13. Broward County, Florida	75
14. Pinellas County, Florida	196
15. San Antonio Independent School District, Texas	191
16. Houston Independent School District, Texas	285
17. San Diego Public Schools, California	200
18. Madison Public Schools, Wisconsin	30
19. Milwaukee Public Schools, Wisconsin	74
20. Southwest Regional Program, Alabama	35
21. Columbia Public Schools, Oregon	30
22. Memphis Public Schools, Tennessee	100
23. Hennepin County, Minnesota	30
24. Low Incidence Program, Illinois	40
25. Nassau Boces, New York	35
26. Orange County, California	185
27. Toledo Public Schools, Ohio	142
28. Vancouver Public Schools, Washington	31
29. Wichita Falls Public Schools, Texas	26
30. Topeka Public Schools, Kansas	30
31. St. Clair Shores Public Schools, Virginia	16
32. Roanoke Public Schools, Virginia	17
33. Greenville Independent School District, Texas	25
Subtotal	2,257
Total	4,726

REFERENCES

Arrowsmith, T. J. 1819. *The art of instructing the infant deaf and dumb.* London: Taylor and Hessex.

Austin v. Beauregard Parish School District, 87 Civ. 741A, M.D.LA., 1988.

Babbidge, H. 1965. *Education of the deaf in the United States, Report of the Advisory Committee on Education of the Deaf.* Washington, DC: U.S. Government Printing Office.

Bartlett, D. 1852. Family education for young deaf-mute children. *American Annals of the Deaf* 5: 32–35.

Bell, A. G. 1883. *Memoir upon the formation of a deaf variety of the human race.* Washington, DC: National Academy of Sciences.

———. 1884. Fallacies concerning the deaf. *American Annals of the Deaf* 28: 124–139.

Chaves, T., and J. Solar. 1974. Pedro Ponce de León: First teacher of the deaf. *Sign Language Studies* 5(1): 48–63.

Commission on Education of the Deaf. 1988. *Report to Congress.* Washington, DC: U.S. Government Printing Office.

Craig, W., and H. Craig. 1975. Directory of services for the deaf. *American Annals of the Deaf* 120 (2).

———. 1987. Directory of services for the deaf. *American Annals of the Deaf* 132 (2).

Day, H., I. Fusfeld, and P. Pintner. 1928. *A survey of American schools for the deaf, 1924–25.* Washington, DC: National Research Council.

Dunn, L. 1968. Special education for the mildly retarded: Is much of it justified? *Exceptional Children* 35(1): 13–20.

Dworkin, G., ed. 1976. *The IQ controversy: Critical readings.* New York: Pantheon Books.

Gordon, J. 1885a. Deaf mutes and the public schools from 1815 to the present day. *American Annals of the Deaf* 30: 121–143.

———. 1885b. Hints to parents. *American Annals of the Deaf* 30: 241–250.

Groce, N. 1980. Everyone here spoke sign language. *Natural History* 89(6): 10–19.

Harvey, J., and J. Siantz. 1979. Public education and the handicapped. *Journal of Research and Development in Education* 12(1): 1–9.

Jones, J. 1918. One hundred years of history in the education of the deaf in America and its present status. *American Annals of the Deaf* 63: 1–43.

Kanner, L. 1967. *A history of the care and study of the mentally retarded.* Springfield, IL: Charles C. Thomas.

Kauffman, J. 1980. Historical trends and contemporary issues in special education in the United States. In *Handbook of special education,* ed. J. Kauffman and D. Hallahan, 3–23. New York: Prentice-Hall.

Mills v. Board of Education of the District of Columbia, 348, F. Supp. 866, 868, 875, D.D.C. 1972.

Moores, D. 1987. *Educating the deaf: Psychology, principles and practices.* Boston: Houghton Mifflin.

Moores, D., and T. Kluwin. 1986. Issues in school placement. In *Deaf children in America,* ed. A. Schildroth and M. Karchmer, 105–123. San Diego: College Hill Press.

Moores, D., T. Kluwin, and D. Mertens. 1985. *High school programs for the deaf in metropolitan areas.* Research Monograph No. 3. Washington, DC: Gallaudet University.

Pennsylvania Association for Retarded Citizens v. Commonwealth of Pennsylvania. 343. F. Supp. 279, E.D.Pa. 1972.

Rehnquist, J. 1982. *Majority opinion. Hendrick Hudson Board of Education v. Amy Rowley.* Case No. 80-1002, Washington, DC: Supreme Court of the United States, June 28.

Ries, P. 1986. Characteristics of hearing impaired youth. In *Deaf children in America,* ed. A. Schildroth and M. Karchmer, 1–32. Boston: Little, Brown and Company.

Rowley v. The Hendrick Hudson Board of Education and the Commissioner of Education of the State of New York, 79 Civ. 2139, VLB, S.D.N.Y., 1979.

Soltow, L., and E. Stevens. 1981. *The rise of literacy and the common school in the United States.* Chicago: University of Chicago Press.

Stedt, J., and D. Moores. 1990. Manual codes on English and American Sign Language: Historical perspectives and current realities. In *Manual communication: Implications for education,* ed. H. Bornstein. Washington, DC: Gallaudet University Press.

6

Consumer Motivated Research to Development: The Rationale for the National Research to Development Network

Thomas N. Kluwin

Cohen and Garret (1975), in a review of the history of social policy research with specific reference to the study of education, concluded that

1. The impact of educational research tends to be in the area of broad assumptions rather than in specific decisions;
2. Improvements in research methods do not necessarily result in improvements in research results, that is, greater agreement within the field; and
3. Educational research does not produce increases in the objective information base.

More recently, writers such as Mosenthal (1985) have tried to justify this third conclusion on the basis of the question of the true effects of educational research. While such further definition of the probable outcomes of educational research is in fact useful, it does not mitigate the obvious fact that educational research results often do not expand the specific knowledge base.

Much concern has been devoted over the past few years to the methods of research and whether or not they are effective in the sense of producing educational innovations. The discussion has reached the point where distinctions are being made about what "effective" means (Mosenthal 1985), with differing interpretations of the effectiveness of research producing different assessments of what research is "useful." An issue that tends to become lost in this discussion is why the research is being done in the first place. Ultimately, research is conducted in education to change practice in some fashion with the hope that the change in practice will result in some benefit.

Assuming that the purpose of educational research is to produce a change in educational practice, the need for change may be conceptualized in several ways, including the historic or progressive tradition, the business or efficiency model, and the radical argument, which is sometimes based on concepts drawn from Hegelian dialectics.

The historic or progressive perspective of school change looks back to the original reasons for free public education in the United States, that is, the Jeffersonian argument of the need for an educated electorate to permit the republic to function as it should. As the definition of the electorate has changed since the nation was founded, so also has the definition of the goals of schooling. These changes have both confused and motivated the definition of appropriate change in the schools.

The efficiency motivation for school change is of more recent vintage in the sense that it finds its roots in the turn-of-the-century progressive social reformers and was expressed by Elwood Cubberly (1911) in his "school efficiency" books. More recently, the case for efficiency was taken up by the Reagan administration in the Office of Educational Innovation, partially in its original form and partially as a cloak for promoting specific educational intervention schemes.

The third current motivation for educational change comes out of a view of the need for the enfranchisement of the powerless, with the resultant dialectical need for struggle. While this view does not represent a broad base of opinion, it is nonetheless used to argue for research to produce changes in schools. Regardless of the philosophy surrounding the discussion of change in schooling, all rationales refer to some set of value assumptions.

A starting point from which to discuss values in educational research is Beyer's (1986) review of Feinberg (1983), in which both writers attempted to define the context in which public school education takes place. Beyer made the point that too often we discuss education without a clear understanding of its role, function, and consequences. Part of the current debate about the quality of American education is the view that it is a product of the highly "specialized, often fragmented, and even antagonistic" disciplines that attempt to define the effectiveness of education without placing it in its appropriate context (p. 88). The sharpest critique of current educational research practice is the tendency of researchers to be absorbed in their own narrowly conceived project and to miss the relationship of their work to the overall purposes of education. There are several outcomes of this position. As Feinberg noted, one is the failure of educational research "to see just how their own activity is internally related to the practices of schooling" (p. 11, cited in Beyer).

Beyer (1986) critiqued educational research in both its social adjustment tradition and its school achievement tradition, variants respectively of the Jeffersonian and the progressive rationales, by remarking that in their failure to deal with the context of schooling, educational researchers see the results of their efforts as neutral and objective rather than as normative. The assertions of both research traditions are normative in the sense that the intent of a statement about teacher behavior or institutional organization is a change in the lives of individual students, and that such a change is structured by the assumptions, stated or ignored, of the individual proposing the action. Ultimately, educational research cannot be value free, because to conduct research or to propose a course of action based on a research result is to make value judgments about the purposes of education. According to Beyer, "the central deficiency of most educational research . . . [is that w]e have tended to view . . . research into these areas, as embodying autonomous, abstracted, fundamentally asocial and nonnormative phenomena" (1986, p. 94). The issue of putting education into a context is an inherently useful one, since education does take place in a very value-laden context, and anyone conducting educational research must at some point deal with the values implicit in any educational system.

Therefore, starting without any attempt to hide the value-dependent nature of educational research, let us consider its alternative conceptualizations and history.

A BRIEF HISTORY OF EDUCATIONAL RESEARCH AND DEVELOPMENT

In 1979, near the end of the largest period of expenditure for educational research in our history and the imminent change in the participation of the federal government in educational research and development, Schutz described four periods in the history of educational research and development. The first period ran from the 1890s to the middle of the 1950s and was characterized by individual activities by university faculty or by graduate students attempting to meet degree requirements. The critical event that ushered in the second stage was the Cooperative Research Act, which created the model of educational research and development (R&D) for the next decade. During this second phase, educational R&D was the product of ad hoc collections of university faculty and subject-matter specialists drawn from the schools in order to create and evaluate curriculum. This period ended in 1965 with the enactment of the Elementary and Secondary Education Act, which established the regional labs and centers systems. Schutz (1979) lamented the passing of this era by decrying both the establishment in the mid 1970s of the National Institutes of Education (NIE) and the decline of the labs and centers as major recipients of R&D dollars. A fifth period would now be added that would run from the movement by Jimmy Carter in the late 1970s to hold down the total federal budget, through the present restrictions on the domestic federal budget.

In the first era described by Schutz, there was little or no formal relationship between the supposed beneficiaries of educational R&D and the knowledge generators. During the second era, the stress was on cooperation between the university and the schools in an indirect fashion. Representatives of the schools were involved as expert practitioners; however, there was no institutional commitment from the schools that the practitioners represented to implement any of the research results. Consequently, direct influence on the schools was accidental at best. The third era saw a gigantic step away from the schools in the attempt to raise educational R&D to the status of a profession through the establishment of the labs and centers that were semiautonomous businesses responsive only to the federal funding agencies that supported them (Schutz 1979). The establishment of NIE was the logical extension of this movement toward professionalization of educational R&D, since educational research was to be raised in the federal hierarchy to the same status as the other scientific and biomedical research establishments. The fifth era has seen the continuing decline of federal involvement in educational improvement, along with the substitution of rhetoric and highly politicized stances for research expansion.

TRADITIONAL MODELS OF SCHOOL–UNIVERSITY COOPERATION

Traditionally, university faculties have viewed themselves as teachers and scholars. They see themselves as the source of information transmission to the schools. This view gives rise to what is probably the most frequent model of university–school relationships: the top–down diffusion approach.

In this model, the university faculty is a source of information, this information is transmitted to a student body that is, by definition, ignorant. The graduates of the program are seen as spreading out in a thin layer, year after year, into the school system, with the understanding that these outstandingly trained individuals will change the system slowly from within. Unfortunately, the graduates are suborned by the personal, economic, and political realities of the system and either are themselves changed into functional members of an existing system or move on to other situations where the percentage of lingering malcontents and misfits is smaller.

A variant on this model was attempted by the Institute for Research on Teaching at Michigan State University when it tried to influence educational practice at the teacher level by taking outstanding practitioners out of the classroom and installing them on a full- or part-time temporary basis as members of the research team (Shalway and Lanier 1978; Florio and Walsh 1978). While the process was very gratifying to the teachers involved and provided a useful perspective for the university researchers, there was no institutional commitment on the part of the schools to enact any of the innovations that the teacher-researchers suggested. In the traditional top–down knowledge diffusion model, the burden of responsibility for educational change is placed on the shoulders of the individual teacher, who is expected to change the system one classroom at a time.

In the bottom–up clinical model, the service role of the university faculty member is stressed. In this approach to creating educational change, service is provided, not to the school, but more directly to the students. Faculty interventions may follow the "trainer of trainers" model, in which teachers or other school professionals are taught to do specific kinds of activities. The limitations of the bottom–up clinical model include the small scale of the projects and the lack of institutional commitment to any project as a permanent change.

The general failure of universities to respond to the ongoing research needs of schools is due to the fiscal needs of the university and the resulting limits placed on the actions of the faculty. Consequently, a radically different kind of relationship is needed if universities are to meet their financial requirements and the research needs of schools. The question to answer is what form that relationship should take.

RATIONALE FOR INTERACTIVE RESEARCH

Cohen and Garret (1975) offered a solution to the problem of how to conduct educational research in a meaningful way. Like Eisner's (1983) notion of connoisseurship in educational evaluation, Cohen and Garret's "discourse" approach to educational research and development steps back from the simplistic, pure science approach to educational research and applies a different model to the methodology. In its rudimentary form (Cohen and Garret 1975, pp. 42–43), all parties in the discourse must be able to

1. Initiate discussion;
2. Establish or influence the rules of conversation;
3. Put forward statements;
4. Request elaboration and clarification; and
5. Call other statements into question.

Such a concept of educational research is foreign to the pure science approach. It is difficult to imagine a physicist negotiating with an electron or a chemist debating a catalyst. While this is an attractive approach to educational research because it involves a method for dealing with the value assumptions implicit in educational systems, some limitations should be noted about the basic assumption of this solution.

There is implicit in any human discourse a set of rules for the conduct of the exchange. In linguistics, these rules are referred to as "turn-taking behavior" or "regulative rules." Consequently, an immediate limitation of Cohen and Garret's proposal is the practical problem of who is to be the referee. Clearly, in any discussion, one side has the potential to dominate. In fact, in multiple participant discussions, there are specific formulae for predicting highly differentiated participation rates.

A further problem with the proposal is the definition of the participants. Is this the university researcher (with or without support staff) engaging students, parents, teachers, administrators, or some other combination of individuals? Do we negotiate with individuals or with their group representatives? What do we do with unreasonable or impractical requests, which can range from the teaching of creationism to requests for double periods for the marching band at the expense of academic instruction? Yet another problem with this approach is the objectivity of results—just as individuals can delude themselves, so can groups. The external observer of this process needs some assurance that the process is valid and the results can be generalized.

An alternative to the problem of validity presented by the discursive model is the notion of reciprocity between the researcher and the subject, a concept that is a given in radical approaches to the conduct of educational research (Lather 1986). The radical view of educational research promotes reciprocity based on the need for the research subject to be empowered to change his or her situation in an "unjust world." However, some familiar themes echo through this radical view, such as the need to state explicitly the values of the individuals involved and the need to develop perceptions of the phenomenon that are shared by the researchers and the subjects. Such explicitness and shared views would benefit educational research practice regardless of one's starting point.

Lather offered a summary of three methodologies that demonstrate the concept of reciprocity between the researcher and the researched.

1. Collaborative interviewing and interactive research in which interviews are repeated several times, primarily for two reasons. First, the researcher wants to respond immediately to the needs of the subject, and acknowledges this desire by reporting the results back to the subject. Second, the researcher can check the descriptive and interpretive validity of the research itself.
2. Expanding the circle of participants through interviews followed by questionnaires. This procedure looks vaguely like a pilot study followed by research. The critical difference is in the source of the items for the questionnaire. In the conventional pilot study method, the researcher generates a set of items and does a "reality test" with a small sample of subjects. The subjects are essentially data emitters, and the purpose of the pilot is to see if a potential audience can and will respond in the way the researcher would prefer. In the expanding circle model, the subjects generate the categories and some of the items, all of which are then used with a larger sample to guarantee generalizability.
3. Collaborative theorizing attempts to move subjects from providing data to theorizing about it. The goal of this research method is to allow participants an opportunity to define the results of the research. Obviously, time imposes constraints on the extensiveness of this process. A variation on this is "co-authored statements" in which the researcher and the subject negotiate a statement about the results of the research. In this form of reciprocal research,

though, a more realistic view is taken of the amount of input the subject can actually have in the results.

While the theoretical underpinnings of these research methods are radical in tone, they are fundamentally variations on accepted practices such as participant observation. What is more critical to the acceptance of the radical view of educational research is a question of the actual degree of subjects' participation in the research process because of practical constraints on researcher-subject communication. The radical approach legitimates the active role of the subject in research through specific procedures, thus moving Cohen and Garret's discursive method a step closer to a workable system.

Overall, one construct must underlie any new approach to educational research: subject participation. A dialogue must exist between those who would provide the basis for change and those who would be changed. Otherwise, the fundamental problem of the role of values in decision making will not be addressed. The "who" in this kind of a system is crucial. To be effective, midlevel managers must be involved, as will be discussed later. In addition, teachers and other school staff must also be involved to as great an extent as is practical in order to ensure the clearest definition of the researchable problem and the widest acceptance of the solution.

A NEW RESEARCH TO DEVELOPMENT PROCESS

To respond to the two challenges of value-implicit research and the need to involve participants in the research process, a seven-step process for the conduct of effective educational research will be defined. The key constructs underlying this new approach are *discussion* and *negotiation*. The discursive model is essentially adopted, but it is amended by the realistic constraints of constituencies with different agendas working to resolve differences through negotiation.

Problem Identification

As the individuals most familiar with the day-to-day operation of their own school programs, the midlevel managers of the programs need to meet regularly with the university research team to define their development needs. Midlevel managers are chosen for this step for two reasons. First, the literature clearly identifies activist principals as a key ingredient in effective schools. Second, midlevel managers share the perspectives of both practitioners and managers in that they have day-to-day contact with the teachers and the students and at the same time have the capacity to set their own schedules in order to accomplish special projects.

The initial meeting to identify problems is an open-ended brainstorming event in which the administrators not only discuss their own situations but also are able to gain a perspective on other programs. The result of this meeting is a collection of perceived needs that is pooled by the research team. Individual program problems are not addressed in themselves; instead, problems are identified that are common to several programs. This produces a manageable set of issues that can be generalized to a wide range of programs. In the dynamics of this meeting, it is the role of the university research team to clarify and identify trends as they appear. It is an option of the university research team during this phase to reject a particular initiative as being out of the range of the team's resources or its expertise.

Problem Definition

Defining the problem takes place after the initial round of problem identification. Part of the activity is the university research team's collection of local problems into themes. This is followed by the school representatives' elaboration and expansion on primary topics (i.e., goal setting for the team), as well as the process of setting priorities for responding to requests for assistance from the team. After the group meeting, the team continues to define the problems through conventional library research and the writing of draft proposals for research or intervention.

Preliminary Research

The initial gathering of research covers a range of activities, including the compiling of background data on potential sites and subjects and the development or pilot testing of specific instrumentation that would be used either in further research or in evaluating an intervention. Small-scale research activities with individual schools could also be planned and executed during this phase if necessary to validate a specific theoretical approach. The emphasis is on assembling information before developing a proposal.

Project Development

In the project development phase, the university research team develops a specific proposal for an activity. Depending on the level of knowledge in the area, this could be a proposal either for research or for an intervention. Obviously this can be point of contention between the school personnel and the university researchers. The school personnel, with their interest in improved practice, prefer intervention projects, while university research teams often show a preference for conducting more research. There is no simple solution to this conflict; however, the mutual respect developed in the relationship, the enthusiasm for the goals of the project, and some innovative thinking can resolve this problem.

The project may be initiated by either side. If the university research team develops the proposal, the school is a source of specific information about conditions and previous experience. If school personnel develop the proposal, the team provides a pool of technical expertise.

Project Review

Because this is a negotiated relationship and not a static one, the team goes to the program administrators with a specific project. The role of the school administrators is to comment on the feasibility of the project itself and to reflect on the match between the values implicit in the proposal and their situations. The simple solution to objections to a theoretical problem is for the school simply not to participate, but such a refusal, if it occurred often, would destroy the essential working relationship. A more constructive resolution is for the school personnel to offer alternatives.

The project review is also the point at which the level of support that the individual program can offer is determined. This is essential because it commits the school program not merely to participating in the project but to supporting it actively. Two obvious problems in any university-proposed intervention are the degree of commitment of the school personnel to the project and the degree of intrusion of the innovation into the system. This early project review phase, where the question of individual program participation remains flexible, allows for varying degrees of involvement at a stage when the feasibility or the utility of the project is still in question.

Pilot Project

Success is often the best justification for an activity. The pilot phase permits the concept to be demonstrated realistically, and this demonstration can be used later to justify an expansion of the project while building institutional commitment to it. There are also certain benefits from a pilot project, such as the field testing of procedures and the development of evaluation techniques.

Proposal Development and External Funding

During the funding phase the local university's procedures for generating external funding are followed. While the funding issue is a tiresome fact of life, this system offers the advantages that firm support from a group of schools is assured and that some preliminary results are available to support the requests.

THE OPERATION OF ONE RESEARCH NETWORK

The national research to development network for public school programs for deaf children grew out of work originated by the Center for Studies in Education and Human Development (CSEHD) of Gallaudet University with three public school programs for deaf students. Out of this initial effort came a national network of sixteen programs that are in direct, regular contact with one another. These programs are providing data for a longitudinal study of public school programs and are participating in various development projects. The network mostly consists of city systems and county-wide systems. The programs in the network are the Horace Mann School in Boston; Bergen County, New Jersey; Philadelphia Public Schools; Allegheny Intermediate Unit #3; Pinellas County, Florida; Broward County, Florida; the regional day programs in Dallas, Austin, San Antonio, and Houston; Orange County and San Diego Unified School Districts in California; Hinsdale South High School in Illinois; the A. G. Bell School in Columbus, Ohio; and the Toronto Metro School District.

The network was initiated during the summer of 1986 at a three-day meeting for personnel from eight school districts. The purpose of the meeting was to explain the network to the school personnel and to solicit their cooperation. In addition, they were given the opportunity to provide feedback on their needs as well as on the feasibility of the project.

One of the unique features of the research to development process is that school personnel participate with the research staff in defining problems, in developing solutions, and in working out appropriate research or intervention procedures. One important step in this process is an annual meeting between representatives from all the schools and members of the research staff. This meeting is held to provide feedback to the school personnel about the previous year's work, to outline future work, to solicit input about problems and solutions, and to develop insights into the interpretation of research results.

We can illustrate how the system works by looking at three projects that grew out of the initial discussions with the school administrators (Kluwin, Moores, and Gaustad in press).

THE FIRST COMPLETED PROJECT: WRITING IMPROVEMENT

The writing improvement project was built around a conventional pretest/posttest model. Pretest data included background information on students and teachers; process data including reactions to the process; and summative data. The summative data included writing sample posttests, which were collected by the teachers.

Forty-three teachers participated in the first year of the project, during which time several meetings were conducted in order to respond to a school-defined need for teacher training in composition. The content of the two-day workshop included developing a rationale for writing instruction, teaching writing as a process and not a product, and the promotion of writing through the nonjudgmental use of journal writing. However, in one group of schools the staff was already familiar with the concepts, and the meetings took a different form. The teachers

Table 6.1
Operation of the Research to Development Process

Project Phase	Projects		
	School Achievement	Social Adjustment	Postsecondary Plans
Problem identification	Completed	Completed	Completed
Problem definition	Completed	Completed	Ongoing
Preliminary research	Completed	Completed	Beginning
Project development	Completed	Beginning	
Project review	Completed		
Pilot project	Completed		
Proposal development/ External funding	Completed		

and the research team reviewed the constructs and organized the implementation of the project and the details of the data collection.

The university research team proposed an innovative way to build on a system already familiar to some of the teachers: dialogue journal writing (Kluwin et al. 1989). The project was instituted in two stages so that hearing students and deaf students could share journals. The first phase took place from November 1987 to February 1988. During this time, those schools in which no journal writing had ever been done began the process of doing journal writing between the deaf students and their teachers. In one school, the students already had considerable experience with journal writing, so they began a small pilot project with fifteen pairs made up of one hearing student and one deaf student. During a meeting of the project director, the chairperson of the English department at the high school where the pilot would be run, and the teachers of English for the deaf students, the problems of instituting a dialogue journal writing project were discussed. The emphasis of the discussion was on local solutions to any problems that might be encountered during the pilot. The participants agreed that an attempt would be made to exchange journals between deaf and hearing students once a week, that the deaf students would initiate the writing, that class time would be allowed for the hearing students to write, and that the students would know in advance to whom they were writing. By the first of November, the fifteen pairs were exchanging journals. This continued until January, when the semester changed. The completed journals were forwarded to the university research team and were used as the basis for developing the coding system for the other journals.

The second phase began in March 1988 and continued until June 1988. During this phase, most of the participants set up dialogue journal writing programs. The details of the individual exchange programs varied due to differing grade levels and school placements.

During the second year of the project, meetings were conducted for the teachers who were participating. They discussed their experiences with the dialogue journal writing process. The project staff members took notes and later wrote a description of how to implement the dialogue journal writing process. This description was then circulated back to the teachers as the basis for replicating the dialogue journal writing project during the second year.

An idea book for teachers of about 125 pages was written (Kluwin and Tobin 1989). The book consisted of a description of how to teach writing to deaf students as a process, sample lesson ideas from the teachers in the writing project, and resources for teachers interested in implementing this kind of a program. Material was received from twenty-seven teachers from this project, and additional material was written. The final document has been sent to the participating teachers as well as to others interested in implementing a similar project.

Day-to-day operation of this project has been the responsibility of Arlene B. Kelly and Blanche Drakeford.

THE SECOND PROJECT:
SOCIAL AND EMOTIONAL ADJUSTMENT

The second area of concern defined during the initial meetings with the program administrators was the social and emotional adjustment of deaf students in public school programs. The administrators' particular concern was that the deaf students in the public school programs appeared to be unnecessarily isolated from their peers.

In response to this concern, the university research team reviewed the available literature on the topic and proposed that a distinction be made between measures of satisfaction with one's current situation and measures of one's ability to cope with new or stressful situations (Blennerhassett, Kluwin, and Sweet 1989). The school personnel accepted the second view of the problem as more appropriate to their situation. While they did not deny that satisfaction was a valid measure, they felt that a better measure, both for making placement decisions and for evaluating the success of intervention programs, would be a measure of the student's ability to cope.

Consequently, the team selected an instrument, the Adolescent Coping Inventory (ACOPE), and modified its form for presentation to a deaf sample with highly varying reading levels. A simplified English version was prepared and pilot tested at two sites. Following the pilot testing, a sign language version was produced on videotape to be shown while the instrument was being administered.

After the completion of the pilot test, the instrument was administered to nearly three hundred adolescents in the sixteen programs in the network. Validity and reliability studies of the coping measure are ongoing. A particular problem with the measure is that most of the twelve scales generated by the test developer are unreliable for use with deaf subjects; however, three "super-scales" created by factor analyzing the output of the twelve subscales are reasonably stable.

It is hoped that profiles of successful and unsuccessful copers can be built so that at-risk populations can be identified and treatment procedures devised.

Upon completion of the validity and reliability studies of the coping measure, the university research team will propose some pilot interventions targeted for groups selected by the school personnel.

THE THIRD PROJECT: POSTSECONDARY PLANS

The third area of concern was defined by the university research team after reviewing the variety of third-choice concerns expressed by the school personnel. At present the problem is being defined more precisely. Issues such as postsecondary training, transition to the workplace, and survival skills have been considered.

During a project review meeting, instrumentation was proposed to the school personnel and rejected because of the language level of the instrument and the perception of the school personnel that they already did a great deal of vocational evaluation. The compromise was that the university research team would review all the vocational evaluation or career planning information used by the schools and develop, if possible, a proposal to use data already collected by the schools as part of the IEP process. That review showed that the schools did quite a bit of vocational evaluation but were not consistent between and within programs in what measures were used.

At the project review meeting, the team proposed an alternative to the use of existing archival information: they offered to modify an existing vocational evaluation instrument. This option was selected, and modifications and pilot testing of the instrument have been completed. When a final version is ready, a validity and reliability study using several hundred of the students in the network will be done.

At present, the university research team needs to review the possible conceptualizations of the problem so that additional instrumentation can be sought or developed and initial plans for interventions can be developed as the basis for a research program.

PUTTING A RESEARCH TEAM TOGETHER

The network is not a single researcher working alone; it requires a team of university faculty members working as a group. Since specialization is a fact of academic life, the network builds on that fact rather than fighting it. The earliest member of the team after Kluwin and Moores was Lynne Blennerhassett of the Gallaudet University Psychology Department, who contributed substantially to the development of the second thread of the current research. Professor Blennerhassett suggested moving away from a static notion of social or emotional satisfaction so often used in research on deaf youngsters toward the more appropriate idea of looking at the capacity of deaf youngsters to cope in public school settings.

Suzanne King of the Douglas Hospital Research Center in Montreal became involved in the project next, through her dissertation work on the career maturity of deaf children. Drs. Michael Stinson of the National Technical Institute for the Deaf and David Stewart of Michigan State University became involved as hearing impaired adults who had experienced public school education and who shared an interest in the social integration of these children in the public school setting. Dr. Stinson is developing instrumentation to assess the degree of social integration of deaf students.

One of the original needs of the project was to assess the communication abilities of the students. This effort brought in Dr. James Woodward of Gallaudet University and Dr. Martha Gonter Gaustad of Bowling Green State University.

And, perhaps most importantly, Catherine Sweet, formerly of Gallaudet University, managed the day-to-day operation of the network.

EXPANDING THE INFLUENCE OF THE NETWORK

The influence of this system has grown in three ways. One is through the direct support and involvement of the administrators of the programs. The second is through the direct contact with teachers and staff members during data collection phases of the project as well as during staff training. One of the more gratifying experiences of the second year of the writing improvement project was the evolution of a self-teaching seminar in which the teachers from around the country came together in small groups to discuss the results of the first year's activities and to share their experiences. An informal secondary network of teaching professionals grew out of those meetings. The third way this system has grown is through the various Gallaudet graduate students who have assisted in the project and have gone on to teaching positions. Kate Tobin at Annandale High School in Virginia, Mary Simpson at the University of Montevallo in Alabama, Lynne Wisman-Horther at the Willie Ross School, and Julie Papalia at the Pennsylvania School for the Deaf all helped to create the sense of camaraderie and hope for the future that is essential to this kind of an undertaking.

PRACTICAL PROBLEMS IN IMPLEMENTING A DISCURSIVE MODEL OF RESEARCH

Four problems will consistently plague the operation of a discursive model of research relationships: cost constraints, time limits, communication problems, and system stability.

Cost constraints are not unique to educational research, but some of the vagaries of funding such a research process may be unique. The primary source of educational research funding is either the federal government or a private foundation. The federal government uses a system that encourages one-time projects with schools. It is not possible to get multiyear commitments from federal sources to develop research ideas. The federal government can only be considered as a funding source for this kind of research during the last stage of the process. The track record of previous work and the ability to demonstrate that the work will result in concrete school changes will make the proposal very appealing to a federal funding agency, but the agency cannot be counted on to support all the effort that goes into the development of the idea. Private foundations should be more amenable to an open-ended working relationship between a university and the schools, but they also want specific projects in advance of funding. The most reliable source of funding for this kind of long-term relationship must come from a university commitment to the improvement of schooling and from school districts that want fundamental changes. Under the current funding systems, this kind of working relationship is a nightmare of economic uncertainty.

A combination of a supportive university administration and hard work can overcome some of the difficulties in funding. The project described in this chapter was initiated under an award from the Office of the President of Gallaudet University and has been continued under the sponsorship of the Gallaudet Research Institute through the Center for Studies in Education and Human Development. Support for major research efforts has come out of the Office of Special Education and Rehabilitation Services. Pilot projects have been jointly supported by CSEHD and the school districts through cost-sharing.

Time for the university faculty member and time for school personnel are very tightly constrained. University faculty members are expected to teach, to provide service, and to do research. Talking to school people about problems and letting the school people set the agenda is not feasible within the limits of time available to university faculty members. Again, a university-level recognition of the utility of this kind of relationship is required. In the school district, there must be a willingness to spend professional time on ideas that may not produce results until some point in the future, or not at all. School districts are increasingly adding to the demands on the teacher's day and to the paperwork requirements of the midlevel administrator. These factors sharply reduce the ability of the school personnel to participate in this relationship.

Communication is a problem in any human system. A national network for research to development compounds the problem because of the distances involved. Understanding must be created within the university research team and between the team and the school personnel. In addition, parents must be informed of the changes so that they have the opportunity to work to support them. Communication costs can be staggering, but innovative technologies, such as computer networking, can ameliorate this problem if all participants can hook up to a single system.

The stability of educational systems is a serious threat to the operation of a national network. The half-life of a midlevel public school administrator is about four years. Consequently, in our national research to development network, about one-quarter of our contact people change each year. New administrators must be initiated into the history and operation of the system, and this process is time-consuming. A university team initiating such a system might mistakenly believe that the programs they work with will remain stable year in and year out. Every year, a portion of the effort that goes into organizing the system must be repeated.

We have attempted to address the substantive problem of the usefulness of educational research findings by initiating a unique form of working relationship between university researchers and school programs. Such a network is feasible, as we have shown, but it is not easy to organize or to maintain. We suspect that the current system for doing research is probably the easiest to maintain, although it may not be the most effective.

REFERENCES

Cohen, D., and M. Garret. 1975. Reforming educational policy through applied research. *Harvard Education Review* 45(1): 17–43.

Cubberly, E. P. 1911. *The school review monograph series.* Chicago: University of Chicago Press.

Beyer, L. 1986. The parameters of educational inquiry. *Curriculum Inquiry* 16(1): 87–114.

Blennerhassett, L., T. Kluwin, and C. Sweet. 1989. Coping skills profile of deaf adolescents in public school settings. Paper presented at the Annual Meeting of the National Association of School Psychologists, Boston.

Eisner, E. 1983. Anastasia might be still alive, but the monarchy is dead. *Educational Researcher* 12(5): 13–14, 23–24.

Feinberg, W. 1983. *Understanding education.* New York: Cambridge University Press.

Florio, S., and M. Walsh. 1978. The teacher as colleague in classroom research. Institute for Research on Teaching: Michigan State University, Occasional Paper No. 4.

Kluwin, T., D. Moores, and M. Gaustad. In press. *Defining the effective public school program for deaf students.* New York: Teachers College Press.

Kluwin, T., and K. Tobin. 1989. Teaching writing as a process: Ideas from teachers. Pre-College Programs at Gallaudet University: Washington, D.C.

Kluwin, T., L. Wisman-Horther, and A. B. Kelly. 1989. Types of relationships found in the dialogue journals of young deaf and hearing writers. Paper presented at the Annual Meeting of the American Educational Research Association, San Francisco.

Lather, P. 1986. Research as praxis. *Harvard Education Review* 56(3): 257–277.

Mosenthal, P. 1985. Defining progress in educational research. *Educational Researcher* 14(9): 3–9.

Schutz, D. 1979. Where we've been, where we are, and where we're going in educational R&D. *Educational Researcher* 8(8): 6–14.

Shalway, L., and J. Lanier. 1978. Teachers attaining new roles in research: A challenge to the education community. Conference Series No. 4. Institute for Research on Teaching: Michigan State University.

7

Factors Predictive of School Achievement

DONALD F. MOORES, CATHERINE SWEET

This chapter presents the results of coordinated yet separate studies of two distinct groups of deaf adolescents—one group consisting of deaf children of hearing parents and the other group consisting of deaf children of deaf parents. Subjects for each group were enrolled in total communication programs from at least age four. The purpose of each study was to identify factors predictive of or related to reading and writing skills of deaf adolescents.

The justification for studying deaf children of deaf parents separate from deaf children of hearing parents is that children in the two categories typically are born into and develop within quite different linguistic, social, and cognitive environments, even though they may attend the same school programs. The deaf child born into a deaf family is immediately exposed to a fully developed manual communication system and matures in a familial environment with direct experience of the impact of deafness. The deaf child born into a hearing family usually is a cause of trauma and threat. Even though the family members are proficient in English or another spoken language, the challenge of establishing effective communication with the child is qualitatively different from that of a family of deaf parents and a deaf child.

The process of instruction may also be quite different as a function of parental hearing status even when children receive instruction via total communication at an early age. The child with hearing parents—along with the family—will first be exposed to one of several manual codes on English. These are prescriptive, pedagogical systems consciously designed to represent spoken and written English in a manual mode. Although all the systems borrow heavily from American Sign Language (ASL) vocabulary, they follow English morphology and syntax. In this way the child and the parents together are learning an English-based manual system, frequently at a time when the parents have been traumatized by the appearance of deafness in their family.

The deaf child of deaf parents, conversely, will be exposed to one or more

Preparation of this chapter was supported by the National Institute of Neurological and Communicative Disorders and Stroke (Contract NO 1-NS-4-2365).

varieties of ASL *prior* to identification of a hearing loss. For such a child, the introduction of a manual code on English represents a second manual communication system to be learned. This system will have a great overlap with the vocabulary of ASL and will share some significant features and constraints but will also possess fundamentally different structures and principles.

Given such different experiences and environments, deaf children of deaf parents may develop along different dimensions and may even structure the world in different ways from deaf children of hearing parents. Consequently, it may be anticipated that factors predictive of and related to literacy may either be different or may manifest themselves in different ways for these two groups.

In identifying for investigation possible factors predictive of or related to literacy in deaf adolescents, previous research with deaf and/or hearing populations provides some guidance. From reviews of the literature and research experience, as presented by Mertens in chapter 2 of this volume, several general factors of potential relevance to reading and writing of deaf adolescents were identified. These include (1) intellectual functioning/world knowledge, (2) academic achievement, (3) English grammar, (4) person-to-person communication fluency, (5) hearing and speech, and (6) family and student background characteristics. The tests and justifications for choosing these factors are presented later.

Unprecedented changes have occurred in the modes of communication used in the education of deaf children over the past two decades. Almost all deaf children educated twenty years ago were taught through oral-only means of instruction at least up to age twelve, whereas by the mid-1970s, approximately 65 percent of classes for the deaf were taught through oral-only means of instruction at least up to age twelve, whereas by the mid-1970s, approximately 65 percent of classes for the deaf were taught via the use of combined oral-manual communication (Jordan, Gustason, and Rosen 1976, 1979). This percentage appears to have remained constant in the ensuing years. For example, using data from the 1983 *Annual Survey of Hearing-Impaired Children and Youth*, Jordan and Karchmer (1986) reported that signs were used in 66 percent of students' instructional programs.

Essentially, then, changes in methodology occurred from 1965 to 1975. Since then, the percentages of children taught through total communication and oral only instruction have remained consistent—approximately two-thirds through total communication and one-third through oral only. The use of total communication increases with age. By high school, about 80 percent of deaf students are being taught through total communication (Allen 1986). For the first time there are some students who have been educated through combined oral-manual instruction throughout their elementary and secondary school years. Educational programs have moved past the point of arguing the relative merits of oralism and total communication and are devoting increasing attention to the individual needs of a child at a particular phase of development.

The research reported herein is designed to study two separate groups of deaf adolescents who have been educated through combined oral-manual instruction from the age of four or earlier. The purpose of the research is not to compare the two groups of students but rather to identify, for each group separately, factors predictive of and related to reading and writing skills. One group consists of 16- and 17-year-old deaf students with deaf parents who employ American Sign Language in their home communication. The second group consists of 16- and 17-year-old deaf students who have been enrolled in total communication programs and who have hearing parents.

It should be stressed again that the rationale for the separate treatment of the two groups is based on the fact that the acquisition of reading and writing skills may be very different for deaf children whose deaf parents signed with them from birth than for deaf children with hearing parents, even when both types of children were instructed through total communication. The areas comprising the research activities in the study are

1. Levels of literacy
   a. Reading
   b. Writing
2. Intellectual functioning and world knowledge
   a. Verbal
   b. Performance
3. Academic achievement
4. Knowledge of English grammatical structure
5. Person-to-person communication
   a. American Sign Language
   b. Simultaneous communication/English-based signing
   c. Oral-aural communication
6. Hearing and speech
   a. Audiological
   b. Articulation
7. Background variables
   a. Student characteristics
   b. Family characteristics

DEVELOPMENT OF ASSESSMENT INSTRUMENTS AND PROCEDURES

A major concern of the study was the identification and/or development of measures that could assess overall competency or fluency, especially in the areas of reading, writing, and interpersonal communication. In order to meet criteria for validity, it was necessary to have functional, holistic measures that could provide measurable process-oriented ratings of fluency in addition to the analytical, elemental measures traditionally employed.

The educational testing movement in the United States has been motivated to develop for a mass audience tests that are easily administered, completed, and scored, with an emphasis on efficiency in time and cost. The outcome of this motivation has been the development of multiple-choice tests to measure academic achievement, including reading and writing skills and English usage. In the case of a deaf student, who may have problems with English syntax or with a limited vocabulary, a multiple-choice test may not take into account the student's ability to process extended narrative through context and prior knowledge.

The use of multiple-choice tests has provided very narrow conceptualizations of writing skills as well as reading skills. Writing is a complex, goal-oriented process which can only be considered within the context of a particular situation, such as writing a description of an event or of a person, or writing a business letter or a friendly letter.

Thus, for the purposes of the study, it was necessary to develop from a consistent framework measures of functional, practical communication under the domains of writing for a purpose, reading comprehension, and person-to-person communication. Because reading and writing skills are treated as outcome, or dependent, variables in the study, attention was devoted to the development of holistic rating systems. Because we consider literate communication within the same framework as person-to-person communication (whether through oral, manual, or mixed oral-manual modalities), for theoretical consistency it was necessary to develop holistic functional measures in this area also. Within this chapter, then, most of the measures employed have been used previously with deaf and/or hearing subjects and will be treated briefly. More detail will be presented on the functional measures that have been developed for this study, which we believe provide important data in consideration of the competency of deaf individuals.

Area	Task
1. Reading comprehension	Story retelling
2. Writing	Narrative essay
	Business letter
3. Person-to-person communication	Language proficiency interviews
	Oral
	English-based signing
	American Sign Language

One other development of importance should be noted: the use of verbal tests for the Wechsler Adult Intelligence Scale (WAIS) as well as performance tests. For good reason, the assessment of intellectual capacity in deaf subjects has been restricted to performance scales, even in the face of reduced reliability, because of the evidence that scores on verbal tests underestimate the intellectual potential of deaf subjects. The inclusion of verbal WAIS tests in this study is not to obtain IQ scores, which would be fallacious, but rather to investigate the relationship of these verbal scores to reading and writing outcome measures and to other variables. Because this is a departure from previous work, background information and justification will be presented in detail.

Preliminary Test Development

Given the range of performances to be tested, a major component of the first stage of the study was the development and testing of a variety of instruments and procedures. In cooperation with the research team at the Central Institute for the Deaf (CID) and with representatives from the National Institute on Neurological and Communicative Disorders and Stroke (NINCDS), a number of tests and procedures were identified for possible inclusion in a test battery.

When available, tests that already had been developed for use with—or had been modified for—deaf subjects were given first consideration. However, because of a dearth of testing instruments of proven reliability and validity for adolescent deaf students, considerable attention was devoted during this period to the feasibility of developing, within the time and resource constraints of the project, appropriate measures in areas such as person-to-person communication and written narrative comprehension. In some cases, this was not possible. For example, there are no existing procedures that the investigators found to be satisfactory measures of comprehension of ASL narrative or ASL syntax. A complex procedure was originally considered that would have required a longer developmental timeline than was available and which, even if it could be successfully developed, would have required a disproportionate commitment of resources for scoring. In this case, it was decided that a completely separate project would be required to develop an adequate measure. In other areas, the prognosis was much more sanguine, and development was carried forward in the seven areas noted above.

Subjects participating in the development activities were adolescent deaf students drawn from the Model Secondary School for the Deaf (MSSD), the Maryland School for the Deaf, Gallaudet University, and the Virginia School for the Deaf.

Following the development activities, representatives from CID, NINCDS and Gallaudet met to agree on a Pilot Test Battery Manual, which would be used in pilot studies with three samples of deaf students: oral, total communication, and students with deaf parents.

Pilot Study

The purpose of the pilot testing was to identify a battery of tests appropriate for use with adolescent deaf students. In some cases, such as the Stanford Achievement Test, Hearing Impaired Battery (SAT–HI), the decision was relatively simple because data were available on validity and reliability, and appropriate age norms existed for both deaf subjects and hearing subjects. As previously noted, tests and procedures specifically developed for the purposes of this study were of particular interest.

The total communication pilot sample consisted of ten deaf students of hearing parents enrolled at the Model Secondary School for the Deaf. Average better ear hearing losses were 105, 107.5, and 111.5 dB at 1000, 2000, and 4000 Hertz

(Hz) respectively. The deaf children of deaf parents pilot sample consisted of eight students from MSSD and two students from the high school department of the Maryland School for the Deaf in Frederick. Average better ear hearing losses were 108.3, 114.4, and 115.6 dB at 1000, 2000, and 4000 Hz respectively. The mean WAIS Performance IQ was 97.1 for the total communication pilot sample and 114.0 for the deaf children of deaf parents pilot sample.

Results of the pilot testing were evaluated along a number of dimensions. For each measure, in addition to questions of reliability and validity, these involved clinical evaluation of the efficacy of the measure, including consideration of problems of test administration as well as time and resources needed for scoring. Because testing for the main study was planned for several sites across the country, portability of equipment and supplies was a major factor. In order to reduce redundancy, cross correlations of all results were run separately for each pilot group as a means of identifying tests that might be eliminated. Following this, representatives from CID, NINCDS, and Gallaudet met once again to agree on a final test battery, which would be administered to subjects from each of the three groups: total communication, deaf parent, and oral. This report addresses results for the first two groups.

Final Test Battery

The listing of measures in the final test battery, by category, is presented in Table 7.1. The following paragraphs briefly describe the measures used.

Stanford Achievement Test–1982 Hearing Impaired Edition

The 1982 Stanford Achievement Test was normed for the hearing impaired in the spring of 1983, on approximately 8,200 students from more than 600 programs for the hearing impaired across the United States (Allen, White, and Karchmer 1983). The norms developed for the Stanford Achievement Test–1982 Hearing Impaired Edition (SAT–HI) allow comparisons of deaf students to both hearing and hearing-impaired subjects across the United States. An additional benefit of the SAT-HI is that hearing impaired students take the same test as do hearing students, but the screening, test administration procedures, scoring, and norms are based on the needs of hearing impaired students.

Narrative Comprehension, "Space Pet"

Recall protocols (retelling) of connected text have been used extensively in research on comprehension and recall (Collins and Quillian 1969; Crothers 1972; Ewoldt 1981; Frederiksen 1975; Meyer 1984; Mandler and Johnson 1977; Yurkowski and Ewoldt 1986). They have also been used in classrooms as a diagnostic tool (Durrell 1955; Goodman and Burke 1972).

Two stories were selected in the pilot phase of the project to assess narrative comprehension: "Space Pet" and "Princess and the Tin Box." Pilot subjects read and retold both stories. "Space Pet" was selected for the final battery because of greater ease in scoring and because there were no floor or ceiling effects. Inter-

Table 7.1
Final Test Battery

I. Literacy
   A. Reading
      1. Stanford Achievement Test–Hearing Impaired, Reading Comprehension
      2. Narrative Comprehension–"Space Pet"
      3. Cloze Task–"Devil's Trick"
      4. Peabody Individual Achievement Test, Reading Comprehension
      5. Gates-MacGinitie Reading Test, Speed and Accuracy
         a. Comprehension
         b. Speed and Accuracy
   B. Writing
      1. Educational Testing Service Written Language Tests
         a. Descriptive Narrative
         b. Business Letter
II. Other Measures
   A. Related Measures of Achievement
      1. California Achievement Test, Vocabulary
      2. Stanford Achievement Test, Hearing Impaired, Spelling
      3. Peabody Picture Vocabulary Test
      4. Clinical Evaluation of Language Function, Producing Word Associations
      5. Expressive One-Word Picture Vocabulary Test
   B. English Grammar/Structure
      1. Test of Syntactic Abilities
      2. Rhode Island Test of Language Structure
      3. Manual Morphology Test
   C. Communicative Fluency
      1. Language Proficiency Interviews
         a. American Sign Language
         b. English-based Signing
         c. Oral
   D. Cognition/World Knowledge
      1. Wechsler Adult Intelligence Scale, Verbal
         a. Information
         b. Comprehension
         c. Arithmetic
         d. Similarities
         e. Digit Span
         f. Vocabulary
         g. Verbal Scale Score
      2. Wechsler Adult Intelligence Scale, Performance
         a. Digit Symbol
         b. Picture Completion
         c. Block Design
         d. Picture Arrangement
         e. Object Assembly
         f. Performance IQ
   E. Speech Production
      1. Speech Intelligibility (SPINE) Test
      2. CID Phonetic Evaluation of Speech
      3. Woodcock Reading Mastery Test, Word Attack

Table 7.1　*(continued)*

F. Hearing
　　1. Hearing Sensitivity
　　　　a. Unaided Thresholds
　　　　b. Aided Articulation Index
　　2. Speech Perception
　　　　a. Monosyllable, Trochee, Spondee Test
　　　　b. Minimal Auditory Capabilities Test, Visual Enhancement
G. Questionnaires
　　1. Parent
　　2. Student

rater reliability was .99. "Space Pet" (developed by Goodman and Burke 1972) was calculated to be at a fourth-grade reading level using the Frye formula (Harrison 1980).

A set of eight questions about the story was developed as a follow-up to the retelling. Each student retold the story on videotape, and then was shown cards with the questions written on them and was asked to answer each question in his or her own preferred mode of communication. Answers were scored as right or wrong, with a range of possible scores from 0–8. Again, inter-rater reliability was .99 in the pilot phase. As with the story retellings, there were no floor or ceiling effects in the responses of pilot subjects to the "Space Pet" questions.

Directions for the "Space Pet" narrative protocol were administered to each subject individually. The directions were presented in simultaneous oral-manual communication, the mode of instruction used in all the schools from which the total communication and deaf children of deaf parent samples were drawn. All sessions were videotaped.

Two measures of reading comprehension of "Space Pet" were obtained—story retelling and questions. The silent reading of "Space Pet" was timed and used as a measure of reading rate. In this way three measures were obtained from the "Space Pet" protocol: story retelling score, responses to questions, and timed reading.

Cloze Procedure, "Devil's Trick"

Reading competence measures normally do not elicit a response until the student has completed the passage. The cloze procedure provides an index of comprehending strategies exhibited during the processing of print. It requires the integrated use of semantic and syntactic cues in the text, and thus this procedure depends heavily upon the reader's ability to predict syntactic structures and construct meaning.

The cloze procedure has been used with a wide range of populations. For instance, Hargis (1972) used the cloze with retarded and nonretarded children. Deaf readers have also been studied extensively through the use of the cloze (Moores 1970; Ewoldt 1981; LaSasso 1980).

Considerable variation in the scoring procedures has been employed by different researchers. This study employs procedures from miscue analysis, using syntactic and semantic acceptability as the criteria. The scoring system has been used by Ewoldt (1977) and Kelly and Ewoldt (1984) in research with deaf subjects.

In the Kelly and Ewoldt (1984) study, all three types of cloze responses (i.e., verbatim, syntactically acceptable, and semantically acceptable) exhibited statistically significant relationships with the SAT–HI. In addition, the semantic acceptability category had a significantly strong relationship with story retellings. There was an overall inter-rater reliability in that study of .82.

Measures of cloze procedures were applied with two stories in the pilot test, "Devil's Trick" and "No Schools for the Deaf Ones." "Devil's Trick" was chosen for the final test battery because it provided a better opportunity for establishing a range without the possibility of a floor or ceiling effect. Inter-rater reliability was .87. The story was calculated at the tenth-grade reading level according to the Frye formula (Harrison 1980).

During the pilot phase, all nonverbatim responses were recorded along with their scoring, reducing the number of decisions required during scoring in the formal study and thereby improving inter-rater reliability. Each of the responses provided by the reader in the main study was scored as to whether the response was verbatim or semantically and/or syntactically acceptable.

Peabody Individual Achievement Test, Reading Comprehension Subtest

The Peabody Individual Achievement Test (1970) is an individually administered screening measure, with norms for hearing children, with an age range of 5.6 years to 18.0 years.

Gates-MacGinitie Reading Test, Reading Comprehension and Speed and Accuracy Subtests

The Gates–MacGinitie Reading Test (1965) is a series of group-administered tests designed to cover grades K through 12. The comprehension subtest is a cloze-type procedure. It contains sentences from which words have been deleted. For each blank space, a choice of five completions is offered, from which the subject is to choose the most appropriate. The Speed and Accuracy Test measures how rapidly subjects can read with meaning. The test consists of a series of paragraphs, with each paragraph ending in a question or an incomplete statement, followed by a choice of four words. The time limit for the test is four minutes.

Written Language Tests, Descriptive Narrative, and Business Letters

In the case of written expression, the purpose was to produce measures suitable for dependent variables; that is, the most appropriate score would be single summary data points for each paper (Cooper and Odell, 1977; White, 1984). The procedures of the National Assessment of Educational Progress (NAEP), as developed by the Educational Testing Service (ETS), were chosen for the study. The

NAEP uses a holistic or primary trait scoring system, which was developed under the premise that writing is done for an audience and can be judged by its effects upon that audience. Successful papers have either a single dominant trait or a collection of characteristics that are appropriate to a particular writing situation (Mullis 1980). Thus, primary trait rating may be considered the most appropriate index of writing success.

Issues of content validity and construct validity also contributed to the adoption of NAEP procedures, which use actual composition as the measure. The procedures measure writing as the complex outcome of a process. They employ constructs to define an ability that may be referred to as "writing ability." This direct measure of writing solves problems posed by more compartmentalized and elemental approaches, such as multiple-choice tests of grammar or usage, that traditionally have been employed. Such elemental tests, although of some utility, can only measure component skills and can never directly assess the actual capacity to compose extended discourse.

The two raters for primary trait and holistic scoring were trained by a consultant from ETS. Each paper was read and scored independently by the two raters. At the end of the scoring session, the scores were compared. If a score differed by more than one level of the scoring system, the papers were discussed and a score was mutually agreed on. If scores were only one level apart, the two scores were used, unless one of the scorers chose to revise the score.

For the major study, two stimuli were used in the assessment of writing ability—a business letter prompt and a general descriptive essay prompt. Scoring categories for the letter and essay were as follows:

	Business Letter	Descriptive Essay
Primary trait rating	x	
Holistic rating		x
Syntactic analysis		x
Error rating scale		x

California Achievement Test, Vocabulary

The California Achievement Test (CAT) is a nationally normed paper-and-pencil group test. The vocabulary subtest is a multiple choice test in which subjects must identify similarities, opposites, and definitions. The test requires ten minutes to administer and the results are presented as grade scores. There are no norms for deaf students.

Stanford Achievement Test–Hearing Impaired, Spelling

The spelling subtest of the Stanford Achievement Test–Hearing Impaired (SAT–HI), is a multiple choice test in which the student must identify misspelled words. It is a timed test of fifteen minutes. Results are reported as grade scores.

Peabody Picture Vocabulary Test

The Peabody Picture Vocabulary Test (PPVT) is an individually administered multiple choice test of 175 items. The tester presents each word orally (or in this case with simultaneous speech and sign). The subject chooses from four simple black and white illustrations the one that best illustrates the meaning of the stimulus. The test was nationally normed on more than 5,000 hearing children and adults and was designed for persons 2.5 through 40.0 years of age. Raw scores are converted to age scores.

Clinical Evaluation of Language Function, Producing Word Associations

The Clinical Evaluation of Language Function (CELF) test, Producing Word Associations subtest was designed to assess quality and quantity of retrieval of semantically related words. Subjects are asked to name as many members of a class as they can within one minute. Classes used were foods and animals. Responses were videotaped, and scoring consisted of counting the total number of appropriate responses.

Expressive One-Word Picture Vocabulary Test

The Expressive One-Word Picture Vocabulary Test (EOWPVT) consists of two components: the first was developed in 1979 for children from 2 to 12 years of age, and the second, published in 1983 and termed the Upper Extension of the EOWPVT, expanded the age range to include 12 to 16 years. The test for ages 2 to 12 is individually administered (although the upper extension may also be group administered and requires a written response) and consists of 110 items. The child is shown a picture and asked to identify it. In this study, students identifying 100 or more items correctly were given the upper extension, which consists of 70 stimulus pictures. Scores are converted to age scores. There are no norms for deaf children.

Test of Syntactic Abilities, Screening Test

The Test of Syntactic Abilities (TSA) is a paper-and-pencil test of the understanding of 9 of the major syntactic structures of English, with norms for deaf students from 10 to 18 years of age. The screening test consists of a pool of 120 items. The test is untimed and is administered on a group basis. Each item consists of a four-alternative, multiple choice task in which only one response is correct. Scores are reported as percentage correct.

Rhode Island Test of Language Structure

The Rhode Island Test of Language Structure was designed as a test of comprehension of simple English syntactic structures. The test booklet is organized so that three contrasting pictures face the subject and the test sentences face the tester.

Of the 100 items, the first 50 consist of simple sentences and the remaining 50 of complex sentences. The test is individual and untimed. Norms for hearing impaired subjects are based on testing of 513 children from 5 to 17 years of age. Scores are obtained by converting the total number of errors to T scores (x = 50, SD ± 10), based on age norms for hearing impaired subjects.

Manual English Morphology Test

A Manual English Morphology Test was developed based on preliminary studies conducted by Gonter (1985), who has been working on the development of imitation, comprehension, and production (ICP) measures of English-based signing. The Manual English Morphology Test is individually administered and consists of a total of 44 sentences presented by videotape. The subject views each sentence and then repeats it. Responses are videotaped.

The presenter in this study was an adventitiously deaf research assistant skilled in English-based signing who has had experience with the development of the Gonter assessment scales. Within the 44 sentences, 77 bound morphemes and 96 function words were identified as follows:

Bound Morphemes (77)		Function Words (96)	
____ S (Pl)	16	Pronoun	31
____ LY	16	Auxiliary Verb/Copula	30
____ ED	13	Preposition	20
____ ING	12	Article	15
____ EST	12		
____ FUL	3		
____ ER	3		
____ NESS	2		

The score is presented as the number of correct morphemes reproduced, out of a possible total score of 173. Scoring was based on the subjects' ability to use English-based signing, not ASL features. Examples from two areas related to the Manual English Morphology Test are presented later in this chapter.

Language Proficiency Interviews

The Language Proficiency Interview (LPI) procedure is an adaptation of the Oral Proficiency Interview, a procedure developed by the Foreign Service Institute and now used widely for rapid, valid, and reliable estimates of proficiency in the use of spoken language (Clark 1975, 1978; Jones 1979; Liskin-Gasparro 1979). Several groups of researchers have recently attempted to apply the LPI to the assessment of sign language proficiency (Johnson et al. 1983; Newell et al. 1983; Francis 1980).

The procedure involves the training of highly skilled native users of a given language to make consistent ratings of an individual's proficiency in that language, based on a face-to-face interactive interview. The ratings emerging from such interviews are keyed to a scale defined in terms of the intersection of the following three variables:

1. *Form*—the extent to which the individual is able to communicate grammatically and fluently in the language;
2. *Content*—the extent to which the individual is able to interact around various levels of topical complexity; and
3. *Function*—the extent to which the individual is able to conduct "business" on a variety of levels of interactional complexity.

The procedures call for the interviewers to conduct a series of "probe and check" techniques in which they attempt to guide the individual being tested to his or her maximum level of proficiency.

In this project, the LPI was used to determine levels of proficiency for each subject in each of the three language varieties: fluent American Sign Language without voice, fluent English signing with the simultaneous use of spoken English by the interviewer, and spoken English with no signing. Under each language condition, an interviewer talked with the student, using the variety of language being assessed. Using information derived from the student interview and several standard topics for discussion, the interviewers determined a global rating of proficiency for that language variety. Levels of proficiency were reported on a five-point scale, with the lowest value representing no skill in the language variety in question and the highest value representing a high level of proficiency.

A different interviewer was used for each language variety assessed. In each case the interviewer was a person who customarily used the variety under consideration. Accordingly, the American Sign Language fluency assessment was conducted by a fluent native signer able to use all signing varieties typically employed by deaf children of this age group; the assessment of English signing with simultaneous voice was administered by two hearing persons skilled at and accustomed to using this variety; and the spoken English interview was conducted by two hearing persons accustomed to communicating orally with deaf people. Each interview required approximately fifteen minutes and was videotaped for later review.

Because the LPI assessment instruments were developed specifically for this project, the scope of the study did not allow for the development of direct reliability and validity indices. However, several factors bear on the issue of the psychometrics of the assessment technique.

The instrument used in the study employs a unified five-point scale of language proficiency designed to apply to each of the three language varieties under examination. The scale describes structural and topical criteria for defining proficiency at each of the following five functional levels:

0 = No functionally useful proficiency
1 = Limited practical proficiency; no school proficiency
2 = Basic practical proficiency; limited school proficiency
3 = Full practical proficiency; basic school proficiency
4 = Full practical proficiency

Each functional level is described in terms of an intersection of formal, structural criteria (vocabulary, pronunciation, grammar, fluency, and comprehension) and topical, content criteria related to the ease or sophistication with which a person can talk about topics at various levels of social and technical complexity.

Concurrent with the development of the scale, a checklist of diagnostic performance factors was designed for each of the three varieties being assessed. These were filled out after the assignment of a global scalar score to be used to attempt to assess the validity of the scale and the procedures. Each checklist also requests the interviewer's assessment of varietal preference and the interviewer's assessment of the interviewee's cooperation).

Wechsler Adult Intelligence Scale

Because of documented problems with standard English, intellectual assessment of deaf individuals has historically posed problems for psychological service providers (Levine 1974, 1981). Ideally, practitioners require evaluation techniques that tap a variety of cognitive, problem-solving skills without testing through linguistic channels.

For this study, the verbal and performance scales of the Wechsler Adult Intelligence Scale (WAIS) tests were individually administered to all subjects by one of five certified school psychologists experienced in intelligence testing with the deaf. Psychological testing was completed within one-and-a-half to two hours for each subject.

The performance scales from each test were used as the measure of nonverbal intelligence. The verbal scales were experimentally administered as standardized measures of verbal comprehension and expression and to investigate the validity of the verbal scales as predictive indices of reading and writing within the population under study.

Test administration and scoring followed the standard procedures established in the Wechsler manuals, particularly regarding the order of subtest administration, time limitations, establishing basal and ceiling points, adherence to permitted demonstrations of items, and prompting of ambiguous responses. All items were administered in a form of Pidgin Signed English (PSE), in which adherence to the Wechsler manual was maintained regarding the English wording and word order of all directions and questions. All examiners were trained on special sign considerations regarding administration of the verbal scale, including uniformity of specific signs to be used, as well as the specific conditions under which fingerspelling, signing, and/or a combination of both was required. Protocols were scored with reference to the standard scoring criteria established in the Wechsler manuals, and raw score performances were converted to standard scores based on the norms published in the WAIS-R manuals.

Hearing Procedures and Protocol
All the subjects were evaluated using the following tests and procedures.

1. Pure tone, air conduction audiometry under earphones at octave and interoctave frequencies between 250–6000 Hertz (Hz) in a monaural condition.
2. The Monosyllable, Trochee, Spondee Test under earphones, monaural condition.
3. The visual enhancement subtest of the Minimal Auditory Capabilities Test.
4. An electroacoustic check for hearing aid(s), including curves meeting ANSI' S 3.22, 1982 guidelines and current use setting(s).
5. Pure tone, air conduction audiometry in sound field, if a hearing aid user.
6. Aided and unaided warbled pure tone, air conduction audiometry in sound field, if a hearing aid user.

In addition, an articulation index was calculated for each subject.

Speech Intelligibility Evaluation
Speech Intelligibility Evaluation Test (SPINE) is designed to elicit the subject's production of 100 words from 10 sets of consonant–vowel–consonant stimulus items. Each set of items contains four different words, although there are two pairs that are acoustically similar. The examiner shuffles the stimulus deck, and ten words are given to the subject for production. After the subject's production, the examiner makes a judgment of what is said, and this is then compared to what the subject actually saw on the printed card. The subject's score is the number of words correctly perceived by the examiner from a total pool of 100 words.

Woodcock Reading Mastery Test, Word Attack
The Woodcock Reading Mastery Test, word attack subtest, is designed to elicit the production of 45 nonsense words. The subject is presented with a written "word" such as *dreek* and is required to produce a natural reading of the word in about five seconds. Following the guidelines of the authors of the test, if the subject did not respond to a word, the examiner encouraged a response. Except for two sample items, the examiner never pronounced the test word for the subject. A score was derived from adding up the total number of correct productions, with a possible total score of 45.

Student Questionnaire

A student questionnaire, modified on the basis of pilot test responses, was administered on a group basis.

Parent Questionnaire

A parent questionnaire, modified on the basis of pilot test responses, was sent to the parents of participating subjects. The questionnaire was designed to elicit family background information as well as information on the subject.

TESTING SCHEDULE

For each site, depending upon resources and the school's preferences, testing schedules were developed before the research team arrived. First priority was given to completion of group testing at an early stage. Schedules were developed and room assignments made for the three language proficiency interviews, psychometric tests, speech and hearing assessment, and individual achievement tests. Facilities and equipment at the schools were ample and were appropriate to the study's needs. The only exception was the heavy reliance of the research team on videotaping procedures. For some schools, complete units were transported from Gallaudet.

FACTORS PREDICTIVE OF ACHIEVEMENT IN
DEAF ADOLESCENTS WITH DEAF PARENTS

Subjects

Information that the principal investigator obtained from the results of the *Annual Survey of Hearing Impaired Children and Youth* indicated that the subject pool was quite limited. In a one-year period, only 210 deaf children of deaf parents were identified from an enrollment of slightly less than 7,000 deaf students in the United States from 16 years, 0 months to 17 years, 11 months of age.

Fortunately, information from the *Annual Survey* indicated that relatively large numbers of deaf children of deaf parents were enrolled in a small number of residential schools for the deaf. The schools were contacted, and all agreed to participate. An unexpected complication arose from the discovery that many deaf children of deaf parents in the participating schools graduated before their eighteenth birthday. Inquiries made to the Gallaudet University Admissions Office indicated that 27 such deaf children of deaf parents entered the freshman class in a two-year period, and several were being offered admittance into the honors program. Because the mandate for the research was to obtain a wide range of achievement in the sample, it was decided that inclusion of all the eligible Gallaudet students would skew achievement to the higher level. Therefore only two Gallaudet students were included.

The deaf children of deaf parents sample consisted of 65 subjects with a mean age of 16 years, 7 months, ranging from 16 years, 0 months to 17 years, 11 months. Average three frequency (500 Hz, 1000 Hz, 2000 Hz) hearing losses were 103.97 dB in the left ear and 105.11 dB in the right ear. The ethnic identity of the deaf children of deaf parents was reported as: White, not of Hispanic origin (57), Black (4), Asian, Pacific Island (3), and Hispanic (Mexican American) (1).

Approximately 12 percent of this group (8 of 65) are of minority status, a much lower percentage than the 30 percent minority enrollment figure in programs for the deaf shown in the *Annual Survey of Hearing Impaired Children and Youth*.

Results

Descriptive Statistics
A mandate for this research was to obtain a sample of subjects with a wide range of achievement in reading and writing in order to investigate factors predictive of success. Descriptive statistics regarding the results are presented in Tables 7.2 through 7.21. The range of Stanford Achievement Test Hearing Impaired Battery (SAT–HI) scaled scores for reading comprehension was from 495 to 779, with a mean of 656. The "Space Pet" narrative comprehension also indicated a diversity in story comprehension.

The "Devil's Trick" cloze task provides further support for the wide intragroup variation. The mean verbatim correct score was 20.06 percent. The mean score for semantically and syntactically appropriate responses increased to 34.95 percent. There were further increases to 47.57 percent for syntactically correct responses and 48.71 percent for semantically correct responses.

A similar pattern is exhibited in each of the remaining standardized tests of reading. Mean grade scores of 6.75 for the reading comprehension subtest of the Peabody Individual Achievement Test (PIAT), 9.82 for the speed measure of the Gates–MacGinitie Reading Test, and 7.80 for the accuracy measure of the Gates were obtained. The range of scores were grades 2.1 to 13.0 for the PIAT, 4.3 to 12.3 for the speed test and 2.1 to 12.4 for accuracy. For the word attack subtest of the Woodcock, the mean grade score was 3.17 with a range from 1.2 to 12.9. These reading measures indicate that the sample consists of subjects with reading skills ranging from the second or third grade to above grade level (i.e. grade twelve and above).

Analyses of writing protocols, as presented in Table 7.2, provides a similar pattern. Primary trait scores for the business letter range from 1 (the letter is in

Table 7.2
Deaf Children of Deaf Parents
Literacy Measures

Measure	Reporting Format	Mean	St. Dev.	Range
Stanford Achievement Test, Reading Comprehension	Scaled Score	655.97	50.46	495–779
Narrative Comprehension, "Space Pet"				
Retelling	Propositional Count	127.58	119.93	0–530
Questions (8)	Number Correct	3.58	2.06	0–7.0
Time	Seconds	253.88	95.59	85–500
Cloze Task, "Devil's Trick"				
Semantic Correct	Percentage	48.71	29.71	0–94
Syntactic Correct	Percentage	47.57	25.68	0–94
Combined (Semantic and Syntactic) Correct	Percentage	34.95	25.39	0–94
Verbatim	Percentage	20.06	16.73	0–94
Peabody Individual Achievement Test, Reading Comprehension	Grade Score	6.75	2.64	2.1–13.0
Gates–MacGinitie Reading Test				
Speed	Grade Score	9.82	2.52	4.3–12.3
Accuracy	Grade Score	7.80	2.87	2.1–12.4
Business Letter				
Primary Trait Score	Rating 0–6	1.34	0.71	0.5–3.0
Descriptive Narrative				
Holistic Score	Rating 0–6	2.76	1.18	0–6.0
Error Score	Rating 0–6	2.65	1.05	0.5–6.0
Syntactic Analysis				
Total Words	Count	154.65	104.98	23–449
Unique Words	Count	80.26	40.98	18–196
Clauses	Count	19.69	14.69	3–58
T-Units	Count	16.15	11.91	3–56
Sentences	Count	12.92	9.05	1–40

some crucial sense incomplete) to 3, in which all elements are included. The range of holistic scores for the descriptive narrative was from 0 (incomprehensible) to 6 (superior).

Related measures of achievement (Table 7.3) reveal a mean California Achievement Test, vocabulary grade score of 6.33 and an SAT–HI spelling grade score of 8.56, with ranges of Grade 2.2 to 13.0 and 2.5 to 13.0 respectively. The Peabody Picture Vocabulary Test produced age scores from 2.58 to 33.67 (mean 9.68) and the One Word Picture Vocabulary Test showed age scores from 3.75 to 18.00 (mean 12.03). The Clinical Evaluation of Language Function produced word association counts from 20 to 60 (mean 40.08). Thus, the related measures

Table 7.3
Deaf Children of Deaf Parents
Related Measures of Achievement

Measure	Format	Mean	Standard Deviation	Range
California Achievement Test, Vocabulary	Grade Score	6.33	2.65	2.2–13.0
Stanford Achievement Test, Spelling	Grade Score	8.56	3.38	2.5–13.3
Peabody Picture Vocabulary Test	Age Score	9.68	5.35	2.58–33.67
Clinical Evaluation of Language Function, Word Associations	Count	40.08	8.29	20.0–60.0
One-Word Picture Vocabulary Test	Age Score	12.03	3.11	3.75–18.00
Woodcock Reading Test, Word Attack	Grade Score	3.17	3.07	1.2–12.9

reinforce the finding that children in the sample represent a heterogeneous group in literacy and school achievement.

Tests of English grammar/structure (Table 7.4) reveal adequate knowledge of English, as evidenced by mean scores of 82.46 percent correct on the Test of Syntactic Abilities and a mean T score of 63.43 on the Rhode Island Test of Syntactic Abilities. Scores on the Manual Morphology Test indicate understanding of the major English-based signed morphemes and function words. Again, it must be pointed out that there is great variation in each of the English grammar/structure tests.

As was anticipated, there was less variation in the Language Proficiency Interviews (LPI) with manual components. The ASL rating of 3.79 reflects native language proficiency in ASL of the subjects, with 53 receiving a "full proficiency" rating. Only two received a rating of 2, indicating basic practical and limited school proficiency. As was also expected from students in total communication programs, the mean score for English-based signing was relatively high (2.97), reflecting full practical and basic school proficiency, and the range was limited, with ratings from 2 to 4. The LPI oral scores, on the other hand, with a mean rating of 1.297, did show a wide range of fluency, with scores from 0 to 4. Approximately two-thirds of the students were rated as having no practical proficiency (0) or limited practical proficiency (1), but nine subjects had full practical proficiency (4). Those nine subjects using oral communication "can converse with sophistication and precision on complex, unfamiliar and technical topics expected for this age." Thus, the range of oral communication skills, as measured by the oral language proficiency interview, varies from no practical proficiency to full proficiency.

The Performance IQ scores (Table 7.5) indicate that the subjects are within the normal range, and on the average they score somewhat higher than the hearing population norm of 100. Verbal scores, of course, do not reflect IQ measures for a deaf sample. They were obtained for the purposes of investigating potential relationships with measures of achievement, to be addressed in a later section.

Table 7.4
Deaf Children of Deaf Parents
English Grammar/Structure and Communicative Fluency

Measure	Reporting Format	Mean	Standard Deviation	Range
English Grammar/Structure				
Test of Syntactic Abilities	Percentage	82.46	16.23	21–100
Rhode Island Test of Language Structure	T Score	63.43	7.23	43.4–91.3
Manual Morphology Test (173)	Number Correct	116.81	34.40	36–167
Communicative Fluency				
American Sign Language	Rating 0–4	3.79	0.48	2–4
English-Based Signing	Rating 0–4	2.97	0.80	2–4
Oral	Rating 0–4	1.30	1.48	0–4

Table 7.5
Deaf Children of Deaf Parents
Cognition/World Knowledge

Measure	Reporting Format	Mean	Standard Deviation	Range
WAIS Verbal Scale				
Information	Scaled Score	8.29	2.69	2–14
Comprehension	Scaled Score	8.59	2.11	3–16
Arithmetic	Scaled Score	9.22	2.46	4–16
Similarities	Scaled Score	8.02	2.11	4–14
Digit Span	Scaled Score	8.99	2.75	4–14
Vocabulary	Scaled Score	6.20	2.06	2–15
Verbal Scale Score	Standard Score	88.25	11.07	62–124
WAIS Performance Scale				
Digit Symbol	Scaled Score	11.79	3.00	5–19
Picture Completion	Scaled Score	11.00	2.40	4–16
Block Design	Scaled Score	12.69	2.70	6–19
Picture Arrangement	Scaled Score	12.06	3.04	6–18
Object Assembly	Scaled Score	11.54	2.94	5–19
Performance IQ	Standard Score	113.02	14.86	84–149

In the case of hearing sensitivity and speech production (Table 7.6), there is only limited variation in a population such as this, which is restricted to individuals with severe and profound hearing losses. However, the subjects do exhibit varying skills to some extent in both speech perception and speech production.

As indicated in the student questionnaire responses, the subjects generally understand what happens in class, feel a part of the school, communicate easily

Table 7.6
Deaf Children of Deaf Parents
Speech and Hearing Measures

Measure	Reporting Format	Mean	Standard Deviation	Range
Hearing Sensitivity/Speech Perception				
Articulation Index	Percentage	6.31	19.41	0–85
Monosyllable, Trochee, Spondee Test				
Word Recognition	Percentage	24.18	26.90	0–100
Word Categorization	Percentage	68.34	19.24	33–100
Minimal Auditory Capabilities Test				
Visual Enhancement				
Aided	Percentage	33.14	22.89	0–100
Unaided	Percentage	27.52	18.51	0–72
Speech Production				
Speech Intelligibility (SPINE) Test	Number Correct	53.52	18.53	22–98
CID Phonetic Evaluation of Speech	Number Correct	70.59	65.99	0–248

with teachers, and can receive help from other students. They communicate with deaf people often (as expected of students in a residential school who have deaf parents), and they use TTYs and watch captioned TV often.

Despite three mailings, parent questionnaire responses were returned for only 30 subjects, less than half the sample of 65. Seven of the fathers and four of the mothers had completed college, with one of the mothers going on to graduate education. The modal occupational categories for the fathers were professional (8) and craft/skilled worker (8). Eleven of the mothers reported doing clerical/semi-skilled work, and four were in professional categories. Twenty-five families reported annual family income as follows: $10,000–14,999—(1); $15,000–24,499—(10); $25,000–34,999—(5); $35,000–49,999—(7); $50,000 and over—(2). Thus the modal family reported income of $15,000–24,999, with nine families above $35,000, two of which were above $50,000.

The parents viewed deafness as a personal characteristic and reported that their child was involved in family activities. Eight agreed that deafness was a major handicap, while one mildly disagreed and 13 strongly disagreed. Parents generally expressed satisfaction with the child's communication ability and reported that communication usually took place through sign (19) or total communication (8). Parents reported heavy involvement in the deaf community, with 21 of 27 families in 3 to 4 activities per month.

In summary, the descriptive statistics indicate that the deaf children of deaf parent sample represents a wide range of achievement in reading, writing, and school achievement. Hearing losses are severe to profound and intellectual capacity is measured within the normal range. There is variation across the spectrum in oral communication proficiency, with proficiency in ASL and English-based sign-ing ranging from adequate to native proficiency. Student self-reports indicate that the subjects understand what is going on in class and participate in curricular and extracurricular activities, especially school sports. On the basis of responses from fewer than half the families, it appears that home communication is natural and fluent. Family incomes range from $10,000 to more than $50,000 annually.

Analysis

The analytical tool used in the analysis, as specified in the original proposal, is multiple regression, a multivariate method of analyzing the collective and separate contributions of two or more independent variables to the variation of a depen-dent variable. The primary goal of this study is the selection of a minimum number of variables necessary to account for almost as much of the variance as is accounted for by the total set.

In this study there are two separate dependent variables—reading and writing—with independent variables clustered into seven categories as shown below.

Dependent Variables	Independent Variables
Reading	Related measures of achievement
Writing	English grammar/structure
	Communicative fluency
	WAIS–Verbal
	WAIS–Performance
	Speech production
	Hearing

In sum, there are seven categories of independent variables, with a total of 31 measures, as listed in Table 7.1. The analysis was conducted to identify mea-sures from each of the categories that would be of importance in the prediction of reading and writing competence of deaf adolescents with deaf parents. Because large numbers of prediction variables, in relation to the number of subjects, reduce the replicability of the results, the goal is to identify from the comprehensive bat-tery of 31 tests a small number of measures that can efficiently predict achievement in reading and writing. Factor analyses were conducted separately on the outcome measures of the two sets of dependent variables—reading and writing.

Table 7.7 presents the factor loadings, in standard scores, for the measures of reading and writing. The factor loadings were used to derive factor scores. For reading, the combined cloze score (.858) and the narrative comprehension score (.826) have the highest factor loadings. For writing, the descriptive narrative error score (.960) and the holistic score (.939) have the highest factor loadings.

Table 7.7
Deaf Children of Deaf Parents
Factor Loadings for Reading and Writing

Measure	Factor Loading
Reading	
SAT Reading Comprehension	.762
Narrative Retelling	.719
Narrative Comprehension	.826
PIAT Reading	.746
Cloze Combined	.858
Gates Accuracy	.803
Gates Speed	.481
Writing	
Primary Trait: Business Letter	.253
Holistic Score: Descriptive	.939
Error Score: Descriptive	.960

The 31 predictors were individually correlated with the two dependent outcome variables, as shown in Table 7.8, in order to establish covariation with the dependent variables.

Some comments are called for concerning the individual correlations. The negative correlation (− .24) for better ear hearing loss (at 250, 500, 1000, 2000, 4,000, and 8,000 Hz) indicates a trend to lower achievement related to greater hearing loss. Looking within categories, correlations of measures of hearing, language proficiency, speech production, and, to some degree, performance IQ, with reading and writing tend to be lower than correlations of measures of verbal functioning, English grammar, and related achievement scores.

Examination of Table 7.9 reveals several variables exhibiting low correlations with reading and writing outcome measures, variables that could be eliminated from consideration for inclusion in a final regression equation for either reading or writing. For writing, these would include, for example, the articulation index, ASL language proficiency, and the CIDPES. For reading, these would include MTS categorization, articulation index, performance IQ object assembly, and ASL language proficiency. There were high correlations between reading and three of the WAIS verbal subtests—vocabulary (.66), information (.65), and arithmetic (.61)—as well as with the TSA (.70) and the Sign Morphology Test (.51). Correlations were also relatively high for the writing of deaf students of deaf parents in the same three WAIS verbal subtests—vocabulary (.67), information (.57) and arithmetic (.57) as well as with the TSA (.70) and Sign Morphology (.51).

In the next phase, predictions were analyzed within each of the seven clusters in stepwise regression procedures in order to reduce redundancy. For each variable, a standardized regression coefficient, Beta, was obtained and the probability

Table 7.8
Deaf Children of Deaf Parents
Bivariate Correlations of Predictors with Factor Scores for
Reading and Writing

Measure	Reading	Probability	Writing	Probability
Hearing				
Better Ear Loss	−.24	.03	−.12	.17
Articulation Index	.01	.46	.04	.39
MTS Recognition	.23	.04	.09	.24
MTS Categories	.11	.20	.005	.484
MAC Aided	.46	.000	.44	.000
MAC Unaided	.41	.000	.35	.002
Verbal Scale				
Information	.65	.000	.57	.000
Comprehension	.35	.002	.45	.000
Arithmetic	.61	.000	.57	.000
Similarities	.50	.000	.39	.001
Digit Span	.40	.001	.34	.003
Vocabulary	.66	.000	.67	.000
Performance IQ				
Digit Symbol	.36	.002	.52	.000
Picture Completion	.44	.000	.21	.05
Block Design	.32	.005	.34	.003
Picture Arrangement	.27	.02	.38	.001
Object Assembly	.15	.12	.10	.20
Language Proficiency				
ASL	−.06	.320	−.02	.424
Oral	.30	.009	−.22	.04
English-Based Sign	.41	.001	.23	.04
Speech Production				
SPINE	.26	.02	.15	.115
CIDPES	.19	.075	.13	.15
English Grammar				
TSA	.70	.000	.61	.000
Rhode Island	.43	.000	.42	.000
Sign Morphology	.64	.000	.51	.000
Related Achievement				
CAT Vocabulary	.56	.000	.43	.000
SAT Spelling	.48	.000	.37	.000
PPVT	.52	.000	.45	.000
CELF	.37	.000	.20	.061
One-Word PVT	.51	.000	.46	.000
Woodcock	.43	.000	.33	.000

Table 7.9
Deaf Children of Deaf Parents
Stepwise Regression Procedures

Measure	Reading			Writing		
	Probability of Beta	Retained in Equation	Selected for Final Equation	Probability of Beta	Retained in Equation	Selected for Final Equation
Hearing						
Better Ear Loss	.855			.84		
Articulation Index	.07			.70		
MTS Recognition	.24			.004	X	
MTS Categories	.034	X		.015	X	
MAC Aided	.000	X	X	.000	X	X
MAC Unaided	.84			.23		
Verbal Scale						
Information	.006	X	X	.180		
Comprehension	.38			.45		
Arithmetic	.27			.30		
Similarities	.14			.27		
Digit Span	.67			.53		
Vocabulary	.005	X		.000	X	X
Performance IQ						
Digit Symbol	.015	X		.000	X	X
Picture Completion	.001	X	X	.807		
Block Design	.52			.49		
Picture Arrangement	.22			.003	X	
Object Assembly	.64			.06		
Language Proficiency						
ASL	.98			.81		
Oral	.37			.35		
English-Based Sign	.001	X	X	.28		X
Speech Production						
SPINE	.04	X				X
CID	.94		X			
English Grammar						
TSA	.000	X	X	.000	X	X
Rhode Island	.78			.49		
Sign Morphology	.09			.46		
Related Achievement						
CAT Vocabulary	.023	X	X	.34		
SAT Spelling	.06			.034	X	X
PPVT	.16			.14		
CELF	.12			.76		
One-Word PVT	.03	X		.003		
Woodcock	.52			.53		

of its difference from zero was computed. Variables surviving in the final equation that had Betas with relatively low probability were considered the best candidates for inclusion in the final predictive equations.

Table 7.9 presents the results of the two stepwise regression procedures, one for reading and one for writing, for each of the 7 sets of predictors. The probability of Beta for each measure is included, as well as whether the measure was retained in the equation. In those categories in which more than one measure from a category was considered eligible for inclusion, correlations with other measures were taken into consideration. For example, as may be seen in Table 7.9, for the verbal scale category both the WAIS vocabulary and WAIS information subtests were considered in reading. Because the vocabulary subtest correlated highly with the TSA and CAT vocabulary measures, the information subtest was chosen instead. Similarly, in reading the CIDPES was chosen over the SPINE in the speech production category because the SPINE had a correlation of .76 with the MAC Aided measure of hearing.

Predictive Factors for Reading
Table 7.10 presents the correlations of all the measures entered into the final equation for reading. In some cases, predictors with high correlations with other predictors were excluded because of interpretability problems, as was the case, for example, of the correlation of .66 between the WAIS vocabulary subtests and the TSA. For the stepwise regression that began with the seven final candidates, one from each category, four of the variables were entered into the equation. As shown in Table 7.10, these were, in order: (1) Test of Syntactic Abilities (grammar), (2) Picture Completion (performance IQ), (3) CAT vocabulary (related measures of achievement), and (4) MAC Aided (hearing). Measures from the verbal scales, Language Proficiency Interviews, and speech production tests were excluded. The four predictors produced an R^2 of .64. Inclusion of the additional three predictors would have increased the R^2 only to .65 while substantially reducing the F (7.10).

Four measures, then, have been identified that account for 64 percent of the variance in the reading score of the deaf children of deaf parents sample. The Test of Syntactic Abilities, the WAIS picture completion subtest, The CAT vocabulary, and the MAC Aided test appear to be the most powerful predictors.

Predictive Factors for Writing
The order of entry for all measures predictive of writing achievement of deaf children of deaf parents, along with a summary of predictors and correlations of all measures considered, are presented in Table 7.11. The variables entered, in order, were: (1) vocabulary (verbal scale), (2) digit symbol (performance IQ), (3) MAC Aided (hearing), and (4) English-based sign (language proficiency). Measures for speech production, related achievement, and English grammar were not included in the final equation. Unlike the situation for the reading prediction, the SPINE

Table 7.10
Deaf Children of Deaf Parents
Categorical Predictors of Reading and Correlations Among Predictors

Category	Measure Selected	Order of Entry into Stepwise Regression	Probability of Beta
Statistics on Predictors			
English Grammar	TSA	1st	.0002
Performance IQ	Picture Completion	2nd	.001
Related Achievement	CAT Vocabulary	3rd	.021
Hearing	MAC Aided	4th	.049
Verbal Scale	Information	Not Entered	.078
Speech Production	CIDPES	Not Entered	.204
Language Proficiency	English-Based Sign	Not Entered	.799
Summary of Prediction	R^2	F	*Probability*
Stepwise (4 Factors)	.64	24.5	.000
Full Model (7 Factors)	.66	14.77	.000

Correlations: Categorical Predictors of Reading

		1	2	3	4	5	6	7
MAC Aided	1	1.00						
Information	2	.27	1.00					
Picture Completion	3	−.003	.33	1.00				
English-Based Sign	4	.54	.24	.21	1.00			
CIDPES	5	.64	−.007	.02	.37	1.00		
TSA	6	.42	.74	.30	.44	.20	1.00	
CAT Vocabulary	7	.42	.47	.10	.35	.24	.54	1.00

was used as the speech production measure despite a correlation of .76 with the MAC Aided test. The trial presence of the CIDPES reduced the R^2 of the seven variables selected, leading to the inclusion of the SPINE. Four variables were retained in the stepwise procedure, which produced an R^2 of .64 as compared to an R^2 of .67 for the full seven-variable model. Thus, four variables account for 64 percent of the variance in the writing of deaf children of deaf parents, with the vocabulary subtest of the WAIS Verbal Scale and the digit symbol subtest of the WAIS performance scale making major contributions. It is interesting to note that four measures account for 64 percent of the variance in both the reading and the writing of deaf adolescents with deaf parents, but that there is little overlap among the measures themselves.

Predictors of Reading	**Predictors of Writing**
1. Test of Syntactic Abilities	1. WAIS Vocabulary
2. Picture Completion	2. Digit Symbol
3. CAT Vocabulary	3. MAC Aided
4. MAC Aided	4. English-based Sign

Table 7.11
Deaf Children of Deaf Parents
Categorical Predictors of Writing and Correlations Among Predictors

Category	Measure Selected	Order of Entry into Stepwise Regression	Probability of Beta
Statistics on Predictors			
Verbal Scale	Vocabulary	1st	.000
Performance IQ	Digit Symbol	2nd	.0001
Hearing	MAC Aided	3rd	.001
Language Proficiency	English-Based Sign	4th	.0416
Speech Production	SPINE	Not Entered	.11
Related Achievement	SAT Spelling	Not Entered	.14
English Grammar	TSA	Not Entered	.52

Summary of Prediction	R^2	F	*Probability*
Stepwise (4 Factors)	.64	24.42	.000
Full Model (7 Factors)	.67	14.0	.000

Correlations: Categorical Predictors of Reading

		1	2	3	4	5	6	7
MAC Aided	1	1.00						
Vocabulary	2	.39	1.00					
Digit Symbol	3	.005	.32	1.00				
English-Based Sign	4	.54	.41	.11	1.00			
SPINE	5	.76	.24	−.12	.48	1.00		
TSA	6	.42	.68	.47	.44	.23	1.00	
SAT Spelling	7	.23	.41	.14	.38	.11	.49	1.00

The only measure in common is the MAC Aided test, which survived as the only major predictor for reading and writing skills for deaf adolescents with deaf parents.

Discussion

Examination of the individual correlations of the thirty-one independent variables with factor scores for reading and writing outcomes provides a somewhat different perspective than is gained from the multiple regression prediction equations that were developed for each outcome. Therefore, the issue of individual correlations will be addressed first.

Table 7.12 lists by category 9 independent measures with correlations of .50 or greater for reading and 6 independent measures with correlations of .50 or greater for writing. For reading, 4 of the 9 measures are subtests of the verbal scale of the WAIS that are vocabulary tests normed on hearing students, and 2 are tests of English grammar developed for deaf students. The high correlations of the

Table 7.12
Deaf Children of Deaf Parents
Independent Measures with Highest Correlations with
Reading or Writing Outcomes

Reading		Writing	
WAIS Verbal		WAIS Verbal	
Vocabulary	.66	Vocabulary	.67
Information	.65	Information	.57
Arithmetic	.61	Arithmetic	.57
Similarities	.50		
English Grammar		English Grammar	
TSA	.70	TSA	.61
Sign Morphology	.64	Sign Morphology	.51
Related Achievement		WAIS Performance	
CAT Vocabulary	.56	Digit Symbol	.52
PPVT	.52		
One-Word PVT	.51		
Categories with No Correlations of .50		Categories with No Correlations of .50	
Hearing		Hearing	
Speech Production		Speech Production	
WAIS Performance		Related Achievement	
Language Proficiency Interviews		Language Proficiency Interviews	

verbal scale subtests are of particular interest because of the reluctance of many psychologists to administer verbal scales of intelligence tests to deaf students due to fears that results would be misinterpreted as low IQ scores. Despite this very real potential danger, the results indicate that verbal subtests correlate very highly with reading achievement of deaf children of deaf parents, and their potential benefit is substantial. High correlations of three vocabulary tests, in addition to the WAIS vocabulary, are consistent with expectations, as are the correlations of two very disparate tests of English grammar: the TSA, which is a paper-and-pencil test, and the Sign Morphology Test, which is a videotaped English-based signing test and that requires a written response. The high correlation with reading for the Sign Morphology test, which was developed in its present form specifically for this study, suggests that it will fill a need in the field.

It should be pointed out that there were no correlations with an arbitrarily established reference point of .50 or greater with reading from any of the independent measures from four categories: hearing, speech production, Language Proficiency Interviews, and WAIS performance scale. The results indicate that there is little relationship between the reading of severely to profoundly deaf adolescents with deaf parents and their hearing and speech skills or their person-to-person skills, as measured by Language Proficiency Interviews. The low correlations between reading on the one hand, and ASL or English-based signing on the other, may be due in part to the fact that there was a limited range of fluency—all subjects tended to be competent. However, the correlation with oral LIP scores was also low, even though there was a range from no proficiency to full proficiency.

The fact that none of the performance IQ subtests correlated at .50 with reading raises some issues. Psychologists consistently use performance measures of intelligence with deaf children, yet, at least for this population, there appears to be little direct correlation with reading outcome. This raises questions about the utility of performance measures in making academic decisions for deaf children of deaf parents. However, performance subtests were part of the regression equations for both reading (picture completion) and writing (digit symbol), indicating that performance IQ scores do play a role.

Correlations with writing outcomes follow the same pattern (Table 7.12) although there are only six independent measures greater than .50. Three of the six are verbal scale subtests, two are measures of English grammar, and one is from the WAIS performance scale. In general, there is similarity with the findings for reading with the major exception that none of the three vocabulary tests in the related achievement category is included, suggesting that vocabulary is more important for reading than for writing in this group. The only other tests that correlated with reading but not writing was the similarities subtest of the WAIS verbal scale. There was only one subtest, digit symbol (performance IQ), that correlated above .50 with writing and did not correlate with reading.

Correlations with reading appear highest with subtests of the WAIS verbal scale and with tests of English grammar (TSA and Sign Morphology). As with the reading outcome measure, there were no correlations at or above .50 with writing from the hearing speech production or language proficiency interview categories, suggesting that these areas tap skills with relatively little direct relationship to the reading and writing of deaf adolescents with deaf parents.

Five of the thirty-one independent measures correlate at .50 or above with factor scores for both reading and writing for deaf adolescents with deaf parents.

| Category | Measure | Correlation | |
		Reading	Writing
WAIS Verbal	1. Vocabulary	.66	.67
	2. Information	.65	.57
	3. Arithmetic	.61	.57
English Grammar	4. TSA	.70	.61
	5. Sign Morphology	.64	.51

Only one of these measures has been used extensively with deaf subjects, the Test of Syntactic Abilities (TSA). As previously noted, subtests from verbal IQ scales have not been utilized as widely as performance tests. The Sign Morphology test has not been used because of its newness. No measures of speech, hearing, or language proficiency correlate at .50 with either reading or writing, let alone both.

Many tests that may be of benefit are used extensively with deaf students in assessing their speech reception and production, person-to-person communication skills, and intellectual potential. These measures, of course, serve important functions, but they tend not to exhibit high correlations with the literacy attainments of deaf adolescents with deaf parents.

The prediction equation for reading presents a somewhat different picture than the individual correlations for deaf adolescents with deaf parents, due to some extent to redundancy of some of the measures that correlate highly with reading achievement. As presented in the results section and in Table 7.10, the Test of Syntactic Abilities (TSA), the picture completion subtest of the WAIS, the vocabulary subtest of the California Achievement Test (CAT), and the Minimal Auditory Capabilities test, MAC Aided, account for 64 percent of the variance on reading of deaf adolescents with deaf parents. These measures represent, respectively, English grammar, a performance IQ subtest, English vocabulary, and use of residual hearing by individuals with severe to profound hearing losses. Although the MAC Aided test was not listed as among the measures with the highest correlations with reading—designated as .50 or greater—it did correlate at .46 and does contribute significantly to the final regression equation. This is the highest correlation of any measure for speech or language proficiency.

The fact that the MAC Unaided test correlated .41 and the MAC Aided test correlated .46 with reading raises some questions about interpretation of results. These represent measures of speechreading under aided and unaided conditions and, to some extent, may be influenced by English language skill. The aided condition in this study represented an ideal or clinical situation, in which testing was done through high fidelity earphones, not through subjects' individual hearing aids. This situation did not represent everyday listening conditions. Since average scores for the aided test were higher than for the unaided (Table 7.10) the results suggest that even for profoundly deaf subjects, even minimal auditory input can improve speechreading.

The results suggest that knowledge of English grammar and vocabulary, along with the ability to utilize even minimal amounts of auditory input, are highly predictive of the reading skills of deaf adolescents whose deaf parents have signed to them from birth. The quality of the child's fluency in speech, English sign, and/or ASL are not major related factors.

The prediction equation for writing (Table 7.11), except for the MAC Aided test, consists of different independent measures than does that for reading. The WAIS vocabulary, the WAIS digit symbol, the MAC Aided and the English-based sign language proficiency interview account for 64 percent of the variance in the writing of deaf adolescents with deaf parents. Although the tests themselves are different from those in the prediction equation for reading, their parameters appear similar. As with reading, these predictors represent a test of vocabulary, a performance subtest, and the MAC Aided test. Instead of a test of English grammar, the final component is communicative fluency in English-based sign. It is interesting to point out that the WAIS performance was part of the prediction equation for writing, although it is not commonly used in formal testing of deaf students. It is also important to point out that for this group, LPI performance in ASL or oral communication is not significantly related, positively or negatively, to reading achievement.

Factors predictive of literacy for deaf adults, then, appear to be related to knowledge of English vocabulary and grammar, the ability to utilize even minimal amounts of residual hearing and, in the case of writing, fluency in English-based sign. Measures of speech, oral communicative fluency, and ASL fluency do not contribute to prediction equations for either reading or writing. Because reliable, valid measures of ASL vocabulary and grammar do not exist at present, it was not possible to ascertain the extent to which such variables may be related to the achievement of literacy in deaf adolescents with deaf parents.

FACTORS PREDICTIVE OF ACHIEVEMENT OF DEAF CHILDREN IN TOTAL COMMUNICATION PROGRAMS

Subjects

Subjects for the total communication study were enrolled in total communication programs at least from age 4 up to the time of testing. At first glance it might seem to be a relatively straightforward task to identify a subject pool, since a large majority of deaf adolescents currently are instructed by means of total communication. However, the predominant mode of instruction was oral-only when subjects in question began their education. Thus, at the time of testing, most deaf adolescents had started in oral-only programs and at some point had been switched over to total communication instruction. The issue was resolved by identifying programs that had initiated total communication during or before the early 1970s.

Efforts were made to identify total communication subjects from public schools. Although the majority of deaf adolescents in public schools are now taught by total communication, most such programs made their transition from oral-only instruction after the mid-1970s. Two public school programs that had total communication preschool components and who had participated in a study by the principal investigator (Moores 1985)—St. Paul, Minnesota and Dallas, Texas—were contacted, but each had only 2 students of 16 and 17 years of age who met the criteria for inclusion. At present approximately 75 percent of deaf students are enrolled in public school programs. Therefore, there is reason for caution concerning the generalizability of results. If the data for this study were to be gathered now, it would include substantial numbers of students in public school programs, including many receiving at least some academic mainstreamed instruction through support from sign interpreters. Given placement practices in some states, it is possible that the subjects tested in this study are not completely representative of upper levels of school achievement.

The average age of the total communication subjects was 17 years, 0 months with a range from 16 years, 0 months to 17 years, 11 months. Average three-frequency hearing losses were 105.04 in the left ear and 106.10 in the right ear.

The reported ethnic identities of the 65 subjects in total communication sample were White, not of Hispanic origin (54), Black (6), and Hispanic (Mexican American) (5).

Blacks and Hispanics are somewhat underrepresented as compared to enrollment figures provided by the *Annual Survey of Hearing Impaired Children and Youth* for 1985–86, in which approximately 30 percent of children in programs for the hearing impaired are classified as minority.

Descriptive Statistics

The total communication sample is very heterogeneous in terms of measures of reading and writing (Table 7.13). Stanford Achievement Test HI reading comprehension scaled scores ranged from 520 to 827 (mean 644.6); grade scores for PIAT reading comprehension ranged from 2.8 to 13.0 (mean 6.01); and the speed (3.2 to 12.3) and accuracy (2.5 to 12.4) grade measures suggest a range of reading scores from second grade to above grade level. "Space Pet" narrative re-tellings produced propositional counts from 0 to 290, and correct responses to 8 questions ranged from 0 to 7. Time required to read the passage varied from under 2 minutes (116 seconds) to almost 14 minutes (825 seconds). The cloze tasks elicited similar variance. Examination of Table 7.13 indicates a similar diversity in writing skills of the subjects, both for the business letter and for the descriptive narrative. The discrepancy in written fluency is striking.

Table 7.14 indicates the same pattern of achievement, ranging from grade 2 to grade 13 in SAT vocabulary and spelling and an even wider range of age normed SAT vocabulary tests. The consistent pattern of diversity continues on measures of English grammar/structure (Table 7.15), strengthening the evidence that the subjects have been drawn from a population with a wide range of English language skills as well as of school achievement.

This pattern does not hold for the ASL and English-based sign language proficiency interviews (LPI), in which all subjects are rated as having some proficiency (Table 7.16). The pattern, however, *does* hold for the oral LPI, with a mean score of 1.523, but a range from 0 to 4. The mean WAIS performance score of 111.83 is within the normal range, with a wide range of scores from 84 to 143.

Because the study was restricted to subjects with severe to profound hearing losses, the mean pure tone air conduction thresholds are quite high, with three-

Table 7.13
Total Communication Students
Literacy Measures

Measure	Reporting Format	Mean	Standard Deviation	Range
Stanford Achievement Test—Reading Comp.	Scaled Score	644.60	62.23	520–827
Narrative Comprehension—Space Pet				
Retelling	Propositional Count	83.65	81.19	0–290
Questions (8)	Number Correct	2.59	1.69	0–7.0
Time	Seconds	303.64	120.01	116–825
Cloze Task—"Devil's Trick"				
Semantic Correct	Percentage	41.59	23.82	0–90
Syntactic Correct	Percentage	40.92	22.05	0–94
Combined (Semantic and Syntactic)				
Correct	Percentage	27.43	20.01	8–88
Verbatim	Percentage	14.00	11.31	0–48
Peabody Individual Achievement Test,				
Reading Comprehension	Grade Score	6.01	2.60	2.8–13.0
Gates-MacGinitie Reading Test				
Speed	Grade Score	7.54	2.79	3.2–12.3
Accuracy	Grade Score	6.00	2.32	2.5–12.4
Business Letter				
Primary Trait Score	Rating 0–6	1.08	0.70	0–3.0
Descriptive Narrative				
Holistic Score	Rating 0–6	2.54	1.90	0.5–5.0
Error Score	Rating 0–6	2.43	1.80	1.0–5.0
Syntactic Analysis				
Total Words	Count	198.46	105.17	27–516
Unique Words	Count	96.28	43.22	21–254
Clauses	Count	25.68	15.55	3–72
T-Units	Count	21.89	13.81	3–65
Sentences	Count	16.28	12.26	1–60

frequency average losses of 105.04 in the left ear and 103.76 in the right ear. Speech perception, on the average, is limited, but again the range is extensive (0–92% for the articulation index, 0–100% for MTS word recognition, and 0–100% for MTS word categorization) (Table 7.17). Unaided and aided visual enhancement scores are 31.48% and 36.73% respectively, but the ranges again extent from no response to perfect or near-perfect scores. As may be seen in Table 7.17, speech production scores also range significantly in the SPINE test, the CIDPES, and grade scores on the word attack subtest of the Woodcock Reading Test (Grades 1.2 to 12.9).

Responses on the student questionnaires indicate an understanding of classroom activity, communication with teachers, and a feeling of being a part of the school. The subjects communicate with other deaf people, use TTYs, watch cap-

Table 7.14
Total Communication Students
Related Measures of Achievement

Measure	Format	Mean	Standard Deviation	Range
California Achievement Test, Vocabulary	Grade Score	5.22	2.49	2.2–12.9
Stanford Achievement Test, Spelling	Grade Score	8.09	3.21	2.7–13.0
Peabody Picture Vocabulary Test	Age Score	8.58	4.77	2.0–33.67
Clinical Evaluation of Language Function, Word Associations	Count	35.70	7.08	13.0–52.0
One-Word Picture Vocabulary Test	Age Score	10.61	3.41	4.17–18.42

Table 7.15
Total Communication Students
English Grammar/Structure and Communicative Fluency

Measure	Reporting Format	Mean	Standard Deviation	Range
English Grammar/Structure				
Test of Syntactic Abilities	Percentage	78.11	15.78	35–98
Rhode Island Test of Language Structure	T Score	60.39	6.03	45.6–74.6
Manual Morphology Test (173)	Number Correct	100.60	33.16	28–157
Communicative Fluency				
Language Proficiency Interviews				
American Sign Language	Rating 0–4	3.31	0.75	2–4
English-Based Signing	Rating 0–4	2.85	0.76	2–4
Oral	Rating 0–4	1.52	1.39	0–4

tioned TV, and communicate with hearing people frequently. They tend to use encyclopedias, and go to libraries sometimes. They report little help from private tutors, and very little or no parental checking of homework. The latter is partially explained by attendance at residential schools. Fifty of the subjects report participation in school sports, and approximately two-thirds (42 of 65) participate in club activities in school. Approximately half read 1 or 2 books a month and 5 of 65 reported reading 10 or more a month.

Communication within the family tends to rely primarily on signs and fingerspelling, with secondary reliance on speech. In 61 of 65 families, the subject signs with the mother, with speech also occurring in 33 families. In families with brothers and sisters, signs and fingerspelling are predominant, with speech occurring in half the families in communication between the student and siblings. Communication with the father represents a somewhat different pattern. Although

Table 7.16
Total Communication
Cognition/World Knowledge

Measure	Reporting Format	Mean	Standard Deviation	Range
WAIS Verbal Scale				
Information	Scaled Score	7.11	2.80	2–15
Comprehension	Scaled Score	7.51	2.14	3–11
Arithmetic	Scaled Score	8.45	2.92	4–17
Similarities	Scaled Score	7.68	2.58	3–17
Digit Span	Scaled Score	7.11	2.69	3–14
Vocabulary	Scaled Score	5.82	1.80	2–12
Verbal Scale Score	Standard Score	83.12	10.67	64–116
WAIS Performance Scale				
Digit Symbol	Scaled Score	10.75	2.56	6–17
Picture Completion	Scaled Score	11.22	2.33	6–15
Block Design	Scaled Score	12.48	3.04	6–19
Picture Arrangement	Scaled Score	11.95	2.85	6–18
Object Assembly	Scaled Score	12.11	2.95	6–19
Performance IQ	Standard Score	111.83	14.55	83–143

Table 7.17
Total Communication
Speech and Hearing Measures

Measure	Reporting Format	Mean	Standard Deviation	Range
Hearing Sensitivity/Speech Perception				
Articulation Index	Percentage	12.45	220.85	0–92
Monosyllable, Trochee, Spondee Test				
Word Recognition	Percentage	19.86	23.95	0–100
Word Categorization	Percentage	61.97	23.33	0–100
Minimal Auditory Capabilities Test				
Visual Enhancement				
Aided	Percentage	36.73	19.31	2–100
Unaided	Percentage	31.48	17.70	0–96
Speech Production				
Speech Intelligibility (SPINE) Test	Number Correct	56.37	17.59	31–91
CID Phonetic Evaluation of Speech	Number Correct	78.77	56.61	0–228
Woodcock Reading Test, Word Attack	Grade Score	2.77	2.55	1.2–12.9

signs and fingerspelling are used with the majority of fathers (40 of 64), and speech is used in 33 cases (as with the mother), in more than one-third of the cases (24 of 64) the student does not communicate in signs and fingerspelling with the father. To a much greater degree than with mothers and siblings, the subjects' communication with the fathers entails a resort to writing.

Parent questionnaires were returned from the families of slightly more than half (36 of 65) of the subjects. Given the numbers of no responses, the following information must be viewed with caution. The extent of generalization to the whole sample is questionable.

From the responses, the average grade completed for mothers of the total communication sample was 14.53, and for fathers, 14.85. Thus, the typical parent had 2 to 3 years of college education. Of the 33 cases reported, 13 fathers had college degrees, of whom 8 went on to graduate education. Of the mothers, 16 of 36 were college graduates and 4 received graduate degrees. Sixteen of the fathers and 16 of the mothers were classified as in professional employment. In addition, 8 fathers were employed in managerial capacities. Other fathers were skilled and semiskilled workers. Mothers' occupations represented a wider range in addition to the professional category and included managerial (3), clerical (4), semiskilled (2) and domestic (2) work.

Family income levels were quite diverse, according to the self-reports of 34 families. The levels broke down as follows: $5,000–9,999—(2); 10,000–14,999—(0); 15,000–24,999—(7); 25,000–35,000—(5); 35,000–49,999—(11); 50,000 and over—(10).

The parents reported the cause of the child's deafness as "unknown" in 13 of 35 cases; 8 reports named rubella; and 5 listed childhood diseases.

Parents returning the questionnaire reported fluent communication with the subject, with all 36 stating that the subject used manual communication with someone at home. Twenty-five of 35 parents expected their deaf child to go to college and strongly agreed with the statement that deafness was seen as a personal characteristic. The child was included in family activities. Opinions as to whether deafness constituted a major handicap was divided, with 11 strongly disagreeing and 11 mildly agreeing. In coping with the stresses of having a deaf child, the total communication parents tended to rely on reading about the subject and receiving advice from other parents of deaf children. Teachers also were a source of support.

Parents tended to rate their children as successful in communicating ideas, feelings, and needs, and in understanding others. Approximately one-third (13 of 36) of the families report participating in the Deaf community 3 to 4 times per month.

To summarize, subjects in the total communication sample represent a range of achievement, using standardized achievement tests, from second grade to above grade level in measures of reading and related areas. Specialized measures of reading such as story retellings and cloze procedures, and adaptations of a writing assessment program, reinforce the finding that the subjects within the group have achievement skills across the spectrum from minimal to quite sophisticated.

The subjects are drawn from a normal distribution in terms of performance IQ measures, with the exclusion of subjects scoring less than 80, and hearing losses are in the severe and profound categories. Oral reception and production, including language proficiency interviews, are limited, but in each case some students exhibit excellent oral abilities. Manual communication, both for ASL and for English-based signs, tends to be proficient. Students appear to communicate well at home and school and participate extensively in extracurricular activities. Parents appear supportive, and communication seems to be good.

Analysis

In this study, as in the study of deaf children of deaf parents, there are two dependent variables—reading and writing—with 31 independent variables, as presented in Table 7.1, categorized into seven clusters: related measures of achievement; English grammar/structure; communicative fluency; verbal scales; performance IQ scales; speech production; and hearing. The purpose of the analysis is to identify separately for reading and writing one predictive variable within each of the seven categories to be considered for inclusion in the development of a prediction equation.

Table 7.18 presents the factor loadings for measures of reading and writing for total communication subjects. From the loadings factor, scores for reading and writing were developed. For reading, the combined cloze score (.878) and the narrative comprehension score (.842) have the highest factor loadings. For writing, the highest loadings are found for the descriptive task error score (.951) and the descriptive task holistic score (.929).

Table 7.18
Total Communication Students
Factor Loadings for Reading and Writing

Measure	Factor Loading
Reading	
SAT Reading Comprehension	.760
Narrative Retelling	.747
Narrative Comprehension	.842
PIAT Reading	.746
Cloze Combined	.878
Gates Accuracy	.788
Gates Speed	.632
Writing	
Primary Trait: Business Letter	.446
Holistic Score: Descriptive	.929
Error Score: Descriptive	.951

Tables 7.19 and 7.20 show the correlations of the 31 independent variables with factor scores for reading and for writing. Examination of the tables reveals that some measures have very low correlations with the outcome measures of reading and writing. Most striking of these are the ASL language proficiency, better ear loss, and articulation index scores, indicating that none of these measures would make it to a final prediction equation. The correlations of individual scores with reading are highest for the One-Word Picture Vocabulary test (.75), the vocabulary subtest of the WAIS verbal scale (.70), the TSA (.70) and the CAT vocabulary (.69). The influence of vocabulary on reading for this group is obvious. For writing, there are similarly high correlations with the TSA (.66) the vocabulary subtest of the WAIS (.62) and the One Word Picture Vocabulary Test (.56).

Table 7.19 presents information on the stepwise regression procedures performed separately for each category of predictors for reading and writing and indicates the predictive measures chosen from each category for the final stepwise analysis.

Predictive Factors for Reading

As shown in Table 7.19, five variables were entered into the final prediction equation for reading of total communication subjects, as follows; (1) TSA (grammar), (2) CAT vocabulary (related achievement), (3) CID phonetic evaluation of speech (speech production), (4) picture arrangement (performance IQ), and (5) similarities (verbal scale). The five predictors accounted for .77 of the variance in reading scores. Forcing the two excluded variables—English-based signing and MAC Unaided tests—would have increased the R^2 to .80 with a reduction of the F value from 25.3 to 19.6. The correlations presented in Table 7.19 indicate that there are no extremely high correlations among the predictive variables entered into the equation.

Predictive Factors for Writing

The order of entry of factors predictive of writing achievement of total communication subjects is presented in Table 7.20, along with a summary of predictors and correlations among independent variables. Of the seven variables selected for analysis, only two were judged to make a significant contribution to R^2: the TSA and the vocabulary subtest of the verbal scale of the WAIS. These two variables accounted for .49 of the variance in writing of total communication subjects. Inclusion of all seven predictors for writing would only increase the R^2 for writing to .52. Thus, we were able to account for a much higher percentage of the variance for reading (77%) than for writing (.49) in total communication subjects. Examination of Table 7.20 reveals that the correlation between the only two variables entered, TSA and vocabulary, is relatively high (.66); however, both made an important contribution and were entered into the final equation.

It is interesting to note that the TSA was the first measure entered into each equation for prediction of reading and writing of total communication subjects, but there is no other commonality across predictors:

Table 7.19
Total Communication Students
Bivariate Correlations of Predictors with Factor Scores for Reading and Writing

Measure	Reading	Probability	Writing	Probability
Hearing				
Better Ear Loss	−.02	.225	−.09	.236
Articulation Index	.007	.482	−.083	.258
MTS Recognition	.25	.05	.20	.06
MTS Categories	.22	.08	.07	.30
MAC Aided	.38	.006	.36	.003
MAC Unaided	.47	.001	.25	.026
Verbal Scale				
Information	.54	.000	.27	.015
Comprehension	.48	.000	.37	.001
Arithmetic	.52	.000	.44	.006
Similarities	.57	.000	.39	.001
Digit Span	.43	.002	.40	.001
Vocabulary	.70	.000	.62	.000
Performance IQ				
Digit Symbol	.34	.01	.36	.002
Picture Completion	.27	.04	.25	.02
Block Design	.18	.111	.22	.04
Picture Arrangement	.38	.006	.20	.06
Object Assembly	.31	.02	.23	.04
Language Proficiency				
ASL	.04	.402	−.10	.230
Oral	.42	.002	−.21	.05
English-Based Sign	.41	.003	.16	.122
Speech Production				
SPINE	.18	.119	.26	.019
CIDPES	.37	.007	.21	.05
Woodcock	.48	.001	.33	.004
English Grammar				
TSA	.70	.000	.66	.000
Rhode Island	.37	.008	.20	.07
Sign Morphology	.55	.000	.35	.005
Related Achievement				
CAT Vocabulary	.69	.000	.46	.000
SAT Spelling	.34	.019	.28	.018
PPVT	.61	.000	.37	.002
CELF	.24	.062	.18	.107
One-Word PVT	.75	.000	.56	.000

Table 7.20
Total Communication Students
Stepwise Regression Procedures

Measure	Reading			Writing		
	Probability of Beta	Retained in Equation	Selected for Final Equation	Probability of Beta	Retained in Equation	Selected for Final Equation
Hearing						
Better Ear Loss	.67			.63		
Articulation Index	.74			.18		
MTS Recognition	.55			.57		
MTS Categories	.56			.40		
MAC Aided	.59			.005	X	X
Mac Unaided	.013	X	X	.83		
Verbal Scale						
Information	.21			.155		
Comprehension	.31			.706		
Arithmetic	.68			.84		
Similarities	.12		X	.98		
Digit Span	.26			.20		
Vocabulary	.000	X		.000	X	X
Performance IQ						
Digit Symbol	.023	X		.0043	X	
Picture Completion	.827			.228		
Block Design	.895			.27		
Picture Arrangement	.012	X	X	.149		X
Object Assembly	.157			.124		
Language Proficiency						
ASL	.79			.52		
Oral	.005	X		.24		X
English-Based Sign	.09		X	.71		
Speech Production						
SPINE	.76			.94	X	X
CID	.01	X	X	.60		
Woodcock	.023	X		.43		
English Grammar						
TSA	.000	X	X	.000	X	X
Rhode Island	.196			.90		
Sign Morphology	.593			.17		
Related Achievement						
CAT Vocabulary	.004	X	X	.34		
SAT Spelling	.304			.43		
PPVT	.993			.87		X
CELF	.843			.62		
One-Word PVT	.012	X		.00	X	

Predictors of Reading	**Predictors of Writing**
TSA	TSA
CAT Vocabulary	WAIS Vocabulary
CIDPES	
Picture Arrangement	
Similarities	

Discussion

Individual correlations of .50 or greater for independent variables with reading and writing outcomes are presented in Table 7.21. For reading, four are WAIS verbal subtests, three are vocabulary tests normed on hearing children, and two are tests of English grammar developed for hearing students. Thus, nine of the thirty-one independent measures correlate at .50 or above with reading outcome. It should be noted that these are identical to the nine measures correlating with reading achievement in deaf adolescents with deaf parents. Again, the potential benefit of the use of verbal intelligence scales should be noted. For students in total communication programs, scores on verbal IQ subtests, vocabulary tests, and tests of English grammar correlate most highly with reading. Measures of speech, hearing, oral communication, English-based signing, performance IQ, and ASL do not exhibit high correlations. The lack of performance IQ subtests raises questions about their efficacy with deaf subjects, at least in relation to the prediction of reading.

The situation is less clear-cut in the case of writing outcomes, in which correlations of .50 or above are found for only three independent measures: WAIS vocabulary, One-Word Picture Vocabulary Test, and the Test of Syntactic Abilities (Table 7.20). All three of these measures also are highly correlated with reading outcomes. They indicate the importance of English vocabulary and English grammar to the writing of total communication students and highlight the relative lack of relationship with writing of measures of hearing, speech, performance tests of intelligence and language proficiency interviews.

Three of 31 measures correlate at .50 or above for both reading and writing of total communication students:

		Correlation	
Category	**Measure**	**Reading**	**Writing**
WAIS Verbal	1. Vocabulary	.70	.62
English Grammar	2. TSA	.70	.66
Related Achievement	3. One-Word PVT	.61	.56

Table 7.21
Total Communication Students
Categorical Predictors of Reading and Correlations Among Predictors

| | | Statistics on Predictors | |
Category	Measure Selected	Order of Entry into Stepwise Regression	Probability of Beta
Grammar	TSA	1st	.015
Related Achievement	CAT Vocabulary	2nd	.0003
Speech Production	CIDPES	3rd	.0008
Performance IQ	Picture Arrangement	4th	.02
Verbal Scale	Similarities	5th	.03
Hearing	MAC Unaided	Not Entered	.08
Language Proficiency	English-Based Sign	Not Entered	.49

Summary of Prediction	R^2	F	Probability
Stepwise (5 Factors)	.77	25.3	.000
Full Model (7 Factors)	.80	19.6	.000

Correlations: Categorical Predictors of Reading

		1	2	3	4	5	6	7
MAC Aided	1	1.00						
Similarities	2	.12	1.00					
Picture Arrangement	3	.18	.13	1.00				
English-Based Sign	4	.29	.35	−.02	1.00			
CIDPES	5	.49	.0005	.05	.29	1.00		
TSA	6	.38	.46	.22	.54	.27	1.00	
CAT Vocabulary	7	.13	.52	.19	.37	−.04	.54	1.00

The prediction equation for reading (Table 7.19) involves five independent measures: the Test of Syntactic Abilities (TSA), the California Achievement Test (CAT) vocabulary subtest, the CID Phonetic Evaluation of Speech (CIDPES), the WAIS picture arrangement subtests, and the WAIS similarities subtest. These variables account for 77 percent of the variance in the reading of total communication subjects. Of the seven categories, only two are not represented—measures of communicative competence and measures of hearing. The first two variables entered into the equation were a test of English grammar and a vocabulary test, followed by a measure of speech production (CID Phonetic Evaluation of Speech) and by performance and verbal scale tests from the WAIS. The results suggest that English-based sign, ASL, and oral communicative fluency are not highly correlated with reading in deaf adolescents taught through total communication. The same holds for measures of communicative fluency, as measured by language proficiency interviews.

For writing, only two variables entered into the prediction equation (Table 7.20), but they accounted for 49 percent of the variance for total communication subjects. These measures were the TSA and the WAIS vocabulary subtests. Measures of hearing, speech, performance IQ, and language proficiency, and related measures of achievement, did not enter into the equation. Thus, for writing, 49 percent of the variance for total communication subjects was accounted for, compared to 77 percent for reading. As with reading, major factors appear to be knowledge of English grammar and English vocabulary. Unlike reading, no verbal or performance IQ measures or measures of speech production entered into the equation.

Factors predictive of literacy in deaf students in total communication programs are most highly related to measures of English vocabulary and English grammar. Measures of hearing and fluency in oral, English-based sign, and ASL communication are not predictive of literacy. For reading, but not for writing, the CID Phonetic Evaluation of Speech, the WAIS similarities and the WAIS picture arrangement subtests contribute significantly to the prediction equation.

Table 7.22
Total Communication Students
Categorical Predictors of Writing and Correlations Among Predictors

Category	Measure Selected	Order of Entry into Stepwise Regression	Probability of Beta
		Statistics on Predictors	
Grammar	TSA	1st	.001
Verbal Scale	Vocabulary	2nd	.01
Speech Production	SPINE	Not Entered	.18
Performance IQ	Digit Symbol	Not Entered	.22
Related Achievement	PPVT	Not Entered	.244
Hearing	MAC Aided	Not Entered	.60
Language Proficiency	Oral	Not Entered	.73

Summary of Prediction	R^2	F	*Probability*
Stepwise (5 Factors)	.49	27.17	.000
Full Model (7 Factors)	.53	8.31	.000

Correlations: Categorical Predictors of Writing

		1	2	3	4	5	6	7
MAC Aided	1	1.00						
Vocabulary	2	.40	1.00					
Digit Symbol	3	.10	.31	1.00				
Oral LPI	4	.73	.24	.01	1.00			
SPINE	5	.51	.17	.15	.49	1.00		
TSA	6	.41	.66	.33	.36	.19	1.00	
PPVT	7	.22	.66	.11	.21	−.10	.54	1.00

Table 7.23
Total Communication Students
Independent Measures with Highest Correlations with
Reading or Writing Outcomes

Reading		Writing	
WAIS Verbal		WAIS Verbal	
Vocabulary	.70	Vocabulary	.62
Similarities	.57		
Information	.52		
Arithmetic	.52	Related Achievement	
		One-Word PVT	.56
Related Achievement			
One-Word PVT	.75	Grammar	
CAT Vocabulary	.69	TSA	.66
PPVT	.61		
Grammar			
TSA	.70		
Sign Morphology	.55		
No Correlations .50		No Correlations .50	
Hearing		Hearing	
Speech Production		Speech Production	
WAIS Performance		WAIS Performance	
LPI		LPI	

SUMMARY AND CONCLUSIONS

Deaf Adolescents with Deaf Parents

The subjects of this study consisted of 65 severely to profoundly hearing impaired 16- and 17-year-old students who used some form of manual communication in the home and who were enrolled in total communication programs. They exhibited a wide range of literacy skills, both in reading and in writing, with corresponding variation in related measures of school achievement, and in communication, with the exception of ASL and English-based sign communication, where all had some levels of fluency. Subjects tended to communicate by sign at school and at home, switching to speech and writing in communication with hearing people. Subjects reported extensive involvement in sports and other extracurricular activities.

Subjects were tested on an extensive battery in order to investigate factors predictive of literacy for deaf adolescents with deaf parents. Using reading and writing as the two dependent variables, thirty-one separate tests, divided into seven categories, were administered to investigate their correlation with outcome measures and to explore their utility in the development of prediction equations for reading and writing. Results indicated that the tests correlating highest with reading consisted of four subtests of the WAIS verbal scale, three tests of vocabulary, and two tests of English grammar. Individual tests of hearing, speech production, and person-to-person communication through oral, English-based sign, or ASL modes were not highly related to reading achievement, suggesting that instructional attention to English grammar and vocabulary were of primary importance in the development of reading skills in deaf students of deaf parents. Similar results were obtained for writing, with the exception that related measures of vocabulary were not highly correlated with writing outcomes.

Regression procedures indicate that the Test of Syntactic Ability, the WAIS picture completion, the CAT vocabulary, and the MAC Aided Test accounted for 64 percent of the variance in reading. For writing, the WAIS vocabulary, the WAIS digit symbol, the MAC Aided, and the English-based sign language proficiency interview accounted for 64 percent of the variance. The results suggest that factors highly predictive of literacy in deaf adolescents with deaf parents are those most directly tied to English grammar and vocabulary. The presence of the MAC Aided test in both equations suggests that good readers may be able to utilize even minimal amounts of auditory input to facilitate speechreading. The failure of measures of speech, oral communication fluency, or sign communication fluency to contribute to the prediction equation for reading or for writing suggests that, for this population, literacy achievement is closely tied to English language skills.

Total Communication

The total communication subjects were 65 severely and profoundly hearing impaired 16- and 17-year old residential students who had been in total communication programs from preschool years. These students had hearing parents. They exhibited a wide range of literacy skills, as well as achievement in related areas. Communication skills also showed variability, with the exception of communication in English-based sign and ASL conditions, where all had some level of fluency. The subjects reported that they were active in sports and other extracurricular activities, and that they understood and participated in classroom activities. Results of student and parent questionnaires showed that there is ease of communication at home, with hearing family members fluent in manual communication. As with deaf adolescents with deaf parents, individual tests correlating most highly with reading outcomes consisted of four subtests of the WAIS Verbal Scale, three tests of vocabulary and two tests of English grammar. Only three of thirty-one independent measures correlated with writing outcomes. A prediction equation involving the Test of Syntactic Abilities, the CAT Vocabulary Test, the CID Phonetic Evaluation of Speech, the picture arrangement subtest of the WAIS, and the similarities subtest of the WAIS accounted for 77 percent of the variance in reading. The TSA and the vocabulary subtest of the WAIS predicted 49 percent of the variance in writing. Results suggest that literacy achievement in total communication subjects is closely tied to specific knowledge of English grammar and English vocabulary.

CONCLUSION

A conscious effort has been made throughout this report not to compare achievement of total communication students with that of deaf students with deaf parents, although the issue has been of interest to professionals in the field of education of the deaf. Given the different constraints on identifying and testing subjects from the two groups, any comparisons of achievement or fluency would be spurious. The results of these two studies, in fact, suggest that the commonalities of the subjects in the two groups far outweigh the differences, especially in view of the correlations of independent measures with reading and writing outcome measures and the types of factors that were entered into prediction equations of both groups. Although the total communication group, who had hearing parents, did not have manual communication in the family from birth, they did have it from early ages. Children from both groups have been taught by total communication and have attended residential schools, which probably has increased their commonality. At present it is unknown whether deaf adolescents in public school total communication programs would evince the same characteristics, but this question is an important one for future study.

REFERENCES

Allen, T. 1986. A study of the achievement patterns of hearing impaired students: 1974–1983. In *Deaf children in America*, ed. A. Schildroth and M. Karchmer. San Diego: College-Hill Press.

Allen, T., C. White, and M. Karchmer. 1983. Issues in the development of a special edition for hearing-impaired students of the seventh edition of the Standard Achievement Test. *American Annals of the Deaf* 128: 34–38.

Clark, J. 1975. Theoretical and technical considerations in oral proficiency testing. In *Testing language proficiency*, eds. R. Jones and B. Spolsky. Washington, DC: Center for Applied Linguistics.

———, ed. 1978. *Direct testing of speaking proficiency: Theory and practice*. Princeton, NJ: Educational Testing Service.

Collins, A., and R. Quillian. 1969. Retrieval time from semantic memory. *Journal of Verbal Learning and Verbal Behavior* 8: 240–247.

Cooper, C., and L. Odell. 1977. *Evaluating writing: Describing, measuring, judging*. Urbana, IL: National Council of Teachers of English.

Crothers, E. J. 1972. Memory structure and the recall of discourse. In *Language comprehension and the acquisition of knowledge*, eds. J. B. Carroll and R. D. Freedle. Washington, DC: Winston.

Durrell, D. 1955. *Durrell analysis of reading difficulty*. New York: Harcourt, Brace and World.

Ewoldt, C. 1977. A psycholinguistic description of selected deaf children reading in sign language. Ph.D. diss. Wayne State University, Detroit, MI.

———. 1981. A psycholinguistic description of selected deaf children reading in sign language. *Reading Research Quarterly* 13(1): 58–59.

Francis, J. 1980. *The evaluation of language proficiency*. Washington, DC: Gallaudet University School of Communication.

Frederiksen, C. H. 1975. Effects of context-induced processing operations on semantic information acquired from discourse. *Cognitive Psychology* 7: 139–166.

Goodman, Y., and C. Burke. 1972. *Reading miscue inventory*. New York: Macmillan.

Hargis, C. H. 1972. A comparison of retarded and non-retarded children on the ability to use context in reading. *American Journal of Mental Deficiency* 76: 726–728.

Harrison, C. 1980. *Readability in the classroom*. Cambridge: Cambridge University Press.

Johnson, R., B. Colonomos, M. Futrell, G. Eastman, and D. Knight. 1983. *Sign language use and evaluation*. Faculty Report, Gallaudet University.

Jones, R. 1979. The FSI oral interview. In *Advances in Language Testing,* ed. D. Spolsky. Washington, DC: Center for Applied Linguistics.

Jordan, I., G. Gustason, and R. Rosen. 1976. Current communication trends at programs for the deaf. *American Annals of the Deaf* 121: 527–531.

———. 1979. An update on communication trends in programs for the deaf. *American Annals of the Deaf* 124: 350–357.

Jordan, I., and M. Karchmer. 1986. Patterns of sign use among hearing impaired students. In *Deaf children in America,* eds. A. Schildroth and M. Karchmer, 125–138. Boston: College-Hill Press.

Kelly, L., and C. Ewoldt. 1984. Interpreting nonverbatim cloze responses to evaluate program success and diagnose student needs for reading instruction. *American Annals of the Deaf* 129: 45–51.

LaSasso, C. 1980. The validity and reliability of the cloze procedure as a measure of readability for prelingually profoundly deaf students. *American Annals of the Deaf* 125: 559–563.

Levine, E. 1974. Psychological tests and practices with the deaf. *Volta Review* 76: 298–319.

———. 1981. *The ecology of early deafness*. New York: Columbia University Press.

Liskin-Gasparo, J., ed. 1979. *Foreign language and proficiency assessment*. Princeton, NJ: Educational Testing Service.

Mandler, J., and N. Johnson. 1977. Remembrance of things parsed. *Cognitive Psychology* 9: 111–151.

Meyer, B. J. 1984. Organization in prose and memory: Research with application to reading comprehension. In *Reading research, theory, and practice,* ed. P. D. Pearson, 214–220. The Twenty-Sixth Yearbook of the National Reading Conference. Clemson, SC: National Reading Conference.

Moores, D. 1970. An investigation of the psycholinguistic functioning of deaf adolescents. *Exceptional Children* 35: 645–652.

———. 1985. Early intervention programs for hearing impaired children: A longitudinal assessment. In *Children's Language: Volume V,* ed. K. Nelson, 159–195. Hillsdale, NJ: Lawrence Erlbaum and Associates.

Moores, D., T. Kluwin, R. Johnson, P. Cox, L. Blennerhassett, L. Kelly, C. Ewoldt, C. Sweet, and L. Fields. 1987. *Factors predictive of literacy in deaf adolescents*. Project No. NIH-NINCDS-83-19. Final Report to National Institute of Neurological and Communicative Disorders and Stroke.

Mullis, I. 1980. *Using the primary trait system for evaluating writing*. Princeton, NJ: Educational Testing Service.

Newell, W., F. Caccamise, K. Boardman, and B. Holcomb. 1983. Adaptation of the language proficiency interview (LPI) for assessing sign communicative competence. *Sign Language Studies* 41: 311–331.

White, E. 1984. *Teaching and assessing writing*. San Francisco: Josey Bass.

Yurkowski, P., and C. Ewoldt. 1986. A case for the semantic processing of the deaf reader. *American Annals of the Deaf* 131: 243–247.

8

Cognitive Theory Guiding Research in Literacy and Deafness

Leonard P. Kelly

The thought processes of readers and writers are elusive quarry: naturally covert, characteristically fleeting, and often unarticulated. Insights about minds engaged in text processing are largely determined by the soundness of the theory that guides how we look "inside the heads" of our subjects. This essay advocates cognitive theory as a sound basis for research into the reading and writing of people who are deaf.

The urgency for refined theory and methodology is seldom greater than among those who study the literacy processes of profoundly deaf children. Educators of deaf children know well that reading and writing present serious problems for their students. Deaf children often misunderstand what they try to read (Allen 1986), and they frequently misrepresent what they try to write (Crandall 1978). Furthermore, although literacy development has attracted substantial amounts of research and of school resources, instructional efforts have not been totally unified because there is still considerable uncertainty about the nature of the problem. Much is still unknown about (1) how deaf students process text during reading and writing, and (2) how they acquire effective literacy skills. It is uncertain both what knowledge about text is most useful to successful deaf readers/writers and what experiences allow them routinely to acquire that knowledge.

This uncertainty is further magnified by differences in learning and processing that may exist among groups within the deaf population: differences among those with varying degrees of hearing loss; differences in children of deaf parents vs. those of hearing parents; and, perhaps, differences between deaf people who tend to process information temporally and those who tend to process information spatially, a tendency that may be relatively common among the deaf (Belmont and Karchmer 1978). There is still an evident need for research in this field, particularly programs of inquiry that are soundly based in theory, methodically con-

Appreciation is expressed to Donald Moores, Karen Saulnier, and Linda Stamper for their helpful reactions to earlier drafts of this chapter and to Vicki Patterson for typing it.

ducted, and responsive to questions that are critical to promoting the literacy of deaf children.

This chapter proposes the cognitive view of literacy as the most desirable theoretical perspective for guiding research into the literacy processes of deaf children. The cognitive view has a number of merits to recommend it.

1. It encourages studies that record the processes as well as the outcomes of reading and writing;
2. It promotes methods of inquiry that are analytical, promising to reveal the specific dimensions of text that are potentially most useful and most manageable for different groups of deaf readers and writers;
3. It asserts the competition among multiple features of text for the limited information processing capacity of humans and encourages the design of investigations accordingly;
4. It combines reading and writing parsimoniously under a single theoretical orientation;
5. It necessitates a focus on working memory (WM), a component of cognition that some researchers consider to be atypical in many deaf people (Rodda and Grove 1987); and
6. It leads logically to studies of metacognition, a focus of inquiry that has only recently emerged in the field of literacy research.

The cognitive approach to literacy research is the next logical step in the ten-year tradition of studying reading and writing acquisition and performance within the Center for Studies in Education and Human Development (CSEHD). The search for factors that produce literate performance links this program of research to related research in the field.

In this chapter, the cognitive view is described in detail. Its particular benefits for illuminating the literacy processes of the deaf are explained, and the application of the cognitive view to a study of deaf students' writing processes is presented. Applications to planned studies of reading are also provided. The most important goal of this program of research is to identify those competencies that distinguish superior deaf readers and writers from those who have average skills. Explication of the nature of reading and writing competence may in turn lead to instructional practices that make advanced literacy more available to the majority of profoundly deaf people who have trouble reading and writing English.

THE COGNITIVE VIEW OF LITERACY

Multiple Constraints Synthesized

Applications of theory from cognitive psychology have contributed to a better understanding of the complexities of reading and writing. Reading, as well as writing, is actually many jobs in one. According to Carpenter and Just (1981), readers arrive at "productions" of text that integrate their knowledge of orthography, phonology, syntax, semantics, pragmatics, discourse structure, and world knowledge. These separate features are commonly called "textual constraints." Stanovich (1980) asserted that readers use their knowledge of textual constraints to "synthesize the stimulus" text so that it represents a reasonable composite of the separate information sources that are present on the printed page. Obviously, these constraints exist as separate and identifiable features of a written text. But equally important, they also reside in the mind of the reader as knowledge of the text's content, of textual patterns, and of procedures for processing those patterns. Smith (1978) described this internal knowledge as the "non-visual information" (p. 5) that a reader brings to text.

Turning to the complexity of written composition, writers have been characterized by Flower and Hayes (1980) as "jugglers" of three constraints: knowledge, language, and rhetoric. Each segment of text must accurately represent what the writer knows about the topic, it must conform to the conventions of written language, and it must contribute to the discourse goals of the full composition. As an example of the multiple constraints affecting one word during writing, a writer settles on "orchards" instead of "forest" because the text calls for a word that (1) represents a group of fruit-bearing trees, (2) indicates that there is more than one cluster of those trees, and (3) communicates meaning to the likely readers of the composition.

Scardamalia (1981) was more specific in listing the features that can be part of every text segment that is inscribed. Her list included handwriting, spelling, punctuation, word choice, syntax, textual connections, purpose, organization, clarity, rhythm, euphony, and audience characteristics. Writers try to take these constraints into account in mentally drafting a text segment and then writing down the words before they escape from working memory. Skillful processing of these constraints helps writers inscribe the text that accurately communicates the meaning they intend, just as, during reading, adroit use of the diverse textual stimuli allows the reader to construct a meaning that closely approximates what the author intended. Table 8.1 displays two of the more complete lists of textual/psychological constraints that guide reading and writing.

During both reading and writing, textual constraints are processed in working memory, our capacity for attending to current information. Working memory has limited volume, and its contents are impermanent (Norman 1976); it is where we hold on to such information as phone numbers that we are about to dial. If an item of information is ignored for more than a second, it will escape from working memory, or short-term memory, as it is also called. Attention to new information tends to erase current contents. According to the work of Miller (1956), working memory seems limited to approximately seven unrelated elements—the now famous "seven, plus or minus two." Reflecting on this limitation, Smith (1978) wryly observed, "It is as if a benevolent providence had provided humanity with

Table 8.1
Textual/Psychological Constraints
Guiding Reading and Writing

Constraints Guiding Readers (Carpenter and Just, 1981)	Constraints Guiding Writers (Scardamalia, 1981)
Orthography	Handwriting
Phonology	Spelling
Syntax	Punctuation
Semantics	Syntax
Pragmatics	Word choice
Discourse structure	Textual connections
Scheme of domain	Purpose
Episodic knowledge	Organization
	Clarity
	Rhythm
	Euphony
	Audience characteristics

just sufficient Short Term Memory capacity to make telephone calls, and then failed to prophesy area codes" (p. 47).

The joint time limits and space limits of working memory are reflected in the obstacles facing novice typists as they compose text. Even if their conscious search for keys does not divert attention from their ideas, their slowed rate of typing planned language frequently causes forgetting before the words can be typed. Given these limits, it is thus important to consider not only how each constraint contributes to the synthesis of text, but also how rapidly it is processed. It should also be noted that constraints are related to each other; that is, the manner in which one constraint is processed may influence the processing of another.

Relationships Among Constraints: Reading

Consider the possible relationships that may occur among certain constraints during reading. When readers have an accessible store of word meanings in long-term memory (LTM), which they retrieve and apply swiftly to the text, their working memory is relatively free to focus on some other constraint like the discourse structure. For example, they may discern and capitalize on the predictable patterns of exposition in an argument or a narrative. When this happens, relatively swift processing of one constraint frees attention so that it can be invested in another, and the reader's synthesis of text benefits more completely from both constraints without a prolonged burden on working memory. Similarly, a rapid recognition of the relations among elements in a passive voice sentence facilitates a swifter construction of a meaning and allows the reader to remain more attentive to the main idea of the complete text.

By contrast, some readers are not automatic in their retrieval of word meanings from LTM; they may be forced to use sentence context (strategically, consciously, and slowly) to discover word meanings. When this happens, their working memories are in danger of being monopolized just long enough that other available constraints are unused and do not contribute to a more refined synthesis of the text. Moreover, the larger representation of text that the reader is trying to sustain in working memory is in greater danger of being forgotten. Returning to the passive voice example, if the grammatical relations do not become apparent quickly, the words of the sentence will have to be sustained in working memory as relatively separate entities, increasing the risk that some of the words may decay before they contribute to the synthesized meaning of the sentence. Instead of understanding "John was bothered by Mary," the reader might construct "John bothered Mary."

So, it is extremely important that some constraints be processed automatically. Naturally, it is most efficient if automatic processing is of lower-level constraints such as word recognition or syntactic analysis, in which the profusion of data would easily monopolize working memory if they each had to be processed slowly and consciously.

Beyond competition with each other, the relationship between two constraints can be facilitative or it can be compensatory. When readers begin to understand the main idea of a text, or when they recognize a text as a standard mode of discourse, they gain tools that sharpen expectations of what words will appear to fill the slots in the emerging text structure. Word recognition is helped because less graphical information is needed to resolve uncertainties, and, equally important, processing time is reduced. Attention to the higher-level discourse constraint actually facilitates the processing of the lower-level data.

Even if one constraint does not stimulate effective use of a second constraint, the first can compensate for the other. Stanovich (1980) describes a compensatory relationship as occurring when a reader's deficient knowledge relative to one constraint is offset by reliance on knowledge of a second constraint in which competence is adequate. For example, Stanovich has conducted experiments to demonstrate how readers who are relatively slow in word recognition compensate by making greater use of sentence context in order to retrieve a word meaning from long-term memory. In a compensatory relationship, attention gravitates toward the constraint in which knowledge seems to be the most accurate or which seems to be contributing best to an understanding of the text.

Relationships Among Constraints: Writing

Constraints can also interact in a variety of ways during the process of composing text, when the writer simultaneously decides on issues related to language, knowledge, and rhetoric to form first an initial mental representation and then a written production that incorporates each of the decisions. For the experienced writer, the various features of text can represent allies, devices used to produce shades of meaning that will be appreciated by the eventual audience. For the novice writer, however, the constraints can represent burdens, obligations that must be satisfied in order for the text to be considered even barely tolerable, let alone informative or enjoyable. If a writer must invest substantial attention in grammatical decision making, for example, then the availability of working memory is correspondingly reduced; there is less attention free for retrieving vocabulary that conveys a desired nuance of meaning. And writers who are frequently concerned with decisions about spelling invest this time at the cost of a vivid image of the substance of their composition.

When a single constraint monopolizes attention, the writer either cannot consciously process the information of another constraint or loses a foothold that had been established in the larger text and that must be recovered at a cost in time and attention. In contrast, writers who invest little time in grammatical decision making and who are accurate and confident spellers are able to concentrate on higher-level rhetorical issues, such as organization of the text. So, in writing, just as in reading, automaticity is at a premium, especially at those lower levels of processing that contain dense arrays of data which, if not processed automatically, would consume working memory in a storm of discrete decisions.

The facilitative and compensatory relationships among textual constraints that are possible during the reading process may also be present to some extent during writing. For example, writers who have a good grasp of their thesis or purpose for writing have an easier time generating specific examples than writers who have only a vague notion of what they are trying to say. The rhetorical constraint facilitates the knowledge constraint.

The compensatory relationship also can operate during the writing process. A writer organizes information in a more logical sequence in order to compensate for a limited repertoire of transitional words and phrases; a more elaborate array of examples might offset a scarcity of definitions; stylistic grace compensates, at least superficially, for deficiencies in substantive knowledge. The writer devotes attention to strengths in order to offset weaknesses. These instances notwithstanding, the compensatory relationship does not necessarily extend to all textual constraints during writing, particularly grammar and spelling, because, in contrast to readers, writers are obligated explicitly to satisfy constraints related to form as well as meaning.

Summary of the Cognitive View

The cognitive view of literacy has implications for performance in both reading and writing. The literate person enjoys reasonably complete and accurate knowledge of textual constraints, including world knowledge (Hirsch 1988), and has procedures for applying that knowledge swiftly during reading and writing. There is a high level of automaticity in the processing of as many constraints as possible, particularly those lower-level constraints that could involve numerous decisions and thus consume working memory. Among those constraints that are processed consciously or strategically, attention shifts rapidly so that the current representation of text is not neglected for long. Finally, those constraints that are not processed automatically tend to facilitate the processing of other constraints or to compensate for deficient knowledge.

CONTRIBUTIONS TO EFFECTIVE LITERACY RESEARCH

This cognitive view of reading and writing processes guides research in several ways.

1. It urges measurement of literacy processes as well as literacy outcomes;
2. It calls for research designs and analyses that isolate the effects of individual constraints but take into account the competition among constraints for the limited space of working memory;
3. It unifies the study of reading and writing;
4. It draws our attention to the allegedly unique working memory processes of deaf people; and
5. It promotes research into metacognition.

These benefits to research are discussed in the following section, along with their practical contributions to the education of deaf children.

Encourages Direct Study of the Process

The refractory interactions that happen among constraints while readers and writers are processing text are very important in the cognitive view of literacy. Hence, more than calling for measurement of behavior at the end of processing, this approach urges research that reveals the process itself. Measurement of the process may be especially important in studies of reading because those behaviors that have traditionally been recorded after reading is concluded may be more an index of postreading thinking processes than a window into the reading process that had occurred earlier.

A number of investigations have monitored the processing of text by recording its rate and direction. Subjects read passages on a computer screen, presenting text to themselves in specified increments as the computer documents the time that each text segment is kept in view. These methods are akin to pressure-sensitive graphics tablets and videotape cameras that have been used to monitor pausing during the writing process (Kelly 1988). The processing time of each text segment is an index of the processing difficulty, the decision making, and the automaticity involved in processing the constraints of that segment (Haberlandt 1984). As mentioned earlier, the duration of processing is a critical index of behavior, because the passage of time tends to erode the contents of working memory. So, the foregoing techniques capture an important, overt indicator of both reading and writing.

Although research that measures text processing variables has become extremely prominent in literacy studies of subjects with normal hearing, applications of these techniques have been very rare in research on deaf subjects. Limited data have been collected to show where deaf writers invest significant amounts of attention in the texts that they read and write. Virtually nonexistent are studies that would record those attention patterns that seem to result in learning of reading and writing skills. These tactics therefore represent untapped resources for exploring the literacy difficulties endured by many deaf people and for explaining the success of the skilled minority.

Calls for Isolating the Effects of Individual Constraints

Reading is largely a covert activity; the processing of textual constraints is usually unobserved. Moreover, even though composing routinely produces a visible written product, the interaction of constraints during the writing process is largely unseen. Hence, performance of reading and writing does not routinely reveal a subject's attention to a certain textual constraint at a specific point in time. Nevertheless, the notion of separate and multiple constraints asserted by the cognitive view commands research tactics that succeed in partitioning the effects of those constraints. This is no minor asset, considering the population that this research is intended to serve.

In the literature on deafness, a variety of textual constraints have shared the blame for the pervasive and chronic reading or writing problems of deaf people. Quigley et al. (1976) cited lack of syntactic knowledge; LaSasso and Davey (1987) blamed deficient lexical knowledge; Conrad (1979) blamed the inability to recode phonologically; King and Quigley (1985) held limited background knowledge responsible. Few constraints have been absolved.

Yet in spite of the prevalence of literacy difficulties and their multiple explanations, some profoundly deaf people do manage to become proficient readers and writers. It stands to reason that, in spite of limited access to spoken English, this minority has somehow compensated by productively channeling their attention to selected textual constraints during reading and writing and while learning to read and write. This would be consistent with Stanovich's theory of compensatory interaction among constraints. The success of this minority discourages the fatalism that would limit the possibilities for helping that larger majority of the deaf population who perhaps are not yet making productive use of textual information that is potentially a resource to them.

But more than engendering optimism, this perspective carries with it uncertainty and attendant questions about the processing of individual textual constraints. It is certain neither what textual knowledge is most useful to successful deaf readers/writers nor what experiences allow them routinely to acquire that knowledge. Which constraints tend to be processed automatically and which are used strategically? Which are routinely deficient and which do successful deaf readers and writers use to compensate for these deficiencies? Which constraints seem to hold very little promise for helping the reading and writing processes of deaf people? Responses to these questions may lead to surer knowledge of the processes that make dramatic differences in literacy performance. This knowledge, in turn, may suggest refinements in the focus and methods of instructional programming for deaf students.

One approach to isolating the effect of a single constraint is selectively to manipulate the task or the text environment, usually altering only one constraint between two experimental conditions and then measuring the differences in processing time and the outcomes of processing. Complementing these design strategies are statistical techniques that isolate the effects of constraints when the analyses focus on a measure of processing. For example, in one such analysis, the multiple constraints of each text segment become categorical variables that theoretically explain processing times as measured by the computer, and analysis procedures such as multiple regression are used to calculate the relative influence of each constraint.

These are tactics that methodically peel away the layers of constraints so that the relative influence of constraints is revealed through a series of investigations. This research approach builds on existing naturalistic lines of inquiry by attempting further closure on some of the questions that earlier investigations have generated. The potential for insight is not confined to the deaf because the special conditions of deafness constitute what amounts to a natural experimental control, making it possible to extend theory as well as to question assumptions regarding literacy acquisition and performance in the general population.

Discourages Studying Constraints in Isolation

The cognitive view asserts that it is crucial to consider an individual constraint as interacting with other constraints within the confines of working memory. It is therefore critical to observe and study the processing of constraints while they are operating "online" in the presence of competing textual constraints. Although almost any study should be designed to peel away the layers of the process somewhat, it is important that not all layers be removed at the same time.

An analytical view of literacy competence is not new to investigations of the deaf. Various studies have purported to isolate the separate effects of such constraints as syntactic knowledge, lexical knowledge, and phonological knowledge (LaSasso and Davey 1987; Lichtenstein 1983; Moores et al. 1987). However, in an effort to isolate the effects of the individual constraints, these investigations have studied the target constraint while it was being processed in isolation. Performance has been measured on instruments such as the Test of Syntactic Abilities or the Gates-MacGinitie test of vocabulary skill, and these separate measures have then been correlated with global measures of reading or writing like the Stanford Achievement Test. However, because constraints were not measured while interacting with other constraints, these studies did not test whether the component skill was being used "online" during actual reading or writing, with other constraints asserting themselves simultaneously.

According to Stanovich (1980), such analytical methods treat knowledge of an individual constraint merely as so much problem-solving skill, which would not necessarily be available to the reader or writer within the environment constituted by the other textual constraints. As Stanovich said, "The question concerns what skills predominate in the actual reading [and writing] situation, not which group of readers [and writers] has more of a certain type of knowledge" (p. 38).

By using the strategies described earlier, this research program will avoid conditions that measure problem-solving skill instead of the knowledge of constraints that is actually accessible during normal reading or writing conditions. So, in addition to arousing skepticism of research that studies knowledge of constraints operating in isolation, the cognitive perspective also invites scrutiny of instruction that teaches knowledge of a constraint in isolation from the competing, compensatory, and facilitative constraints present in communicative discourse.

Consolidates Reading and Writing Research

The present paradigm combines multiple constraint theories that were derived separately for reading (Carpenter and Just 1981; Stanovich 1980) and for writing (Flower and Hayes 1980). Beyond its compatibility with the recent trend (Stein 1984) to merge reading and writing under the term *literacy*, this consolidation has several practical benefits. The deaf have problems with both reading and writing, and both of these processes warrant attention. Having them grouped in this way decreases the chances that either of them will be neglected. Second, because both processes will be viewed with the aid of similar theoretical constructs, effective methods and helpful insights gained from the study of reading will be more easily generalized to the study of writing and vice versa. Third, this union facilitates an increasingly popular and important line of research (i.e., investigations that illuminate the symbiotic relationships between reading and writing). This more elegant treatment may even encourage teachers of the deaf to accelerate their efforts to integrate instruction in the two processes.

Encourages Study of Working Memory and the Deaf

Working memory is integral to the cognitive view of literacy. It is our capacity for temporarily storing textual constraints and words while we are processing text. For deaf people in particular, the functioning of working memory may represent a key to understanding reading and writing. This has become apparent from a growing literature that explores the potentially unique nature of, and also questions the effectiveness of, the working memory strategies and capacity of some deaf people. By promoting a sustained focus on working memory, the cognitive view of literacy increases the chances of revealing psychological processes that influence deaf people's reading and writing.

According to this literature, readers with normal hearing use speech recoding to hold individual words in working memory until a meaning for a segment of text can be synthesized (Conrad 1979). The reader does not necessarily speak out loud or even move the lips, but there is an internal conversion of the print into its speech equivalent. This strategy is considered akin to phonological recoding, articulatory recoding, and auditory memory. Phonological recoding seems to support psychological processing that is temporal in nature; it preserves the order in which items are perceived, earliest to most recent. Temporal processing contrasts with visual/spatial processing, a strategy that captures the appearance, physical location and spatial relationships of the items perceived and held in working memory.

According to Ellis and Hunt's (1983) review of research on hearing subjects there is a consensus that information encoded in working memory with a phonological/temporal strategy is substantially more enduring than information that is encoded visually. In theory, readers who skillfully apply a phonological recoding strategy ought to be able to sustain a more complete and more lasting record of the words in text segments than readers who use a visual strategy. It follows that the meaning synthesized in working memory is based on information that is more complete.

This body of research is extremely relevant to the literacy of deaf children because a number of empirical studies have produced evidence that visual/spatial processing is far more prevalent in the deaf population than among people with normal hearing (Belmont and Karchmer 1978; Lake 1978; O'Connor and Hermelin 1973). These findings have led to suspicions that the inferior reading performance of many deaf people is due to a greater reliance on visual processing instead of phonological recoding. In addition to phonologically encoded material being less in danger of decay, according to Hanson (in press), "A phonological code may be an efficient medium for retaining the sequential information that is represented in English" (p. 16). This means that readers who encode information visually are suspected of being more in danger of altering the actual sequence of the words held in working memory, thus doing violence to the grammatical relations among those words.

Regardless of the greater prevalence of visual processing among people who are deaf, there is research to indicate that some deaf readers do use a phonological strategy to encode information in working memory. Hanson and Fowler (1987) theorized that, in spite of a profound hearing impairment, deaf people can acquire phonological information in one of several ways: either by noticing regularities in the orthographic system, "which maps on to the phonological representation of words" (p. 200), or by learning to speak or speechread English. Separate studies by Conrad (1979), Hanson and Fowler (1987), and Lichtenstein (1983) concluded that some deaf readers do use phonological information during experimental tasks that involve working memory. They also found that use of a phonological recoding strategy tended to be characteristic of superior deaf readers. All three studies found correlations between a phonological recoding tendency and a separate measure of reading performance. They reasoned from these correlational data that the superior performance may be due to the greater availability in working memory of more complete and more accurately sequenced textual information.

Although these results alert us to the presence of a potentially important influence on reading performance, they are not sufficiently conclusive to guide instructional practice. Again, the results are correlational in nature; reading performance and phonological recoding were measured separately. Assuming that phonological recoding does require attention, and recognizing the limited capacity of working memory, it is worth questioning whether phonological information can be routinely applied during reading while other textual constraints are competing for working memory.

Our knowledge of phonological reading might be advanced by two kinds of experiments, which would contrast the performance of confirmed phonological recoders and visual/spatial recoders. One kind of experiment might interrupt subjects during the reading process and determine the relative completeness and sequential accuracy of working memory contents. To date, research has not verified that visual recoders do in fact have a less complete record of textual information in working memory. And related to the question of whether word order is disturbed by visual processing, reading miscue data (Quigley et al. 1976) have indicated that the only consistent trend is for some deaf readers wrongly to impose a Subject–Verb–Direct Object structure (S–V–O) on imbedded clauses and on passive voice constructions. The S–V–O pattern does in fact retain the sequence of the original sentences. It is important to note that if one preserves the spatial sequence of words, then the temporal sequence is also maintained, since in English the left-to-right spatial sequence and the first-to-last temporal progression are one and the same.

A second kind of experiment might also employ a contrast between phonological recoders and spatial recoders. The experimental conditions might be manipulated in such a way that it would be more difficult for phonological recoders to apply their sound-based strategy for sustaining words in working memory. If phonological skill is what truly determines their superiority, then the experimental performance of phonological recoders ought to begin to resemble that of the visual recoder. Using an analogous strategy, Conrad (1979) induced a decline in the performance of visual recoders by requiring them to read aloud instead of silently.

Working memory is obviously a topic that has potential to inform our understanding of the reading process of the deaf. Adoption of the cognitive view of literacy will assure that the study of working memory is not neglected.

Studies of Metacognition

Informal notes to family members often do not require extensive investment of conscious attention. By the same token, comprehension of the sports page often occurs simply as a result of the print being exposed to the reader's casual gaze. There are other occasions, however, when cognitive functions must be intentionally controlled for performance to be successful. It is then that literate people take into account their personal strengths and limitations, combine this assessment with knowledge of the reading or writing task, and then apply intentional strategies that maximize the chances of success. Garner (1988) labels this knowledge and use of our cognitive resources as *metacognition*.

Research into how we succeed or fail at marshalling our intellects during reading and writing is a logical outgrowth of studies of literacy and cognition. It may be especially called for in a program of research meant to produce insights into the literacy of deaf people.

Many people somehow discover that composing is difficult because of the considerable cognitive burden that they face during writing, and they take conscious steps to limit the burden on working memory. As the most obvious example, they may jot down a tentative outline of the points that they plan to cover in their compositions. Later, during actual generation of text, this reasonably complete record of ideas allows the writer to focus less on what to write and more on how to write it. Experienced writers may also know that such outlines needn't be exhaustive, since the act of writing about a topic tends to refine our thinking, alerting us to what we really do know (Shanklin 1982). In both cases, self-knowledge and knowledge of the composing process guide the adoption of a prudent strategy.

Reading also can be the focus of metacognitive activity. It is becoming increasingly apparent that reasonable knowledge of a certain subject domain usually facilitates comprehension of new text about a topic within that domain (Walker 1987). Thus, when readers take active steps to stimulate recall of relevant background knowledge before they begin reading a text, they have engaged in metacognitive activity. As a different example of reading and metacognition, Palincsar and Brown (1984) have verified the effectiveness of four strategies (summarizing, questioning, clarifying, and predicting) as procedures for intentionally monitoring and promoting reading comprehension. Again, the reader takes active steps to apportion cognitive resources so that performance is maximized.

Study of exceptionally proficient deaf readers may reveal that they are capitalizing on certain selected cognitive resources during reading and writing. Although they may be marshalling their capabilities intentionally, the process may be virtually intuitive for many. Identification of these capabilities could lead to instruction in self-directed strategies that would make these same cognitive resources more instrumental in the reading and writing of the majority of the deaf population who are not exceptionally skilled. Metacognitive research (Garner

1988) is a relatively recent field of inquiry; applications to the reading and writing of the deaf are virtually nonexistent. This line of investigation thus represents a source of information on literacy and deafness that is as yet untapped. Findings of investigations of literacy, deafness, and cognition have the potential to inform subsequent research on literacy, deafness, and metacognition.

A STUDY OF COGNITION, LITERACY, AND DEAFNESS

The cognitive view can provide excellent theoretical guidance to studies meant to illuminate literacy processes of deaf people and the general population as well. What follows is a description of a study of the composing processes of deaf college students. It has been reported at greater length elsewhere (Kelly 1986, 1987, 1988, 1989) but the following account gives an indication of how research design, data analysis, conclusions, and discussion of implications can benefit from an application of the components of cognitive theory.

Background of the Study

When writers frequently make grammatical errors, they often spend a substantial portion of their composing time making decisions about grammar. Studies of unskilled writers with normal hearing indicate this hyperconcern for correctness and lack of automaticity (Perl 1979). Krashen (1978) describes such concern for grammar as "monitor over-use." The monitor is a writer's conscious knowledge of grammar, also called learned competence, which usually results from formal instruction and error correction. Conscious use of learned competence contrasts with a writer's use of acquired language knowledge, which is the intuitive, fluent competence that the language user has "picked up" and that guides performance with a minimal draw on working memory. Based on cognitive theory, we would thus predict that monitor over-users have greater difficulty allocating working memory to the management of the other constraints of composing because their attention is so focused on the correctness of their language. Moreover, heavy use of learned competence does not guarantee the absence of errors in the completed composition.

Prior to Kelly's research on the composing process, there had been reason to believe that the attention of deaf writers who make errors is less consumed by grammatical decision making than that of hearing writers. Even highly educated deaf writers reportedly failed to detect certain errors in their prose. Persistent errors include the misuse of pronouns, determiners, verb inflections, copulas, and prepositions. The presence of such mistakes in the writing of deaf writers with advanced academic degrees had aroused a suspicion that profoundly deaf adults are relatively inattentive to certain nuances of English grammar. As Crandall (1978) noted, English is, after all, a language that is rooted in sound. Given their limited access to spoken English, the form in which language is usually acquired, it is logical that profoundly deaf people may use a less elaborate, less constraining version of English.

Beyond this logic, empirical research on the language skills of deaf people also had suggested this phenomenon. According to Charrow (1974), certain errors may be reflections of a pidgin that has resulted from the interaction between standard English and sign language, the first language of many deaf people. Wilbur (1977) blamed a flawed instructional system for certain chronic errors, asserting that the prevalence of grammar drills in deaf education has led to a set of nonstandard but well-learned grammatical generalizations that are applied with a minimal draw on attention.

The very terms that have been used to describe these errors suggest that they may be the products of nonstandard language intuitions instead of repeated wrong decisions that have been made consciously. Such terms include "deafisms" (Eachus 1971), "meta-language" (Lenneberg 1967), "distinct rule-ordered syntactic structures" (Quigley, Power, and Steinkamp 1977), and "fossilizations" (Goldberg, Ford, and Silverman 1984). Whatever the exact source of the errors, it was reasoned that the flawed English written by many prelingually deaf people is produced with relative automaticity, without the same hyperconcern for correctness that seems to affect unskilled writers who have normal hearing. It would follow that the intellects of deaf writers are relatively free, if sometimes not adequately skilled, to address constraints of writing other than language.

Although freedom from the constant nag of grammatical decision making may have certain advantages, such freedom is a mixed blessing. A writer whose intuitive acquired language competence is either incomplete or inaccurate will have to compensate with learned competence in order to produce correct, conventional English. Deaf writers, isolated from spoken English, may be faced with just such a heavy reliance on learned competence. Moreover, instructional practices in programs for the deaf have stressed grammar drills and error correction (Meath-Lang, Caccamise, and Albertini 1982), the kinds of experiences thought to contribute more to learned language than to acquired fluency. Finally, if certain errors are so well learned that they are produced almost automatically, avoidance of such errors will require intentional use of learned language. In sum, there are strong reasons to believe that deaf writers may be more reliant on learned competence than are writers with normal hearing.

It may be that certain deaf writers do not produce correct English automatically, forcing them to rely on learned competence. However, their learned competence sometimes is not brought to bear, either because errors remain hidden or because use of learned competence requires too much working memory. It is worthwhile to summarize this multiple predicament, which may be faced by many deaf writers.

Most important is the likelihood that native-level acquired competence does not guide the fluent production of conventional English by many deaf writers. The ungrammatical writing samples of many deaf writers provide ample evidence.

For these writers, many errors remain hidden during editing because the language may "sound right;" more precisely, it does not sound wrong enough to attract attention and to stimulate the use of explicit learned competence. The competition for attention posed by the other textual constraints during composing also makes it difficult to apply learned competence. Finally, it is quite possible that, for many of these writers, learned competence is either incomplete or flawed. At least in theory, there appear to be many psychological forces militating against correct grammatical performance by deaf writers.

Kelly's study (1987) compared deaf writers to unskilled writers with normal hearing in terms of their apparent attention to grammatical correctness. Subjects' patterns of pausing under three composing conditions were combined with their error correction behavior to infer the relative attention that the two groups paid to grammatical decision making. A finding of differences in attention to grammar would imply additional differences in the amounts of working memory that could be invested in other constraints of composing, such as organization, elaboration, and content accuracy. Differential attention to grammar would also have implications for instruction.

Methodology

Subjects
Ten deaf subjects were profoundly, prelingually deaf college freshmen with no additional handicaps. They all had hearing parents. The comparison group was comprised of five hearing subjects between 18 and 21 years old who were attending their first year of college. They were native speakers of English and, like the deaf subjects, their prior writing samples contained errors from selected categories in the classification system used in the study (Crandall 1980).

Data Collection
In the initial (generating) phase of data gathering, subjects produced separate written accounts of two short stories that they had viewed on videotape. The stories were both signed and spoken on the tape. This condition required them to manage all the constraints of the writing process to some extent; even though the need actually to generate original ideas had been minimized by the use of the videotaped story, it was theoretically more difficult for the subjects explicitly to monitor their language for its correctness because of the competition from the other constraints. That is, they had to search memory for what they wanted to say.

In the next phase, revising self, subjects reviewed and revised their original drafts during sessions that occurred a number of days after the generating phase. Subjects were instructed to inspect their texts and make changes that they thought would improve the grammar of their original versions. They recopied the sentences of the original composition after they had separately inspected them and decided on any necessary changes. Because subjects were discouraged from adding new story information to their original texts, this condition was considered to have less of a cognitive burden, making it easier to monitor grammar explicitly.

Finally, subjects processed text under a third condition, revising other, when they reviewed and revised a passage with standard content after representative errors had been imbedded in the passage. To produce these common passages, the investigator composed an account of one of the videotaped stories that the subjects had written about during the earlier sessions. Then a common set of errors (modeled after the examples of deaf students' errors that appear in Crandall's [1980] manual for classifying errors) were inserted in the 554-word text. Subjects reviewed and revised the passage, presented to them as "another student's" composition.

While they were writing under each condition, subjects' pauses were observed and recorded. The subject's stationery was positioned on a pressure-sensitive graphics tablet that was connected to an Apple II computer. During each writing session, the computer recorded the exact tablet locations, accurate to within one-tenth of an inch, where the writer's pen either established or ended contact with the tablet's surface. These locations were stored as a series of Cartesian (X,Y) coordinates in the computer's memory. Meanwhile, the computer's internal timekeeping system monitored the passage of time in increments of one-tenth of a second and stored the time when each episode of writing and pausing had started and stopped. The computer was later programmed to print out a record of exact tablet and page locations where interruptions in writing had occurred and of the duration of associated pauses.

Data Reduction

Later, subjects' texts were segmented into T-units (independent clauses with their dependent attachments, Hunt, 1965) and their rates of pausing were calculated separately within T-units and at T-unit boundaries. Errors were identified, and their severity was classified according to the system developed by Crandall (1980). Error frequencies were tabulated, as were the percentages of errors that subjects corrected in each category. Intergroup comparisons of mean pausing and error correction rates constituted the primary analyses.

Inferring Grammatical Decision Making from Pausing

This study did not draw its conclusions on the basis of individual pauses. Rather, because of the large number of grammatical errors made by the subjects included in the study, the conditions under which they wrote, and the text location of pauses included in calculation of pause rates, it was reasoned that a large portion of the pause time would be associated with grammatical decisions. If there were large differences in pause time between the two groups, then they would likely be due in large part to differences in the durations of grammatical decision making. Again, the analyses of error-correction patterns provide an additional basis for testing the hypothesis of interest.

Results and Conclusions

Compared to the hearing group, the deaf writers made more errors and corrected fewer of them when they were working with their own texts. However, when correcting errors in the revising other text, they demonstrated proficiency that was comparable to the hearing subjects. In the category that contained the largest number of errors, the deaf writers actually performed slightly better than the hearing subjects. These combined results suggest that the deaf subjects were attending less to grammatical decision making during their own writing.

The same conclusion was supported by differences between the pausing patterns of the two groups. Particularly indicative were the significantly longer rates of pausing by the hearing writers within T-units (hearing 35.9 sec/10 words; deaf 14.3 sec/10 words). This measure, in contrast to pausing at T-unit boundaries, is considered the most direct index of time spent on making decisions about grammar. Based on these findings, the major conclusion of the study was that the deaf subjects invested significantly less attention in grammatical decision making. This happened even though their inferior performance in almost every category of grammar errors would have predicted a greater investment of attention than the hearing subjects.

Implications

The differences between the deaf students and the hearing students in this study show that the mere presence of comparable errors in the compositions of two students does not guarantee that both will be equally attentive to correctness. The deaf writers in this study made many more errors than the hearing subjects, but they attended less to grammatical decision making.

Therefore, teachers ought to anticipate differences among their students in this regard. They cannot routinely assume that during writing a student's working memory is consumed by worry over grammar. Some students will be able to focus attention on the other features of their ungrammatical compositions and to improve them accordingly. As partial evidence of this, the compositions of the deaf students in this study were approximately 50 percent longer than the texts of the hearing group. The attention that was not consumed by grammar apparently was invested in preparing more complete first drafts of the stories that had been viewed on videotape. It follows that complex writing tasks in many cases may be assigned by teachers even when glaring grammatical errors are present in a student's compositions.

These results also imply that deaf subjects who attend less to grammar may be less in danger of a paradoxical phenomenon that was suggested by the performance of one hearing subject who seemed particularly concerned about correctness. This subject's pausing and revising behavior suggested that concern for error actually seemed to produce error.

In her first drafts of the two generating episodes, this subject made more than thirty serious word omissions. For example, in the sentence "The father told him the first thing you must learn," she omitted "father" and "him." Many of these omissions were proximate to episodes of extended grammatical decision making, as suggested by her patterns of pausing and editing. In these cases, it appeared that the writer had mentally formulated the substance of a phrase, but before inscribing it, she had encountered grammatical uncertainty related to a lexical item near the end of the phrase. By the time the uncertainty had been resolved, the initial part of the phrase may have escaped from working memory, and the subject inscribed only what remained.

These serious omissions were in most instances obvious to the writer at a later time, and she corrected them during the revising self condition, when the burden of working memory was less severe. But under the more demanding generating condition, the concern for grammar actually seemed to produce errors. This would also be consistent with cognitive theory. Failure to reach rapid closure on a text segment can increase the risk that its constituents may fade from working memory before the complete segment is inscribed.

This study also provides insights into the cognitive demands of the editing process; namely, why writers have greater difficulty finding and correcting errors in their own texts compared to the texts of a peer. Although few are puzzled by the finding that writers are more adept at detecting errors in standard experimental texts than in their own work, explanations for the discrepancy are neither unanimous nor conclusive. Hull (1987) reasoned that the novelty of the errors in standard texts produces greater detectability. Each writer's errors are unique, so the mistakes intentionally inserted stand out during inspection of a standard text. In an alternative explanation, Bartlett (1982) and Hull (1987) point to the possibility that writers' intentions for their texts—their "privileged information"—tends to mask certain kinds of flaws, such as referential ambiguities. In these instances, writers tend to overlook the information needs of their audiences.

Both of these explanations emphasize the properties of the errors that make them more or less detectable. Less emphasis, however, is placed on differences between the two textual environments. It may simply be that writers have less attention available when searching for errors in their own compositions.

The design of this study, contrasting hearing subjects and deaf subjects, furnished an opportunity to test whether differential error detection performance between the two conditions may be due to differential availability of attention. It may be harder to attend to our own grammar errors when our attention is being constantly drawn to the meaning of our compositions. Intrusion of meaning would be indicated if writers whose error correction processes are more dependent on the availability of attention show a greater improvement in performance when more attention becomes available under the revising other condition. Writers less dependent on attention for error detection would benefit less from the greater freedom of attention.

In theory, deaf writers need to pay more attention than hearing writers in order to produce accurate grammar. Thus, if their revising other performance shows a greater improvement over revising self than it does for the hearing writers, this improvement would suggest that attention is more available during the revising other condition. Unlike the case of the revising self condition, the writer's meaning may pose less competition for working memory resources during revising other, and thus there may be plenty of attention available for the conscious error-detection process. If, however, the novelty of the errors is the explanation, then the hearing writers ought to improve at a greater rate because the errors imbedded in the revising other text were modeled after those made by deaf writers, as indicated in Crandall's (1980) scoring manual.

First, it is useful to explore theoretically why reading our own writing makes it difficult to focus only on form. There is a growing body of literature that shows the connection between writing and learning. Langer and Applebee (1986) and Newell (1984) produced findings to indicate that the process of writing about information, in contrast to more passive forms of learning such as listening to a lecture or reading, tends to store the information in long-term memory in a more effective fashion, as indicated by its enhanced retrievability at later times. We can reason that systematic storage of information through writing may work in two ways to jeopardize detection of errors in passages that we have written ourselves. First, as we are reading our own texts, the meaning stored earlier is quickly retrieved from long-term memory, takes up residence in working memory, and thus circumscribes the sustained attention originally intended for the error search. Second, because the information is so well known, writers-as-readers need very little graphic information in order to resolve meaning uncertainties. They are thus prone to giving only superficial scrutiny to the text's surface correctness.

In contrast, the information of a standard passage written by an experimenter is not systematically stored in long-term memory. Reading of a standard text does not, therefore, stimulate retrieval of a vivid mental representation of text that would tend to capture working memory and reduce the attention invested in the search for errors. The effect of attention being captured by meaning should be particularly dramatic on the error detection of writers whose error detection processes rely on the availability of attention, as is likely the case with deaf writers.

According to the data from this study, the deaf subjects demonstrated improvements between the self-written and standard conditions that far surpassed those of the hearing group. Particularly dramatic were the improvements in error Type 6, free functor errors, which improved 240 percent for the deaf subjects compared to 65 percent for the hearing subjects; and in Type 8, inflectional morpheme errors, an improvement of 217 percent for the deaf writers compared to 88 percent for the hearing writers. These two categories are especially important because they contained the greatest frequencies of errors.

The deaf subjects may have improved to the greater degree because, under the standard text condition, their intentional processes for detecting grammar errors were not preempted by the meaning of their texts. Meaning tended to monopolize attention during the revising self condition.

Teachers and writers should be aware that the meaning of their own texts constitutes a threat to error detection. They need to devise metacognitive strategies for overcoming that threat, and there is a need for greater emphasis on improving acquired competence, which consumes minimal attention.

The conclusions of this study have an additional implication regarding the theoretical relationship between degree of mastery and degree of automaticity of a reading or writing task. Until a task is mastered, its performance ordinarily requires substantial attention. However, Bereiter (1980) has concluded that a reasonable level of automaticity can occur without mastery of certain subskills of writing. Bereiter distinguished between the theoretical state of automaticity, which is reflected by performance that requires minimal attention, and mastery, which is reflected by accurate performance. He emphasized that automaticity does not require mastery "but only proficiency such that the behavior in question requires little or no conscious attention" (p. 89). As examples, he cited inaccurate but swift handwriting and spelling.

The many grammatical errors produced by the writers in this study indicate that neither group of writers had mastered certain conventions of English. However, by devoting less conscious attention to their grammar, the deaf subjects demonstrated relative automaticity, even though they made more errors. Their writing behavior supports Bereiter's contention that a writer's performance need not be error free before it is relatively fluent. Bereiter cited confident but inaccurate spelling and swift but illegible handwriting to illustrate his notion of writing proficiency. The writing of the deaf subjects in this study extends the concept of relative automaticity to include the grammaticality of a writer's text. The mere presence of errors in a text does not guarantee that the writer has invested large amounts of time in grammatical decision making.

Bereiter implied that advanced proficiency will be accompanied by increased automaticity. Indeed, for many tasks and performers, advances in accuracy predict greater freedom of attention. If the hearing writers and the deaf writers had demonstrated equal grammatical proficiency, the present study's findings might not have illuminated this point. However, the hearing writers did demonstrate substantially less automaticity, even though they also showed somewhat greater proficiency, especially in terms of correcting their own texts, indicating that superior performance is not necessarily accompanied by limited use of conscious attention. This finding suggests further that any conclusion about how the management of grammar may influence the writing process of an unskilled writer needs to consider the potential variability in the actual costs in attention resources. Ungrammatical performance does not uniformly indicate a hyperconcern for correctness.

Turning to the key instructional implication of this study, although there are advantages to reducing students' overattention to error, their teachers' instructional attention is almost unavoidably attracted by mistakes. The errors are a source of embarrassment, and they need to be reduced. With writers like those in this study, young adults who make so many mistakes, is it more efficient to focus on improving explicit learned knowledge of language rules, what Krashen (1978) calls the *monitor*? Alternatively, is it more realistic to concentrate on improvement of acquired competence?

The findings of this study suggest that explicit knowledge of grammar conventions is not completely at a writer's disposal during composing and editing. Even if a set of rules is accurate and complete, it may be inaccessible if application requires the writer's attention. The multiple features of the composition (organization, word choice, and audience characteristics) are competing for the limited amount of processing space in working memory. Teachers thus ought to promote the kind of language competence that does not require excessive use of attention, namely the competence that Krashen refers to as *acquired*.

Acquired competence is the intuitive, fluent competence that the language user has picked up through frequent opportunities to communicate. According to Krashen, such competence does not result from formal instruction and error correction. The literature related to second-language learning stresses the value of the communicative approach to learning language (Brumfit and Johnson 1979; Burling 1982) as a way to augment acquired competence. This view of classroom instruction urges teachers to use activities and exercises that are valid acts of communication. Zamel (1983) described and endorsed the communicative philosophy based on the finding that

> The most recent approaches to language instruction have underlined the fact that language learning can best be promoted when language is used purposefully and communicatively, when language is viewed as the means for true expression, when language accuracy serves linguistic fluency and is subordinate to it. (p. 184)

Frank Smith (1984), long an advocate of an approach to reading instruction that focuses on meaning, also endorsed the communicative philosophy for writing. He argued that if students are made to feel like writers, like "members of the Writers Club" (p. 53), they will begin to read like writers. Students will pick up the nuances of written expression when, as "spontaneous apprentices," they read the texts of established writers. He warns, however, that "emphasis on the elimination of mistakes results in the elimination of writing" (p. 56).

Carroll (1986) emphasized that while communicative events may be necessary conditions for development of acquired competence, they are certainly not sufficient. He argued that in order for language acquisition to occur, the learner must "notice regularities" (p. 103) in the target language. The noticing need not be the result of explicit instruction. According to Carroll, "the process may be subconscious in the sense that the learner may not notice that he is noticing something, or not notice that what he is noticing is a regularity. The noticing of regularities seems, in any event, to be a minimal cognitive process necessary in acquiring [a second language]" (p. 103).

Carroll also suggested that the target regularity must be within the learner's current span of apprehension, it must occur in some particular context, it must occur on different occasions in highly similar contexts, and the regularity must be noticed in contrast to other regularities of the language. According to this line of reasoning, the greatest challenge to teachers is to arrange appropriate "patterns of noticing" by their students.

In its purpose, design, analysis, conclusion, and discussion of implications, this study benefited greatly from the key conceptual components of cognitive theory.

1. Automaticity—differences in how rapidly subjects processed grammatical decisions;
2. Competition among constraints for the limited space in working memory—the language constraint limited the working memory of the hearing subjects during generating (the texts of deaf subjects were 50 percent longer) and meaning seemed to intrude excessively on the deaf writers during revising-self (they were substantially less successful in correcting their own errors); and
3. Information and processing procedures from long-term memory can intentionally or unintentionally invade working memory, limiting the attention that can be invested in managing multiple constraints.

At the center of the entire investigation was the concept of working memory, with its limits on accommodating new data and the impermanence of the information that it does accommodate.

The cognitive perspective will guide future studies of writing. These studies will focus on how deaf writers process grammar as well as higher level constraints, such as organization, sense of audience, and word choice. Furthermore, this same conceptual framework has provided the basis for planned investigations of reading processes.

PLANNED STUDIES OF READING AND COGNITION

An understanding of the cognitive processes used by skilled deaf readers could guide the instruction of the many deaf people who have deficient reading skills. A planned program of study has been designed to determine whether two specific subprocesses tend to distinguish the minority of deaf readers who have exceptional reading skills from most deaf readers, whose reading skills are somewhat deficient. One of the target subprocesses is the ability to activate relevant knowledge of a topic in order to facilitate processing of text; the other is the ability to apply superior syntactic knowledge in order to process sentence patterns (such as relative clauses and the passive voice) that have been identified as potentially disruptive to deaf readers.

Although deafness rarely enhances reading performance, it does not guarantee illiteracy. A select population of deaf students do read with considerable skill. At one school, Gallaudet University's Model Secondary School for the Deaf, during 1987–88, the average reading performance of 41 students in the Advanced English program was comparable to that of typical hearing students who were nearing high school graduation (Center for Curriculum Development, 1988). This occurred in spite of a better ear average hearing loss of 96.2 decibels for students in the program. Even though they were virtually isolated from the sounds of spoken English, these students managed to become adept at processing English text.

Their superior literacy skills suggest that these students are processing selected constraints with exceptional effectiveness. It stands to reason that they have somehow compensated for certain deficiencies by productively channeling their attention to selected textual constraints during reading. On theoretical grounds, it is highly plausible that the literacy processes of exceptional deaf readers are benefiting from Stanovich's conception of a compensatory relationship among textual constraints.

The success of these students encourages at least some optimism regarding the potential for helping the majority of the deaf population who have inferior reading skills. Whatever the paths of these skillful students to their current levels of competence, they command arrays of cognitive processes that permit proficient processing of written English. Hence, rather than trying to discover the factors that, over time, have promoted skills of this high order, the purpose of this study is to explicate the nature of this competence. Identification of critical subprocesses will make it more feasible to devise ways of making those subprocesses more readily available to other deaf readers.

There were several reasons for narrowing the focus of this investigation to topic familiarity and syntactic knowledge as potentially important factors in reading process differences between skilled and average deaf readers. First, although there are theoretical reasons and some empirical evidence to suggest that both may be influential, conclusive evidence has not been found for either factor. Second, a research paradigm—measurement of reading time—has been perfected in studies of hearing readers, and it can be appropriately applied to the investigation of these two subprocesses. Third, these subprocesses warrant study because clarifying how each contributes to competent performance will have important practical implications for teachers who want to promote reading skills.

To date, those investigations that have studied the influence of syntactic knowledge have produced data that are correlational in nature. Syntactic knowledge was measured in isolation from other textual constraints that would have competed for the reader's attention in a more natural reading context. Recalling the limitations of working memory, it is entirely conceivable that a reader's full repertoire of syntactic knowledge, as demonstrated on a separate test, might not be readily available during the reading process. Thus, better readers don't necessarily apply all their superior syntactic knowledge during reading, especially if their knowledge is of the learned (vs. acquired) variety.

Moreover, at present we do not know the manner in which difficult structures, such as relative clauses and the passive voice, affect attention during the reading process. Do skilled deaf readers process these structures swiftly, devoting very little conscious attention to processing, or do they invest time in a methodical inspection of these structures? Does the familiarity of the text affect the manner in which these difficult structures are processed? Do unfamiliar topics induce methodical processing by skilled readers? Are skilled readers distinguished from average readers by their facility in processing difficult syntactic structures? The answers to these questions will have significant implications in the education of deaf children.

Differential world knowledge is also a plausible explanation for the differences in the reading performance of skilled and average deaf readers, justifying this constraint, too, as an appropriate focus of investigation. It is obvious that deaf children are hampered in their ability to acquire, incidentally yet methodically, extensive knowledge of the world around them. In *Reading and Deafness*, King and Quigley (1985) cite lack of background knowledge as one of the principal explanations for the inferior reading performance of deaf people in general. Yet, in spite of the pervasiveness of this culturally held and anecdotally supported belief, there has been little systematic research on how superior world knowledge may benefit the deaf reader. We have little evidence at present that increasing familiarity with many topics will increase reading performance substantially.

In contrast, various studies of hearing subjects have documented the facilitating effect of applying relevant world knowledge during the reading process. Walker (1987) found that relatively unskilled readers who had a good knowledge of baseball understood more from written accounts of baseball games than did highly skilled readers who had a minimal knowledge of the game. Spilich, et al. (1979) found comparable results in a similar experiment. As McNeil (1984) observed, "It is knowledge stored in memory that plays an important role in the interpretation of new information" (cited in Garner 1988, p. 3). This study would begin to estimate the extent to which world knowledge represents an asset to superior deaf readers. Conclusive results would provide considerable guidance to teachers of the deaf.

The study will compare the reading processes of fifteen skilled deaf readers and fifteen average deaf readers recorded under four reading conditions: (1) passages that have a familiar topic and are free of difficult syntax (high familiarity/ simple syntax); (2) passages that do not have a familiar topic but are free of difficult syntax (low familiarity/ simple syntax); (3) passages that have a familiar topic and contain relative clauses and passive voice structures (high familiarity/complex syntax); and (4) passages that do not have a familiar topic and contain relative clauses and passive voice structures (low familiarity/complex syntax).

Subjects will present passages to themselves on the screen of a personal computer using the "moving window" paradigm (Just, Carpenter, and Woolley 1982). During episodes of reading, the time-keeping mechanism of the computer will keep track of how long each word of text is kept in view. (Reading time has become an accepted index of processing difficulty and investment of cognitive resources.) The computer system will allow subjects to regress in the passage in order to reread earlier segments, and all instances of looking back will be recorded.

Word reading times will be analyzed using multiple linear regression, with particular attention to the contributions made to explained variance by two inter-action terms: skill level by passage familiarity and skill level by syntactic complexity. In conceptual terms, if topic familiarity is a significant contributor to the processing differences between skilled and average deaf readers, then reading time differences ought to shrink when the skilled readers are prevented from applying their world knowledge in the low familiarity passages. If superior syntactic knowledge is an important subprocess, then skilled/average differences observed in the simple syntax passages ought to widen when the complex syntax passages are read. The skilled readers will be able to apply their superior syntactic knowledge in order to sustain skillful processing in spite of being challenged by more complex syntax.

As mentioned, the expected findings of this investigation will have implications for instruction. First, the documented importance of world knowledge would underscore the importance of content learning, especially in social studies, history, and literature, and it would discourage the teaching of reading skills in isolation from content. Parents would be prompted to find ways to compensate for their children's isolation from incidental learning. Second, teachers would be encouraged to foster strategies for activating their students' knowledge of relevant background before they begin reading. Third, as Walker (1987) suggested, the documented facilitation effect of topic familiarity during reading would induce teachers occasionally to base instruction on books about familiar topics, so that students could recognize and practice their ability to apply cognitive skills that had not been tapped when they read about less familiar topics. Finally, a finding that familiarity with the topic is an important difference between superior and average deaf readers would suggest that current tests of reading may underestimate the cognitive functioning of many deaf students.

There also will be important implications related to syntax. A finding that skilled readers process these structures methodically, combined with a finding of relatively inattentive processing of syntactic structures by average deaf readers, would encourage development of enlightened methods of drawing these conventions to the attention of average readers. A finding that certain syntax tends to draw the attention of skilled readers only when they are reading unfamiliar material would alert teachers to another possible need for instructional intervention. They might either provide instruction that would promote greater fluency in processing these structures or teach strategies for activating relevant background knowledge, stimulating the potential facilitation of such knowledge during reading. At minimum, superior students could be warned of the additional draw on attention during more difficult reading, perhaps of technical college textbooks. A finding that difficult structures draw inordinate amounts of attention by average readers compared to superior readers would indicate the need for the development of instruction that promotes both greater automaticity and improved accuracy of processing. Finally, if processing of syntax is not an important component of skilled/average differences, teachers would be advised to focus less attention on syntactic instructional goals.

SUMMARY AND CONCLUSION

Readers and writers process several different kinds of information while they construct meaning from another writer's text or while composing their own. The information is available as visible characteristics within the text itself and as competence present in the mind of the literate reader or writer. For readers, textual constraints constitute clues that can guide construction of a meaning that closely approximates the intentions of the text's author. During composition, the constraints are more akin to tools at the disposal of the writer. They can facilitate composition of a text that evokes specific thought processes in the mind of the expected audience. However, unskilled writers may see these constraints, especially those related to correctness of form, as obligations rather than as assets.

The multiple constraints are processed within working memory, where capacity is limited and contents are fleeting. Because of this twofold limitation, it is highly desirable that certain textual constraints be processed with relative automaticity. These constraints ought to be processed without intruding on working memory for an extended period, thus avoiding encroachment on necessary processing of other textual constraints.

Competition for working memory is only one of the relationships that textual constraints can have with one another. Certain constraints can facilitate the processing of others, or they can compensate for deficient processing of other constraints. The primary underpinnings of the cognitive view of literacy form the basis for the orientation that will continue to guide much of the literacy research in the Center for Studies in Education and Human Development.

The cognitive view of literacy encourages research that, in essence, puts the mind on display while it is engaged in text processing. True enough, controlled experiments guided by this orientation do not re-create the conditions of natural reading and writing; that is not their intent. Rather, through repeated attempts to isolate the contributions of individual textual constraints, we will begin to identify the psychological and textual dimensions that seem to distinguish skilled deaf readers and writers.

The cognitive view is an aggressive research perspective propelled by the search for clarity. An aggressive approach is precisely what is called for in our field because deficient literacy has long been a source of vexation among deaf people, their parents, and their teachers. The cognitive view of literacy has the potential to better illuminate reading and writing processes, enlighten our methods of helping deaf people become more literate, and reduce the sense of failure associated with their attempts to read and write English.

REFERENCES

Allen, T. 1986. Patterns of academic achievement among hearing impaired students: 1974 and 1983. In *Deaf children in America,* ed. A. Schildroth and M. Karchmer, 161–206. San Diego: College-Hill Press.

Bartlett, E. 1982. Learning to revise: Some component processes. In *What writers know: The language, process, and structure of written discourse,* ed. M. Nystrand, 345–364. New York: Academic Press.

Belmont, J. M., and M. A. Karchmer. 1978. Deaf people's memory: There are problems testing special populations. In *Practical aspects of memory,* ed. M. M. Gruneberg, P. E. Morris, and R. N. Sykes, 581–588. London: Academic Press.

Bereiter, C. 1980. Development in writing. In *Cognitive processes in writing,* ed. L. Gregg and E. Steinberg, 73–96. Hillsdale, NJ: Lawrence Erlbaum and Associates.

Brumfit, C., and K. Johnson, eds. 1979. *The communicative approach to language teaching.* London: Oxford University Press.

Burling, R. 1982. *Sounding right: An introduction to comprehension-based language instruction.* Rowley, MA: Newbury House.

Carpenter, P. A., and M. A. Just. 1981. Cognitive processes in reading: Models based on readers' eye fixations. In *Interactive processes in reading,* eds. A. M. Lesgold and C. A. Perfetti, 177–213. Hillsdale, NJ: Lawrence Erlbaum and Associates.

Carroll, J. 1986. Second language. In *Cognition and instruction,* ed. R. Dillon and R. Sternberg, 83–126. New York: Academic Press.

Center for Curriculum Development, Training, and Outreach, Pre-College Programs, Gallaudet University. 1988. *Final report Model Secondary School for the Deaf annual profile.* Washington, DC: Gallaudet University.

Charrow, V. 1974. Deaf English—An investigation of the written English competence of deaf adolescents. Ph.D. diss., Stanford University.

Conrad, R. 1979. *The deaf school child.* London: Harper and Row.

Crandall, K. 1978. Reading and writing skills and the deaf adolescent. *Volta Review* 80: 319–332.

———. 1980. *Written language scoring procedures for grammatical correctness according to reader intelligibility.* Rochester, NY: National Technical Institute for the Deaf.

Eachus, T. 1971. Modification of sentence writing by deaf children. *American Annals of the Deaf* 116: 29–43.

Ellis, H. C., and R. R. Hunt. 1983. *Fundamentals of human memory and cognition.* Dubuque, IA: William C. Brown Company.

Flower, L., and J. Hayes. 1980. The dynamics of composing: Making plans and juggling constraints. In *Cognitive processes in writing,* ed. L. Gregg and E. Steinberg, 31–50. Hillsdale, NJ: Lawrence Erlbaum and Associates.

Garner, R. 1988. *Metacognition and reading comprehension.* Norwood, NJ: Ablex Publishing Company.

Goldberg, J. P., C. Ford, and A. Silverman. 1984. Deaf students in ESL composition classes: Challenges and strategies. *Teaching English to the Deaf and Second-Language Students* 2(2): 4–9.

Haberlandt, K. 1984. Components of sentence and word reading times. In *New methods in reading comprehension research,* ed. D. Kieras and M. Just, 219–252. Hillsdale, NJ: Lawrence Erlbaum and Associates.

Hanson, V. In press. Phonology and reading: Evidence from profoundly deaf readers. In *Solving the puzzle of reading disability,* ed. D. Shankweiler and I. Y. Liberman. International Academy of Research on Learning Disabilities Monograph Series. Ann Arbor: University of Michigan Press.

Hanson, V., and C. A. Fowler. 1987. Phonological coding in word reading: Evidence from hearing and deaf readers. *Memory and Cognition* 15: 199–207.

Hirsch, E. D. 1988. Cultural literacy: Let's get specific. *NEA Today* 6(6): 15–21.

Hull, G. 1987. The editing process in writing: A performance study of more skilled and less skilled college writers. *Research in the Teaching of English* 21(1): 8–29.

Hunt, K. 1965. *Grammatical structures written at three grade levels.* Research Report No. 3. Champaign, IL: National Council of Teachers of English.

Just, M. A., P. A. Carpenter, and J. D. Woolley. 1982. Paradigms and processes in reading comprehension. *Journal of Experimental Psychology: General* 111: 228–238.

Kelly, L. 1986. *The relative attention to English grammar during composition of deaf college students and unskilled college writers with normal hearing.* Ph.D. diss., The Catholic University of America, Washington, DC.

———. 1987. The influence of syntactic anomalies on the writing processes of a deaf college student. In *Writing in real time: Modeling production processes,* ed. A. Matsuhashi, 161–196. Norwood, NJ: Ablex Publishing Company.

———. 1988. Relative automaticity without mastery: The grammatical decision making of deaf students. *Written Communication* 5(3): 325–351.

———. 1989. The interference of meaning in error detection during editing. Paper presented at the Annual Meetings of the American Educational Research Association, San Francisco.

King, C., and S. Quigley. 1985. *Reading and deafness.* San Diego: College-Hill Press.

Krashen, S. D. 1978. Individual variation in use of the monitor. In *Second language acquisition research,* ed. W. C. Ritchie, 175–184. New York: Academic Press.

Lake, D. 1978. Syntax and sequential memory in hearing impaired children. In *Proceedings of the Gallaudet Conference on Reading in Relation to Deafness,* ed. H. Reynolds and C. Williams, 193–212. Washington, DC: Gallaudet University.

Langer, J., and A. Applebee. 1986. *Moving toward excellence: Writing and learning in the secondary school curriculum.* National Institute of Education Grant No. NIE-82-0027. Stanford, CA: Stanford University School of Education.

LaSasso, C., and B. Davey. 1987. The relationship between lexical knowledge and reading comprehension for prelingually profoundly hearing impaired students. *Volta Review* 89: 211–220.

Lenneberg, E. 1967. *Biological foundations of language.* New York: John Wiley and Sons.

Lichtenstein, E. H. 1983. *The relationships between reading processes and English skills of deaf college students. Parts I and II.* Rochester, NY: National Technical Institute for the Deaf, Communication Program.

McNeil, J. D. 1984. *Reading comprehension: New directions for classroom practice.* Glenview, IL: Scott, Foresman.

Meath-Lang, B., F. Caccamise, and J. Albertini. 1982. Deaf persons' views on English language learning: Educational and sociolinguistic implications. In *Interpersonal communication and deaf people,* ed. H. Hoemann and R. B. Wilbur. Washington, DC: Gallaudet University.

Miller, G. 1956. The magical number seven, plus or minus two: Some limits on our capacity for processing information. *Psychological Review* 63: 81–97.

Moores, D., T. Kluwin, C. Ewoldt, R. Johnson, P. Cox, L. Blennerhassett, L. Kelly, C. Sweet, and L. Fields. 1987. *Factors predictive of literacy in deaf adolescents.* Project No. NIH-NINCDS-83-19, Contract No. NO1, NS-4-2365. Washington, DC: Gallaudet University.

Newell, G. 1984. Learning from writing in two content areas: A case study/protocol analysis. *Research in the Teaching of English* 18(3): 265–288.

Norman, D. 1976. *Memory and attention: An introduction to human information processing.* New York: John Wiley and Sons.

O'Connor, N., and B. Hermelin. 1973. Short-term memory for the order of pictures and syllables by deaf and hearing children. *Neuropsychologia* II: 437–442.

Palincsar, A. S., and A. Brown. 1984. The reciprocal teaching of comprehension fostering and comprehension monitoring activities. *Cognition and Instruction* 1: 117–175.

Perl, S. 1979. The composing processes of unskilled college writers. *Research in the Teaching of English* 15(4): 317–336.

Quigley, S. P., D. J. Power, and M. W. Steinkamp. 1977. The language structure of deaf children. *Volta Review* 79: 73–83.

Quigley, S. P., R. Wilbur, D. Power, D. Montanelli, and M. W. Steinkamp. 1976. *Syntactic structure in the language of deaf children.* Urbana, IL: University of Illinois, Institute for Child Behavior and Development.

Rodda, M., and C. Grove. 1987. *Language, cognition, and deafness.* Hillsdale, NJ: Lawrence Erlbaum and Associates.

Scardamalia, M. 1981. How children cope with the cognitive demands of writing. In *Writing: The nature, development, and teaching of written communication,* ed. C. Frederiksen and J. Dominic, 81–103. Hillsdale, NJ: Lawrence Erlbaum and Associates.

Shanklin, N. 1982. *Relating reading and writing: Developing a transactional theory of the writing process.* Bloomington, IN: Indiana University School of Education.

Smith, F. 1978. *Understanding reading: A psycholinguistic analysis of reading and learning to read.* New York: Holt, Rinehart, and Winston.

————. 1984. Reading like a writer. In *Composing and comprehending,* ed. J. Jensen. Urbana, IL: ERIC and NCRE.

Spilich, G., G. Vesonder, H. Chiesi, and J. Voss. 1979. Text processing of domain related information for individuals with high and low domain knowledge. *Journal of Verbal Learning and Verbal Behavior* 18: 275–290.

Stanovich, K. 1980. Toward an interactive-compensatory model of individual differences in the development of reading fluency. *Reading Research Quarterly* 16: 32–71.

Stein, N., ed. 1984. The development of literacy in the American schools [special issue]. *American Journal of Education* 93(1).

Walker, C. 1987. Relative importance of domain knowledge and overall aptitude on acquisition of domain-related information. *Cognition and Instruction* 4(1): 25–42.

Wilbur, R. B. 1977. An explanation of deaf children's difficulty with certain syntactic structures. *Volta Review* 79: 85–92.

Zamel, V. 1983. The composing process of advanced ESL students: Six case histories. *TESOL Quarterly* 17: 165–187.

9

Home and Classroom Communication

SUSAN M. MATHER

In developing its program of research in communication, the research team of the Center for Studies in Education and Human Development (CSEHD) operates within the framework of several principles and assumptions. First, it is anticipated that deaf professionals will play increasingly important roles at all levels and that the field will incorporate deaf professionals into areas where they have been underrepresented or excluded. This includes early education programs and educational administration positions, especially in the public schools. CSEHD members are aware that deaf individuals are greatly underrepresented in teacher training programs, thus depriving prospective teachers of the views of those with direct experience in schools and programs for deaf children. There is also a lack of deaf researchers working in the areas of education and communication.

Deaf and hearing teachers have much to learn from each other. Because of the lack of research on the effectiveness of both deaf and hearing teachers, some of CSEHD's first work in communication research has focused on what might be teachers' special skills. Most people would accept the statement that deaf teachers tend to have better signing skills. For example, Kluwin (1981) reported that hearing teachers required a period of years to acquire the same level of signing skills exhibited by deaf teachers. The research team's interest is developing along a somewhat more general dimension (i.e., the use of the visual-motor channel in communication). Because of their experience, deaf teachers are likely to use more elements of the visual and motor systems to monitor and direct classroom activities. This possibility is the basis for a preliminary study on eye-gaze, which is reported later in this chapter.

Some of the material in this chapter is from S. Mather, Visually Oriented Teaching Strategies with Deaf Preschool Children, in *Sociolinguistics and the Deaf Community,* ed. C. Lucas (New York: Academic Press, 1989), 165–187. Copyright © 1989 by Academic Press, Inc. Reprinted by permission of the publisher. The author also wishes to thank Dr. Patricia Spencer for permission to use data videotaped for a research project of the Center for Studies in Education and Human Development.

COMMUNICATIVE COMPETENCE

The CSEHD research team began with the belief that if one group of teachers evidences a particularly effective behavior, it can be taught to all teachers. However, the field is operating under a set of constraints that can limit the access of qualified deaf students to appropriate educational positions. The difficulty is best illustrated by Serwatka, Anthony, and Simon (1986), who reported on comparative effectiveness among deaf and hearing teachers. The authors found that there was no difference on an observational instrument, although deaf students rated deaf teachers higher. However, Serwatka et al. reported that while the overall failure rate for persons taking the Florida state teachers exams was 22 percent, over 57 percent of deaf persons who took the test failed it. The authors argue that

> If these paper/pencil tests are found to be accurate predictors of teaching effectiveness, this difference in failure rate may be acceptable. However, if as some researchers have hypothesized, performance on these tests is not significantly related to effective teaching practice, this difference in failure rate is unacceptable and possibly indicative of discriminatory testing. (p. 339)

The same criticisms of teacher competency tests have been made in regard to members of racial and ethnic minorities. In the case of education of the deaf, rigid adherence to a paper and pencil test unfairly based on a frozen English model could severely limit the exposure of deaf students to deaf teachers. The very limited results obtained to date suggest that (1) deaf and hearing teachers both can be effective teachers of the deaf; and (2) the failure rate for deaf teachers may be higher on paper and pencil teacher competency tests than that of hearing teachers. The explanation for these contradicting facts is that performance on such tests probably is not related to effective teaching performance in deaf teachers.

More attention should be focused on the development of standards or evaluations to determine teachers' competence in the kinds of communication necessary for the effective teaching of deaf students. Specifically, studies are needed to determine what an appropriate level of competence should be and what components should constitute it.

The projected program of research will be much more concerned with process than with product. In this applied functional program of research, the emphasis will be on the teachers' and the pupils' communicative behaviors. This work will concentrate on communication instead of language or English in order to emphasize the need for competence in communicating information. One problem in deaf education is that educators and administrators tend to emphasize learning English or language in the classroom without ever considering the importance of acquiring communicative competence. The concept of learning a language in a classroom and that of developing one's communicative competence in a classroom are overlapping but distinct. It is not sufficient to be linguistically competent in order to be an effective communicator. Hymes (1964) observed that speakers who could utter any and all of the grammatical sentences of a language would be fossilized if they did not know the social or cultural rules for the use of that language. Communicative competence relates to the social and cultural comprehension that proficient communicators use to express and interpret linguistic forms. Such competence represents a confluence of syntactic, semantic, and situational features.

Communicative competence also deals with both knowledge and expectation of who may or may not speak in certain settings, when to speak and when not to speak, to whom one may speak, how one may talk to persons of different status, how one may talk in different social roles, appropriate nonverbal behaviors in various contexts, the routines for turn-taking in conversations, how to ask for information, and how to give information; in short, everything involving the use of language and other communication in social settings (Trudgill 1985).

In order to be an effective teacher, one needs to be competent not only in a particular language but also in communication. For example, Mather (1987) found that a failure to use appropriate eye gaze may produce conflicts in turn-taking exchanges with deaf children.

Social situations produce differential language uses or registers (Ferguson 1983). A person may use one register in an informal setting and a different one in a formal setting (Trudgill 1985; Lakoff 1975; Kochman 1981). American Sign Language (ASL), like other languages, has different registers for various social situations, for example, a scientific lecture (Roy 1989); audience presentations (Zimmer 1989); mother-baby talk (Erting, Prezioso, and O'Grady 1987); Deaf Black Signing (Woodward 1976; Hairston and Smith 1983); and formal and informal social situations (Stokoe 1969).

For those children who have not had an opportunity to develop their communicative competence before entering school, one of the challenges is to use appropriate registers in and out of the classroom. Two strategies in developing communicative competence that are employed frequently by native signing teachers are *evocative* and *visually oriented* teaching strategies.

Communicative Competence in Home and Classroom

Day (1982) reported that hearing mothers tend to employ yes-no questions but not Wh-questions (who, what, where, when, why) with their deaf children. Mather (1989) found similar communicative patterns with nonnative signing teachers of deaf students. Those teachers did not use Wh-questions to encourage the students to think about important parts of the story but tended instead to use yes-no questions in classrooms. This occurred even in classrooms of students with communicative competence. Rodda and Grove (1987), in a similar vein, noted

> The teachers of deaf students tend to monopolize the classroom conversation. They prefer to exercise a directive control, rather than fostering natural interactive language development. (p. 233)

Rodda and Grove suggested that if teachers fostered communicative competence in deaf classrooms (e.g., using Wh-questions), deaf students would be able to progress further in academic achievement and in social-emotional development. That strategy would allow for active interaction between teachers and students.

The program of research under development will maintain a focus on communication and will be cautious in the use of the term *language*. This is due to the belief that educators of the deaf and other professionals too frequently have treated *language* and *English* as synonymous. References to the language problems of deaf children and even statements to the effect that deaf children don't have language have long been common within the field of deaf education. These statements, of course, refer to standard English and ignore the fact that deaf children might have access to a nonstandard English. Even more damaging, such statements ignore the legitimacy of American Sign Language. Therefore, the team plans to specify English or American Sign Language and to use the term *communication* in a more inclusive way.

Within this global framework, the issue of parent-child communication will be approached with a sensitivity for the needs of both parent and child. Parents do not have to be teachers, but certain ASL principles of visual-motor communication can be identified and taught to parents and hearing siblings to assist them in communicating with the deaf children. Areas ripe for investigation and application include the use of dimensional space, pronominalization, signs that show visual concepts, the use of classifiers, body shifting, paralinguistic/linguistic nonmanual cues, and eye gaze. Of course, research already has been conducted in these areas to varying degrees with ASL. From observations, fluent signers also incorporate principles of ASL into the invented manual codes on English, thus making such codes more efficient in the expression and reception of information.

EXPLORATORY STUDIES

For purposes of illustration, this chapter will discuss two exploratory studies that have been conducted as part of the process of developing a program of research. One deals with communicating via eye gaze with deaf toddlers, and the other discusses evocative and visually oriented teaching strategies with preschool deaf children.

Linguistic Features of Eye Gaze

The process of language development in all children, hearing and deaf, should include rich patterns of interaction between parents and children. In the case of hearing parent/hearing child families, the use of vision is important but is not a necessary component of spoken communication. A mother may and often does talk to her child when she is out of the child's range of vision. She may keep up a stream of conversation even from another room, secure in the knowledge that the child is hearing her voice. Hearing parents do this naturally because of their own years of experience as hearing persons. On the other hand, deaf parents must use the visual system to communicate effectively with their children. They do this naturally because of their own years of experience as deaf persons. However, a large majority of deaf children have hearing parents. These parents should be helped to use the visual environment more effectively. Achieving this goal, of course, is more easily said than done. The primary goal is to help parents develop new skills without losing their sense of delight, excitement, and spontaneity with their children.

Mother/Child Interaction

Harding (1983) reported that infants whose mothers were more responsive displayed higher levels of communicative development than infants whose mothers assumed a more directive role.

Wells and colleagues (Wells 1985; Barnes et al. 1983; Wells and Gutfreund in press) indicated that preschool children acquire language more rapidly when their mothers are more responsive, providing them with language contingent upon their existing interests and behaviors rather than language unrelated to themselves. Tomasello and Farrar (1986) reported that infants would be more likely to learn modeled vocabulary that was contingent on their spontaneously established focus of attention than if the adult directed the infant's attention to an object and provided the infant with vocabulary.

Day, Gutfreund, and Bodner-Johnson (1987) reported that deaf mothers tend to take an opportunity to present a topic to interact with the infant's interest when an infant averts gaze, whether to look at an object or without any definite new attention focus. Day et al. found these maternal reactions to be facilitative of infant language acquisition because their utterances often consist of semantics related to the infant's attention to a certain object. Thus deaf infants can benefit from their mother's communicative responses and linguistic input based upon the infant's attention focus.

Eye Gaze

Baker (1977) emphasized the importance of eye gaze as a regulator of turn-taking in everyday signed discourse. She noted that spoken discourse differs from signed conversation in that a deaf speaker cannot initiate signing until the specified addressee is looking at the would-be speaker. A person cannot sign something and be seen if the other person is not paying attention. Baker's ethnographic study showed that those who are not aware of or do not employ eye gaze rules find signed discourse to be awkward in that there is a lack of a smooth exchange, or confusion about turns to sign. This constraint makes eye gaze one of the most powerful regulators in sign communication because it determines when a speaker can sign.

Mather (1987) identified two major types of eye gaze used by a deaf native signing teacher to regulate classroom interaction. The first was an individual gaze (I-Gaze); it requires mutual eye gaze between speaker and an individual addressee. This gaze is held until the speaker finishes or gets a reply from the addressee. When a teacher signs to an individual student and asks, "What is your name?" the question is understood as I-Gaze (i.e., directed at an individual, not the class). If the teacher wants to speak to a particular student in a group, the teacher must use I-Gaze to signal everyone in the group that only one student is being addressed.

The second type of eye gaze observed, used with two or more addressees, was a group-indicating gaze (G-Gaze). Its purpose is to tell the group that the speaker is treating the group as a unit. G-Gaze is evenly directed to all members of the group and moves constantly across or around the group without pausing. It typically takes the form of a smooth arc-like gaze (i.e., the head smoothly turning from one side of the group to the other). Both types of gazes are customarily used by native signing teachers.

There are many variations of the I-Gaze and G-Gaze procedures in the classroom, depending on the age of the students, the size of the class, and the content being taught or discussed. For the parent/young child dyad, only the I-Gaze paradigm applies.

Gregory (1988a, 1988b) recorded that the deaf mother of the deaf child has little difficulty in gaining her child's attention and in establishing a joint focus of activity with him or her, just as hearing children of hearing parents. However, the hearing mother and the deaf child have great difficulties.

Erting, Prezioso, and O'Grady (1987) studied the interaction of deaf mothers with deaf infants less than six months old. They focused on the mothers' strategies for gaining and maintaining the infants' visual attention and the mothers' linguistic communication through sign language. They noted that these mothers were in physical contact with their deaf infants throughout much of their interaction, engaging in a variety of touching behaviors such as tapping, stroking, tickling, and moving the infant's limbs. Deaf mothers alter the type of movement, location on the infant's body, intensity and speed of movement, and rhythmic patterning of tactile behaviors as they seek to get and maintain the infant's attention. Finally, deaf mothers modify the sign language they use with their infants by producing signs that appear slower, formationally different, and grammatically less complex than they normally use during adult-directed discourse. The signing space is usually related to the infant's direction of gaze: If the infant is looking at the mother, she usually signs near her face rather than making use of fixed signing space available in adult-directed discourse; if the infant is looking away or at an object, the mother will sometimes sign near or on the object or reach into the infant's visual field to sign. As in babytalk varieties of spoken language, the content is often associated with the immediate context, the baby's behavior, and the mother's interpretation of the baby's feelings.

The observations of Erting, Prezioso, and O'Grady closely follow the findings of Maestas y Moores (1979, 1980a, 1980b) in her earlier pioneering studies of deaf parents and their hearing and deaf infants from birth to 18 months. In the first study, involving ten deaf parents, Maestas y Moores (1979, 1980b) found that all the deaf parents established communicative interaction by the first month of life, utilizing speech, manual communication, and touch. For very young children, physical contact was utilized along with eye contact in orienting the child's attention. With very young children, the mother would take the child's face in her hands and gently move it to face her while she was speaking and/or just prior to signing. With older children, this was accomplished by moving the face with one hand or with two fingers under the chin. With children over six months old, the mother would place her hands on the child's body or tap his or her shoulder to gain attention.

Maestas y Moores reported more than 40 variables in a typology of deaf parent child interaction. Because of proximity between parent and child, the signs tended to be smaller. When holding the infant or using one hand for child care activities, parents would use one-handed instead of two-handed signs. Parents would also sign on a child's body as well as using visual signing space.

In an intensive follow-up study, Maestas y Moores (1980a) investigated the communicative modes and pragmatic functions used by deaf mothers with hearing and deaf infants from the first through the sixth month of life. She found that through the complementary use of oral and manual communication systems, deaf mothers utilize the same pragmatic functions as hearing mothers in their communication with infants during the first six months. The only difference between deaf mothers and hearing mothers is that the former use manual as well as vocal forms of communication.

Kyle and Ackerman (1987) noted that, since eye gaze is a prerequisite for receiving communication, the patterns of interaction between deaf mothers and their children and hearing mothers and their children are different, in spite of the fact that the pragmatic functions are the same. Mather (1987, 1989) observed in her study of parent-child communication that a fluent signing deaf teacher employed one of the strategies identified by Maestas y Moores. Building on a student's gaze to a book, the teacher used "miniature" signs by signing smaller near the book, enabling the student to look at the pictures and see the teacher's signs at the same time.

Those findings indicate that eye gaze can serve several functions, such as to regulate turn taking; to invite individual and group response; to initiate discourse; to invite response from members in a group; to communicate with a particular person; to ask a question directly; and to gain or maintain the infant's visual attention. In Mather's current study, eye gaze can also serve to use signs in space depending on the toddler's eye gaze.

Based on the information presented above, Mather has begun explanations and observations on three types of activity that a teacher (or parent) may use with a deaf toddler. These are (1) child's eye-level gaze, (2) directional use of (normally) nondirectional verbs, and (3) miniature signs. The results reported herein are observational.

Toddler's Eye-Level Gaze (EL-Gaze)

Fluent signers appear to be able to take advantage of the interest of the toddler, as indicated by the toddler's eye gaze, and to modify their sign behavior to accommodate to the demands of a situation. Frequently, deaf communicators sign within a toddler's line of vision whether or not the toddler is paying attention. The signer may also change the orientation of the signs, depending on the circumstances. One example of this occurred when a toddler was looking at an object to his right. The teacher physically moved into the toddler's line of vision to comment. In another example, a toddler was putting a picture of a house on a poster. The deaf teacher, standing behind the student, reached around him and signed *That is house* directly in his line of vision with the picture.

A similar incident occurred when an eight-year-old boy employed toddler's eye-level gaze discourse to provide information to a toddler. The older boy shifted his body to the left side and signed *ship* at the toddler's eye level while the child was looking to the right at the ship, which was on the floor. The older boy did not attempt to get the child's attention but simply bent to the toddler's eye level. It was clear that the older boy knew the strategy of "filling in" without disrupting a toddler's activity.

Unfortunately, analysis of classroom videotapes indicated that the younger child's hearing classroom teacher did not employ the strategy in class. She did not use toddler's eye-level gaze at all throughout the class period, unlike the deaf teacher-aide and the older student. Thus the toddler missed nearly all the output from the hearing teacher. She used her voice continually when she signed either because she was not aware of the importance of using toddler's eye-level gaze in discourse, or because she assumed the toddler heard her since she used voice continually when signing.

In a related study, Day (1987) found that a hearing mother tended to try to force her infant child to pay attention by moving the child's chin or face to her so the mother could direct her I-Gaze at the infant. Mather found a similar strategy with a hearing teacher who forced the toddler to look directly (I-Gaze) at the teacher by turning his body to face her. The toddler resisted by pulling away. This behavior, which is different from that used by deaf mothers to direct the attention of children under six months, seems to be recurrent among hearing mothers and teachers.

To sum up the finding, one does not need to direct I-Gaze at the toddler as long as the signer signs along the direction of child's gaze without disrupting his or her activity. It is appropriate to sign without disruption in this manner any time the signer wants to supply more information while the toddler is maintaining his or her interest.

Directional Use of (Normally) Nondirectional Verbs

ASL has a number of directional verbs that can be modulated for a variety of purposes; that is, their form can be changed in specific ways to show different meanings (Klima and Bellugi 1980; Baker and Cokely 1986). For instance, some modulated verbs can indicate subject or object in sentences. These directional verbs use the space around the signer's body to express grammatical relationships, usually by varying the verb's direction of movement, palm orientation, and/or location. Many verbs in ASL can use these spatial locations for pronominalization (i.e., to indicate first, second, or third person).

During extensive observations, Mather has found that the directional use of (normally) nondirectional verbs is a striking aspect of adult-toddler communication because it highlights a type of communication that does not exist between adults. It should be noted that these nondirectional verbs are part of ASL registers (adult-toddler discourse). Two cases are discussed below.

A teacher repeatedly signed *Please sit down* to a toddler, who just stood facing her and made no response. The nonnative signing teacher used correct signs in a fixed space with proper I-Gaze, all without effect. The native signing teacher-aide walked over and signed, *please* (in citation location), then moved her hands nearby to where the toddler's chair was located and signed *sit down*. The sign was made with larger movements, and the handshapes were held through movement to the chair. The child obviously comprehended and quickly walked and sat down on the chair. The connection of the chair to the sign SIT DOWN added needed information.

Upon learning of this incident, a hearing parent of a deaf toddler reported that the toddler did not respond to the mother's repeated admonition not to touch a TV set. The mother concluded that she should have made her signs with the set.

A teacher was taped employing a similar strategy to initiate a class activity. She waited with arms down (away from signing position) (Mather 1987) and at the same time fixed her gaze (I-Gaze) continually at a child to signal that she wanted his attention. After the toddler established eye contact, the teacher signed *Please* in a fixed location, then moved her hand toward a ball and signed *get* in a bigger sign, and finally moved her hands back into a fixed space and signed *ball*. As she moved her hand toward the ball, she gazed briefly at the ball and then back to the child to monitor his response.

These directional uses of (normally) nondirectional verbs such as *sit, touch* or *get* do not occur with adults. It is possible that they represent a development process with children who may need more sensorimotor and linguistic input and who may benefit from reference to an object in the environment.

The signer uses I-Gaze to signal that he or she wants to talk to a toddler. Often the signer will use a nondirectional verb and sign in proximity to the object. It is not necessary to sign exactly on the object, at least for preschool age children. It is quite possible that for children three years old and younger, direct signing on an object would be more common. In the examples just cited, both the ball and the chair were somewhat at a distance. The signer had to make sure that the child was gazing at the spot where the object was and then sign within the child's visual field. If that fails, the signer may move closer to the object and repeat the phrase to the child.

Miniature Signs

Mather (1987, 1989), Day et al. (1987), and Maestas y Moores (1979, 1980a, 1980b) have reported that deaf teachers and deaf mothers often employ special linguistic techniques to make signed messages within a student's or infant's visual space, so that the object and the signs can be seen simultaneously by the child.

An example of this process is provided by a sequence of events that occurred between a teacher and a toddler. The teacher first showed several pictures of objects to a child and asked him to identify them. He was able to identify them all until she introduced a picture of a horse. When he did not respond, she used her right hand and signed *horse* while her left hand held the picture near her face. Enabling the student to connect the sign and the picture, she then signed and said, "I pet this horse." When she signed *pet,* she actually put her hand on the picture and repeated the movement of petting. She repeated the petting several times on the picture with her direct gaze on the picture. She then proceeded to several more pictures, which the student identified correctly. When shown a picture of a faucet with running water, the student signed *car* repeatedly. The teacher bent to his eye-level gaze, pointed to the picture and signed *You know?* The child said something that was not clear on the videotaping. The teacher replied and signed *you turn on water.* Again she pointed to the picture of running water (not to the faucet) and used the inflectional signing of running right on the picture, as if the water were running. She then directed her gaze from the picture back to him and said, "You like to play with water. Also you like to drink water," and pointed to the picture of running water again. She repeated the statement about running water and then pantomimed turning water on in the picture. She gazed back at him and reinforced the form and meaning *turn on* before proceeding to the next picture. Both activities enabled the student to make a connection between form and language.

The use of miniature signs occurred at the next step. After the teacher told the student that they were going to see pictures of flowers, she pointed to a picture and handed it to him. Then she turned her gaze toward a wall, where there were three pictures of different objects. She signed *where* on the picture. She used a miniature sign with a very small movement, turned his gaze away from her, and she employed his eye-level gaze by moving her hands and signing, *Where does it match?* with very small movements. He turned his gaze halfway to her, and the teacher repeated the question. He put the picture on one of the three pictures on the wall. The teacher waited until he looked back to her before she looked back to his picture match and she signed *no* twice on the picture, not to the student directly. He stood there and looked at her. She repeated the phrase, *No, not that* directly to the picture. She took the picture off the wall, pointed to another picture, and signed *No* directly to the picture. She went on to the next picture and waited for him to reply. Then she signed *no.* Again she moved on to the third picture on the wall. She repeated it twice to show that those two pictures were the same. One would normally sign SAME horizontally, but in this case the teacher made the sign vertically to convey the intended meaning of sameness between the pictures of flowers on the wall and another on the floor. When the student then signed *flower,* the teacher confirmed his statement by signing *flower* and nodding her head.

It should be noted that the teacher did not sign *no* directly to the child, but to the picture. Apparently, she acted so as not to penalize the student for a wrong answer. In effect, the teacher encouraged the student to take risks in much the same way that Mather (1989) reported in a related study.

When introducing a new concept, the signer does not have to direct I-Gaze at the student, but may directly gaze at an object and make miniature signs so that the student can see both the object and the sign simultaneously.

Background

Mather (1987, 1989) conducted two ethnographic studies involving two teachers with different backgrounds in sign language. In these studies, the teachers reviewed the story "Three Little Kittens" with two classes of deaf preschool students. One teacher had learned Signing Exact English as an adult and taught a class of deaf preschool children of deaf parents; the other teacher acquired ASL as a native language and taught deaf children of hearing parents who had just learned sign language.

During the story review, the teachers did not read the story but rather asked the students about it. This study focuses on the two major strategies that the native signing teacher used: evocative and visually oriented teaching strategies. The evocative strategy relates to a certain pattern of behaviors that the teacher used in prompting a discussion with the students. Visually oriented strategies involve the use of special linguistic devices of ASL as teaching tools.

Evocative Strategies

To encourage the students to engage in a discussion or to answer a question, the native signing teacher used at least three strategies: using Wh-questions, eliciting answers, and responding to students' answers. The teacher's selection of one strategy or a combination of two or more strategies depended on the level of each student's class participation, either highly active (high) or relatively inactive (low) (Gearing and Epstein 1982); and the type of answer the student gave.

Using Wh-Questions
Mather was concerned with two different kinds of question forms: yes-no questions and Wh-questions. These types of questions have an impact on the degree of interaction among students and teachers.

Many teachers are trained to use questions to confirm what students have learned in the classroom (Heath 1983). The question-answer format is the most prevalent method of turn-taking in American classrooms. The goal of this communication is to be correct as often as possible and incorrect as infrequently as possible. Heath (1983) and Shuy (1979) argue that inherent in this form of communication is the assumption that incorrect answers are the fault of the child. For example, if a teacher raises a question and the child does not answer correctly, it is often assumed that the problem is the child's.

Wood et al. (1986), Dillon (1982), and Rodda and Grove (1987) suggested that Wh-questions are important in extending students' understanding, encouraging them to reflect, and helping them to reanalyze their thinking. In other words, teachers should make every effort to facilitate the development of their students' communicative competence by using two-way communication.

In those activities where the interaction between the teacher and the children is limited, the teacher selects a student as next speaker, but when the student finishes a turn, the turn to speak automatically returns to the teacher. Mehan (1979) pointed out that the turn-taking mechanism for classroom discourse is almost exclusively of the "current speaker selects next speaker" type (i.e., control always reverts to the teacher). The interaction between the teacher and the students appeared to be more active when the teacher used Wh-questions. The turn-taking strategy for classroom discourse is different from that in everyday conversation in which one speaker begins and the next speaker "takes the floor" at the end of a turn.

At the beginning of the review of the story, the teacher with native signing skills asked what the title of the book was. There was no response. Then the teacher rephrased the question and signed *What is the book about?* The children responded, "Cats." The teacher nodded. She asked, "How many cats?" When there was no response, she quickly repeated the question with an additional clue by quickly signing *1, 2, 3, or 4?* She then had the students participate actively in counting the cats in the book. Two students counted while the teacher nodded. Then the teacher took the hands of another student to help her count the cats. She then repeated herself, counting three cats in order to reinforce the question, and signed and said loudly, *These are three little kittens.*

In contrast, the questions used by the teacher who was a nonnative signer are a mixture of Wh- and yes–no questions. The nonnative signer used questions to confirm that students had learned something. The first three questions were *What is the title?*; (to a particular student) *Do you know the title?*; and (to the same student) *Do you remember the title?* When there were no responses from the students, the teacher eventually gave the answer herself.

Another contrast between the native and the nonnative signers' types of questions revolved around a picture showing the mother cat frowning and turning a timer. The native signer asked, "What did Mom say?" The nonnative signer asked, "Do you think Mom was crabby?" The native signer's question was the type that required information. It required the students to participate and think actively in a discussion either with other students in the group or with the teacher. The nonnative signer's question required only a yes or no answer, although the question itself was high level.

Unlike the native signer, the nonnative signer used different types of questions, similar to the ones described by Heath (1983) in the Roadville case. The nonnative signer asked questions that required specific information, such as "What is the title?" Throughout the review of the story, the native signer asked Wh-questions, such as "What happens?" "What kind of pie does Mother make?" or "Where is one more kitten?" The students were very active in discussing or discovering what kind of pie the mother cat made, in trying to find where one more cat was, and in counting the numbers of cats.

Eliciting Answers

When the native signing teacher found that using Wh-questions did not evoke an answer from the students, the teacher would then make further efforts to elicit an answer. In the course of reviewing the story, the native signer prepared the students to adapt when they were expected to meet the needs of the situation. She said what they should say and directed them to participate by encouraging them to talk with her. Before the native signer asked any particular student a question, she always asked the class the question. Often the more fluent students volunteered to answer her questions. After those students answered, she asked other students questions with additional clues, such as pointing to the picture. If there was no response or if the students gave an incorrect answer, instead of providing an answer, she helped the students adapt to the situation by giving even more clues, pointing more to the picture or playing a role to help the students grasp the idea of what the kittens in the story did. In contrast, the nonnative signer did not attempt to have the students adapt to the situation by indicating what she expected them to say or by directing them toward what they should say. Instead, after one or more questions with slight modification or rephrasing, she provided the answer herself.

This difference in teaching strategies appears to have an impact on the process of eliciting answers. Throughout the initial portion of the review session, the native signer asked forty-one questions, and all of them were answered by the students themselves. In contrast, the nonnative signer asked only nine questions, and only two were answered by the students. It showed that the native-signing teacher and the students were engaged in a rich communicative environment.

The different ways in which the two teachers discussed the story's opening illustrate the contrast in strategies between them. The native signer opened the book. The picture on the opening page showed the kittens' footprints, a bike on the floor, and a ball on the bench. The teacher orally exclaimed "Ah" with a surprised look. She looked at all the students and signed and asked, *What happened?* Sasha (high) responded *Bike.* The teacher signed *Yes, you remember* to the student and then looked back at the class. She showed the book around and then put it on her lap. She rephrased her question and asked whether the house was clean or dirty. She repeated the question, *Is the house clean or dirty?* Kevin responded by putting his hands on the floor, in pantomime, as if he were a cat walking all over the floor. The teacher nodded and responded, *Yes, there are dirty footprints all over the floor.* Then she asked Barb the same question, *What happened?*, and pointed to the picture of the dirty footprints. The student responded, *Dirty footprints.* The teacher acknowledged her answer with *Yes, there are dirty footprints all over the floor.* The teacher then asked the same student (Barb) another question, *Whose footprints?* There was no response. Then she rephrased the question by saying *Barb's footprints?* Barb responded, but her signs were unclear on the videotape. The teacher answered her, *No, whose footprints?,* but there was no response.

The teacher next shifted her gaze to Ted and asked the question *Whose footprints?* He responded *Ball.* The teacher nodded and responded, *See the ball.* She then pointed to the picture of footprints and signed, *The cats went out to play. Later they were ready to come in the house again.* Then the teacher got up and repeated the first statement, *The cats went out to play.* She started to play the role of a cat and signed *Play outside and then entered the house.* Portraying a cat again, she used her legs and hands to bend forward with her hands on the floor. Using the nonverbal gesture of *knowing nothing,* she acted as if she walked without knowing that her paws were dirty. She then signed that the floor became dirty all over. She then sat down, looked at everyone, and smiled. The students responded, *Dirty floor.* The teacher nodded.

In contrast, the nonnative signer requested an answer from a particular student to a question about the title of the story. When asked, the student did not have a chance to answer the question because the teacher switched her gaze to the student on her right side and repeated the last part of the question, *Title of?* Another student sitting in the middle replied *Cats* several times, but the teacher did not see him. Then the teacher asked if someone could help the first student and repeated the question, *What is the title?* Shortly thereafter, she gave the answer herself. Unlike the native signer, the nonnative signer did not use any special methods to elicit answers from the group, such as giving a clue or playing a role, as the native signer did. She simply repeated questions a few times with little modification, such as *What is the title of this story?, Do you remember the title?,* or *You forgot.*

Responding to Students' Answers

How a teacher responds to a student's answer plays a critical role in keeping the student's participation active. In responding to answers, the native signer encouraged the students to take risks. When a student gave a wrong answer, the teacher did not penalize the student. Instead, she focused both on the answer and on the intended meaning. In the earlier example, when the teacher asked "Whose footprints?", the student responded "Ball." Instead of penalizing the student for the incorrect answer, the signer nodded and responded "See the ball." She then went back to the original topic and performed the role of a cat playing outside and then entering a house with dirty paws. Then the student answered "Dirty floor." The intent of the teacher was to acknowledge what the student said or to request clarification.

The following example shows that the native signer repeatedly responded by acknowledging the student's utterance and clarifying it. When one student played the role of a kitten, he used the biting-from-the-plate classifier predicate, which is not correct. Then the teacher imitated his classifier with a slight modification, producing the chewing-from-the-plate classifier predicate.

Later, another student corrected the teacher indirectly by using her mouth movement to indicate licking, not chewing. The teacher responded positively and said that the student was correct. Then the teacher used the licking-the-plate classifier predicate to show that the kittens were licking their plates. Then all the students excitedly imitated the teacher's actions.

Consistent patterns appear in the native signer's ways of responding to students' answers throughout the story review. The teacher usually responded positively to students' answers, whether they were correct, partially correct, or incorrect. For example, if a student's answers were incorrect, the teacher would say, "Yes, you remember" or "Yes, I see that." She would then restate the question or point to the picture in the book to give another hint for a correct answer. If the student gave a partially correct answer, the teacher would repeat the student's answer and clarify it with additional information. For instance, when asked what happened on the opening page, one student answered "Footprints." The teacher responded, "Yes, there are dirty footprints all over the floor." If the student answered correctly, the teacher would acknowledge the answer. Then she would either repeat the previous question to other students or move on to the next question or page.

The nonnative signer, on the other hand, did not create an environment that promotes risktaking on the part of the students. The teacher would respond negatively to answers when they were partially correct or incorrect; for example, "No, don't you remember?", "You forgot", or "Could someone else help?" She often responded to the students' answers by saying, "Oh, you think so." And if a student answered correctly, she sometimes failed to acknowledge the correct answer.

Visually Oriented Teaching Strategies

Communicative competence in deaf education needs to be weighed within the broad context of the relationship between cultural norms and classroom discourse. The teacher's and the students' rules in a classroom setting are operating on at least two sets of behavior rules and discourse rules. The teacher brings to the classroom his or her own socially conditioned ways of behaving and a value system that explicates the role of teacher and accepts, refuses, or tries to modify the behavior of the children. Students bring to the classroom socially conditioned ways of behaving, both paralinguistically and linguistically. They learn the language of their parents and of other significant persons in their surroundings. Communication problems can arise when a teacher uses a different linguistic repertoire than that of the children in the classroom (Matluck 1978; Heath 1983).

LaForge (1983, p. 3) suggested that language as social process is "different from language as communication." Thus education in the classroom is viewed as a cultural process (Richards and Rodgers 1986). Intrinsic to this view is the understanding that learning is a social act. The process is shared by the teacher and students who cooperatively accomplish their social interactions. Members of a culture share "a system of standards for perceiving, believing, evaluating, and acting" (Goodenough 1971, p. 41).

There is evidence that in classrooms either ASL users or minority students may correct the errors made by "nonnative" teachers (Chesterfield et al. 1983; Johnson and Erting 1989; and Mather 1989). Students as young as three years old often interrupt when the teacher breaches the grammatical rules of ASL, that is, incorrectly produces in sign the intended meaning of concepts or information in the story review. For instance, since ASL gives grammatical information via modulations (verb inflections) (Klima and Bellugi 1980), one would inflect the sign CLEANING by repeating it in a circular movement on the vertical plane to indicate the meaning *I-am-cleaning-the-room* (or the whole house). If one wants to use *clean* as an adjective, one will not inflect the sign CLEAN and will use the sign only once, as in *Now the mittens are clean*, using the sign only once to indicate that it is an adjective. Since the nonnative signing teacher was not aware of verb signs in ASL, she used the inflected verb *cleaning* and signed, "NOW THE KITTENS ARE *CLEANING-THE-WHOLE-HOUSE*" (repeating the sign CLEAN in the circular motion on the vertical plane). The three-year-old deaf students discussed among themselves what the teacher meant. Eventually one of the students asked her if she meant cleaning the house. The nonnative signing teacher was puzzled by the question. She replied, "No, the kittens are *cleaning incessantly*" (repeating her sign CLEAN with a short, tense, iterated movement). The students' attitudes toward the teacher are apparently affected adversely by the teacher's seeming lack of awareness of the importance and appropriateness of transmitting correct information.

The studies described above often refer to visually oriented teaching strategies where teachers, both native and nonnative, bring their own socially conditioned ways of behaving, and their value systems, into the classroom.

Unlike evocative strategies, visually oriented teaching strategies are used by teachers who transmit information by teaching, lecturing, telling a story, or describing an event to students who sit and listen. These teaching strategies involve linguistic methods, such as classifier predicates, role playing, miniature signs, adapting signs to the specific actions depicted in pictures, and changing English words that show sound-related concepts to signs that show visual concepts. The linguistic methods in those strategies have been found to be effective in two ways: first, patterns of language that create involvement by sweeping the students along in their rhythm, signs, and form; and second, those that create involvement by requiring audience participation in sense-making, such as indirectness, imagery, detail, and dialogue, with many of these intertwined in storytelling (Tannen 1988). Labov (1972), Chafe (1982), Ochs (1979), Tannen (1985), and Schiffrin (1981) have observed that narration is more graphic when speech is presented as first-person dialogue (usually called "direct quotation" or "direct speech") rather than third-person discourse ("indirect quotation" or "indirect speech").

Labov (1972) described two different evaluative devices for storytelling, known as internal evaluative and external evaluative.

The narrator uses the external evaluative device by stopping the narrative, turning to the listener, and telling what the point is. As an example, throughout the storytelling, the nonnative signing teacher usually informed the students how the mother cat felt by presenting her signing speech as third-person dialogue: . . . The mother cat put her hands on her hips and said that she is cross with her kittens for losing their mittens.

The native signing teacher would use an internal evaluative device by letting the narrative itself convey this information to the listener—to give the students the experience. She performed what the mother cat did rather than what it said, as if the dialogue took place between the mother cat and the kittens. This carried more dramatic and graphic force:

> The teacher put her hands on her hips and played a role of mother cat. She bent her body as if she actually looked down at the three kittens standing before her. She scolded them and used a direct quotation, "What, you-plural lost your mittens?!"

In using the internal evaluative device, the teacher did not step out of her narration and tell the students that the mother was angry. Her strategy helped get them involved in the dialogue.

ASL linguistic devices are often employed by teachers who are fluent in ASL. Many deaf teachers employ the devices as part of their visually oriented teaching strategies at all levels, from preschool deaf classrooms to college deaf classrooms.

The ASL linguistic devices used in the strategies include, as previously noted, using classifier predicates, role playing, miniature signs, adapting signs to the specific actions depicted in pictures, and changing English words that show sound-related concepts to signs that show visual concepts.

Using Classifier Predicates

Consciously or not, the teacher who is a native signer respected the importance and appropriateness of transmitting information in a way that conforms to the grammatical rules of ASL. Moreover, she adapted her signs to the specific actions depicted in the pictures rather than to the printed words that accompanied each picture. To adapt the signs, this teacher used classifier predicates, a feature of ASL structure.

In one picture, the mother cat used her rolling pin to scold the kittens. The standard sign for the word *naughty* entails the use of one index finger to scold, but the teacher did not use this sign. Instead, she used an instrumental classifier predicate in which her handshape signalled holding onto the rolling pin and scolding at the same time, to mean *naughty.* Since Signed English does not involve the use of classifier predicates, the nonnative signer correctly signed the form that means *naughty* in Signed English, but this sign does not exactly convey the intended message of the picture.

The native signer also used classifier predicates when she discussed the picture that showed one cat sliding down a rail. She used a RAIL classifier handshape to convey *slide,* together with her left hand serving as a rail. She also used the HOLDING GLOVES classifier predicate and said, "I found my mittens." Playing the role of the third cat riding the bicycle, she used a classifier predicate in which both hands portrayed the cat's speed in riding the bicycle, and said to the mother, "I found my mittens." Then she shifted to the role of the mother and said, "Oh, I am so happy that you found your mittens."

The nonnative signer did not use classifier predicates as often as the native signer because she learned Signed English, which does not have that feature. She did attempt to borrow some ASL classifier predicates, but she did not use them correctly or she failed to transmit several actions going on at the same time. As a result, the signed messages are in conflict with their intended meanings. Unlike the native signing teacher, the nonnative signing teacher did not describe exactly how the kittens informed the mother cat of the good news. The teacher signed:

> Three little kittens ran and slide down the rail (using the wrong classifier of person sliding down) "Mom, Mom, look. We are happy. We found mittens." They clapped their hands and cheered.

The intended meaning of this message was not consistent with that of the picture. Not all of the three kittens were seen to slide, or clap, or cheer.

What is striking about the native signer's use of classifier predicates is its positive impact on the students' responses. Despite their initially low communicative competence, the students are encouraged by the teacher's use of the classifiers to take risks in answering questions and developing language. One possible explanation is that classifiers involve the use of certain handshapes, locations, and movements that not only serve to convey the intended meanings clearly, but also to present them in an active sense as opposed to a passive sense. In any case, classifier predicates seem to be an effective strategy in promoting linguistic risk taking among the students.

Role Playing

Rather than limiting herself to the printed word, the native signer used role playing to expose the students to the actions portrayed in the pictures. For example, the teacher pretended to be the mother cat. To explain that the mother cat was mad, the teacher started by detaching her eye-gaze from the group and looking down, her head and body leaning forward as if three kittens were standing before her. In this manner, she shifted her role from that of a teacher to that of a mother cat. Imitating the picture exactly, she put her hand on her hip, pretended to scold with the rolling pin, and signed I AM ANGRY. She scolded each kitten once and, while looking down at the three little kittens, signed THREE LITTLE KIT- TENS, YOU (you-plural) LOST YOUR MITTENS AND SO YOU WON'T HAVE PIE. YOU (you-plural) GO AND LOOK FOR YOUR MITTENS. Then she put her hands on her hips and frowned. Returning to the role of teacher, she showed the picture to the students and pointed to the mother cat. She then re- peated the role of the mother cat. She asked if the mother cat was happy. NO, she signed (with both hands), SHE IS SAD. She showed the picture around again and signed THE MOTHER CAT IS MAD. The teacher deliberately scolded three times to reflect the number of kittens.

The native signer also used role playing when she shifted her role to that of the mother cat kissing the kittens. She leaned forward and pretended to kiss the kittens three times. By leaning back, she returned to the role of teacher and signed THREE BABY CATS. She then showed the picture around. One student (high) signed something that is unclear on the videotape. The teacher responded, "Yes, Mom hugged the three kittens. Mom said you can have some pie, but take the pie outside." She then showed the picture around again. In other portions of the story review, the teacher accurately used the mathematical concept of three when play- ing the role of the mother cat hugging or kissing the kittens three times. The same student corrected the teacher when she played the role of a mother cat kissing the three kittens separately, which conflicted with the picture portraying the mother cat hugging all the kittens at the same time.

Unlike the native signer, the nonnative signer violated the mathematical con- cept of three several times. Sometimes the students who were native ASL signers interrupted the teacher to correct signing that was not consistent with the mathe- matical concept. For instance, in playing the role of the mother cat, the nonnative signer kissed each of the five students directly, as if all of them were the three kittens. The three students whose native language is ASL discussed among them- selves the teacher's act of kissing each of them, and one student counted the five students. Another student whose native language is ASL then protested the num- ber of kisses, saying that it was three, not five. The nonnative signer, throughout the story review, often played the role of the mother cat in a way that was incon- sistent with the specific actions portrayed in the pictures.

Adapting Signs to the Specific Actions Depicted in Pictures

ASL has different signs for the word *crying* depending on the intended meaning. For *weeping,* the signer will use two fingers to indicate tears dripping down the cheeks. For *calling,* the signer will use the inflected verb *shouting,* repeating its sign in a small and intense circular movement.

Instead of signing the printed sentences, the native signing teacher often adapted her signing to reflect what was portrayed in the pictures. For example, under the picture of three kittens holding their mittens high and running toward the mother cat, the printed sentences read: "And they began to cry, 'Oh, mother dear, see here, see here.'" Instead of signing *they began to cry,* she signed, *Ah* (orally), THE CATS RUN TO THEIR MOM AND SAID, "WE FOUND OUR MITTENS." If the teacher had followed the strict principles of Signing Exact English, the story might have been misinterpreted.

Changing English Words for Sound-Related Concepts to Signs for Visual Concepts

The native signer chose signs that had relevance to the visual background experience of her deaf students. For example, there is no standard means in sign language (except fingerspelling) for recoding the English word *meow.* Instead of fingerspelling it, the native signer translated the word as *cry* (in the sense of *whimper*). Compared with the word *meow,* the sign CRY appears more consistent with the intended meaning of the picture. The native signer used signs that showed visual concepts. First, the teacher signed three times, THE CATS CRY. Later, she changed her choice of mouthing from "cry" to "meow" and signed (while meowing orally) THE CATS CRY, repeating the sign CRY three times.

Unlike the native signer, the nonnative signer signed the printed sentence THEY BEGAN TO CRY and then said "Meow" several times while not manually signing. This shows again that the nonnative signer literally followed the printed words in Signed English. Whether she was aware that her signing coded a meaning different from the intended one is not known.

CONCLUSION

The research team of the Center for Studies in Education and Human Development is in the preliminary stages of a program of research to foster the development of communicative competence in deaf children and their teachers and family members. The focus of the research represents something of a departure from the traditional concentration on objective outcome measures involving standardized tests of achievement. Rather, we are more process-oriented; that is, we are concerned with the dynamics of home and classroom interaction and with identifying procedures, registers, and strategies that can be used by all to increase the quality and quantity of home and classroom learning.

This chapter has provided information on exploratory studies of the effective use of eye-gaze by parents and teachers and of the use of questioning strategies in discussions of stories and use of special linguistic techniques of ASL. In both cases, the interaction dynamics were much more complex than was apparent on first examination. Over the next several years, the Center plans to establish an empirical base of research that can provide insights to improve the communication environment, both in the home and in the classroom, for deaf children.

REFERENCES

Baker, C. 1977. Regulators and turn-taking in American Sign Language. In *On the other hand*, ed. L. Friedman, 215–236. New York: Academic Press.

Baker, C., and D. Cokely. 1986. *A teacher's resource text on grammar and culture.* Silver Spring, MD: T. J. Publishers.

Barnes, M., M. Gutfreund, D. Satterly, and G. Wells. 1983. Characteristics of adult speech which predict children's language development. *Journal of Child Language* 10: 65–84.

Chafe, W. 1982. Integration and involvement in speaking, writing, and oral literature. In *Spoken and written language: Exploring orality and literacy*, ed. D. Tannen, 35–53. Norwood, NJ: Ablex Publishing Company.

Chesterfield, R., Barrows, K. Chesterfield, K. Hayes-Latimer, and R. Chavez. 1983. The influence of teachers and peers on second language acquisition in bilingual preschool programs. *TESOL Quarterly* 17(3): 401–420.

Day, P. 1982. The expression of communicative intention: Deaf children and hearing mothers. In *Interpersonal communication and deaf people*, ed. H. Hoemann and R. Wilbur. Washington, DC: Gallaudet University.

Day, P., M. Gutfreund, and B. Bodner-Johnson. 1987. Face to face interaction between hearing mothers and hearing-impaired infants. Paper presented at the Convention of the American Speech-Language-Hearing Association, New Orleans.

Dillon, J. T. 1982. The effect of questions in education and other enterprises. *Journal of Curriculum Studies* 14: 127–165.

Erting, C., C. Prezioso, and M. O'Grady. 1987. Mother signs in babytalk. Paper presented at the Fourth International Symposium on Sign Language Research, Lappeenranta, Finland.

Ferguson, C. 1983. Sports announcer talk: Syntactic aspects of register variation. *Language in Society* 12: 152–172.

Gearing, F., and P. Epstein. 1982. Learning to wait: An ethnographic probe into the operations of an item of hidden curriculum. In *Doing the ethnography of schooling*, ed. G. Spindler, 243–267. New York: Holt, Rinehart, and Winston.

Goodenough, W. 1971. *Culture, language, and society.* Reading, MA: Addison-Wesley.

Gregory, S. 1988a. Communication between deaf mothers and their deaf babies. Final report to the Nuffield Foundation, Cardiff, England.

———. 1988b. Parent-child communication: The implications of deafness. Paper presented at the Conference of the Developmental Section of the British Psychological Society, Cardiff, England.

Gregory, S., and S. Barlow. 1986. Interaction between deaf babies and their deaf mothers and hearing mothers. Paper presented at the Language Development and Sign Language Workshop, Bristol, England.

Harding, C. 1983. Setting the stage for language acquisition: Communication development in the first year. In *The transition from prelinguistic to linguistic communication*, ed. R. Golinkoff, 93–113. Hillsdale, NJ: Lawrence Erlbaum and Associates.

Hairston, E., and L. Smith. 1983. *Black and deaf: Are we that different?* Silver Spring, MD: T. J. Publishers.

Heath, S. 1983. *Ways with words.* New York: Cambridge University Press.

Hymes, D. 1964. *Language in culture and society.* New York: Harper and Row.

Johnson, R., and C. Erting. 1989. Ethnicity and socialization in a classroom for deaf children. In *The sociolinguistics of the deaf community*, ed. C. Lucas, 41–83. New York: Academic Press.

Klima, E., and U. Bellugi. 1980. *The signs of language*. Cambridge, MA: Harvard University Press.

Kluwin, T. 1981. The grammaticality of manual representations of English in classroom settings. *American Annals of the Deaf* 126: 417–421.

Kochman, T. 1981. *Black and white styles in conflict*. Chicago: University of Chicago Press.

Kyle, J., and J. Ackerman. 1987. *Signing for infants: Deaf mothers using BSL in the early stages of development*. Centre for Deaf Studies, School of Education Research Unit, Bristol, England.

Labov, W. 1972. The transformation of experience in narrative syntax. In *Language in the inner city*, ed. W. Labov, 354–396. Philadelphia: University of Pennsylvania Press.

LaForge, P. G. 1983. *Counseling and culture in second language acquisition*. Oxford, England: Pergamon Press.

Lakoff, R. 1975. *Language and woman's place*. New York: Harper Colophon Books.

Mather, S. 1987. Eye gaze and communication in a deaf classroom. *Sign Language Studies*, 54: 11–30.

———. 1989. Visually oriented teaching strategies with deaf preschool children. In *The sociolinguistics of the deaf community*, ed. C. Lucas, 165–187. New York: Academic Press.

Matluck, J. H. 1978. *Cultural norms and classroom discourse: Communication problems in the multiethnic school setting*. Austin: University of Texas.

Mehan, H. 1979. *Learning lessons*. Cambridge, MA: Harvard University Press.

Maestas y Moores, J. 1979. Language acquisitions: Mother-child interaction. Paper presented at NATO Advanced Institute on Sign Language and Cognition. Copenhagen, Denmark.

———. 1980a. A descriptive study of communication modes and pragmatic functions used by three prelinguistically profoundly deaf mothers with their infants one to six months of age in their homes. Ph.D. diss., University of Minnesota.

———. 1980b. Early linguistic environment. *Sign Language Studies* 26: 1–13.

Ochs, E. 1979. Planned and unplanned discourse. In *Discourse and syntax*, ed. T. Givon, 51–80. New York: Academic Press.

Richards, J., and T. Rodgers. 1986. *Approaches and methods in language teaching*. New York: Cambridge University Press.

Rodda, M., and C. Grove. 1987. *Language, cognition and deafness*. Hillsdale, NJ: Lawrence Erlbaum Associates.

Roy, C. 1989. Features of discourse in an American Sign Language lecture. In *The sociolinguistics of the deaf community*, ed. C. Lucas, 231–252. New York: Academic Press.

Schiffrin, D. 1981. Tense variation in narrative. *Language* 57(1): 45–62.

Serwatka, T., A. Anthony, and S. Simon. 1986. A comparison of deaf and hearing teacher effectiveness. *American Annals of the Deaf* 131: 339–343.

Shuy, R. 1979. The unexpected by-products of fieldwork in discourse. Washington, DC: Georgetown University and the Center for Applied Linguistics.

Stokoe, W. C. 1969. Sign language diglossia. *Studies in Linguistics* 21: 27–41.

Tannen, D. 1985. Relative focus on involvement in oral and written discourse. In *Literacy, language, and learning: The nature and consequences of reading and writing*, ed. D.

Olson, N. Torrance, and A. Hildyard, 124–147. New York: Cambridge University Press.

———. 1988. Hearing voices in conversion, fiction, and mixed genres. In *Linguistics in content: Connecting observation and understanding.* Norwood, NJ: Ablex Publishing Company.

Tomasello, M., and M. Farrar. 1986. Joint attention and early language. *Child Development* 57: 1454–1463.

Trudgill, P. 1985. *Sociolinguistics: An introduction to language and society.* Middlesex, England: Penguin Books.

Wells, G. 1985. *Language development in the preschool years.* New York: Cambridge University Press.

Wells, G., and M. Gutfreund. In press. The development of conversation. In *Language topics,* ed. T. Threadgold and R. Steele. Amsterdam: J. Benjamin.

Wood, D. J., H. Wood, A. Griffiths, and I. Howarth. 1986. *Teaching and talking with deaf children.* New York: John Wiley and Sons.

Woodward, J. 1976. Black southern signing. *Language in Society* 5(1): 211–218.

Zimmer, J. 1989. Toward a description of register variation in American Sign Language. In *The sociolinguistics of the deaf community,* ed. C. Lucas, 253–272. New York: Academic Press.

10

Intellectual Assessment

Lynne Blennerhassett

> Science, since people must do it, is a socially embedded activity. . . . Much of
> its change through time does not record a closer approach to absolute truth,
> but the alteration of cultural contexts that influence it so strongly.
> Stephen Jay Gould, *The Mismeasure of Man*

In their pioneer treatise on the intelligence of deaf people, Rudolph Pintner
and Donald Paterson (1917) acknowledged the pragmatic foundation of mental
measurement.

> Theoretical considerations have lagged behind practical application of mental
> tests. We have been measuring intelligence long before we have decided what it
> really is. (p. 1)

Pintner (1923) further acknowledged that intelligence testing "appeared as the
fulfillment of a need that existed. It came to supply a want in society" (p. 3).

Indeed, the development of the original Binet-Simon Intelligence Scale
(1905) was motivated by the practical need to identify mentally retarded children
who were in need of special education. Created under the auspices of the French
Minister of Education, Binet's original scale measured intelligence by sampling
thirty different tasks arranged in order of increasing difficulty. In 1908, the scale
was revised, with overall intelligence expressed in a single score, the "mental age."
By 1916, the ratio intelligence quotient (IQ) was established as the assessment
product used to identify children in need of special education.

Stephen Jay Gould credits Binet with pragmatic, educational motives for intelligence testing. Binet's purpose was to identify and provide services to students,
not to label them as deficient or to limit their opportunities. As such, Gould distinguished between Binet's original intentions and later hereditarian uses of intelligence tests. Gould (1981) explained that

> Hereditarians view their measures of intelligence as markers of permanent, in-
> born limits. . . . Antihereditarians, like Binet, test in order to identify and help

. . . they emphasize the power of creative education to increase the achievement of all children, often in extensive and unanticipated ways. Mental testing becomes a theory for enhancing potential through proper education. (pp. 152–153)

For children identified in need of special education, Binet recommended small class size (fifteen to twenty students) and instruction tailored to individual needs. Special "mental orthopedic" exercises were described to increase attention span, mental discipline, and other prerequisites of learning.

The early intelligence theorists offered only vague definitions of the construct they attempted to measure. Stern (1914), the original proponent of the ratio IQ, broadly defined intelligence as "a general capacity of an individual consciously to adjust his thinking to new requirements: it is general mental adaptability to new problems and conditions of life" (p. 3). Binet and Simon (1916) were no more specific in their definition of intelligence as "judgement, otherwise called good sense, practical sense, initiative, the faculty for adapting oneself to circumstances. To judge well, to comprehend well, to reason well, these are the essential activities of intelligence" (pp. 42–43).

Although the construct was not adequately defined, intelligence tests were developed, and the numeric product, or IQ, was offered as an index of some single, general mental capability. As history progressed, single-factor intelligence models gave way to multiple-factor models, exemplified by Wechsler's (1974, 1981) performance IQ and verbal IQ; Kaufman and Kaufman's (1983) Simultaneous Processing and Sequential Processing scales; and the Stanford-Binet Intelligence Scale, Fourth Edition, factor scores for verbal comprehension, nonverbal reasoning/visualization, and memory (Sattler 1988). Although factor-analytic theories of intelligence evolved, assessment remained product-oriented, with standard scores or deviation IQs used as the index of ability.

As early as 1927, Charles E. Spearman described a two-factor theory of intelligence consisting of a common, general ability factor (g), plus numerous specific factors (s1, s2, s3, etc.). Performance on a given mental task involves both the g factor, which impacts upon all task performance, and the specific factors, which are unique to the task at hand. The 1986 revision of the Stanford-Binet Intelligence Scale (Thorndike, Hagan, and Sattler 1986) maintains a hierarchical construction in which measurement of the g factor is expressed in the composite IQ score, and the second-order specific factors for crystallized, fluid-analytic, and memory abilities are assessed on scales from fifteen subtests.

Raymond B. Cattell and John Horn (Cattell 1963; Horn and Cattell 1967) were the first to describe crystallized and fluid intellectual abilities. Crystallized abilities refer to the acquisition of culturally transmitted information, facts, and skills. Fluid abilities refer to nonverbal, culture-free, and novel mental operations. The Wechsler Intelligence Scales (1967, 1974, 1981) attempt to measure both types of intelligence. Performance scale subtests, such as block design and coding, measure fluid abilities; whereas verbal scale subtests, such as vocabulary and information, measure crystallized abilities (Sattler 1988).

L. L. Thurstone and T. G. Thurstone (Thurstone 1938; Thurstone and Thurstone 1941) developed a multiple-factor model of intelligence comprised of numerous, equally weighted factors. Primary mental abilities were identified and assessed by their Primary Mental Abilities Tests, published by Science Research Associates (SRA) (Thurstone and Thurstone 1962). Five of the primary abilities were scored on the SRA tests (verbal meaning, perceptual speed, number facility, reasoning, and spatial reasoning), with ability level expressed as a deviation IQ. Moderate correlations among the Thurstones' primary factors were attributed to a higher level ability factor similar to Spearman's g factor (Sattler 1988).

J. P. Guilford's (1967) Structure of the Intellect (SIO) model defines mental activities according to 120 possible factors along three dimensions. Intellectual activities involve a mental operation (memory, cognition, evaluation, divergent production, convergent production) that is performed on some type of content (figural, symbolic, semantic, behavioral) and results in a product (units, classes, relations, systems, transformations, implications). Sattler (1982, 1988) presents SIO classifications for a number of intelligence tests, including the Wechsler Scales (1967, 1974); the Extended Merrill-Palmer Scale (Ball, Merrifield, and Stott 1978); and the Stanford-Binet Intelligence Scale, Third Edition (Terman and Merrill 1973).

In a more recent model, Jan-Eric Gustafsson (1984) describes a three-level structure of intelligence, with the g factor at the highest level, followed by the crystallized, fluid, and general visualization factors at the second level. The lowest level consists of ten specific factors that resemble abilities previously described by Guilford, the Thurstones, and others. Three abilities form the crystallized intelligence factor: verbal comprehension, verbal achievement, and numerical achievement. Four abilities make up the fluid intelligence factor: speed of closure, cognition of figural relations, induction, and memory span. The general visualization factor is comprised of three abilities: spatial orientation, visualization, and flexibility of closure.

With only minor exceptions, intellectual assessment of deaf people mirrored practices established for hearing populations, emphasizing psychometric properties of the tests and development of norm score distributions. Although early researchers in the field of deafness understood that intelligence testing of deaf students necessitated elimination of language items (Drever and Collins 1936; Pintner and Paterson 1915, 1917), their efforts to develop and use nonverbal scales of performance nevertheless embraced the psychometric, product approach established by the scientific community. Only recently have process-oriented assessment techniques surfaced, first developed for hearing populations (Feuerstein 1979) and subsequently adapted to deaf populations (Jonas and Martin 1985; Katz and Buchholz 1984; Keane 1983; Krapf 1985; Martin and Jonas 1987, 1989). The goal of process assessment is to identify cues, aids, and techniques needed to teach higher performance levels, as opposed to product assessment goals, which simply identify current levels of functioning.

This chapter examines historic and current trends in intellectual assessment of deaf students. The discussion traces product assessment approaches, including the preoccupation with hearing–deaf comparisons; the drive to develop deaf norms; and the search for predictive validity of global and subtest scores of deaf students. Product assessment approaches will be contrasted to the process techniques currently being applied to deaf children.

PRODUCT-ORIENTED ASSESSMENT

Comparing Deaf Performance to Hearing Norms

Deafness researchers initially administered nonlanguage intelligence tests to deaf groups in order to compare deaf performance to hearing norms. This practice spurred debates that persisted and evolved for decades concerning whether deaf people, as a group, possessed intelligence comparable to the general hearing population. Throughout decades of research, dozens of studies reported lower IQs of deaf compared to hearing controls, with mean deaf scores hovering in the high 80s to mid-90s. However, during the same period, an almost equal number of studies challenged that assumption, citing equal, and occasionally higher, mean scores of deaf groups compared to hearing groups (see Lunde [n.d.] and Vernon [1967] for a review of these early studies).

The tests used in the early studies included the Scale of Performance Tests (Pintner and Paterson 1917); Kohs' Block Designs (Kohs 1923); Porteus Mazes (Porteus 1924); the Draw-A-Man Test (Goodenough 1926); the Pintner Non-Language Test (Pintner 1929); the Grace Arthur Performance Scale (Arthur 1930); the Performance Tests of Intelligence (Drever and Collins 1936); the On-tario School Ability Test (Amoss 1936); Raven's Progressive Matrices (Raven 1938); and the Nebraska Test of Learning Aptitude for Young Deaf Children (Hiskey 1941). It is interesting to note that only three of these early nonlanguage tests were specifically developed for, and normed on, the deaf: the Drever-Collins Performance Tests of Intelligence; the Ontario School Ability Exam (Amoss 1936); and the Hiskey–Nebraska Test of Learning Aptitude. The vast majority of tests were developed and normed specifically for hearing children; deaf children's intelligence was judged relative to hearing, rather than deaf, peers. Even today, the majority of intelligence tests used with deaf children were developed and normed for hearing populations (Gibbins 1989; Spragins, Blennerhassett, and Mullen 1987).

Many items from these early scales are still in use today. For example, the Manikin puzzle from Pintner and Paterson's 1917 test (Figure 10.1) is currently

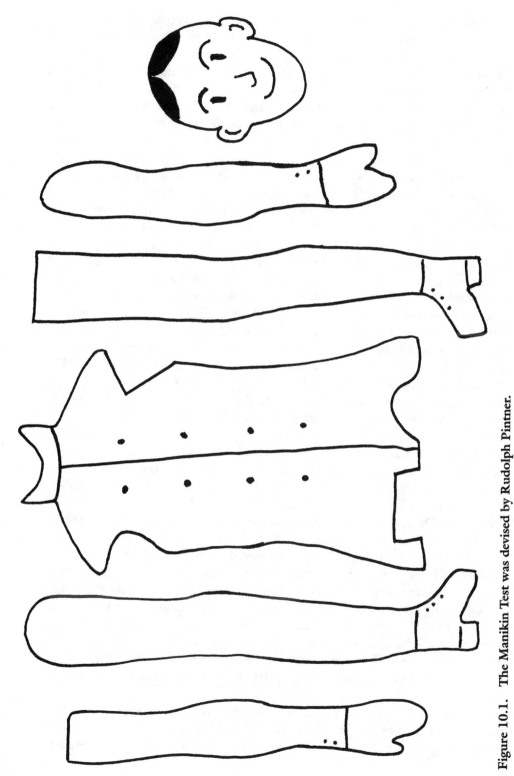

Figure 10.1. The Manikin Test was devised by Rudolph Pintner.

Source: R. Pintner and D. G. Paterson, *A Scale of Performance Tests.* (New York: D. Appleton and Company, 1917), 45.

used in Wechsler's 1981 Adult Intelligence Scale-Revised (WAIS-R), the Merrill-Palmer Scale of Mental Tests (Stutsman 1948), the Central Institute for the Deaf (CID) Preschool Performance Scale (Geers and Lane 1984), and the Smith-Johnson Nonverbal Performance Scale (Smith and Johnson 1977). Pintner's Form Board Test (Figure 10.2) was included in Drever and Collins' (1936) intelligence test for deaf children and still appears in the current CID Performance Scale. Figure 10.3 shows the Substitution Test by Woodworth and Wells (1911), which was borrowed by Pintner and Paterson for their Scale of Performance Tests, and is still in use as part of Wechsler's Intelligence Scale for Children-Revised (WISC-R) (Wechsler 1974). Figure 10.4 shows Knox and Kempf's Feature Profile Test (Knox 1914), which also was incorporated into Pintner and Paterson's early test, and which closely resembles the profile puzzle currently used in the WAIS-R object assembly.

When deaf children scored lower than hearing children on such nonlanguage tasks, several interpretations evolved to account for the differences. The first wave of interpretations held that deaf children were inherently inferior because, as Pintner (1923) claimed, "the disease which produced the deafness caused at the same time the mental backwardness" (p. 323). Although this interpretation primarily applied to the adventitiously deafened population, Pintner (1923) extended it to the congenitally deaf as well, stating that "the results indicate that the adventitious and congenital groups show the same general inferiority in these traits" (p. 323).

But not all measures resulted in significantly lower scores for deaf subjects; consequently, inquiry switched from examining overall IQ to analyzing subtests. Investigation of subtest scatter marked the second wave of interpretations regarding deaf intelligence. Myklebust and his contemporaries held that the deaf subjects performed comparably to hearing subjects on concrete tasks, but were significantly lower on subtests that measured abstract abilities (McAndrew 1948; Myklebust 1953, 1964; Myklebust and Brutten 1953; Oleron 1950; Templin 1953).

Concrete tasks required no generalization or deduction, as exemplified by Kohs' Block Design Test and the block design subtests of the WISC-R and WAIS-R. Abstract abilities were measured with tests such as Raven's Progressive Matrices, in which "the problem cannot be solved without deducting a principle" (Myklebust 1964, p. 87). Figure 10.5 presents an example of abstract thinking on the Raven's Progressive Matrices test. The correct answer (option 5) is obtained by performing subtraction across the rows, down the columns, or both. The solution requires the assignment of negative values to internal angles and positive values to external angles. For example, the equation in the row across the top is $+2 - (+4) = -2$. The same operation reading down the far left column is $+2 - (-1) = +3$. Option 5 satisfies the equations across the bottom row and down the third column.

The Myklebust interpretation held that deaf children performed lower on abstract tasks than hearing children because of differences in their intersensory organization. He argued that any sensory deprivation (e.g., deafness) altered all

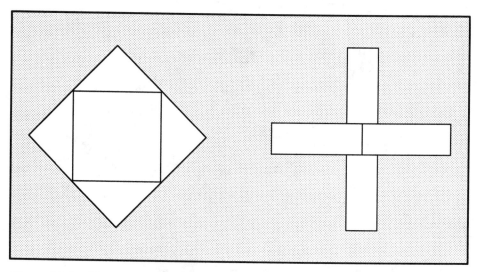

Figure 10.2   Pintner's Form Board Test was adapted for the Drever-Collins Performance Tests of Intelligence.

Source: J. Drever and N. Collins, *Performance Tests of Intelligence,* 2d ed. (London: Oliver and Boyd, 1936), 27.

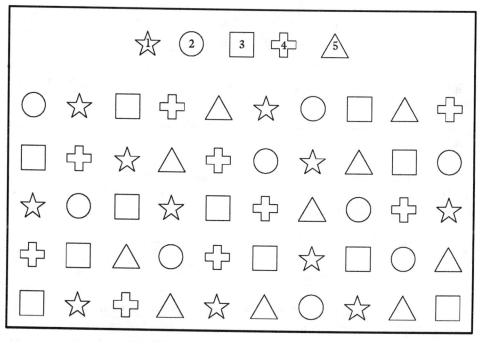

Figure 10.3.   The Substitution Test by Woodworth and Wells was included in Pintner and Paterson's scale.

Source: R. Pintner and D. G. Paterson, *A Scale of Performance Tests.* (New York: D. Appleton and Company, 1917), 64.

Figure 10.4.   The Feature Profile Test by Knox and Kemp was included in Pintner and Paterson's scale.

Source: R. Pintner and D. G. Paterson, *A Scale of Performance Tests*. (New York: D. Appleton and Company, 1917), 57.

subsequent intersensory organization and rendered deaf children fundamentally different from hearing children in more ways than just hearing sensitivity. Myklebust (1964) claimed

> a specific sensory experience is interpreted on the basis of what had been learned from all sensory experience. When a certain sensory input is lacking, however, the experience gained from the remaining senses is structured differently. (p. 50)

According to this interpretation, the source of the performance deficit was located within the child; poor performance was due to predetermined differences in the sensory-perceptual organization of the child. Myklebust's interpretation was attacked by the philosophers and researchers of the 1960s and 1970s, whose focus was to examine the social, cultural, and experiential determinants of behavior.

The social-experiential interpretation argued against the notion of the deaf

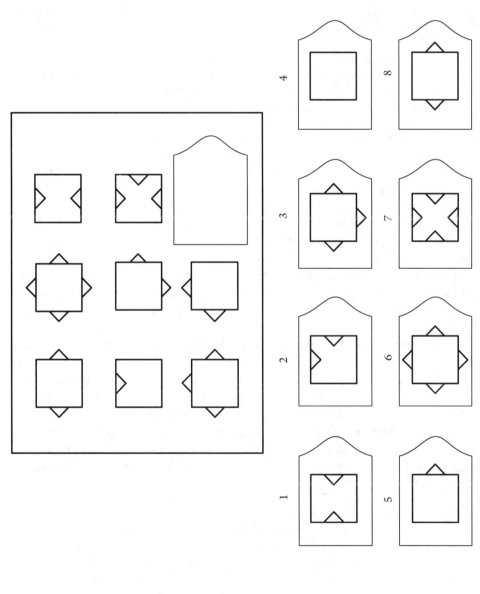

Figure 10.5. Raven's Progressive Matrices test requires the subject to deduct a principle.

Source: J. C. Raven, *Progressive Matrices*. (London: H. K. Lewis, 1938). Reprinted by permission.

as intellectually inferior, citing cultural differences that could account for score discrepancies. For example, the different social, cultural, linguistic, and educational experiences of deaf children were suspected of lowering performance during test sessions (Levine 1960; Levine and Wagner 1974; Rosenstein 1960, 1961). Poor performance was attributed to educational experiences that trained deaf children to respond rigidly in test situations. Over-reliance on copying or matching strategies discourages the use of alternate strategies that would be more successful. Levine (1960) explained

> Anyone who has observed the education of the deaf would not be surprised to see deaf children repeatedly sticking to a choice once declared correct, for they learn very early to repeat and repeat in parrot-like fashion. The attitude of repeating what has been learned is drilled into them. (pp. 147–148)

In addition, poor performance might result from unfamiliarity with test expectations, communication breakdowns between deaf clients and hearing examiners, and lack of rapport during test sessions.

In her classic survey of psychological tests and practices with deaf clients, Levine (1974) found that 96 percent of the practitioners reported major barriers in assessing their deaf clients, citing lack of training, inadequate tests and norms, communication and rapport problems, and difficulty with test administration and interpretation. Of the practitioners surveyed, 65 percent had received no specialized training to work with deaf people, and 50 percent could not express themselves in sign language or understand the sign communication of their clients. Even those familiar with sign language tended to rate their skills as only "fair" or "poor."

One response to these charges was to develop special training opportunities for practitioners who work with deaf clients (Spragins 1979). Ecological models of intellectual assessment were also proposed, stressing the need to gather assessment data from a number of sources and to use a variety of techniques (Barnett 1983; Levine 1981). Public Law (PL)94-142 formalized the requirement for nondiscriminatory, multisourced, multifactored evaluations, placing new demands for appropriately normed tests and evaluations in the child's native language. The Office of Education's (1977) implementation plan for PL 94-142 required that:

1. Tests and other evaluation material
   a. Are provided and administered in the child's native language or typical mode of communication, unless it is clearly not feasible to do so;
   b. Have been validated for the specific purpose for which they are used; and
   c. Are administered by trained personnel in conformance with instructions provided by their producer.
2. Tests and other evaluation materials include those tailored to assess specific areas of educational need and not merely those which are designed to provide a single general intelligence quotient.

3. Tests are selected and administered so as best to ensure that when a test is administered to a child with impaired sensory, manual, or speaking skills, the test results accurately reflect the child's aptitude or achievement level or whatever other factors the test purports to measure, rather than reflect the child's impaired sensory, manual, or speaking skills (except where those skills are the factors which the test purports to measure . . .). (pp. 42,496–42,497)

Nondiscriminatory assessment procedures are especially important in deaf education, not only because of the linguistic and cultural implications of hearing loss, but also because more than 32 percent of deaf children come from Black, Hispanic-American, Oriental, and multiethnic backgrounds (Center for Assessment and Demographic Studies 1988; Fischgrund, Cohen, and Clarkson 1987).

During the late 1970s, the Spartanburg conference was convened to review the state of psychological services for the deaf population. The conference (*The Preparation of Psychological Service Providers to the Deaf*) recommended minimum competencies for psychologists and other practitioners who serve deaf clients (Levine 1977, 1981). The list (Levine 1981) included

The ability to express and receive messages in whatever communicative modes and concept levels are habitually used by a deaf subject; or until this point is reached . . . the ability to understand the art and skills of interpreting for the deaf, and to work effectively through interpreted communication. . . .

For lack of psychological tests standardized on deaf youth and adults, the ability to select from a pool of hearing-standardized tests those best suited to a particular deaf subject, and to make whatever adaptations are required in language and administration that will elicit best-performance yet preserve test objectivity. (p. 226)

Despite awareness and training opportunities that resulted from the Spartanburg conference, psychologists continue to identify the enhancement of sign language skills and the availability of tests normed on deaf clients as primary needs in working with the deaf population (Gibbins 1989).

In response to social forces in the 1970s, researchers turned their attention to the establishment of deaf norms, seeking tools that would help to differentiate needs within the deaf population and help to identify individuals at risk for school failure compared to deaf peers. The approach remained product-oriented, although research focused on score distributions within the deaf population, rather than relative to hearing peers.

The Search for Deaf Norms and Within-Group Differences

In defense of intelligence assessment, Sattler (1988) stated that the tests "provide standardized ways of comparing a child's performance with that of other children observed in the same situations represented by the test items" (p. 78). Although

Table 10.1
Intelligence Measures Standardized with Deaf Students

Test	Researchers	Administration Standardized	Deaf Norm Tables Provided
CID Preschool Performance Scale	Geers and Lane, 1984	Yes	Yes
Hiskey–Nebraska Test of Learning Aptitude	Hiskey, 1966	Yes	Yes
Smith-Johnson Nonverbal Performance Scale	Smith and Johnson, 1977	Yes	Yes
WISC-R Performance Scale	Anderson and Sisco, 1977	No	Yes
WISC-R Performance Scale	Ray, 1979	Yes	No
WPPSI Performance Scale	Ray and Ulissi, 1982	Yes	No

this may be true when testing hearing children, assessment of deaf children typically requires alteration of the instructions, thus violating the standardization assumption. Over the past two decades, researchers increased their efforts to standardize intelligence tests with deaf children. The rationale was to provide appropriate norms against which individual differences and unique abilities within the deaf population could be identified.

Table 10.1 presents a list of intelligence tests that provide norm tables and/or standardized administration procedures specifically for deaf students. The largest standardization effort was Anderson and Sisco's (1977) renorming of the WISC-R performance scale. Working through Gallaudet University's Office of Demographic Studies (now the Center for Assessment and Demographic Studies), Anderson and Sisco collected protocols of 1,228 students from residential schools and day schools throughout the country. The students ranged in age from six to sixteen years; all had hearing losses of 70 decibels (dB) or greater in the better ear. Seventy-seven percent were tested using total communication; 2.2 percent were tested using speech only; 4.0 percent using fingerspelling and speech; and the remainder were tested using gestures, pantomime, or other (unspecified) methods. The sample resembled the original WISC-R hearing sample (and the 1970 census statistics) with regard to percentage of representation across sex, race, urban/rural residence, geographic region, and parental occupation variables.

Anderson and Sisco found that although the deaf students scored significantly higher on the object assembly subtest, performance IQ was significantly lower (deaf mean was 95.70). Significantly lower performance was also noted on picture arrangement, coding, block design, and picture completion subtests. However, much of the difference was attributed to the younger, lower scoring children in the sample, and Anderson and Sisco (1977) concluded that in most cases, "deaf children performed similarly to hearing children on all performance subtests except coding and picture arrangement" (p. 6). The analysis resulted in new norm tables that rank an individual's performance relative to deaf peers.

The data were also analyzed for within-group differences, specifically comparing deaf students of deaf parents with deaf students of hearing parents. Sisco and Anderson (1980) reported significantly higher performance IQ for deaf students with deaf parents (mean was 106.7) compared to deaf students with hearing parents (mean was 96.0). This finding was supported by Kusché, Greenberg and Garfield's (1983) report of a significantly higher performance IQ among residential school students with deaf parents (mean was 111.89) compared to deaf peers with hearing parents (mean was 100.74).

Ray's (1979) adaptation of the WISC-R provided special verbal instructions and practice materials for the performance scale. Because administration procedures were uncontrolled in the Anderson and Sisco (1977) study, Ray devised a consistent set of "alternate instructions" in which the syntax and semantic content of the verbal directions were modified for the deaf test takers. Supplemental materials provide further assistance to children who do not understand the directions. Figure 10.6 shows a supplemental item for the picture arrangement subtest. Figure 10.7 shows the supplemental worksheet for the coding subtest. Supplemental items are demonstrated and allow the student to practice before completing the actual test item. These items are intended only for those students who, after receiving the alternate instructions, still do not understand the task. With modified administration, the scores of deaf children increased to the same level as hearing children, lending support to the social-experiential hypothesis.

Ray and Ulissi (1982) developed similar materials to accompany the performance scale of Wechsler's (1967) Preschool and Primary Scale of Intelligence (WPPSI). With the modified instructions and supplemental materials, deaf children's performance on the WPPSI was comparable to that of hearing children, eliminating the need for specific norm tables. However, within-group differences were noted in the test profiles of the deaf sample. Deaf preschoolers with deaf parents earned a mean performance IQ of 108.55 compared to 101.79 earned by deaf peers with hearing parents. In addition, the subtest profile of deaf children with deaf parents was relatively consistent, whereas significant scatter was noted for deaf children with hearing parents.

Wechsler subtest comparisons help identify another group within the deaf population: the learning-disabled hearing-impaired (LDHI). LDHI students account for the largest percentage of deaf students with additional handicaps, representing between 6.0 percent and 8.6 percent of that population (Center for Assessment and Demographic Studies 1988; Craig and Craig 1987; Powers, Elliot, and Funderburg 1987). Wechsler profiles for learning-disabled students generally show average intelligence accompanied by atypical subtest scatter and unique learning styles. For LDHI students, Rush, Blennerhassett, and Alexander (1989) found atypically low scores on picture completion, picture arrangement, and

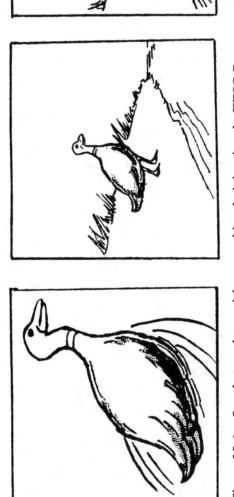

Figure 10.6. Supplemental materials are used in administering the WISC-R Picture Arrangement subtest to deaf children.

Source: S. Ray, *An Adaptation of the Wechsler Intelligence Scale for Children-Revised*. (Northridge, CA: Steven Ray Publications, 1979). Reprinted by permission.

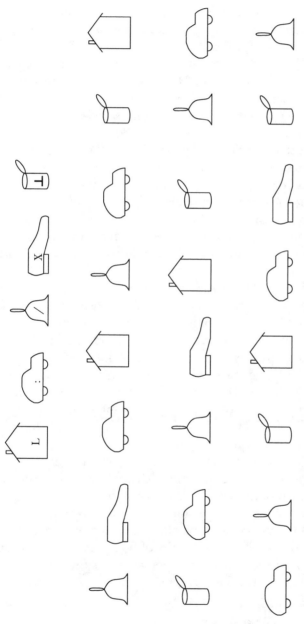

Figure 10.7. A supplemental practice sheet is used in administering the WISC-R Coding subtest to deaf children.

Source: S. Ray, *An Adaptation of the Wechsler Intelligence Scale for Children-Revised*. (Northridge, CA: Steven Ray Publications, 1979). Reprinted by permission.

arithmetic. Although the arithmetic subtest from the verbal scale is not generally administered to deaf students as a measure of intelligence, the deaf typically score higher on arithmetic than on other verbal scale subtests (Geers and Moog 1987; Hine 1970; Kohoutek, Pulda and Zemanova 1971; Moores et al. 1987). Further research is needed to determine whether the atypical low cluster on the arithmetic, picture completion, and picture arrangement subtests provides a useful index for identifying students at risk for LDHI status.

Although the Wechsler performance scales remain the most frequently used intelligence tests for deaf children, the Hiskey–Nebraska Test of Learning Aptitude maintains a popular status despite out-of-date norms (Hiskey 1966). Standardization of the Hiskey–Nebraska was based on a sample of 1,079 deaf students and 1,074 hearing students between the ages of 2½ and 17½ years. The sample was drawn from ten states, including Florida, New York, and Utah. Raw scores from the twelve subtests were converted to age scores, and a composite Learning Quotient (LQ) replaced the traditional IQ for the deaf group. Separate norms for the deaf and hearing subjects were provided, as hearing children tended to perform at higher levels than the deaf sample. The difference was attributed to differences in administration: deaf children were administered the test in pantomime; hearing children were given the benefit of verbal instructions, which clarified performance expectations.

Although the Hiskey–Nebraska is generally not administered to children below three years of age, two newer preschool scales provide norms for deaf children as young as two years. The Smith-Johnson Nonverbal Performance Scale (Smith and Johnson 1977) was normed on a sample of 632 orally trained preschool students between the ages of twenty-four and forty-eight months. All subjects attended the John Tracy Clinic at some time over a nineteen-year period spanning the 1960s and 1970s. The CID Preschool Performance Scale (Geers and Lane 1984) provides an expanded set of norms for orally educated children between the ages of two years and five-and-a-half years. This scale was normed on 521 deaf children who attended the Central Institute for the Deaf at some time over the past two decades. The sample consisted of children with hearing losses of 30 dB or greater in the better ear. As with most intelligence measures, the observed level of performance on each of the six CID subjects is converted to a standard score and, in turn, to an overall IQ that ranks the child relative to same-age, deaf peers.

Although deaf norms provide a psychometric base upon which atypical or unique students can be identified, the validity of IQ scores as achievement predictors remains a separate issue. The next section examines the degree to which IQ scores of deaf children correlate with academic success.

Predictive Validity of Intelligence Scores of Deaf Children

In a discussion of the pros and cons of intelligence testing, Sattler (1988) cited several advantages of the tests. The list, in part, reads:

The IQ has a larger collection of correlates predictive of success in a wide variety of human endeavors than does any other variable. . . .

IQs may be regarded as a measure of the child's ability to compete in our society in ways that have economic and social consequences. . . .

IQs are excellent predictors of scholastic achievement. (p. 78)

IQ tests were developed at the request of educational institutions, and their use is grounded in the assumption that IQ scores predict academic success. Although only vague definitions of "intelligence" are offered by test developers, the "something" that is measured by the tests is believed to have predictive validity. These claims may be true for hearing populations; however, they cannot be assumed true for deaf populations, especially since the strongest correlations between achievement and intelligence occur within the verbal scale (Sattler [1988] provides a review of predictive validity of IQ scores with hearing populations).

For deaf students, performance IQ appears to be relatively stable and shows respectable concurrent validity with other nonverbal intelligence measures (Gibbins in press; Hirshoren, Hurley, and Hunt 1977; Geers and Lane 1984). Reports of criterion-referenced validity, however, have been less consistent and somewhat contradictory. For example, some researchers find performance IQs to be among the best predictors of reading, math, and language achievement, with correlations reaching into the .50s through .70s (Brill 1962; Kusché, Greenberg, and Garfield 1983; Pollard and Oakland 1985; Ulissi, Brice, and Gibbins in press; Watson, Goldgar, Kroese, and Lotz 1986; Watson, Sullivan, Moeller, and Jensen 1982).

Other researchers question the predictive validity of nonverbal IQ. Clarke and Leslie (1971) claimed that the Wechsler Performance Scale subtests "did not significantly differentiate between deaf retarded readers and non-retarded readers" (p. 263). Hirshoren, Hurley, and Kavale (1979) found only modest correlations (.09 to .35) between performance IQ and Scholastic Aptitude Test (SAT) scores for deaf children between the ages of eight and thirteen years. Brooks and Riggs (1980) also reported no significant correlation between performance IQ and SAT Hearing-Impaired reading scores for deaf students in public schools. And inconsistent results were reported by Giangreco (1966), who found that Hiskey–Nebraska scores correlated with Gates Reading achievement at grades 2, 11, and 12 ($r = .640$ and $.599$), but not at grades 5 and 8 ($r = -.086$ and $.232$).

As with hearing populations, verbal scale scores may correlate higher with achievement than performance scale scores, even though the verbal scales are not administered as measures of intelligence per se. When used with deaf students, the verbal scales assess specific types of verbal comprehension and expression (e.g., information, vocabulary, arithmetic). As Miller (1984) explained,

Use of the verbal scales of intelligence tests with deaf students, administered in their own language system, would provide useful information regarding their ability to use symbols to comprehend and transmit verbal concepts. (p. 172)

When administered in their own language system, significant differences between verbal and performance scale IQs were found for deaf adolescents with hearing parents and deaf adolescents with deaf parents, supporting the long-standing hypothesis that verbal scale scores do not provide the measure of intelligence enabled by the performance scales (Blennerhassett et al. 1988).

As measures of verbal comprehension and expression, the verbal scales appear to be valid predictors of academic achievement for deaf students. Davis, Elfenbein, Schum, and Bentler (1986) reported a correlation of .76 between WISC-R verbal IQ and reading achievement in a sample of mildly to moderately deaf children between the ages of five and twelve years. Moores and his colleagues (1987) administered both the verbal and performance scales to a sample of profoundly deaf students, of whom half had deaf parents and half had hearing parents. For both groups, the strongest correlations between reading and writing achievement were found within the verbal scale.

Table 10.2 shows the correlations between WAIS-R subtest scores and achievement for the deaf sample with deaf parents. The strongest correlations were observed between reading achievement and three verbal scale subtests: vocabulary (.66), information (.65), and arithmetic (.61). The same three subtests correlated with written language. Of the performance scale subtests, picture completion and digit symbol were among the best predictors of reading and writing, with correlations reaching only .44 and .52, respectively.

Correlations between Wechsler scores and achievement for deaf students with hearing parents are presented in Table 10.3. The vocabulary subtest correlated with both reading (.70) and writing (.62) achievement. Similarities, information, and arithmetic subtests also correlated with reading achievement, evidenced by coefficients of .57, .54, and .52, respectively. The strongest correlation within the performance scale was observed on the picture arrangement subtest with a coefficient of only .38. These data were among several measures that were subsequently included in a multiple regression study of factors predictive of achievement in deaf adolescents (Moores et al. 1987; chapter 7 provides further discussion).

THE SHIFT TO PROCESS ASSESSMENT

Although product assessment has dominated the field, process approaches are evolving as supplemental, if not alternate, evaluation techniques. Process assessment follows a test-teach-test model, altering standard procedures and materials for the purpose of enhancing intellectual performance. In contrast to the norm-based, psychometric information derived from product assessment, the goal of process assessment is to identify the cues, aids, and supports needed to alter cognitive ability.

Process assessment provides educators with specific guides for instructing and enhancing intellectual development, information not furnished by IQ scores

Table 10.2
Correlations Between WAIS-R Scores and
Achievement for
Deaf Students of Deaf Parents

Scale	Reading Achievement	Writing Achievement
Performance Scale		
Picture Completion	.44	.21
Picture Arrangement	.27	.38
Block Design	.32	.34
Object Assembly	.15	.10
Digit Symbol (Coding)	.36	.52
Verbal Scale		
Information	.65	.57
Similarities	.50	.39
Vocabulary	.66	.67
Arithmetic	.61	.57
Comprehension	.35	.45
Digit Span	.40	.34

Source: D. Moores et al., *Factors Predictive of Literacy in Deaf Adolescents,* Report No. NO1-NS-4–2365. (Washington, DC: National Institute of Neurological and Communicative Disorders and Stroke, 1987), p. 111. Reprinted by permission.

Table 10.3
Correlations Between WAIS-R Scores and
Achievement for
Deaf Students with Hearing Parents

Scale	Reading Achievement	Writing Achievement
Performance Scale		
Picture Completion	.27	.25
Picture Arrangement	.38	.20
Block Design	.18	.22
Object Assembly	.31	.23
Digit Symbol (Coding)	.34	.36
Verbal Scale		
Information	.54	.27
Similarities	.57	.39
Vocabulary	.70	.62
Arithmetic	.52	.44
Comprehension	.48	.37
Digit Span	.43	.40

Source: D. Moores et al., *Factors Predictive of Literacy in Deaf Adolescents,* Report No. NO1-NS-4–2365. (Washington, DC: National Institute of Neurological and Communicative Disorders and Stroke, 1987), p. 139. Reprinted by permission.

alone. Salvia and Ysseldyke (1981) recognized the importance of process evaluations in meeting the needs of teachers.

> Teachers have long expressed concern that mere knowledge of the extent to which a student deviates from normal is of little help in their efforts to devise an appropriate educational program for that student. They repeatedly ask for specific information about a student's skill development strengths and weaknesses and for effective strategies to move students from where they are to where teachers want them to be. (p. 517)

Salvia and Ysseldyke also recognized that "administrators need the scores and interpretations of pupil performance on norm-referenced tests to document placement decisions" (p. 516); these needs are typically met by psychologists. The outstanding challenge seems to be how to incorporate process assessment into research and practice.

Process assessment techniques have been described as "testing of limits" (Sattler 1988); "mediating learning experiences" (Feuerstein 1979); and assessing the "zone of proximal development" (Vygotsky 1978). (Also, Lidz's (1987) dynamic assessment process provides an interactional approach to evaluating learning potential.) Of these techniques, the most detailed model is Feuerstein's Learning Potential Assessment Device (LPAD) which was originally developed for low functioning Israeli children and was recently adapted for deaf children (Martin and Jonas 1987).

The theoretical basis of Feuerstein's (1979) LPAD describes cognitive development as the result of both "direct learning experience" and "mediated learning experience" (MLE). MLEs require interactions with a mediating agent (e.g., teacher, adult, or examiner) who promotes intellectual development by "selecting, focusing, and feeding back environmental experiences in such a way as to produce . . . appropriate learning sets and habits" (p. 71).

The LPAD model (Feuerstein 1979) views low intellectual performance as the result of insufficient MLEs. Assessment goals are redefined to identify the number and nature of input variables needed to move the child to higher mental functioning. The traditional examiner-client interaction is qualitatively altered to that of teacher-learner. During the interaction process, the child's mental tasks are analyzed and modified in an effort to enhance performance. Mental acts are analyzed along seven dimensions.

1. Content: familiar, unfamiliar
2. Modality: pictorial, verbal, numerical
3. Phase: input, elaboration, output
4. Operations: classification, seriation, reasoning by analogy
5. Level of Complexity: quantity
6. Level of Abstraction: concrete, abstract, propositional
7. Level of Efficiency: speed or slowness

Deaf students exposed to mediated learning experiences with the LPAD achieved significantly higher performance scores compared to control subjects tested in more traditional ways (Keane 1983; Krapf 1985). The LPAD was also used in a single-subject study of a "slow learning" (IQ of 85) deaf adolescent whose intellectual performance on Raven's Progressive Matrices was increased to above the 90th percentile (Katz and Buchholz 1984). Use of Instrumental Enrichment, the curriculum Feuerstein (1980) developed to accompany his LPAD, further expanded the student's repertoire of cognitive abilities to include "searching for cues, making appropriate comparisons, using problem-solving strategies, capitalizing on logical evidence, and viewing the information within a task in a holistic way when appropriate" (Katz and Buchholz 1984, p. 104).

Martin and Jonas studied the effectiveness of Feuerstein's techniques in longitudinal studies of deaf adolescents. Treatment of high school students resulted in improved cognitive performance on Raven's Matrices. Achievement-related classroom functioning also increased, as evidenced by improved problem-solving, organization, completeness, and peer cooperation (Jonas and Martin 1985; Martin and Jonas 1987). A subsequent study of college preparatory students and freshmen reinforced the efficacy of Feuerstein's system with deaf populations. Exposure to mediated learning experiences resulted in improvements in logical reasoning, math concepts, math calculations, and reading comprehension. Improved self-confidence in class and in test situations was also noted (Martin and Jonas 1989).

Although process assessment provides educators with the type of information needed to advance the ability and achievement of students, its use is threatened by historic, product-oriented models of training and service delivery. Psychometric assessment models are the standard for university training and practica, whereas process models are accorded peripheral status. Special training is required to purchase and administer the LPAD, and this training is available only at regional centers or the University of Maryland (Palmer 1983). Training on the Instrumental Enrichment curriculum, which accompanies the LPAD, is also required (Braden 1985).

Despite these challenges, Steven Jay Gould's proposition that social forces influence the direction of science may still prevail. Traditional product approaches to intellectual assessment may shift in response to pragmatic needs within educational institutions, replacing static, psychometric intelligence scores with dynamic prescriptions for altering cognitive ability.

REFERENCES

Amoss, H. 1936. *Ontario school ability examination*. Toronto, Canada: Ryerson Press.

Anderson, R. J., and F. H. Sisco. 1977. *Standardization of the WISC–R performance scale for deaf children*. Washington, DC: Gallaudet University, Center for Assessment and Demographic Studies.

Arthur, G. 1930. *A point scale of performance tests.* New York: Commonwealth Fund.

Ball, R. S., P. Merrifield, and L. H. Stott. 1978. *Extended Merrill–Palmer scale.* Chicago: Stoelting Company.

Barnett, D. W. 1983. *Nondiscriminatory multifactored assessment: A sourcebook.* New York: Human Sciences Press.

Binet, A. and T. Simon. 1905. Methodes nouvelles pour le diagnostic du niveau intellectuel des anormaus. *L'Annee Psychologique* 11: 191–244.

———. 1916. *The development of intelligence in children,* trans. E. S. Kite. Baltimore: Williams and Wilkins.

Blennerhassett, L., D. F. Moores, J. Hannah, and L. Woolard. 1988. *The impact of parental deafness on WISC–R and WAIS–R verbal and performance scores of deaf adolescents.* Paper presented at the National Association of School Psychologists, Chicago.

Braden, J. 1985. LPAD applications to deaf populations. In *Cognition, education, and deafness,* ed. D. S. Martin, 149–150. Washington, DC: Gallaudet University Press.

Brill, R. G. 1962. The relationship of Wechsler IQs to academic achievement among deaf students. *Exceptional Children* 28: 315–321.

Brooks, C. R. and S. T. Riggs. 1980. WISC–R, WISC, and reading achievement relationships among hearing impaired children attending public schools. *Volta Review* 82(3): 96–102.

Cattell, R. B. 1963. Theory of fluid and crystallized intelligence: A critical experiment. *Journal of Educational Psychology* 54: 1–22.

Center for Assessment and Demographic Studies. 1988. *Annual survey of hearing impaired children and youth, 1986–1987* (Unpublished data). Washington, DC: Gallaudet University.

Clarke, B. R. and P. T. Leslie. 1971. Visual motor skills and reading ability of deaf children. *Perceptual and Motor Skills* 33: 263–268.

Craig, W. N. and H. B. Craig. 1987. Programs and services for the deaf in the United States. *American Annals of the Deaf* 132: 2.

Davis, J. M., J. Elfenbein, R. Schum, and R. A. Bentler. 1986. *Journal of Speech and Hearing Disorders* 51: 53–62.

Drever, J., and N. Collins. 1936. *Performance tests of intelligence.* London: Oliver and Boyd.

Feuerstein, R. 1979. *The dynamic assessment of retarded performers: The Learning Potential Assessment Device theory, instruments, and techniques.* Baltimore: University Park Press.

———. 1980. *Instrumental enrichment.* Baltimore: University Park Press.

Fischgrund, J. E., O. P. Cohen, and R. L. Clarkson. 1987. Hearing impaired children in black and hispanic families. *Volta Review* 89(5): 59–67.

Geers, A. E., and H. S. Lane. 1984. *CID preschool performance scale.* Chicago: Stoelting Company.

Geers, A. E., and J. S. Moog. 1987. *Factors predictive of the development of reading and writing skills in the congenitally deaf: Report of the oral sample,* Report No. NIH-NINCDS-83-19. Washington, DC: National Institute of Neurological and Communicative Disorders and Stroke.

Giangreco, C. J. 1966. The Hiskey–Nebraska test of learning aptitude (revised) compared to several achievement tests. *American Annals of the Deaf* 8: 566–577.

Gibbins, S. 1989. The provision of school psychological assessment services for the hearing impaired: A national survey. *Volta Review* 91(2): 95–103.

———. In press. Use of the WISC–R performance scale and the KABC nonverbal scale with deaf children in the United States and Scotland. *School Psychology International.*

Goodenough, F. L. 1926. *Measurement of intelligence by drawings.* New York: World Book Company.

Gould, S. J. 1981. *The mismeasure of man.* New York: W. W. Norton and Company.

Guilford, J. P. 1967. *The nature of human intelligence.* New York: McGraw-Hill.

Gustafsson, J. E. 1984. A unifying model for the structure of intellectual capabilities. *Intelligence* 8: 179–203.

Hine, W. D. 1970. The abilities of partially hearing children. *British Journal of Educational Psychology* 40(2): 171–178.

Hirshoren, A., O. L. Hurley, and J. T. Hunt. 1977. The WISC–R and Hiskey–Nebraska Tests with deaf children. *American Annals of the Deaf* 122: 392–394.

Hirshoren, A., O. L. Hurley, and K. Kavale. 1979. Psychometric characteristics of the WISC–R performance scale with deaf children. *Journal of Speech and Hearing Disorders* 44: 73–79.

Hiskey, M. S. 1941. A new performance test for young deaf children. *Education and Psychological Measurements* 1: 77–84.

———. 1966. *Hiskey–Nebraska Test of Learning Aptitude.* Lincoln, NB: Union College Press.

Horn, J. L., and R. B. Cattell. 1967. Age differences in fluid and crystallized intelligence. *Acta Psychologica* 26: 107–129.

Jonas, B. S., and D. S. Martin. 1985. Cognitive improvement of hearing impaired high school students through instruction and instrumental enrichment. In *Cognition, education, and deafness,* ed. D. S. Martin, 172–175. Washington, DC: Gallaudet University Press.

Katz, M. A., and E. S. Buchholz. 1984. Use of the LPAD for cognitive enrichment of a deaf child. *School Psychology Review* 13(1): 99–106.

Kaufman, A. S., and N. L. Kaufman. 1983. *Kaufman Assessment Battery for Children.* Circle Pines, MN: American Guidance Service.

Keane, K. J. 1983. Application of Feuerstein's mediated learning construct to deaf persons. In *Cognition, education, and deafness,* ed. D. S. Martin, 141–147. Washington, DC: Gallaudet University Press.

Knox, H. A. 1914. A scale based on the work at Ellis Island, for estimating mental defect. *Journal of the American Medical Association* 62: 741–747.

Kohoutek, R., M. Pulda, and A. Zemanova. 1971. A contribution to the problem of intellectual achievement in the deaf. *Psycholgia A Patopaychologia Dietata* 6(2): 147–154.

Kohs, S. C. 1923. *The Block Designs Test.* Chicago: Stoelting Company.

Krapf, G. F. 1985. *The effects of mediated intervention on advanced figural problem solving with deaf adolescents: Implications for dynamic process assessment.* Ph.D. diss. Philadelphia: Temple University.

Kusché, C. A., M. T. Greenberg, and T. S. Garfield. 1983. Nonverbal intelligence and verbal achievement in deaf adolescents: An examination of heredity and environment. *American Annals of the Deaf* 128: 458–466.

Levine, E. S. 1960. *The psychology of deafness.* New York: Columbia University Press.

———. 1974. Psychological tests and practices with the deaf: A survey of the state of the art. *Volta Review* 76: 298–319.

————. 1977. The preparation of psychological service providers to the deaf (monograph). *Journal of Rehabilitation of the Deaf* 4.

————. 1981. *The ecology of early deafness: Guides to fashioning environments and psychological assessments.* New York: Columbia University Press.

Levine, E. S., and E. E. Wagner. 1974. Personality patterns of deaf persons: an interpretation based on research with the hand test. *Perceptual and Motor Skills* 39: 1167–1236.

Lidz, C. S. 1987. *Dynamic assessment: An interactional approach to evaluating learning potential.* New York: Guilford Press.

Lunde, A. S. n.d. *Conflicting results of psychological testing of the deaf.* Washington, DC: Gallaudet University.

Martin, D. S., and B. S. Jonas. 1987. Cognitive modifiability in the deaf adolescent. In *Proceedings of the Tenth World Congress of the World Federation of the Deaf,* Vol. I, ed. R. Ojala, 277–282. Finland.

————. 1989. *Cognitive enhancement of hearing impaired post-secondary students.* Paper presented at the Second International Symposium on Cognition, Education, and Deafness, Washington, DC: Gallaudet University.

McAndrew, H. 1948. Rigidity and isolation: A study of the deaf and blind. *Journal of Abnormal and Social Psychology* 43: 476–494.

Miller, M. S. 1984. Experimental use of signed presentations of the verbal scale of the WISC–R with profoundly deaf children: A preliminary report of the sign selection process and experimental test procedures. In *International Symposium on Cognition, Education and Deafness, Working Papers,* Vol. I, ed., D. S. Martin 167–185. Washington, DC: Gallaudet University.

Moores, D., T. Kluwin, C. Ewoldt, R. Johnson, P. Cox, L. Blennerhassett, L. Kelly, and C. Sweet. 1987. *Factors predictive of literacy in deaf adolescents,* Report No. NO1-NS-4-2365. Washington, DC: National Institute of Neurological and Communicative Disorders and Stroke.

Myklebust, H. R. 1953. Toward a new understanding of the deaf child. *American Annals of the Deaf* 98: 345–357.

————. 1964. *The psychology of deafness.* New York: Grune and Stratton.

Myklebust, H. R., and M. Brutten. 1953. A study of the visual perception of deaf children. *Acta Oto Laryngologica, Supplementum* 105: 1–126.

Office of Education 1977. Education of handicapped children: Implementation of part B of the education of the handicapped act. August *Federal Register* 42,496–42,297.

Oleron, P. 1950. A study of the intelligence of the deaf. *American Annals of the Deaf* 95: 179–195.

Palmer, L. L. 1983. Reuven Feuerstein's instrumental enrichment: A program for the teaching of thinking? *Developmentalist* 2(3): 5–12.

Pintner, R. 1923. *Intelligence testing.* New York: Henry Holt and Company.

Pintner, R., and D. G. Paterson. 1915. The Binet scale and the deaf child. *Journal of Educational Psychology* 6: 201–210.

————. 1917. *A scale of performance tests.* New York: D. Appleton and Company.

Pollard, G., and T. Oakland. 1985. Variables associated with educational development of residential deaf children. *Special Services in the Schools* 1(4): 67–82.

Porteus, S. D. 1924. *Guide to Porteus Maze Test.* Vineland, NJ: The Training School.

Powers, A., R. Elliot, and R. Funderburg. 1987. Learning disabled hearing impaired students: Are they being identified? *Volta Review* 89(2): 99–105.

Raven, J. C. 1938. *Progressive Matrices*. London: H. K. Lewis.

Ray, S. 1979. *An adaptation of the Wechsler Intelligence Scale for Children-Revised*. Northridge, CA: Steven Ray Publications.

Ray, S., and S. M. Ulissi. 1982. *An adaptation of the WPPSI for deaf children*. Northridge, CA: Steven Ray Publications.

Rosenstein, J. 1960. Cognitive abilities of deaf children. *Journal of Speech and Hearing Research* 3: 108–119.

———. 1961. Perception, cognition, and language in deaf children. *Exceptional Children* 27: 276–284.

Rush, P., L. Blennerhassett, and D. Alexander. 1989. *WAIS-R verbal and performance profiles of deaf adolescents referred for atypical learning styles*. Paper presented at the Second International Symposium on Cognition, Education, and Deafness, Washington, DC: Gallaudet University.

Salvia, J., and J. E. Ysseldyke. 1981. *Assessment in special and remedial education* (2d ed.). Boston: Houghton Mifflin.

Sattler, J. M. 1982. *Assessment of children's intelligence and special abilities* (2d ed.). Boston: Allyn and Bacon.

———. 1988. *Assessment in children* (3d ed.). San Diego: Jerome M. Sattler Publications.

Sisco, F. H., and R. J. Anderson. 1980. Deaf children's performance on the WISC–R relative to hearing status of parents and child-rearing experiences. *American Annals of the Deaf* 125: 923–930.

Smith, A. J., and R. E. Johnson. 1977. *Smith-Johnson Nonverbal Performance Scale*. Los Angeles: Western Psychological Services.

Spearman, C. E. 1927. *The abilities of man*. New York: Macmillan.

Spragins, A. B. 1979. *Training for specialty: The school psychologist and deafness*. Paper presented at the convention of the National Association of School Psychologists, San Diego, CA.

Spragins, A. B., L. Blennerhassett, and Y. Mullen. 1987. *Review of tests used with the hearing impaired in five assessment areas*. Paper presented at the convention of the National Association of School Psychologists, New Orleans, LA.

Stern, W. 1914. *The psychological methods of testing intelligence*. Baltimore: Warwick and York.

Stutsman, R. 1948. *Guide for administering the Merrill-Palmer Scale of Mental Tests*. Los Angeles: Western Psychological Association.

Templin, M. C. 1953. *The development of reasoning in children with normal and defective hearing*. Minneapolis: University of Minnesota Press.

Terman, L. M., and M. A. Merrill. 1973. *Stanford-Binet Intelligence Scale*. Boston: Houghton Mifflin.

Thorndike, R. L., E. P. Hagan, and J. S. Sattler. 1986. *The Stanford-Binet Intelligence Scale: Fourth Edition*. Chicago: Riverside Publishing.

Thurstone, L. L. 1938. Primary mental abilities. *Psychometric Monographs* 1.

Thurstone, L. L., and T. G. Thurstone. 1941. Factorial studies of intelligence. *Psychometric Monographs* 2.

———. 1962. *SRA Primary Mental Abilities*. Chicago: Science Research Associates, Inc.

Ulissi, S. M., P. Brice, and S. Gibbins. In press. Use of the KABC for children with hearing impairment. *American Annals of the Deaf.*

Vernon, M. 1967. Relationship of language to the thinking process. *Archives of Genetic Psychiatry* 16: 325–333.

Vygotsky, L. S. 1978. *Mind in society: The development of higher psychological processes.* Cambridge: Harvard University Press.

Watson, B., D. Goldgar, J. Kroese, and W. Lotz. 1986. Nonverbal intelligence and academic achievement in the hearing impaired. *Volta Review* 88(5): 151–158.

Watson, B. U., P. M. Sullivan, M. P. Moeller, and J. K. Jensen. 1982. Nonverbal intelligence and English language ability in deaf children. *Journal of Speech and Hearing Disorders* 47: 199–204.

Wechsler, D. 1967. *Manual for the Wechsler Preschool and Primary Scale of Intelligence.* New York: Psychological Corporation.

———. 1974. *Manual for the Wechsler Intelligence Scale for Children–Revised.* New York: Psychological Corporation.

———. 1981. *Manual for the Wechsler Adult Intelligence Scale–Revised.* New York: Psychological Corporation.

Woodworth, R. S., and F. L. Wells. 1911. Association tests. *Psychological Monographs* 8(5): 53–55.

PART TWO

The Deaf Child at Home

11

Research on Developmental Aspects of Deafness

Kathryn P. Meadow-Orlans

A developmental perspective encompassing the entire life span has become a more widespread approach to the study of human behavior during the past two decades. It is recognized that an understanding of all stages of life is important for appreciation of a single developmental period. When deafness is involved, a life-span perspective is both more important and more difficult to acquire. It is more important because events, institutional/societal arrangements, and family/educator responses may be different for the deaf person at different developmental periods, thus creating unexpected life experiences. This life-span perspective is also difficult to acquire because systematic study of some developmental periods is lacking (particularly studies of infancy and old age).

Professionals who have intensive experience with deaf individuals at one period of the life span may lack experience with them at other ages. It has long been my contention that the violent conflicts and controversies surrounding education and communication for deaf people are fueled by rigid specialization among the (hearing) professionals who serve them. Teachers of young deaf children often have little contact with those children after they leave school. Rehabilitation counselors who work with deaf adults know little about deaf children and even less about the experiences and feelings of hearing parents.

Educational provisions for deaf children are necessarily "special" in order to create environments that cater to their reliance on visual cues. This maintains a focus on educational or academic/cognitive development to the detriment of social/emotional development. This emphasis results in deaf children with widely varying needs being grouped together in the same schools and classrooms. (For example, deaf children whose parents have normal hearing and have not learned sign language are placed together with deaf children who have a native knowledge

Some of the material in this chapter was adapted from K. P. Meadow-Orlans, Understanding Deafness: Socialization of Children and Youth, in *Understanding Deafness Socially,* ed. P. C. Higgins and J. E. Nash (Springfield, IL: Charles C. Thomas, 1987), 29–58. Courtesy of Charles C Thomas, Publisher, Springfield, Illinois.

of Sign). Such grouping also excludes the hearing children of deaf parents from any special provisions. A life span perspective on deafness and development should include that group plus the siblings and the grandparents of deaf children. In other words, a life span or developmental perspective should be broader than an educational perspective, in terms of age levels included and in terms of the total social environment of the deaf individual.

It is no accident that the setting for research on deaf children more often has been the school than the home. One reason is merely demographic: the low incidence of deafness means that it is easier to locate groups of children for testing or observation in schools. The children's homes are widely scattered and difficult to reach. There are other, more complex reasons, however. Education begins earlier for deaf children than for their hearing counterparts. Mandatory educational provisions begin at either five or six years of age for children in regular classrooms. For children receiving special education, provision is made no later than age three. Increasingly, school districts are required to offer special programs from birth onward. This trend toward early intervention is seen as a positive influence—a "head start" for children with special educational and developmental needs. Thus school teachers and administrators have an earlier and more intense role in the lives of deaf children, compared to children in regular educational settings.

While early intervention is a desirable goal, there are some dangers in transferring a major responsibility away from the home. One danger is that the parents may be delayed in feeling responsible and competent in relation to their own child, and those feelings may even be permanently reduced. Another is that cognitive/educational tasks may be overemphasized for deaf children relative to social/emotional development.

Research with deaf children both reflects and lags behind existing educational provisions. More research has been done on educational/cognitive development over the years, with less emphasis on social/psychological growth; more research has been done on children of school age, less on very young deaf children or on postgraduate deaf adults. An important reason for the absence of research on deaf infants has been the difficulty of diagnosing hearing loss at an early age. Technical capabilities have improved so that this obstacle is decreasing. Unfortunately, as we have found in our efforts to recruit deaf infants for our current research, improved technology does not always result in immediate and widespread increases in the number of children who receive an early diagnosis.

Another reason for the importance of a life-span approach to an understanding of deafness and development is the influence of prior experience on the patterns influencing the next generation of deaf individuals. We neglect the obvious truth that today's deaf children of hearing parents are tomorrow's deaf parents of deaf (or hearing) children. The fact that they are the children of hearing parents makes their parenting different from that of their peers with deaf parents. We also neglect the influence that grandparents (and even great-grandparents) have on families with deaf members. The control exerted by the older hearing generation is often greater than that found in comparable families with no deaf members.

One lesson we have learned from the many deaf individuals and families who have participated in our developmental research at the Center for Studies in Education and Human Development (CSEHD) over the years is that a wide range of normal variation exists within groups of deaf children or deaf adults. Sometimes it seems that each individual or family is a case study in itself. In the presentation of group data, these individual differences must be blurred. It is necessary to work back and forth between individuals' experiences and group summaries to reach an understanding of the developmental process.

BUILDING ON PREVIOUS DEVELOPMENTAL RESEARCH

Like all research, the developmental research done by members of CSEHD has built on that done by others. In addition, research has been shaped by the interests, training, and orientation of individuals responsible for carrying out projects. In some cases, it has been influenced by legislation affecting the education of deaf children (especially by Public Law [PL] 94-142). Another factor is our location in the Kendall Demonstration Elementary School (KDES). Until the creation of the Gallaudet Research Institute and the Center for Studies in Education and Human Development, we were part of the KDES structure, reporting to the dean or to the principal.

Despite the range of interests, trends, and institutional demands that has shaped the nature of developmental research within CSEHD, the most important influences have been the historical experiences of deaf people, and the research knowledge gained from previous work of others. As a background for the chapters included in Part Two, it may be helpful to summarize this work.

The Early Years: Diagnosis and Linguistic Choices

Most parents of deaf children have never known a profoundly deaf individual. More than 90 percent of the parents of deaf children have normal hearing themselves (Rawlings and Jensema 1977). These parents immediately confront two related problems when deafness is diagnosed in their infant. First, the parents must cope with the shock of learning about an unexpected handicap. Second, they must face the difficulties of communicating with their child in the absence of a common (that is, a spoken) linguistic system. This is the central feature of the early experiences of deaf children: The language readily available to deaf children is not the language used by their parents.

One group of parents does have command of a linguistic system enabling them to communicate easily with their deaf children. These are parents who are deaf themselves and who, therefore, are fluent in sign language. The experiences of deaf children from these two kinds of families are very different indeed. There are wide variations in socialization patterns and problems of the deaf children in these two groups (that is, the group with deaf parents and the group with hearing parents), but this one dimension helps to explain and underline some of the most basic social processes at work in the lives of deaf children.

For deaf parents, deafness is a familiar condition. They have a wide circle of deaf friends. They probably participate in a community composed primarily of deaf people (Padden 1980). They know the educational opportunities available for deaf children, and the vocational possibilities that lie ahead. They can anticipate rearing their deaf child as they themselves were reared, or perhaps with modifications based on experiences they want to avoid. For parents with normal hearing, all these areas provide unknown vistas. Their own family experiences provide few guidelines for the socialization of their deaf child. From their first suspicion of their child's hearing loss, through their contacts with medical, audiological, and educational specialists, into the child's preschool, elementary, high school, college or technical training experiences, the deaf parents and the hearing parents of deaf children will have differing understandings and differing expectations. Contrasting the hopes and fears, the expectations, and the obligations of deaf and hearing parents of deaf children, it is possible to come to a deeper understanding of the developmental process as it is influenced by the condition of deafness.

For most parents with normal hearing, the diagnosis of deafness in a young child comes as a profound shock. Often, the diagnosis confuses deafness with other kinds of impairments, such as mental retardation or emotional disturbance. The struggle to achieve a firm medical opinion about the child's condition may be debilitating for parents, and this concern and confusion interferes with early child-rearing practices. Parents sometimes are made to feel incompetent to deal with their child's needs, particularly when they are told by medical professionals that their suspicions of "something wrong" are false (Williams and Darbyshire 1982). Thus, the earliest experiences of hearing parents around their child's deafness can create strong feelings of inadequacy. Their own feelings of stress and helplessness can be communicated to the child, resulting in spirals of tension and helplessness that may contribute to general family chaos. This unhappy scenario is even more likely in families where the deaf child is the firstborn. Confidence that other parents gain from prior parenting experience cannot emerge in these parents. Sometimes they can look to a supportive extended family for help. For others, this support may come from educational professionals or from other parents with similar experiences. However, many families face the dark days of diagnosis alone.

Some professionals who have worked extensively with parents and children believe that the diagnosis of a handicap in a young child evokes a response of grief in the parents similar to the grief felt for the death of a loved one. Many parents find disability to be the great spoiler of their dreams and fantasies about who or what their child was to be. Most dreams require an unimpaired child; therefore, the initial diagnosis of disability often marks the point when a cherished and significant dream has been shattered (Moses 1985, p. 86). The particular processes experienced by many parents of handicapped children have been discussed by professionals who are experienced in counseling them. The response to the diagnosis of hearing loss has been described as similar to the reaction to other kinds of crises:

shock, recognition, denial, and acknowledgement, followed by constructive action (Kubler-Ross 1969; Luterman 1984).

Although parents may not experience these emotions in any particular order, most hearing parents probably feel this way about their hearing-impaired children at various times and in various ways. Some of the "states of grief" identified by Moses include denial, guilt, depression, anger, anxiety, and coping.

Schlesinger (1985) also observed a sense of powerlessness in parents of a newly diagnosed deaf child. That is, parents may feel that they should be able to do something to reverse the unwelcome diagnosis. When they are told by medical specialists that "nothing can be done," their sense of being unable to influence the destiny of their young child is overpowering for them. Schlesinger believes that the sense of powerlessness continues beyond the child's infancy and becomes particularly intense when parents begin to try to communicate with the child and are unsuccessful. They then become more and more domineering as they try harder and harder to break through the communication barrier.

The responses of deaf parents to the diagnosis of deafness in a young child may have quite a different quality, compared to those of hearing parents. We expect that deaf parents will not be upset with the diagnosis of deafness in a child, that, indeed, they may welcome it with a feeling that they are better prepared to parent a child whose hearing status is like their own. However, in this area as in so many others, there is a wider variation in parental reaction than might be expected. Some parents who are deaf themselves may hope that the child's pattern of hearing loss is similar to their own. They may be just as anxious to get a confirmed diagnosis—that is, to *know* what to expect—as are hearing parents. Or, they may be just as upset as any hearing parents when the diagnosis of deafness comes unexpectedly.

A deaf couple tells a particularly striking story of the effect of their child's diagnosis of hearing impairment. Both husband and wife believed their deafness to be the result of nongenetic causes and therefore assumed their children would have normal hearing. When their first child was two years old, the director of a nursery program for hearing-impaired children urged them to enroll him as part of a "reverse mainstreaming" project. One month later, the parents were shocked to receive a call saying a hearing loss was suspected in the child. The wife reports, "I remember my shock and disbelief when [my husband] came home to tell me the news. It just couldn't be. It was as if someone we loved had died. Certainly something in us died" (Thompson, Thompson, and Murphy 1979, pp. 338–339).

The meaning this situation has for parents is influenced by their own hearing status, by their prior experiences with deafness, by the expectations and attitudes of family members about hearing loss, and by whether the diagnosis represents a shift in their understanding of the child's hearing status. All of these factors help to create a context for parents' definitions of the diagnosis. This definition, in turn, creates a context for the socialization of the child at successive stages of life. For parents who know very little about deafness (primarily parents who themselves have normal hearing), the manner in which they are informed of the hearing loss may have an important influence on later behavior as well.

Just as the diagnosis of hearing loss creates a context for socialization that cuts across the childhood and adolescence of the deaf child, so does the linguistic orientation of the parents. For hearing parents, decisions about the use of sign language vs. cued speech vs. only spoken English are the ones that will probably be most critical.

Nash and Nash (1981, pp. 47–61) have proposed a typology for describing hearing parents of deaf children in terms of their orientation to language mode. They describe one group of oralists as "recruiters" who see the use of sign language as a last resort "used only when a child is hopelessly handicapped" (p. 48). These parents proselytize others to their views and follow an active strategy of convincing parents of other deaf children that theirs is the preferred way. The second group of oralists is called "the searchers"—not completely convinced that oral-only education is the correct answer, but continuing to search for medical remediation to normalize their child. The third group, "the aloof," rely on special schools and teachers to "make oralism work" for their deaf child, while they engage in other kinds of activities.

Hearing parents who support the use of sign language are also divided into three types. The first is resigned to its use, feeling that it is the best that can be expected for deaf children, even though sign language is considered second best to oralism. The second type of sign language users are called "sign changers." They try to become familiar with the experiences of deaf people, but they prefer to change the sign language of deaf adults into a more English form—one of the artificial sign languages that follows the grammar and syntax of spoken English. The third group of signers among hearing parents are the "friends of the deaf." These parents may attempt to participate in the Deaf community to a greater extent than any of the other groups of deaf parents. Although they probably will not become fluent in American Sign Language, they are sympathetic to the experiences of deaf people and to their attachment to their own language as an expression of culture or ethnicity.

Regardless of hearing parents' linguistic orientation, if they are committed to the use of sign language, there will be times when the use of a new and unfamiliar language with their child will become taxing.

There is variation in the linguistic orientations of deaf parents of deaf children as well as in hearing parents. Much of the variation is related to the parents' own childhood experiences. Erting (1987) has described in rich detail the ideas and linguistic attitudes of a group of deaf parents in a school for deaf children in which she was closely involved. She describes some of the background of their approach to education in their children as follows:

> Deaf parents' emphasis on communication rather than language (structured English lessons) as a central part of the curriculum for preschoolers was a realistic response to the constraints imposed by deafness as they had experienced them.

They remembered their own school experiences, with time spent day after day in drill and memorization of English sentences that could have been spent acquiring knowledge and developing cognitive skills. They remembered their frustration and low self-esteem as they tried to attain the perfect speech and English skills their hearing teachers worked so hard to teach. In contrast, they remembered the freeing experience of communicating with other deaf people—perhaps their parents, their peers, and Deaf teachers who often were responsible for rekindling curiosity and a desire for learning through information not previously accessible. They wanted their children to have this experience in their formative years so they would develop the positive self-image and eagerness to learn important to their future academic and linguistic success (p. 148).

Deaf Children: Development from Birth to Age Five

Until CSEHD studies of deaf infants began in 1984, little information was available about the first year in the life of a hearing-impaired infant. A limited number of research studies had been completed that gave us some notion of how socialization might differ for deaf or hearing infants who have deaf parents. Deaf parents had been observed to use touch in a variety of ways to reinforce interaction, to sensitize their infants to basic aspects of space and time in signing and fingerspelling, and to help the infants to attend visually (Maestas y Moores 1980). They were observed to sign on the infant's body and to mold or physically guide their infant's hands, sometimes in shapes that approximated sign language.

In an effort to expand understanding of events in the first year of the deaf child's life, our research group began a series of pilot studies with deaf and hearing infants of hearing and deaf parents. Three chapters in this volume (chaps. 14, 15, 16) report data from these studies; this topic is also discussed by Erting, Prezioso, and Hynes (1990).

For hearing mothers, concerned about the nature of the "difference" they feel in their hearing-impaired infants and worried about the implications, it is likely that normal early interaction would also be impaired. The results of one study of two deaf infants with hearing mothers (Nienhuys and Tikotin 1983) suggests that some differences between these sets of mothers and infants and others with normal hearing were attributable to the mothers' depression. The mothers were observed to play less with their infants compared with mothers of hearing babies studied previously. Clearly, it is difficult for parents to engage in their normal behaviors when they are deeply concerned about the health and normal development of their infants. It would seem clear that these parents need support services and supportive social networks if they are to face the difficulties of parenting their deaf children. (This need is addressed in chapter 12 by Koester and Meadow-Orlans.)

A recently reported study of stress and support in families with deaf children suggested that support services have improved greatly in the past ten years for families with children younger than five years of age. However, the quality and quantity of these services declines abruptly after the age of five (Calderon, Greenberg, and Kusché 1989).

While any number of studies of deaf children with deaf parents indicate that these children acquire sign language at the same rate and in the same progression as hearing children acquire spoken language, deaf children of hearing parents are almost inevitably delayed in their language acquisition. Apparently this delay has a pervasive effect on interactions between parent and child. The eight studies of interactions of deaf children and their mothers published between 1970 and 1986 report a consistent set of findings (Day 1986; Goss 1970; Greenberg 1980; Henggeler and Cooper 1983; Hyde, Power, and Elias 1980; Meadow et al. 1981; Schlesinger and Meadow 1972; Wedell-Monnig and Lumley 1980). Hearing mothers of deaf children were clearly found to be more dominating and intrusive with their children. They tended to spend more time teaching their children and were rated as tense and antagonistic. The deaf children, on the other hand, were described as less compliant, less attentive, and less responsive than were the hearing children with whom they were compared. Perhaps the conflict between teachers' imperatives to communicate more and the deaf child's inability to communicate orally created pressure on mothers to try harder and harder to elicit responses. Thus, deaf children may be bombarded increasingly with messages they do not understand; they then become less attentive to their mothers and less compliant. The very behaviors that are sought appear less frequently than they otherwise might (Meadow 1980).

When communication between parents and a preschool child is dramatically reduced, parents become more protective of that child. The parents' definition of a child's fragility may be the critical factor, rather than the child's actual ability to perform a developmental task. One study of English families with deaf children reported that more than half of the mothers said they made concessions to their deaf children that were not made to siblings with normal hearing. For example, they were less strict about bedtimes and overlooked rule infractions that would have been punished in the other children. Of some significance is the fact that mothers of deaf children seemed more likely to make concessions than did a comparison group of mothers whose children had cerebral palsy. The kinds of punishment utilized with deaf children also were different from those used with hearing siblings (Gregory 1976). A laboratory study of hearing mothers and deaf children indicated that demands were relaxed for performance of simple tasks (Stinson 1974, 1978).

Parents feel it necessary to supervise their preschool deaf child more than they would if the child had no hearing loss. One group of parents reported a narrower range of disciplinary techniques, a heavier reliance on spanking, and more frustration around child-rearing techniques generally than did a comparison group of parents of children without hearing impairments (Schlesinger and Meadow 1972).

Deaf parents of deaf children appear to be less anxious about their deaf preschoolers' abilities to navigate within their neighborhood independently, about environmental dangers, and generally about their ability to care for themselves.

Deaf Children in Elementary School

Like most other tasks of childhood and adolescence, development of independence begins in the preschool years, if not in infancy. When a child starts elementary school, however, he or she is generally expected to be able to operate in many situations without parents. Hearing parents tend to shield their deaf children in the early years, and this extra protection carries over into middle childhood. The ability to care for oneself and to act independently influences classroom behavior as well as educational achievement and social relationships. Deaf children seem to have more difficulty in demonstrating independence than do children without hearing handicaps. Teachers tend to describe their deaf students as dependent on others for help; as giving up quickly and expecting to fail; and as demanding attention and help constantly and taking a disproportionate share of their teachers' time (Zwiebel, Meadow-Orlans, and Dyssegaard, chapter 19, this volume).

An early study of deaf children of deaf parents reported that their teachers saw them as more mature, more independent, and more capable of taking responsibility compared to deaf children of hearing parents, whether the children were enrolled in residential schools or in day schools (Meadow 1968; Schlesinger and Meadow 1972).

A study utilizing the Scales of Independent Behavior (Bruininks et al. 1984) reported interviews with twenty-five (hearing) parents of deaf children and twenty-five (hearing) parents of hearing children. The deaf children's scores were similar to those of the hearing children on subscales reflecting gross and fine motor skills and on subscales for personal and community living skills. The deaf students scored lower on subscales for social interaction, language comprehension, language expression, money and value, and home-community orientation. The authors suggested that the "independence" required for making a dental appointment or completing an application for a savings account are related to communicative ability, and that it is in these areas that the deaf students are deficient. (Klansek-Kyllo and Rose 1985).

Two other areas in which many deaf children seem to need special help are those of empathy and impulse control. The ability to think about the consequences of an action before impulsively rushing to an act or to a conclusion are important to the success of many interactions. The ability to understand the feelings of others as a possible basis for their actions, and to understand one's own emotions, are important for the child to grow successfully to adulthood. One psychologist studied impulsivity in deaf children of deaf parents and of hearing parents and found that deaf children of deaf parents were more capable of impulse control (Harris 1978).

As in other areas where deaf children are sometimes seen as deficient, lack of communication skill rather than auditory deprivation is the major basis for the deficiencies. A group of psychologists interested in the whole area of deafness and development have formulated the complex links between communication ability and impulse control in a useful way. They propose that misbehavior on the part of deaf children is punished not by verbal admonishment or by denial of privilege related to the misdemeanor, but by removal from a situation or by physical discipline. This is the case because too often parents do not have the level of communicative ability that would allow them to do otherwise. As a result of this general situation at home (and perhaps at school as well), deaf children have few experiences in which they learn exactly what was wrong about their behavior, how it affected other people, and what substitute behaviors would be more acceptable. In addition, parents are demonstrating that avoidance and physical action are acceptable ways of solving problems, and the children have few opportunities to learn from past difficulties. "Quite simply, the impact of these limited explanations and restricted experiences is to deny them their rightful opportunity to understand others" (Greenberg et al. 1984, p. 245).

Several studies of self-image or self-concept in deaf children and adolescents suggest that generally they may have less positive ideas about themselves than do comparable groups of hearing peers. Of more interest to us, perhaps, are differences among various subgroups of deaf children. Again, differences have been reported between groups of deaf children with deaf parents and those with hearing parents. One study subdivided the deaf children in each of these groups (that is, the group with deaf parents and the group with hearing parents) in terms of rankings for what was termed "family climate" (Meadow 1969). This grouping took account of socioeconomic factors as well as intactness of the family and interpersonal problems within the family. In the group of deaf children with deaf parents, those from the most positive family climates had the highest scores for positive self-image, followed by those with intermediate family climate ratings, with those in the lowest family climate group having the most negative self-image scores. However, in the group of deaf children with hearing parents, those with intermediate ratings for family climate received the highest scores for self-image. A possible explanation for this reversal of the expected finding was that hearing parents in the most positive family climates had the greatest expectations for their children's academic and oral language performance, and were, therefore, most disappointed in their children's achievements. The inability of the deaf child to meet parental expectations led to a poor self-evaluation.

In this same study, it was reported that children of hearing parents who had better oral communication skills had more positive self-image scores, while communication skill level made no difference in the self-image scores of children of deaf parents. The effect of school achievement on self-image scores was similar to the effect of communication skill acquisition. For the deaf children of deaf parents, school achievement had little relationship to self-image. For the deaf children of hearing parents, those with higher achievement test scores also had higher self-image scores.

Rodda and Grove (1987) discussed the complexities of factors influencing self-esteem in deaf children, and the difficulties of language and communication that compound the problems of measuring feelings about the self. They suggested that there is probably an interaction between academic achievement and self-esteem whereby each influences the other to accelerate either a positive or a negative outcome (pp. 87–91).

Deafness and Social Development in Adolescence

As deaf children reach high school age, it becomes more likely that they will be found in mainstream school situations. For adolescents who are in the process of learning "who they are" and who want badly to fit in with their peers, this can be an isolating, negative experience for students who are "different" in an important way, and whose communication skills set them apart from the group.

Ladd, Munson, and Miller (1984) reported on social interactions of high-school-age mainstreamed hearing-impaired students with their normally hearing peers. This research was carried out with students who were mainstreamed in vocational courses only. During a three-year period, increasing rates of interaction between deaf students and hearing students were observed, and the deaf students received average ratings on sociometric measures. Parents and teachers felt that the social situations of 60 percent of the hearing-impaired students were positive. Nevertheless, more than half of the hearing-impaired students had difficulty making friends with their hearing peers at school and had almost no contact with them outside of school hours.

Moores and his colleagues recently completed an in-depth review of the social and educational effects of mainstreaming placement on hearing-impaired students (Moores, Kluwin, and Mertens 1986). They concluded that the amount of social interaction taking place in mainstream environments is directly related to structured activities involving both deaf and hearing students. They also believe that the provision of support services can be an important influence.

Learning social expectations and the dimensions of socially approved behavior is another task of socialization that is continuous throughout childhood and adolescence. This is an area that psychologists often describe as *social adjustment*. Students who are at the extreme end of the continuum of social maladjustment might be considered emotionally or behaviorally disturbed. If the disturbance takes the form of acting out or aggressive behavior, and disrupts the classroom, the student would probably be excluded from school. Thus, this topic has been the focus of a good deal of attention from educators as well as from psychologists and others who deal with deaf students.

Deaf children generally are reported to show more problems in social adjustment than do hearing children (Meadow 1980). Deaf children of deaf parents are less frequently identified as exhibiting problems in emotional and behavioral adjustment than do deaf children of hearing parents (Stokoe and Battison 1981). A study of students between the ages of ten and fifteen compared the social and emotional adjustment of deaf students in residential and public schools with hard-of-hearing public school students and with public school students who had normal hearing. It was reported that deaf students in public school received lower ratings from teachers than did students in any of the other three groups. Hard-of-hearing students were rated significantly below the other two groups on items reflecting self-esteem (Farrugia and Austin 1980). Another study indicated that integration (or mainstreaming) appears to be beneficial for the academic achievement of deaf students, but that mainstreamed deaf students may have more personal and social problems than deaf students in segregated settings (Reich, Hambleton, and Houdin 1977).

Deafness and Experience

Concern has been expressed recently about negative descriptions of deaf persons that often emerge from social and psychological research findings. It has been said that "children learn what they live." When we realize that most deaf children do not have easy communication with their parents at home, that all their life experiences are skewed by this fact, and that a reduced ability to communicate has an impact on every area of human development, it does not seem strange that many deaf children and adolescents demonstrate behavioral difficulties or social developmental lags. Indeed, the fact that most deaf children are well-adjusted and "normal" is almost miraculous—their normality is a tribute to the resiliency of the human organism.

It is important to guard against research that takes only the perspective of the hearing world. Any researcher whose background, experience, or culture is different from that of the subjects of study must guard against an ethnocentric point of view. Collaboration with members of the cultural or linguistic group is extremely important. Training for researchers whose roots are in the deaf culture is of great importance for the future of significant research. This does not mean that all research done by hearing persons should be negated, only that it be evaluated with a view to the sensitivity, the knowledge, and the insight with which it was designed and conducted.

An inescapable component of the deaf experience is a dependency on hearing people fostered in deaf children during their early years and continued by the condition of deafness into adulthood. An important part of Schlesinger's (1985) theory about the feelings of powerlessness in parents of deaf children can be compared to the dependency and helplessness that exist in members of many disadvantaged and handicapped groups. She contended that individuals who have little power to influence their environment, to create their own destinies, become defeated and cease the effort to take responsibility for themselves. Another part of her theory relates to behaviors that are characteristic of many hearing mothers of deaf children—behaviors labelled "intrusive" and "controlling." Schlesinger suggests that these parental behaviors arise from feelings of powerlessness because the mothers "have brought forth a child with a disability that they cannot directly influence" through the usual communicative channel (p. 105). This is a persuasive argument, and it provides an explanatory developmental strand for some of the difficulties of autonomy experienced by deaf adolescents.

Erting (1987) has made an insightful point about the "dependency constraint" for deaf persons, an idea that may be complementary to Schlesinger's theory of powerlessness. Erting's point is that deaf people's reliance on the visual mode results in a certain amount of dependence on hearing people because the world is set up for persons who hear. Many everyday needs (to say nothing of emergency events) can only be taken care of through the auditory sense.

> For most people born to hearing parents . . . dependence begins at birth. Their dependence on people who hear has its roots in the emotionally powerful and influential experiences of early childhood and the parent-child relationship. Dependence continues in the spheres of education, religion, employment, and in the acquisition of goods and services provided and controlled primarily by those who infrequently confront or even think about deafness as a life experience . . . [Deaf people] continue to find their fate dependent, to a large extent, on the willingness of hearing people to interact with and accommodate them. (p. 131)

Although this appears to be an extremely illuminating insight, and (like many brilliant observations) obvious once it has been stated, there have been some interesting responses to Erting's idea. Deaf people generally are prepared to nod in agreement: "Yes, this describes an important part of our life experience." Hearing people who have often served as "brokers" for deaf persons in the hearing world—many interpreters, for example—find this notion quite unacceptable and argue bitterly that it is not true that deaf people are forced into dependency by the way things are structured in the hearing world. Perhaps it is more than a coincidence that interpreters find this idea unacceptable, since the need for an interpreter in public situations is certainly an unwelcome, and obvious, example of the dependency constraint.

Joining the ideas of Schlesinger and Erting, it might be suggested that the thrust toward dependency in deaf people arises from a combination of two sources: early experience and the existing social structure. One reason for dependency may come from early and continuing experiences that neither foster nor allow the development of autonomy as a habit or as a personality characteristic. The other reason for dependency is that which is embedded in the social structure and which is forced on deaf people even if their characters or personalities are strongly autonomous.

SUMMARY

During the ten years of research on developmental aspects of deafness within the Center for Studies in Education and Human Development, efforts have been made to maintain a life-span perspective. Whether the research has focused on infants or adolescents, on deaf parents or hearing parents, on prelingually or post-lingually deafened children, we have tried to keep the context of the life span intact. A second principle has been a continuing effort to avoid the pitfalls of the ethnocentric view of the hearing world when looking at deaf parents, and to remember the particular needs and problems faced by hearing parents. Third, we have tried to build on research efforts made in the past while expanding the horizons of knowledge for the present and the future.

REFERENCES

Bruininks, R. H., R. W. Woodcock, R. F. Weatherman, and B. K. Hill. 1984. *Scales of independent behavior.* Allen, TX: DLM Teaching Resources.

Calderon, R., M. T. Greenberg, and C. Kusché. 1989. The influence of family coping on the cognitive and social skills of deaf children. Paper presented at the Second International Symposium on Cognition, Education, and Deafness, Gallaudet University, Washington, DC.

Day, P. S. 1986. Deaf children's expression of communicative intentions. *Journal of Communication Disorders* 19: 367–385.

Erting, C. J. 1987. Cultural conflict in a school for deaf children. In *Understanding Deafness Socially,* ed. P. C. Higgins and J. E. Nash, 123–150. Springfield, IL: Charles C. Thomas.

Erting, C. J., C. Prezioso and M. O. Hynes. 1990. Mother signs in baby talk. In *From gesture to language in hearing and deaf children,* ed. V. Volterra and C. J. Erting, 97–106. Heidelberg: Springer-Verlag.

Farrugia, D., and G. F. Austin. 1980. A study of social-emotional adjustment patterns of hearing-impaired students in different educational settings. *American Annals of the Deaf* 125: 535–541.

Goss, R. N. 1970. Language used by mothers of deaf children and mothers of hearing children. *American Annals of the Deaf* 115: 93–96.

Greenberg, M. T. 1980. Social interaction between deaf preschoolers and their mothers: The effects of communication method and communicative competence. *Developmental Psychology* 16: 465–474.

Greenberg, M. T., C. A. Kusché, R. N. Gustafson, and R. Calderon. 1984. The PATHS project: A model for the prevention of psychological difficulties in deaf children. In *The habilitation and Rehabilitation of Deaf Adolescents,* ed. Anderson, G. B. and D. Watson, 243–263. Proceedings of the National Conference on the Habilitation and Rehabilitation of Deaf Adolescents, Wagoner, Oklahoma.

Gregory, S. 1976. *The deaf child and his family.* London: George Allen and Unwin.

Harris, R. 1978. Impulse control in deaf children: Research and clinical issues. In *Deaf children: Developmental perspectives,* ed. L. S. Liben, 137–156. New York: Academic Press.

Henggeler, S. W., and P. F. Cooper. 1983. Deaf child-hearing mother interaction: Extensiveness and reciprocity. *Journal of Pediatric Psychology* 8: 83–95.

Hyde, M. B., D. J. Power, and G. C. Elias. 1980. *The use of verbal and nonverbal control techniques by mothers of hearing-impaired infants.* Research Report No. 5. Mt. Gravatt, Australia: Mt. Gravatt College of Advanced Education, Centre for Human Development Studies.

Klansek-Kyllo, V., and S. Rose. 1985. Using the scale of independent behavior with hearing-impaired students. *American Annals of the Deaf* 130: 533–537.

Kubler-Ross, E. 1969. *On death and dying.* New York: Macmillan.

Ladd, G. W., H. L. Munson, and J. K. Miller. 1984. Social integration of deaf adolescents in secondary-level mainstreamed programs. *Exceptional Children* 50: 420–428.

Luterman, D. 1984. *Counseling the communicatively disordered and their families.* Boston: Little, Brown.

Maestas y Moores, J. 1980. Early linguistic environment: Interactions of deaf parents with their infants. *Sign Language Studies* 26: 1–13.

Meadow, K. P. 1968. Early manual communication in relation to the deaf child's intellectual, social, and communicative functioning. *American Annals of the Deaf* 113: 29–41.

———. 1969. Self-image, family climate and deafness. *Social Forces* 47: 428–438.

———. 1980. *Deafness and child development.* Berkeley: University of California Press.

Meadow, K. P., M. T. Greenberg, C. Erting, and H. Carmichael. 1981. Interactions of deaf mothers and deaf preschool children: Comparisons with three other groups of deaf and hearing dyads. *American Annals of the Deaf* 126: 454–468.

Moores, D. F., T. N. Kluwin, and D. M. Mertens 1986. *High school programs for deaf students in metropolitan areas, progress report* Research Monograph No. 3. Washington, DC: Gallaudet University.

Moses, K. L. 1985. Infant deafness and parental grief: Psychosocial early intervention. In *Education of the Hearing Impaired Child,* ed. F. Powell, T. Finitzo-Hieber, S. Friel-Patti, and D. Henderson, 85–102. San Diego: College-Hill Press.

Nash, J. E., and A. Nash. 1981. *Deafness in society.* Lexington, MA: Lexington Books.

Nienhuys, T. G., and J. A. Tikotin. 1983. Pre-speech communication in hearing and hearing impaired children. *Journal of British Association of Teachers of the Deaf* 6: 182–194.

Padden, C. 1980. The deaf community and the culture of deaf people. In *Sign language and the deaf community, Essays in honor of William C. Stokoe,* ed. C. Baker and R. Battison, 99–104. Washington, DC: National Association of the Deaf.

Rawlings, B. W., and C. J. Jensema. 1977. *Two studies of the families of hearing impaired children.* Series R, Number 5. Washington, DC: Gallaudet University, Office of Demographic Studies.

Reich, C., D. Hambleton, and B. Houdin. 1977. The integration of hearing impaired children in regular classrooms. *American Annals of the Deaf* 122: 534–543.

Rodda, M., and C. Grove. 1987. *Language, cognition and deafness.* Hillsdale, NJ: Lawrence Erlbaum and Associates.

Schlesinger, H. S. 1985. Deafness, mental health, and language. In *Education of the hearing impaired child,* ed. F. Powell, T. Finitzo-Hieber, S. Friel-Patti, and D. Henderson, 103–116. San Diego: College-Hill Press.

Schlesinger, H. S., and K. P. Meadow. 1972. *Sound and sign: Childhood deafness and mental health.* Berkeley: University of California Press.

Stinson, M. S. 1974. Maternal reinforcement and help and the achievement motive in hearing and hearing-impaired children. *Developmental Psychology* 10: 348–353.

————. 1978. Effects of deafness on maternal expectations about child development. *Journal of Special Education* 12: 75–81.

Stokoe, W. C., and R. M. Battison. 1981. Sign language, mental health, and satisfactory interaction. In *Deafness and mental health,* ed. L. K. Stein, E. D. Mindel, and T. Jabaley, 179–194. New York: Grune and Stratton.

Thompson, R. E., A. Thompson, and A. Murphy. 1979. Sounds of sorrow, sounds of joy: The hearing-impaired parents of hearing-impaired children—a conversation. *Volta Review* 81: 337–351.

Wedell-Monnig, J., and J. M. Lumley. 1980. Child deafness and mother-child interaction. *Child Development* 51: 766–774.

Williams, D. M. L., and J. O. Darbyshire. 1982. Diagnosis and deafness: A study of family responses and needs. *Volta Review* 84: 24–30.

12

Parenting a Deaf Child:
Stress, Strength, and Support

LYNNE SANFORD KOESTER, KATHRYN P. MEADOW-ORLANS

All families, even the most cohesive and seemingly invulnerable, must weather many stormy passages in the normal course of development. Within the family unit, individuals are bound together by strong emotional ties and mutual influences. It is therefore inevitable that changes in patterns of behavior or deviations from expected development by one member will have an impact on others in the family. Learning that a child is handicapped, whether this knowledge comes at birth or at some later date, is one of the most stressful of family experiences. As Howard (1978) noted, "Instead of appreciating the baby's abilities, the family will see instead evidence of his deficiencies . . . each member of this unit, including the handicapped child, influences marital quality and family interaction" (p.275).

This chapter has two purposes: (1) to review the current level of knowledge about the effects of family stress and the roles of social support in mediating or buffering that stress; and (2) to relate these effects to the presence of a deaf child in the family as the child progresses through various developmental milestones requiring renewed adaptation by each family member.

This discussion emphasizes hearing families with deaf infants, rather than families with older children, because (1) the demographic/assessment trend is toward earlier diagnosis; and (2) less attention has been paid in previous literature reviews to this important period, primarily because most deaf children are not diagnosed before the age of three. The last part of this chapter is devoted to short sections on the stress of hearing loss and the family's response during older childhood and adolescence, since we believe that each period in the developmental cycle brings new stress and requires additional creative methods of coping for families with deaf children.

We have chosen to focus primarily on those families with hearing parents and deaf children because we believe that this combination creates a great deal

Research for this chapter was supported, in part, by the Division of Maternal and Child Health, Bureau of Health Care Delivery and Assistance (Grant MCJ-110563).

more stress and a greater need for coping skills than is experienced by deaf parents with deaf children. That is, deafness itself is not necessarily a handicap in a family context that already includes sign communication, participation in and support by the Deaf community, and familiarity with the educational choices and resources available to the child. Despite the increasing awareness in Western culture about the competence, potential, and contributions of deaf individuals, it is nevertheless still the case that most hearing parents *perceive* their child's deafness as a handicapping condition. In reality, parents who are part of the hearing world and expect to be able to share that experience with their children are—at least initially—greatly affected by the communication difficulties that they assume will be inevitable after they learn that their child is deaf. Thus, the impact of deafness on dynamics within the family depends largely upon the meaning which that family attributes to it. Being deaf does not, in itself, predetermine a given child's path of development any more than does the fact of being left-handed or being six-feet tall. Rather, the context in which deafness occurs, and the interpretations placed on it by others, will be far more influential in shaping the child's future progress and adjustment.

The experience for parents who are themselves deaf is obviously very different. These parents have their own needs, expectations, and self-concepts, all of which are less easily threatened by the diagnosis of the child's deafness than are those of hearing parents. Furthermore, deaf parents are likely already to be part of the linguistic community to which their child will eventually belong, and they are knowledgeable about opportunities and philosophies related to the education of deaf people.

EFFECTS OF STRESS ON THE FAMILY

McCubbin and Patterson (1983) defined *stressor* as a life event or transition experienced by the family that has the potential or actual effect of producing change in the family system. Family responses following a crisis are the result of interactions among multiple psychological, familial, and social factors, all of which should be addressed in order to deal satisfactorily with the ensuing stress. Thus, the family's resources, or its ability to prevent a *change* from becoming a *crisis,* must be considered. That is, what is the family's capacity for resisting disruption in the light of a serious stressor such as diagnosis of deafness in one of its members? In addition, the family's own subjective interpretations of the meaning or impact of the event must be taken into account, as these may differ from the societal norm. It is this subjective definition that may determine whether stress becomes *dis*tress: "A family's outlook can vary from seeing life changes and transitions as challenges to be met to interpreting a stressor as uncontrollable and a prelude to the family's demise" (p. 9).

Family disruption resulting from a crisis depends partly on the family's ability to restore equilibrium while simultaneously making necessary changes in its own structure and patterns of interaction. If the family has access to existing sources of support and is able to utilize them, and if family members define the situation so as to resist disruption and maintain stability, then even the extraordinary stress of diagnosis may not reach crisis proportions. Unfortunately, a stressful event is rarely experienced in isolation, as all too often the onset of one stressor is followed by others.

Stress in Families with Exceptional Children

The relationships among parenting stress, social support, and psychological adjustment have been investigated recently with a variety of populations: teenage mothers, single parents, and families with a handicapped or premature child are among the most frequently cited in the literature. While all these special populations may be distinctly different from that of parents with a deaf child, they all share the phenomenon of additional stress beyond that normally associated with the birth of a child, and they all share the need for additional strength and resources both within and beyond the family itself.

The Importance of Social Support

Social support may be found at various levels, beginning with intimate relationships; progressing to friends and extended family members; and including neighborhood, community, and educational resources on a more formal level. According to Crnic and Greenberg (1987), an effective social support system is a source of assurance that one is valued, cared for, and accepted as a member of a network with shared obligations to one another. Results of their studies with mothers of preterm and full-term infants suggest that the support these mothers receive during the first year of an infant's life does influence parenting behaviors and early parent-child interactions: "Mothers' perceived satisfaction with their intimate, friendship, and community supports showed generally positive relationships to their reported life satisfaction, satisfaction with parenting, and the quality of their behavioral interactions with their infants" (p. 34).

Boukydis, Lester, and Hoffman (1987) have argued convincingly that the availability of social support is positively related to maternal psychological outcome, to mother-infant interactions, and by logical extension, to the infant's own development. Moreover, in reviewing comparisons of different populations of infants, of how individual differences (such as variations in temperament) affect parenting, and of the differing responses of social networks according to the health of the infant, they conclude that *infant* status must be included as a variable which itself influences the quality and functions of social support to the parents.

In one study of social support and maternal behavior with high-risk infants (comparing both sick and healthy preterm and full-term infants), the researchers included infant risk status as a variable and found a relationship with the amount and type of support the mother received (Feiring et al. 1985). A control group of mothers with healthy full-term infants was matched with mothers in the risk groups according to income, education, occupation, family size, and ethnic background. Ironically, those mothers with the greatest need (that is, those with sick premature babies) reported the fewest friends and the fewest people providing support through gifts and baby supplies. By contrast, mothers with sick full-term infants (who are expected to survive their illness) seemed to be the ones who received goods from the greatest number of people. Nevertheless, mothers of sick infants in general were the recipients of fewer offers of supportive services by others (such as housekeeping or babysitting), despite the fact that having a sick infant is more exhausting and demanding in terms of routine caregiving tasks. This point has been illustrated in interviews with mothers of deaf children who report greater difficulty finding others who are willing to help care for their child. As one parent of a twelve-month-old reported,

> It's gotten to the point now that even my family will bow out. . . . With the neighbors, once they find out he's hearing-impaired, it makes them nervous. Not that they think it's catching or anything like that, but they're afraid they won't be able to communicate with him, or they won't know what to do if his hearing aids fall out.

Feiring and her colleagues suggested that since mothers of sick infants receive fewer services from others, they are more vulnerable to stress and feel more inadequate as parents. Mothers who received adequate support engaged in more episodes of close, proximal stimulation with their infants: "Again, provision of support to a mother of a sick infant may reaffirm her faith that her infant will survive and encourage her caretaking behavior" (Feiring et al. 1985, p. 16).

As others have also found (e.g. Crockenberg 1981; Weinraub and Wolf 1983), the responsiveness of the social network may mediate parental interactions with high-risk infants, so that support to the mother reinforces positive qualities of her interaction with the child during infancy. Another study of premature and full-term infants (Crnic et al. 1983) showed that mothers reporting high stress but little social support were less sensitive to their infants' cues and less likely to use behaviors that foster healthy social-emotional development in the infant than were mothers experiencing equally high stress but also reporting high levels of support. In contrast, Crockenberg found that stressful life circumstances after the birth of a child (such as loss of a job or the absence of the father) negatively influenced the effectiveness of social supports for teenage mothers. That is, when stress was particularly high, interactions with their infants lacked many of the verbal, visual, and tactile components characterizing optimal dyadic relationships. Only under conditions of relatively little stress did social support predict such behaviors as smiling and eye contact between the teen mothers and their babies.

For families with young deaf children, it is possible for professionals representing formal intervention programs to become an important part of a support network. Greenberg's evaluation study (1983) of two contrasting intervention programs for deaf toddlers showed significant differences in measured stress levels experienced by families. Families reporting lower levels of stress were those participating in the program where counseling for the emotional response to the diagnosis of deafness was a major component.

Disruption of Normal Parenting Behaviors

It is important to emphasize that the psychological state of the mother, either due to her own personality or due to temporary alterations caused by stress (such as that brought on by the diagnosis of a handicapping condition), has been shown to influence interactions with, and developmental outcomes for, the infant. Studies of disruptions in normal parent-infant interactions, such as those using the "still-face" condition in which the adult is instructed to look at the infant without responding or showing any expression, have shown two patterns of infant behavior: (1) the infant tries to repair the interactive failure but is unable to do so as long as the distortion continues; and (2) negative affect continues to build as long as the infant is still motivated to interact but is unsuccessful (Tronick and Gianino 1986).

If interactive distress is prolonged, the infant may attempt to use both positive and negative affect to signal or reengage the partner, may push away or withdraw from the source of stress, or may shut down visual perception of the stressful stimuli by "looking without seeing"—staring blankly as if the partner were not even there. While all these may be effective coping strategies in helping the infant reduce negative affect, only the behavior of *signalling* is also effective in maintaining the infant's involvement with the partner. An infant who repeatedly resorts to the use of other coping strategies sacrifices potential social interaction in the interest of maintaining its own internal regulation. "The infant turns inward, away from social engagement, and increasingly utilizes self-directed regulatory behaviors that reduce his sensitivity to the inappropriate emotional feedback provided by the mother" (p. 9).

If the infant's partner is in the process of grieving for the wished-for child, it is easy to imagine that there may be a period of prolonged interactive failure during which the infant's attempts to engage in satisfying interactions, or to repair the imperfections and mismatches expected within the normal range of parent-infant relationships, will be continually frustrated.

In the case of mothers with clinical depressive symptoms, another research group reported that the mothers appeared to be detached, impatient, and insensitive to their seven-month-olds, and that there were few instances of contingency, turn-taking, or mutual responsiveness in the behaviors within the dyad (Cohn et al. 1986). Furthermore, the depressed mothers spent less time playing with their babies than did nondepressed mothers. The infants were less able to refocus on an object and to continue to interact with the environment at some level even when confronted with a nonresponsive partner. Thus, prolonged distortions in early interactions have the effect of disrupting the infant's emerging interpersonal skills *and* object skills. The negative affect engendered may well lead to a vicious cycle of continued interactive failure. If a parent learns that an infant is deaf and reacts with depressive symptoms and nonresponsive interaction patterns, the child may be subjected to the further disadvantage of a partner who is psychologically incapable of meeting the child's developmental needs.

THE CONTINUING NEED FOR FAMILY SUPPORT

Research literature related to parenting a mentally retarded child sometimes suggests that it is the initial diagnosis that initiates disequilibrium in the family, but that when this is followed by eventual adjustment to the special demands and the reality of life with this child, the family is able to proceed without further ill effects (Wikler 1981). However, recurrent discrepancies between parental expectations and the actual performance of the child may elicit renewed emotional stress and continuing need for support far beyond the years of infancy. Parents may find that the normal channels for seeking child-rearing advice are inadequate when a child has special needs, and that most information and support come from other parents with similar children. Even in this case, however, the wide variations among experiences may make this network an additional source of confusion and conflicting opinions.

It is important, as Boukydis (1987) has emphasized, to differentiate between a social *network* and social *support:* some people in one's social network may not provide support, and may, in fact, add to the burden by demanding additional output of time and energy. The extended family should not be overlooked as a potential source of much-needed help. However, it may also magnify parental stress by encouraging denial of the situation or by contributing to feelings of guilt, humiliation, and inadequacy (Mendelsohn and Rozek 1983).

The Particular Case of Deafness

Although in the past there often has been a tendency to treat the deaf individual separately, as an isolated entity (Murphy 1979), clearly the impact of deafness on the entire family dictates a very different approach. That is, the family itself should be considered the primary group interfacing with both the deaf child and society, and therefore also in need of resources, counseling, and ongoing support as the child develops. Each member of the family must be accepted and valued in a mutually nurturant family environment, including the often-overlooked siblings.

> Brothers and sisters play vital parts in the entire family drama, serving as a source of both nurturance and discomfort. They frequently find themselves recipients of uneven expectation standards, as 'compensators' for parental disappointment, as targets of jealousy, or as overworked caretakers of their impaired siblings. In addition, they might find it difficult to handle their friends' or neighbors' attitudes toward their 'special' family and feelings of frustration in communication may occur. On the other hand, many siblings appear to develop stronger characters in the presence of a handicapped sister or brother. (Murphy 1979, pp. 272–273)

Parents of children with special needs have certain experiences in common—searching for the best services, explaining their own needs as well as those of the child in a society that often rejects differences, and living with the fear of social isolation. Although moderate or "marginal" handicaps may, on the surface, appear to be less disruptive, they actually have the potential for more serious adjustment problems within the family compared to more extreme and obvious conditions (Fewell and Gelb 1983). Perhaps it is human nature to be made anxious by ambiguity. Certainly in the case of intermediate handicaps, parents experience great uncertainty about their child's future. For hearing parents with a deaf child, there is always the lingering hope that the child will be completely accepted in the "normal" world, or that professionals will provide them with a "solution" to a problem for which there is no solution. As Erting (1982) pointed out,

> A deaf child challenges a hearing parent's notion of selfhood at a very basic level, since hearing and speaking in order to communicate are aspects of the self which are so fundamental and taken for granted that they are not usually brought to consciousness for reflection unless challenged in this way. (p. 91)

For hearing parents, the discovery that their child is deaf may result in an abrupt change in their lives and in their perceptions of themselves as parents. The natural vocal communication between parent and child is now precluded, and in order to establish satisfactory communication the parents may well decide to incorporate visual-gestural methods to some degree, even if they remain basically committed to an oral approach. If they decide to learn American Sign Language instead, they may essentially forego their own language and that of their social sphere (that is, vis à vis the deaf child), and replace it with a system that will become their child's primary language (Erting 1982).

Quittner (in press), in a study of parental adjustment to the chronic stress of having a deaf child, reports that mothers of deaf preschoolers not only had smaller networks than those with hearing children, but that they also had more problematic relationships with friends and relatives in this network. Misconceptions about the child, advice-giving, and underestimates of the deaf child's abilities by friends, relatives, and community members were the most commonly reported problems, and parents may withdraw from those members of the network who are critical or whose attempts at support are not appreciated. It is also possible that middle-class parents may *over*estimate their deaf child's abilities, pushing the child to excel and disregarding evidence of limitations. The conflict that this can create is illustrated in parental responses to an interview question about the tensions between their own estimations and expectations of their child compared with those of other people. Both parents perceived that other people, such as school personnel, treated their seventh-grade daughter more like a fourth grader; on the other hand, the father felt that as parents they had always expected her to behave as if she were much older. This expectation was reflected in the fact that the child had been accepted into a summer Gifted and Talented Program at a nearby university. For this family, then, the dilemma centered around an apparent discrepancy between the daughter's social immaturity and her academic acceleration. [Material from interviews not otherwise identified are from unpublished data collected as part of the development of the research instrument "Impact of a Child's Hearing Loss on the Family."]

THE PROCESS OF FAMILY ADAPTATION

The initial period after diagnosis has a unique and highly emotional quality that is potentially a crisis for most families. Furthermore, immediate decisions must be made regarding the child's special training and education and regarding the approach that the rest of the family will take in developing effective means of communicating with the child. Nevertheless, as Mendelsohn and Rozek (1983) have pointed out, "These decisions need to be reexamined at different developmental points, from childhood through adulthood, and with each reexamination the family must struggle again to adjust to the disability" (p. 40). As one of the mothers interviewed explains,

> I think when she was an infant it hit us for the first time. We lost a lot of dreams at that point. You didn't know what you were getting into at all. . . . Now it's coming again at the teenage years when the kids now don't really want to be associated with someone that's different. . . . But luckily for us she's smart and she's got compensation so we have new hopes too.

The unique adjustment that the individual family makes to a child with special needs will depend greatly on the extenuating circumstances and the context of the particular family at the time the situation first becomes known. Previous stability and communicative effectiveness within the family will be of critical importance on the positive side, as will sources of negative external pressure, such as economic privation. A family with inadequate financial resources, or one for which unemployment is already (or potentially) a fact of life, faces an increased burden that may limit its ability to cope with the added demands of an exceptional child.

If this child is the firstborn, the parents' sense of competence and willingness to follow their own intuitions about appropriate caregiving and interaction styles may be severely tested. If there are other children in the home, their relationship with the parents may suffer as they, too, share the unique responsibilities of accepting, caring for, and loving the sibling who requires so much of the parents' time and attention. The mother in particular may feel the added pressures to remain at home with a special needs child: not to return to work if she had been employed (thereby adding further strain to the family's economic resources), and to assume the role of teacher herself.

The emotional reactions which have been shown to follow the birth of a congenitally malformed or seriously premature infant (Irvin, Kennell, and Klaus 1982; Kennell and Klaus 1982) may also be applicable to the response of most parents to the diagnosis of their child's hearing loss, particularly when the diagnosis is unexpected. Depression, mourning, and grief at the loss of their anticipated and idealized child are frequently reported parental responses to the birth or diagnosis in each of these cases (Howard 1978; Irvin et al. 1982; Wikler 1981). However, in light of individual family circumstances, and the strengths and resources that each family brings to the situation, we would argue that a strict delineation of "stages of adaptation" may not adequately represent the wide variability in parental responses. Typically, parents do experience an initial reaction of shock after the diagnosis, during which the normal feelings of joy and pleasure in the growing relationship with the child are suddenly disrupted. Feelings of irrationality and helplessness may take over, accompanied by frequent crying and an urge to flee or escape this undesired situation.

One complication noted frequently in relation to the diagnosis of deafness is that the initial response of pediatricians (implying that the parents are simply being overly concerned, for example) leads to unnecessary delays before referral for testing is made (Williams and Darbyshire 1982). At the time of diagnosis, parents need all the sympathetic help they can get just to manage this serious personal crisis—not, as one parent recalled, a doctor who refers to their child as "just one bad apple." As Williams and Darbyshire found in their study of parental perceptions of the way the diagnostic outcome was communicated to them, such help was critical to "parents' realistic acceptance of permanent hearing losses and their subsequent involvement in constructive training procedures with their children" (p. 25). Furthermore, they suggested that doctors should be more aware of the possibility of hearing loss in their young patients, more willing to view the parents as the "experts" regarding their own child, and consequently more ready to make referrals. "Phrases such as 'It's just a stage' and, 'Wait and see' should be struck from the vocabulary of primary care physicians when there is even a remote possibility of a communicative disorder" (p. 29).

Again, the unfortunate experience of one family, revealed in interviews, makes this point all too well.

Mother: We took her to our doctor and we said 'Well, she doesn't hear us. . . .' And he said, 'She hears.' We'd wait and we'd wait and he'd never read the charts. . . . He kept saying, 'Some kids don't talk until they're three, some kids don't talk until they're three and a half. Don't worry, don't worry.' We didn't look around.

Father: But we went—finally—we impressed upon them to have the hearing test done at the [hospital]. . . . We finally pushed for it.

Mother: But you know, it took me eight years until I could finally say to the same pediatrician, "From now on when somebody asks you and thinks their child is hearing-impaired would you please refer them right away?" It took me that long to get my courage to speak to him and he says, "Oh, come on!" I mean, he still was not accepting what I said.

Recovery from the initial shock may manifest itself in disbelief and denial, efforts to avoid admitting the problem, or unrealistic attempts to cushion the blow brought on by the child's condition. As Josefowitz comments (in Irvin et al. 1982), the anger that parents feel may be turned against some higher being who is perceived as having betrayed them, or against the medical professionals with whom the parents are in daily contact. No matter how much one does to help them through this difficult phase, it can never be enough, for "of course the only help really wanted is to have the child made whole again, and nothing short of that will do" (p. 232).

In the continuing process of accepting and adjusting to an exceptional child, parents often experience varying degrees of sadness, anger, and anxiety. They are sometimes hesitant to become closely attached to the baby, particularly in the case of a premature or congenitally malformed infant. However, since diagnosis of hearing loss usually occurs after the immediate postpartum period is over, the parents and the child usually have had time to develop a healthy attachment before the diagnosis of deafness.

One mother of an adopted child reports that it was actually *helpful* that the diagnosis came some time after they initially suspected their infant's hearing loss. She felt that after finally making the decision to adopt, discovering that their "beautiful baby was handicapped" would have thrown them into a very self-focused kind of despair: "We would have thought that God had doomed us and that we just weren't supposed to be happy." By the time of the diagnosis, however, she believed their bond with the child was so strong that their grief focused instead on the baby herself, and on their concern for *her* because she would never be able to hear.

On the other hand, it is also possible that the parents' efforts to establish vocal communication with their infant have failed or have been thwarted by the infant's lack of response to their voices, in which case the attachment process itself may have also been compromised (Howard 1978).

As the initial intense emotional reactions gradually subside, equilibrium is reestablished in the family, the parents regain their confidence, and the family finds the ability to accept and to deal with the situation that will continue for the life-time of the child. As the family undergoes this reorganization, eventually accept-ing the additional responsibility required, some family members may even go be-yond acceptance to the point of actively becoming advocates for the child with special needs. This positive, long-term acceptance evolves gradually out of mutual support within the family during the early years, assurances from friends and pro-fessionals that parents need not feel guilty, and the parents' renewed sense of com-petence in their abilities as parents.

Irvin and her colleagues (1982) have pointed out that family members may progress at different rates and with different styles through the process of regain-ing equilibrium after a major family crisis. The result may be only temporary emo-tional asynchrony between individuals in the family unit, or long-term difficulties in communication and understanding among them. It is important that professionals not deny the parents' need to experience these aspects of adjustment, as the unfortunate result may be that the parents simply intellectualize the problem without sufficiently working through it and coming to terms with their own emotional needs and responses. As with any challenge or crisis, successful mastery at one level helps to strengthen the individual's ability to continue coping, to respond adaptively to the next stressful event or upheaval.

The Effects of Deafness on Parent-Infant Interactions

As Erting (1982) has asserted, one of the most important concepts to remember in understanding deafness is that it is primarily a *visual* experience. Hearing parents who are confronted with a deaf infant may require special help in learning to respond to and fostering the child's reliance upon visual stimuli and signals as a unique communicative style is developed. Parents may need to be taught, for example, to respond to the child's early gestures by also using the visual-gestural modes themselves, rather than relying primarily on the auditory channel that is typically used by hearing parents in an exaggerated form ("Motherese" or baby-talk) with infants. They may also need to be sensitized to the importance of eye contact and the infant's shifts in eye gaze (Erting 1982), as ways of interpreting the infant's interests, level of attention, and receptiveness to environmental input.

Nienhuys and Tikotin (1983) elaborated on these points in their effort to understand how interactional synchrony between mothers and infants is affected by infant deafness. Reporting results from a pilot study of two mother-infant dyads (one with a normally hearing child and one with a profoundly deaf child), they pose the following questions:

> To what extent do the emotional stress and affective aspects which are introduced with the diagnosis of infant handicap affect the dyadic interchange? If the dyadic interchange is affected by infant hearing-impairment, what long term effects, reversible or otherwise, might be expected for the infant's subsequent communicative development? (p. 183)

As they noted, the deaf child cannot simultaneously attend to the visual surroundings *and* receive the ongoing vocal commentary about the world which is so often provided by an infant's partner. Instead, the deaf infant must divide its attention sequentially between the communication itself and the subject of communication (e.g., the infant looks toward the ceiling at a light, then looks back at the partner, who may then provide the appropriate label or comment about the light).

This may explain Nienhuys and Tikotin's finding that the deaf infant spent a much greater amount of time in either avert or attend behaviors than in play or talk (which were much more characteristic of the hearing infant). The same pilot study found that the mother may have a greater need to monitor the deaf child's behavior, leaving less time for her to initiate playful interactions. Nienhuys and

Tikotin also observed the expression of affect between the two partners: as shown in other studies with deaf infants, a large proportion of interaction time (98.5%) was characterized by neutral or negative affect, compared to 45.6 percent in the case of the dyad with a hearing baby.

Meadow-Orlans, Erting et al. (1986) have used the monadic-phase coding system (Tronick, Als, and Brazelton 1980) to examine the interactions between mother-infant dyads when the infants were between fourteen and sixteen weeks old (three deaf infants with deaf parents, three hearing infants with deaf parents, and three normal hearing dyads). By including both hearing and deaf mothers, Meadow-Orlans and her colleagues were able to determine that neutral affect may actually be more characteristic of the hearing mothers than of the deaf mothers. That is, mothers in the deaf/deaf pairs were much more likely to show positive facial affect than those in the hearing/hearing pairs. The authors concluded that, since facial expression is such an important component of communication among deaf people, these mothers intuitively begin to socialize their babies in these subtle nuances very early. By contrast, deaf infants with deaf mothers spent a higher percentage of time in behaviors categorized as *neutral attend* than infants in either of the other dyadic combinations (hearing/hearing or deaf/hearing). In this case, it may well be that a deaf infant who appears to be neutral in response to the mother's displays of positive facial expression is actually reading information from the face, rather than responding only to affect.

In another study of nine mother-infant dyads videotaped when the infants were three- and six-months old, the same research team concluded that the greater amount of positive facial affect observed in the deaf mothers may be their way of substituting for the positive vocal expressions of affect so commonly used by hearing parents with their babies. In addition, the greater amounts of neutral affect observed in the deaf infants with deaf mothers may be related to their heightened need for visual attentiveness. As Meadow-Orlans and her colleagues (1987) have stated: "Increased neutral affect from infants with deaf mothers may be a response to the fact that their mothers provide large amounts of information by means of the visual modality. If there is more happening visually for these infants (expressions on the mother's face, movements of her hands and her body), they may become accustomed quite early to focusing intently in order to process the additional volume of information provided in the modality that requires them to attend visually" (Meadow-Orlans, MacTurk et al. 1987, p. 3).

One implication of these findings is that hearing parents may need assistance in interpreting a deaf infant's signals, and in particular to avoid interpreting the child's seemingly neutral facial expressions as negative or expressionless. That is, we can learn a great deal by observing the ways in which deaf parents quite naturally seem to develop communication with their deaf infants, and much of this observation can be used to help hearing parents accept and foster the positive ways in which the deaf child approaches the world and relies upon personal strengths developed through other sensory channels.

Studies of the numerous forms of nonvocal stimulation provided by parents to their hearing infants (Koester 1987; Koester et al. in press) have shown that hearing parents typically supplement their vocalizations with a rich variety of temporally-patterned stimulation in the visual, tactile, kinesthetic, and vestibular modes during their normal face-to-face interactions with young infants. Therefore, the nonvocal behaviors that may be so important in eliciting and maintaining attention, and in communicating with a deaf infant in general, are already evident and used by most parents regardless of the hearing status of their child.

In the case of a deaf infant, then, the initial task for the parents will be to bring these behaviors to a more conscious level in order to emphasize them and to make them more dominant, rather than relying primarily on the auditory mode, as they may be inclined to do at first. Although the new behaviors initially may seem awkward and unnatural to the parents, the eventual goal should be to arrive at a style of interaction that is effective and mutually satisfying, in which the parent and the infant are responding to each other and influencing each other's behaviors. After the new method of interaction begins to take hold, the parents can once again rely on their intuitions instead of being preoccupied with the goal or outcome at every step. As these behaviors become more automatic and natural to the parent, the smooth flow of interactional synchrony should become increasingly apparent, allowing both members of the dyad to gain confidence in their newfound communication skills.

Beyond Infancy: Later Developmental Issues for the Deaf Child's Family

The context and emotional support provided at the time of a child's hearing loss is diagnosed may be crucial for setting the tone of parental acceptance of suggestions regarding early training and methods of communicating with the child. In the case of hearing parents, the most immediate decisions will relate to the use of some form of sign language, cued speech, or only spoken language. As Erting (1982) has noted, advocates of each method are often highly emotional in their rhetoric as they urge parents to make the "right" choice at a time when the parents themselves may not be sufficiently well informed of all the alternatives available to them. When this occurs soon after the diagnosis, as is often the case, the parents may be overwhelmed by conflicting information and controversy as they try to make a decision that will influence the child's future in school as well as in the home. For parents with more than one child, this decision will clearly have implications for the siblings as well. The entire family must adapt its style of communication in some very fundamental ways in order to accommodate the needs of the deaf child, and it is quite possible that this will entail learning a new language altogether—a task that is easier at younger ages and therefore may be less arduous for the children than for their parents.

Once the parents have committed themselves to a particular method of communication, they may also feel locked into that decision as if it were irreversible and may find themselves easily influenced by its proponents. According to Schlesinger and Meadow (1972),

From the time that deafness is diagnosed, mothers are exposed to a multitude of dicta related to what they should or should not do with, for, and to the deaf child. . . . However, if a mother is to retain her own style, and to incorporate the teacher's style rather than being engulfed by it, she needs self-confidence that often has been diluted by the difficult, guilt-producing process of adjusting to a handicapped infant. (p. 109)

Protectiveness vs. Autonomy

The development of a healthy sense of autonomy—a self-concept in which one is perceived as an independent and competent individual able to meet age-appropriate challenges alone and successfully—is a task that recurs in various dimensions throughout the life span. According to Erikson (1963), it is first and perhaps most dramatically evident during the stage of toddlerhood, when the infant is emerging as a being with distinct personality, motoric, and communicative characteristics that effectively allow a gradual separation from the primary care-givers, even though their support and protection are still very much needed. When the child has a sensory deficit, however, the parents may feel compelled to become more protective, to allow less active exploration of the environment (with its inherent risks), and to perceive the child as being more fragile or vulnerable than may actually be the case (Harvey 1989).

Again, the parents' own prior experience may be a crucial factor. Deaf parents with deaf children grant independence earlier than hearing parents. One hearing mother who acknowledged that she tended to treat her child as if she were much younger than her actual age, spoke about the issue of giving her child freedom: "I won't let her go somewhere because I'm afraid she couldn't communicate if she got in trouble or something . . . her freedoms are real limited." Aside from protectiveness, another reason for parents' inadvertently limiting their deaf child's steps toward autonomy may be the fear of social stigma or ostracism, and a resultant tendency toward withdrawal or isolation by the parents. Nevertheless, denying a toddler the opportunity to develop a sense of autonomy has long-term implications for his or her later development, as Meadow-Orlans (1987) has noted.

These early patterns may bear the fruit of less mature deaf teenagers and adults. It has often been observed that only those who have the opportunity to take responsibility for themselves become capable of doing so. Although it is difficult for hearing families to provide these opportunities for deaf children, it seems to be very important. (p. 43)

Early Childhood Education for the Deaf Child

Preschool programs designed specifically for handicapped children and those that integrate such children into classrooms with nonhandicapped peers both offer advantages and disadvantages that must be carefully considered in light of the particular needs of individual families. Turnbull and Blacher-Dixon (1980) reported a number of positive outcomes of preschool mainstreaming, including the opportunity for the special needs child to observe and model appropriate social and academic skills; the possible enhancement of the child's self-image; and the opportunity for the child's peers and teachers to develop sensitivity towards the needs and feelings of the handicapped. Many preschool programs require a high level of parent involvement, the primary goal of which is to support the developmental needs of the child. However, parents who are themselves working through the difficult process of adapting to the special situation of having a deaf child will need support for their own emotional needs and vulnerabilities. Their reaction to the efforts of the preschool program staff, and to their child's adjustment to the program, may depend largely upon the point they have reached in this adaptation process and the options they perceive as being available to them.

As Turnbull and her colleague asserted, a number of dilemmas face those parents who decide to place their preschooler in a mainstreamed setting, including

> the daily reminder of discrepancies between developmental deficits and normal development, the problem of 'shared stigma,' lack of interests in common with other parents, the responsibility associated with enhancing the social adjustment of the handicapped child, and the likelihood of supportive services available through the preschool program not being specifically geared to the needs of handicapped children and their families. (p. 34)

Furthermore, in a mainstreamed setting, the parents may feel compelled to sensitize teachers, children, and other parents to the special attributes of their child.

By contrast, a program specifically designed for deaf children offers an environment in which the child's developmental patterns are similar to those of classmates, amplification devices and stimulating visual input are the norm, and other parents are coping with similar adjustments in their own lives.

> Rather than being put in the position of supporting others, parents who themselves need support in coping with their emotional disorganization may need the implicit acceptance of others . . . The vulnerability of parents at a particular point in their adjustment process can be the determining factor in whether or not they can handle the additional responsibilities and stress of serving as change agents for the social acceptance of their child. (Turnbull and Blacher-Dixon 1980, p. 39)

For parents who are still working to accept the reality of having a deaf child, daily comparisons between their own child's progress and that of peers with normal hearing can be an additional source of anxiety and frustration and may result in undue pressure for the child to achieve. In some cases, then, segregated preschool settings may be particularly advantageous in helping the parents recognize, accept, and value their child's positive qualities. Exposure to models of other children and adults who have made successful adjustments to deafness may offer needed solace to these parents while providing an environment of acceptance and mutual support for the child.

In any discussion of the relative merits of mainstreamed vs. segregated classrooms, it is important to remember that decisions are rarely final or permanent, and that the needs of a particular family (including the emotional support required by both adults and children) may fluctuate over time and thus dictate new arrangements or changes in schooling as the child develops. For both deaf and hearing children, it is as important to interact with those of different backgrounds and capabilities as it is to share experiences with those similar to oneself. For the parents of deaf children, having a variety of options available regarding the upbringing of their child offers an additional degree of flexibility and sense of control over these difficult decisions.

The School Years: Education and Communication Revisited

Some of these issues will recur again and again throughout the deaf child's development, although the nature of the choices and decisions facing parents changes with each new milestone. Entry into elementary school, for example, may involve choices not only between mainstreaming and education with other deaf students, but also between residential schools and local day schools. Although this dichotomy is perhaps less frequently encountered now than it was several decades ago, many states do continue to offer both options, and the choice may be a very difficult one for hearing parents. For deaf parents who were educated in residential schools, who made many of their closest friends at such a school and who became a part of the deaf community there, sending their child to a residential school may represent a viable and comfortable option. For hearing parents, however, considering sending their child away to school is often both traumatic and confusing, bringing many of the earlier emotional reactions to diagnosis to the surface once again; issues of grief, blame, protectiveness, vulnerability, and autonomy may never be fully resolved in these families.

Regardless of the school setting, impulse control and discipline are important aspects of the school-age child's early socialization. Anticipating the consequences of one's actions and reflecting on a variety of possible solutions to a particular problem both influence the effectiveness not only of social interactions but of cognitive problem-solving as well. But teaching these skills is often a language-mediated process and therefore one that may be inherently more difficult for any child with poor communication skills or for whom the communication environment is less than adequate. It has been found, for example, that parents who cannot communicate effectively with a deaf child are less likely to provide sufficient explanation and feedback about what is wrong with a child's behavior. When faced with misbehavior, such parents are more likely to resort to removal or physical discipline. The child does not receive the information needed about the effect of the action on others or about more positive and acceptable behaviors; thus, instead of learning something constructive to guide his or her future behavior, the child has learned from the parents that avoidance and physical solutions are appropriate responses to social problems (Greenberg et al. 1984).

As the child grows older, communication within the family may continue to be a problem even when other family members have mastered at least the rudimentary skills of sign language. Mendelsohn and Rozek (1983), writing from a clinical perspective, emphasized the need for the hearing family members to respect the visual needs of the deaf child. They listed specific questions that need to be kept in mind to help these families become more aware of this issue.

> Do they face the child when speaking? Do they keep the visual field clear, i.e., no hand covering the mouth? Do they mouth words clearly and slowly? Do they pay attention to whether the child is paying attention and receiving the information? If the child uses sign language, do the family members sign and how well? Does one family member communicate better than others with the child? Does that family member become the interpreter for all other family members? Do the family members pay attention to slowing the pace of conversation sufficiently to include the child? Do family members enhance conversation by use of body language, facial expression, gestures, homemade signs, fingerspelling? (p. 41)

Similar points have been made by parents struggling to treat all their children fairly, while also recognizing the particular individual needs of each one. As one mother recounted in an interview,

> I wish his older brother would just try a little harder. He has the skills. *R.* [the deaf child] is an excellent lip-reader. But [his brother] has his own pidgin signing, he's real sloppy with it and doesn't always take the time to even face *R.* . . . . I find myself getting into the role of the interpreter between the boys, which I don't like to do. Everybody talks at the same time. I mean, it's just awful. He must want to just take his aids right out and put them down—especially at the dinner table.

Deafness and the Adolescent

By the time the deaf child reaches adolescence, many of the important early decisions about schooling and about forms of communication to be used within the family have been made, and the appropriate adjustments have become largely unconscious aspects of the interactions among the family members. Nevertheless, in most Western cultures, adolescence connotes a period of "storm and stress," of renewed conflict surrounding issues of dependence and independence, and of gradually moving away from the influence and protection of one's own family in favor of greater involvement with age-mates. Most developmental theorists would see these changes as age-appropriate and predictable, based on the developmental tasks that predominate during adolescence: defining one's individual identity (which may initially be derived from that of the larger peer group), coming to terms with physiological and reproductive changes that inevitably influence this identity, preparing for future roles in the larger society, and anticipating the establishment of enduring personal relationships beyond that of one's initial family.

Many of these issues cause friction even in the most well-functioning family, but they may cause proportionately greater disruption when a deaf child is involved. While the parents may continue to perceive the child as vulnerable and in need of their protection, the adolescent is striving to separate and to assert his or her own autonomy, much the same as during toddlerhood. At this point, however, there is indeed another "family" or protective group to take over and support the adolescent's efforts, as the peer group becomes increasingly important and influential. The adolescent's friends, most of whom are experiencing similar struggles in their own families, may create an expectation of conformity to certain styles, mannerisms, and behavior patterns as confirmation of their own identities. For many adolescents, acceptance by one's peers becomes a primary focus, and the idea of being different therefore becomes increasingly abhorrent. But within most social groups outside the deaf community, the deaf adolescent *is* different, even if the source of the difference is in fact insignificant when compared to the many similarities. One parent of a teenage daughter expressed concern that the efforts to make hearing aids almost invisible actually contribute to the social problems the child experiences.

> I think part of the problem is having it invisible, so people don't know [she is deaf]. Here we sent our daughter off to a summer college program. I said, "You're going to have to tell the people." I said, "You might even put your hair back a little so they can see because it's invisible. Nobody knows; they're not going to remember. They're going to think you're rude or something because you're not responding when you're talked to because it can't be seen."

Accompanying the dilemmas of personal identity and peer group loyalties, there is often a communication gap between adolescents and adults in general. Whether adults are parents, teachers, therapists, or coaches, it is often assumed that they are not on the same "wave length" as a teenager. It is not difficult to understand, then, that for a deaf child with whom there may have been a long history of communication problems within the family, adolescence is likely to exacerbate this vulnerability. As one parent sums it up, "everyone has heard about the communication gap. But 90 percent of parents of deaf adolescents are hearing. We are hearing and our kids are deaf. For us the communication gap becomes a chasm" (Mendelsohn and Fairchild 1984, p. 114).

If hearing parents reject the deaf world of their adolescent—or vice versa— this chasm may never be successfully bridged. Accepting the deaf adult whom this adolescent will become is part of the reality that many parents become acutely aware of for the first time during this stage of their child's development. As Mendelsohn noted,

> What happens in adolescence is that the realization hits—no magic, no miracles are going to happen. . . . The realization is that there *is* a future, and that the future involves deafness. It is the period of time when parents begin to think of life after family—life after hearing family. Life as a deaf person. It is as big a shock for many families as the initial diagnosis of deafness. (p. 113)

CONCLUSION

In this chapter, we have reviewed some of the changes and stresses often experienced by a family of hearing parents following the diagnosis of hearing loss in one of their children. While the emphasis has been primarily on the infancy and early childhood stages of development, this does not imply that the influence of deafness on family functioning and interaction ceases to be important at later stages. Clearly, decisions and adjustments and the search for appropriate services will continue throughout life, taking many different forms and requiring varying levels of resourcefulness and tolerance according to each new circumstance. Nevertheless, the initial acceptance of a child's hearing loss, and the necessity for developing effective means of communicating with that child within the family, are critical for the child's successful progression through later stages. For many hearing parents, the diagnosis itself may precipitate a crisis that interferes with family interactions on many different levels. Dealing with this crisis requires the support of the extended family, friends, and a network of professionals to assist the parents in making the first decisions about their child's education and upbringing as a deaf person. Other parents who have experienced the anxiety associated with the presence of a child with any kind of handicap can be particularly important sources of advice, support, and reassurance; they provide models of effective parenting and of informed decision making and advocacy. Their children can provide models of successful handicapped children.

As with any child, the period of time surrounding major developmental milestones often brings about a temporary phase of instability for the entire family. Even a child's learning to walk interrupts many of the family's established patterns of interaction, calling for increased watchfulness, safety precautions, and energy output from the parents. Similarly, the lack of attainment of an important skill, such as speech, can bring about a painful awareness of a child's limitations and of the need to compensate in other areas of proficiency. As the deaf child develops, periods of vulnerability may recur repeatedly for the family, especially as peers are seen to master communication skills that are much more difficult for a child with hearing loss. Transitions to new levels of competence may take longer and may be more demanding, thus causing greater disequilibrium for the family with an exceptional child. In the long run, however, the sense of accomplishment and pride in the child's newly acquired skills may also be greater when their acquisition was not assumed to be automatic. As stated earlier, the interpretation or *meaning* attached to a child's hearing impairment may be one of the most crucial factors determining parents' response to the diagnosis, how decisions are made regarding the child's future, how the parents support the child's needs, and whether they can encourage the development of the child's other achievements that need *not* be affected by deafness.

REFERENCES

Boukydis, C. F. Z. 1987. *Research on support for parents and infants in the postnatal period.* Norwood, NJ: Ablex Publishing Company.

Boukydis, C. F. Z., B. M. Lester, and J. Hoffman. 1987. Parenting and social support networks in families of term and preterm infants. In *Research on support for parents and infants in the postnatal period,* ed. C F. Z. Boukydis, 61–83. Norwood, NJ: Ablex Publishing Company.

Cohn, J. F., R. Matias, E. Z. Tronick, D. Connell, and K. Ruth-Lyons. 1986. Face-to-face interactions of depressed mothers and their infants. In *Maternal depression and infant disturbance,* ed. E. Z. Tronick and T. Field. New Directions for Child Development, 34: 31–45. San Francisco: Jossey-Bass.

Crnic, K., and M. T. Greenberg. 1987. Maternal stress, social support, and coping: Influences on the early mother-infant relationship. In *Research on support for parents and infants in the postnatal period,* ed. C. F. Z. Boukydis, 25–40. Norwood, NJ: Ablex Publishing Company.

Crnic, K. A., M. T. Greenberg, A. S. Ragozin, N. M. Robinson, and R. Basham. 1983. Effects of stress and social support on mothers and premature and full-term infants. *Child Development* 54: 209–217.

Crockenberg, S. B. 1981. Infant irritability, mother responsiveness, and social support influences on the security of mother-infant attachment. *Child Development* 52: 857–865.

Erikson, E. H. 1963. *Childhood and society.* New York: W. W. Norton.

Erting, C. J. 1982. Deafness, communication, and social identity: An anthropological analysis of interaction among parents, teachers, and deaf children in preschool. Ph.D. diss., American University, Washington, DC.

Feiring, C., N. Fox, J. Jaskir, and M. Lewis. 1985. The relationship between social support, infant risk status and mother-infant interaction. Presentation at the Biennial Meeting of the Society for Research in Child Development, April, Toronto, Ontario.

Fewell, R. R., and S. A. Gelb. 1983. Parenting moderately handicapped persons. In *The family with a handicapped child: Understanding and treatment,* ed. M. Seligman, 175–202. New York: Grune and Stratton.

Greenberg, M. T. 1983. Family stress and child competence: The effects of early intervention for families with deaf infants. *American Annals of the Deaf* 128: 407–417.

Greenberg, M. T., C. A. Kusché, R. N. Gustafson, and R. Calderon. 1984. The PATHS project: A model for prevention of psychological difficulties in deaf children. In *The habilitation and rehabilitation of deaf adolescents,* ed. G. B. Anderson and D. Watson, 243–263. Proceedings of the National Conference on the Habilitation and Rehabilitation of Deaf Adolescents, April, Wagoner, Oklahoma.

Harvey, M. A. 1989. *Psychotherapy with deaf and hard-of-hearing persons: A systemic model.* Hillsdale, NJ: Lawrence Erlbaum and Associates.

Howard, J. 1978. The influence of children's developmental dysfunctions on marital quality and family interaction. In *Child influences on marital and family interaction: A life-span perspective,* ed. R. M. Lerner and G. B. Spanier, 275–298. New York: Academic Press.

Irvin, N. A., J. H. Kennell, and M. H. Klaus. 1982. Caring for the parents of an infant with a congenital malformation. In *Parent-infant bonding* (2d ed.), ed. M. H. Klaus and J. H. Kennell, 227–258. St. Louis, MO: C. V. Mosby.

Kennell, J. H., and M. H. Klaus. 1982. Caring for the parents of premature or sick infants. In *Parent-infant bonding* (2d ed.), ed. M. H. Klaus and J. H. Kennell, 151–226. St. Louis, MO: C. V. Mosby.

Koester, L. S. 1987. Multimodal, repetitive stimulation in parent-infant interactions: A look at micro-rhythms. Presentation at the Biennial Meeting of the Society for Research in Child Development, April, Baltimore, Maryland.

Koester, L. S., H. Papoušek, and M. Papoušek. In press. Patterns of rhythmic stimulation by mothers with three-month-olds: A cross-modal comparison. *International Journal of Behavioral Development.*

McCubbin, H. I., and J. M. Patterson. 1983. The family stress process: The double ABCX model of adjustment and adaptation. In *Social stress and the family: Advances and developments in family stress theory and research,* ed. H. I. McCubbin, M. B. Sussmann, and J. M. Patterson. Marriage and Family Review, 6 (1 and 2): 7–37. New York: Haworth Press.

Meadow-Orlans, K. P., C. J. Erting, C. Prezioso, F. Bridges-Cline, and R. H. MacTurk. 1986. Effects of deafness on mother-infant interaction. Presentation at the Annual Meeting of the American Psychological Association, August, Washington, DC.

Meadow-Orlans, K. P., R. H. MacTurk, C. Prezioso, C. J. Erting, and P. S. Day. 1987. Interactions of deaf and hearing mothers with three- and six-month-old infants. Presentation at the Biennial Meeting of the Society for Research in Child Development, April, Baltimore, Maryland.

Mendelsohn, J. Z., and B. Fairchild. 1984. Years of challenge: Parents, adolescence and deafness. In *The habilitation and rehabilitation of deaf adolescents,* ed. G. B. Anderson and D. Watson, 110–122. Proceedings of the National Conference on the Habilitation and Rehabilitation of Deaf Adolescents, April. Wagoner, Oklahoma.

Mendelsohn, M., and F. Rozek. 1983. Denying disability: The case of deafness. *Family Systems Medicine* 1(2): 37–47.

Murphy, A. T. 1979. The families of handicapped children: Context for disability. *Volta Review* 81(5): 265–278.

Nienhuys, T. G., and J. A. Tikotin. 1983. Pre-speech communication in hearing and hearing-impaired children. *Journal of the British Association of Teachers of the Deaf* 7(6): 182–194.

Quittner, A. L. In press. Coping with a hearing-impaired child: A model of adjustment to chronic stress. In *Advances in child health psychology: Proceedings of the first Florida conference,* ed. J. H. Johnson and S. B. Johnson. Gainesville, FL: University Presses of Florida.

Schlesinger, H. S., and K. P. Meadow. 1972. *Sound and sign: Childhood deafness and mental health*. Berkeley: University of California Press.

Tronick, E. Z., H. Als, and T. B. Brazelton. 1980. Monadic phases: A structural descriptive analysis of infant-mother face to face interaction. *Merrill-Palmer Quarterly* 26(1): 3–24.

Tronick, E. Z., and A. F. Gianino. 1986. The transmission of maternal disturbance to the infant. In *Maternal depression and infant disturbance,* ed. E. Z. Tronick and T. Field. New Directions for Child Development 34: 5–11. San Francisco: Jossey-Bass.

Turnbull, A. P., and J. Blacher-Dixon. 1980. Preschool mainstreaming: Impact on parents. *New Directions for Exceptional Children* 1: 25–46.

Weinraub, M., and B. M. Wolf. 1983. Effects of stress and social supports on mother-child interactions in single- and two-parent families. *Child Development* 54: 1297–1311.

Wikler, L. 1981. Chronic stresses of families of mentally retarded children. *Family Relations* 30: 281–288.

Williams, D. M. L., and J. O. Darbyshire. 1982. Diagnosis of deafness: A study of family responses and needs. *Volta Review* 84(1): 24–30.

13

The Impact of Childhood Hearing Loss on the Family

Kathryn P. Meadow-Orlans

The impact of a child's congenital handicap on the family is a concern for both clinicians and researchers. A few questionnaire forms have been developed for use with parents of children with handicaps other than deafness (Holroyd 1973; Stein and Reissman 1980), but no instruments of this kind that are specific to deafness have been constructed. A number of research reports that record data from parent interviews are available (Erting 1982; Freeman, Malkin, and Hastings 1975; Gregory 1976; Meadow 1968). Other sources of published information are from clinicians (Mindel and Vernon 1971; Freeman, Carbin, and Boese 1981; Moses 1985; Schlesinger 1985) and from parents' personal accounts (Thompson, Thompson, and Murphy 1979; Schwartz 1987; Mendelsohn and Fairchild 1984). Greenberg (1983) utilized a short stress inventory and his own adaptation of the Holroyd Questionnaire on Resources and Stress. (This was revised further and is described in Friedrich, Greenberg, and Crnic 1983).

Distinct differences exist between the richness of experience conveyed through a narrative and the quantitative response provided to a written question. Generally, the more sensitive the nature of the content area to be covered, the more desirable it is to collect the information during an interview. Questions that might be perfectly acceptable in an interview setting, after rapport has been established between the interviewer and the respondent, can seem out-of-bounds and objectionable when printed on a form. A trained interviewer can serve as a resource to diminish the distress associated with recounting a traumatic event, and

Lita Aldridge, coordinator of parent education for the Affiliated Schools Project, Pre-College Programs, at Gallaudet University, was extremely helpful during the distribution phase of the project. She distributed many questionnaires and discussed items with groups in several different states. She provided a major source of data by distributing the final version of the questionnaire to many groups of parents. In addition to Ms. Aldridge, I am grateful to Judith Houk, Sister Bernadette Kenney, Richard Lytle, and Susan Schwartz for coordinating distribution of questionnaires to various parent groups. Preparation of this chapter was supported by the Division of Maternal and Child Health, Bureau of Health Care Delivery and Assistance (Grant MCJ-110563).

respondents are free to expand upon or to qualify their answers. Barsch's (1968) description captures some of the advantages of the interview approach.

> For many of the parents the perceptual set of giving information in a research project became a secondary consideration to the personal dynamics, to the excitement and threat of systematic self-appraisal, to the revelations being experienced in relation to their own feelings. . . .
>
> There was a general characteristic of . . . release in almost all of the interviews. . . . Some parents [commented] . . . that they had "never been so confidential with anyone before" or "have never told this to anyone before."
>
> The . . . interviewers . . . were understandably distressed by the necessity to code a response in some arbitrary manner and convert it mechanically to some statistical form. It left a feeling that the lifeblood of the response had been drained out, the tone had gone and the empty barren statistic remained. (p. 28)

While an interview is the preferred means of collecting information, the realities of research sometimes dictate the use of a questionnaire. When that is the case, researchers attempt to work with previously constructed instruments that have been used with a population similar to the one with which they are dealing.

The instrument described in this chapter was developed as part of a larger project (in collaboration with Richard Lytle) designed to provide a description of the family and school backgrounds of new students entering the Model Secondary School for the Deaf (Lytle and Jonas 1984; Lytle, Feinstein, and Jonas 1987). It was not practical to interview parents of these students, who lived at varying distances from the school, so a questionnaire was used. The questionnaire was designed for assessing the impact of a child's hearing loss on the family.

FRAMEWORK FOR DEVELOPMENT OF
QUESTIONNAIRE ITEMS

Based on a large number of earlier interviews with parents of deaf children (Meadow 1967, 1968; Schlesinger and Meadow 1972; Erting and Meadow 1978) and on the work of other investigators cited above, five general areas of major concern were defined.

1. The effect of a young child's deafness on his or her parents and other family members:
   a. the parents' feelings of grief, sorrow, guilt, anger, and pride in successful coping;
   b. the feelings and responses of grandparents and siblings;

   c. the family's response to the financial and energy demands of special educa-
      tional needs;

   d. family stress;

   e. the responses of friends and neighbors.

2. Parental concerns about the difficulties of communicating with a deaf child:

   a. efforts to include the child in family conversations;

   b. success in acquiring special skills and techniques for improving language
      and communication at home and school.

3. Relationships between parents and a wide range of professionals who provide
   services for the special needs of the deaf child:

   a. members of the medical profession and audiologists who are involved with
      the family at the critical period when the hearing loss is diagnosed;

   b. educators who are likely to be intensely involved with the family very early
      in the child's life.

Many parents feel caught between professionals who have conflicting ideas
about effective intervention with deaf children. This conflict is a frequent cause
of parental stress.

4. The level of parental satisfaction with the deaf child's current performance and
   future prospects:

   a. educational progress, often painfully slow for deaf children, can be partic-
      ularly disappointing for parents with high expectations for their child's aca-
      demic performance;

   b. areas of social-emotional development that may be problematic for parents
      who find it difficult to grant independence to their deaf child;

   c. parents' worries about the occupational future of their child;

   d. parents' concerns about the attitudes of the general public.

5. The treatment of the deaf child by others in his or her environment:

   a. possible problems with siblings competing for parental attention;

   b. thoughtless behavior by friends and neighbors;

   c. support or the lack of support from friends and members of the extended
      family.

    With these general areas of concern forming the framework, questionnaire
items were constructed to fit a true-false response format. This format was chosen
because it forces a choice in the research edition of the questionnaire and enables
the detection of items with innate ambiguities and those that respondents are un-
willing or unable to answer without qualification. Also, the forced choice format
provided a less ambiguous basis for the later factor analysis of items.

    An early version of the questionnaire was distributed to approximately 100
parents from diverse backgrounds. Extensive revisions of that version were made,
based on questions and comments from the respondents. Items were written and
rewritten by several colleagues experienced in working with groups of parents of
deaf children. The final research version of the questionnaire contained thirty-nine

items, distributed among the five subject areas identified above. A two-page list of questions designed to provide demographic information about the deaf children and their families was also developed and distributed to parents with the impact questionnaire (see Notes).

SOURCES OF DATA

Five major sources of data accounted for 363 of the 395 completed sets of questionnaires. These included

1. Parents of deaf children enrolled in a wide range of programs that participated in the Gallaudet University Affiliated Schools Program. The programs were located in many different states in all regions of the United States, and served families living in large metropolitan areas, small towns, and rural areas. Ninety-seven completed questionnaires were received from parents of children with a mean age of 8.1 years.
2. A residential school for the deaf in the midwestern part of the United States supplied twenty-nine questionnaires from parents whose children had a mean age of 10.2 years.
3. A suburban public school system provided eighty-nine questionnaires. Children of parents responding had a mean age of 10.1 years.
4. A residential high school for deaf students supplied eighty-nine completed questionnaires. The mean age for students in this group was 16.6 years.
5. A combined residential/day facility for deaf students, located in a major eastern seaboard city, supplied fifty-nine questionnaires. The mean age of the students was 13.3 years.

Clearly, these groups did not constitute a true random sample. The parents were volunteers, and the universe from which they came was unknown. However, the summary of child and family characteristics in Table 13.1 shows that they were a heterogeneous group. The entire age spectrum of children, from infants through age twenty-one, was represented. While children with profound hearing losses comprised the largest group (44%), a significant number of the children (15%) had only mild or moderate losses. All types of educational programs were represented, including residential, day, and mainstream. Twenty percent of the families were other than Caucasian, with a full range of social class representation (based on the Hollingshead Two-Factor Index). Massachusetts and Maryland were the two states with the largest single groups (17% and 26%, respectively), but thirty-seven other states were represented by at least one family, as well as one family each from Guam and Puerto Rico.

The total number of children represented in the sets of returned questionnaires was 395. Both parents replied to the questionnaires in 221 cases; mothers only replied in 132 cases, and fathers only replied in 42 cases.

Table 13.1
Characteristics of Children and Families ($N = 395$)

A. Sex		B. Age (in years)	
Boys	54.5%	0–3	6.2%
Girls	45.5	3.1–6	13.8
(N)	(363)	6.1–9	16.5
		9.1–12	11.5
		12.1–15	17.4
		15.1–21	34.7
		(N)	(357)

C. Cause of Hearing Loss		D. Age at Onset of Hearing Loss (cumulative percentages)			
			Suspected	Confirmed	Educ. began
Heredity	15.2%	By 6 months	32.6%	10.8%	3.8%
At birth:		By 12 months	50.7	28.9	11.6
Maternal rubella	22.3	By 18 months	68.4	51.0	26.6
Other	12.1	By 24 months	85.9	67.1	51.2
After birth:		By 36 months	93.1	88.9	80.1
Meningitis	11.3	By 48 months	96.7	94.2	90.8
Other	8.5	(N)	(304)	(343)	(346)
Unknown	30.7				
(N)	(355)				

E. Degree of Hearing Loss		F. Likes/Wears Hearing Aid		G. Additional Handicapping Conditions	
Profound	44.0%	NO	8.9%	None	81.5%
Severe	25.6	no	16.5	One or more	18.5
Moderate-Severe	14.9	yes	23.5	(N)	(357)
Moderate	10.6	YES	51.1		
Mild	4.9	(N)	(358)		
(N)	(348)				

H. Communication with Child			I. Type of Education Program		J. Deaf Relatives	
	Home	School	Residential	19.3%	None	75.0%
Speech only	35.6%	24.6%	Day	29.6	Parent(s)	5.6
Speech + signs	55.8	67.7	Partial mainstr.	26.1	Sib(s)	7.8
Cued speech	5.2	5.4	Mainstreamed	21.0	Other(s)	11.7
Signs only	2.5	0.8	Home teacher	3.2	(N)	(360)
Other	0.8	1.4	Other	0.9		
(N)	(362)	(353)	(N)	(348)		

K. Child's Home Life		L. Race/Ethnic Background		M. Home Language	
Both parents present	68.3%	Caucasian	79.8%	English	96.1%
Mother only	22.2	Black	12.6	Spanish	2.0
Father only	1.6	Hispanic	3.2	Sign	1.1
Adoptive/other	7.8	Oriental	2.0	Other	0.8
(N)	(360)	Other	2.4	(N)	(356)
		(N)	(342)		

Table 13.1 (*continued*)

N. Social Position			O. Geographical Location		P. Number of Siblings	
Class	Mother	Father	Massachusetts	17.3%	None	13.5%
1 (high)	8.3%	14.2%	Maryland	26.4	One	36.1
2	19.8	20.8	Other*	56.3	Two	24.6
3	50.1	40.3	(N)	(371)	Three +	25.7
4	17.7	18.6	*39 states + Guam and		(N)	(349)
5 (low)	4.1	6.3	Puerto Rico			
(N)	(339)	(318)				

SELECTION OF FINAL QUESTIONNAIRE ITEMS

Selection of the twenty-four items for the final version of the questionnaire involved a series of processes including (1) the consideration of the comments from the respondents who completed the second research version; (2) an analysis of the distribution of nonresponses to the thirty-nine items in the research version; and (3) an analysis of the distribution of "true" and "false" responses.

Table 13.2 shows the fifteen items from the research edition that did not appear in the final version of the completed instrument. Item 1 offended many parents, who were affronted by the suggestion of a truly positive aspect of life with a handicapped child. This is an example of an item that might have received a less negative review if it had been embedded in an interview schedule. Although 85 percent of those responding to this question answered it affirmatively, the item was eliminated because it received a large number of written negative comments.

Items 3 and 10 were eliminated from the pool because 90% or more of the respondents answered in the positive direction. Item 6, which related to the child's ability to speak clearly, seemed to have different meanings for different parents. Since it did not contribute to the factor analytic solution, it was dropped from the final version.

Items 9 and 11, which related to the child's job opportunities, had high nonresponse rates (up to 15%). Many parents indicated that they lacked the factual information needed to respond to these questions. Also, some of the questions related to future occupational opportunities were undoubtedly less salient for parents with younger children.

After eliminating items with high nonresponse rates and negative comments, the remaining items were subjected to a varimax rotated factor analysis. The best selection criteria appeared to be the three-factor solution composed of scale 1, stress; scale 2, communication; and scale 3, relationships with professionals. Twenty-four items with the highest loadings on these three factors were selected for inclusion in the final instrument.

Tables 13.3, 13.4, and 13.5 provide the factor loadings for individual items, the proportion of parents responding in the "positive" (i.e., scored) direction, and

Table 13.2
Questionnaire Items Eliminated from Final Instrument

Item	Proportion with Positive Score* (N = 352)
1. Our family life has been more interesting because of our experiences related to deafness... (true)	85%
2. Sometimes I still have strong feelings of grief and sorrow about my child's deafness.. (false)	36
3. Being the parent of a deaf child has made me a stronger person ...... (true)	90
4. My other children are often impatient with their deaf brother/sister.... (false)	55
5. I adjusted fairly quickly to the news of my child's hearing loss......... (true)	58
6. My child's inability to speak more clearly is a disappointment to me .. (false)	68
7. There are many things my family can't afford because we spent so much on the special needs of our deaf child............................ (false)	84
8. Sometimes I feel that my hearing children have been cheated because of the time I devote to my hearing-impaired child .... (false)	72
9. I worry about whether my deaf child will be able to find a good job .. (false)	33
10. Opportunities for deaf people have improved. This gives me more hope for my child's future... (true)	94
11. Today, young deaf people have job opportunities much like those of young people with normal hearing............................... (true)	58
12. I have always given my deaf child the same amount of freedom that I would give a hearing child .... (true)	56
13. I have many wonderful friends that I know only because of my child's hearing loss.. (true)	59
14. Many friends and family members have been helpful and supportive about my child and his/her hearing impairment................... (true)	83
15. Sometimes I worry that my deaf child will prefer to be with deaf people rather than with our family .... (false)	72

*True or false response scored "0" or "1" depending on content of question. Responses that received a positive score of "1" are indicated in parentheses at the end of each question.

the number of responses available for each item. Reliability for the three scales (Cronbach's alpha) was .74 for Scale 1, with item loadings ranging from .375 to .624; for Scale 2, reliability was .75 with factor loadings ranging from .365 to .554; for Scale 3, reliability was .71, with factor loadings ranging from .304 to .587. The format and content of the final instrument appears in the Notes section at the end of this chapter. Responses (*SA* for strongly agree, *a* for agree, *d* for disagree, and *SD* for strongly disagree) are arranged so that the most positive response appears in the last or far right column in every case.

SCALE SCORES AND DEMOGRAPHIC CHARACTERISTICS

After the final items were selected and the scales determined, scores were computed for the respondents. A maximum score of 8 was possible for each of the

Table 13.3
Scale 1: Stress Factors

Item	Factor Loading	Percentage with Positive Scores	Number of Responses
1. I often regret the extra time our family must devote to the problems of hearing impairment.	.375	85	527
2. We have more family arguments about our hearing-impaired child than we have about other things.	.618	81	471
3. Much stress in my family is related to deafness/hearing impairment.	.624	83	521
4. My hearing-impaired child's behavior has often been a source of worry to me.	.401	59	524
5. Family and friends usually treat my hearing-impaired child the same as they would treat a hearing child of the same age.	.386	73	523
6. Because of hearing loss, it was (is) necessary for me to forget many hopes and dreams that I had for my child.	.470	79	522
7. In the preschool years, my child's hearing loss created so many demands that I never had time for myself.	.449	73	514
8. Parents of hearing-impaired children are expected to do too many things for them. This has been a burden for me.	.402	76	518

Note. Reliability (Cronbach's alpha) = .74

Table 13.4
Scale 2: Communication Factors

Item	Factor Loading	Percentage	Number of Responses
1. I can feel proud of the way I have responded to the special needs of my hearing-impaired child.	.475	89	525
2. My communication skills are quite adequate for my child's needs.	.554	60	522
3. I wish I could communicate as well with my hearing-impaired child as I do with (my) hearing child(ren).	.536	32	461
4. I wish some of the other members of my family could communicate more easily with my hearing-impaired child.	.374	30	529
5. I tend to treat my hearing-impaired child like a child who is a good deal younger.	.373	63	529
6. My hearing-impaired child is often left out of family conversations because of communication problems.	.540	48	524
7. I feel confident that my hearing-impaired child can handle most situations as well as a hearing child.	.365	72	521
8. There are many things I can't seem to communicate to my hearing-impaired child.	.554	50	527

Note. Reliability (Cronbach's alpha) = .75

Table 13.5
Scale 3: Relationship Factors

Item	Factor Loading	Percentage	Number of Responses
1. Differing opinions from professionals have made it hard for me to make decisions about schooling for my hearing-impaired child.	.470	60	523
2. I feel satisfied with the educational progress of my hearing-impaired child.	.398	67	526
3. I have had a lot of good professional advice about my hearing-impaired child's education.	.491	64	515
4. Sometimes my friends and neighbors have been thoughtless or cruel about my child's hearing impairment.	.304	70	526
5. Many times I have been angry because of the way professionals treated me as the parent of a hearing-impaired child.	.578	64	520
6. I have no regrets about the educational opportunities that have been available to my hearing-impaired child.	.587	62	523
7. It was really hard to find a doctor who could tell us that our child has a hearing loss.	.356	62	512
8. It is frustrating for me as a parent to have so many different opinions among professionals who work with hearing-impaired children.	.465	32	514

Note. Reliability (Cronbach's alpha) = .71

three scales (high scores reflected greater positive adjustment). Mean scores of mothers and fathers were compared, first as two groups (Table 13.6), then as subgroups with various demographic or educational characteristics (Tables 13.7, 13.8, 13.9).

Table 13.6 shows that the fathers' scores on the "stress" scale were marginally higher than those of the mothers (i.e., fathers expressed somewhat less stress in regard to their deaf child ($t = -1.7$; $p \leq .10$). Mothers expressed more confidence in their abilities to communicate with their deaf child, compared to fathers ($t = 2.5$; $p \leq .01$). There were no differences in the satisfaction expressed by mothers and fathers concerning their relationships with professionals ($t = -1.1$; $p > .10$).

The sex of the deaf child did not affect the parents' scores. Although both mothers and fathers of boys achieved more positive scores than did parents of girls, the differences were not statistically significant. However, both mothers and fathers of older children (age thirteen and above) felt less positively about their relationships with professionals and others outside the family than did parents of children younger than age six. Table 13.7 shows the relationship of the child's age and birth order to parents' scores on the three scales. Parents of middle children scored significantly less positively on the communication items compared to par-

Table 13.6
Mean Scores of Mothers and Fathers on Scales 1, 2, 3

Scale	Mean Score	t	p
1. Stress			
Mothers	6.2		
Fathers	6.4	-1.7	$\leq.10$
2. Communication			
Mothers	4.9		
Fathers	4.6	2.5	$\leq.01$
3. Relationships w/ Professionals and Others			
Mothers	4.7		
Fathers	4.8	-1.1	$>.10$

Table 13.7
Relationship of Parents' Scale Scores to Child's Age and Birth Order

		Stress		Communication		Professionals	
	Group	Mother	Father	Mother	Father	Mother	Father
Child's Age							
Under 6 yrs.	1	6.0	6.6	4.4	4.5	5.3	5.9
6 to <10 yrs.	2	5.6	6.3	4.8	5.5	5.3	4.9
10 to <13 yrs.	3	6.0	6.2	4.0	4.5	4.6	5.5
13 to <16 yrs.	4	5.9	6.3	4.7	4.5	4.4	4.6
16+ yrs.	5	6.2	6.5	4.3	4.1	4.5	4.4
F		n.s.	n.s.	n.s.	2.05	3.05	2.44
p					$\leq.10$	$\leq.05$	$\leq.05$
group difference		—	—	—	5<2	4,5<1,2	4,5<1
Birth Order							
Only	1	6.0	6.8	5.3	5.3	4.7	5.0
Oldest	2	5.7	5.7	4.4	4.2	4.5	4.5
Youngest	3	6.0	6.9	4.7	5.0	5.0	5.1
Middle	4	6.1	6.3	3.8	3.8	4.9	4.7
F		n.s.	4.14	4.89	3.33	n.s.	n.s.
p			$\leq.01$	$\leq.01$	$\leq.05$		
group difference		—	2<1,3	4<1,3 2<1	4<1,3	—	—

ents of both older and younger deaf children. Fathers of oldest children expressed lesser degrees of stress than did fathers of only or youngest children.

Table 13.8 shows the relationship of the scale scores for mothers and fathers to the cause of deafness and the presence or absence of additional handicaps. Mothers of rubella children expressed more general stress (marginally significant in comparison with mothers who named heredity as the etiology), more stress related to communication ($F = 4.9$; $p \leq .001$), and much less satisfaction about

Table 13.8
Relationship of Parents' Scale Scores to Cause of Deafness and
Presence of Additional Handicaps

	Group	Stress		Communication		Professionals	
		Mother	Father	Mother	Father	Mother	Father
Cause of Deafness							
Rubella	1	5.6	6.4	3.7	4.0	4.1	4.3
Other Prenatal	2	5.6	6.8	4.5	4.8	4.6	5.0
Heredity	3	6.5	6.2	5.4	5.6	5.1	4.8
Postnatal	4	5.8	6.6	4.5	4.8	5.1	5.0
Unknown	5	6.1	6.3	4.6	4.3	5.1	5.0
F		2.2	n.s.	4.9	2.3	3.2	n.s.
p		≤.10		≤.001	≤.10	≤.01	
group difference		1<3		1<2,3,4,5	1,5<3	1<3,4,5	
Additional Handicaps							
None		6.1	6.4	4.7	4.6	5.0	4.6
One or more		5.2	6.6	3.6	4.0	4.3	5.8
t		2.8	n.s.	3.7	n.s.	2.0	−2.2
p		≤.01		≤.001		≤.05	≤.05

their relationships with professionals ($F = 3.2; p ≤ .01$). A similar pattern appears for mothers of multihandicapped children. Indeed, these two variables are probably confounded so that there is overlapping influence.

Table 13.9 shows the relationship of the parents' scale scores to the degree of hearing loss reported for their child (profound vs. less than profound), and the communication mode reportedly used at home (speech only vs. speech plus sign). No significant differences among the four groups appeared in Scale 1 (stress) scores, either for mothers or for fathers. Mothers with profoundly deaf children, using either speech only or speech plus sign, were significantly less satisfied with their communication, compared to mothers whose children were less than profoundly deaf *and* who used speech only at home ($F = 6.0; p ≤ .001$). Mothers of profoundly deaf children using speech plus sign were significantly less satisfied about their relationships with professionals compared to the three other groups. Fathers showed similar, although less dramatic, patterns.

The final analysis involved a series of stepwise multiple-regression equations, one for each of the three scale scores for mothers and for fathers. Demographic variables to be entered for each equation were selected if they correlated significantly ($p ≤ .05$) with a particular subscale. The variable with the strongest relationship was entered first, followed by additional variables in order of strength. Table 13.10 provides a summary of the Beta weights of those factors that contributed significantly to the analysis for each of the six subscales. Mothers whose deaf children have no additional handicaps reported better adjustment to stress compared to fathers whose children use hearing aids and are middle or last in birth

Table 13.9

Relationship of Parents' Scale Scores to Severity of Child's Hearing Loss and Home Communication Mode

Group		Stress		Communication		Professionals	
		Mother	Father	Mother	Father	Mother	Father
	Profound loss						
1	Speech only	6.3	6.2	4.5	4.4	5.2	4.8
2	Speech + sign	5.9	6.3	4.0	3.7	4.0	4.0
	< Profound loss						
3	Speech only	6.2	6.6	5.2	5.0	5.2	5.2
4	Speech + sign	5.7	6.2	4.0	4.3	5.1	4.8
	F	2.2	n.s.	6.0	3.2	5.6	2.4
	p	<.10		≤.001	≤.05	≤.001	≤.10
	group difference	n.s.	—	2,4<3	2<3	2<1,3,4	2<3

Note. Profound loss is greater than 90 dB

Table 13.10

Stepwise Multiple-Regression Analyses of Parents' Scale Scores, for Mothers and for Fathers: Beta Weights

Predictor Variables	Stress		Communication		Professionals	
	Mother	Father	Mother	Father	Mother	Father
Additional handicap[a]	−.14		−.19			.17
Home communication[b]			−.23	−.24		−.24
Cause of deafness[c]			−.17			
Use of hearing aid[d]		.17	.18			
Race[e]					−.19	−.25
Child's age[f]					−.23	−.28
Mother's sign skills[g]					−.19	
Child's birth order[h]		−.22				

Note. This analysis was conducted by Dr. Donna Mertens.
[a] 1 = yes; 0 = no
[b] 1 = sign only or speech + sign; 0 = speech only or speech + cues
[c] 1 = rubella; 0 = other
[d] 1 = yes; 0 = no
[e] 1 = Caucasian; 0 = other
[f] 14 to 259 (in months)
[g] 6 = excellent; 0 = none
[h] 1 = first-born; 0 = other

order. On items in the communication subscale, mothers reported better communication with their children if (1) children have no additional handicaps, (2) the children use speech only or speech plus cues, (3) the cause of deafness was other than rubella, and (4) the child uses a hearing aid. Fathers reported better communication if speech only or speech plus cues constituted the home communication mode. Positive relationships with professionals were more likely for mothers if (1) they belonged to a minority racial group, (2) the children were of younger ages, and (3) their sign language skills were less proficient. Fathers were more likely to have positive relationships with professionals if (1) the deaf child has an additional handicap, (2) speech or cues are the home communication mode, (3) the family is non-Caucasian, and (4) the child is younger rather than older.

The one surprising relationship to emerge from this analysis was that of minority group membership with professional subscale scores. In an effort to propose some possible reasons for this finding, several cross-tabulations were undertaken, none of which provided explanatory ideas. The experiences of minority group families with deafness needs further investigation.

The better relationships with professionals reported by parents of younger children might suggest that services have been improved since parents with older children were receiving diagnostic and early educational interventions.

SUMMARY

1. Three scales of eight items each were constructed from a pool of thirty-nine questionnaire items related to the impact of childhood deafness on the family. These sets of items were categorized as (1) family stress, (2) communication with the deaf child, and (3) relationships with professionals and others outside the family.

2. Generally, the responses of mothers and of fathers to individual items did not differ. Fathers tended to express less stress related to deafness. Fathers showed significantly less satisfaction or comfort in their ability to communicate with their deaf child, compared to mothers.

3. Both mothers and fathers of older children evaluated their relationships with professionals less positively than did parents of younger children. Parents of middle children felt their family's communication to be less satisfactory than parents whose deaf children were first-born, last-born, or only children.

4. Mothers of rubella children and of children with additional handicaps expressed heightened levels of family stress and less satisfaction about communication and relationships with those outside the family, compared to mothers of children with other etiologies and of children without additional handicaps.

5. When stress scale scores were compared between groups of parents who have profoundly deaf children and those whose children have lesser hearing impairments, no differences were found related to home communication (speech only vs. speech plus sign). Mothers who use speech plus sign with their less-than-profoundly deaf children scored below mothers who use speech only on items related to communication and on satisfaction about relationships with professionals.

NOTES

Demographic Questionnaire

PLEASE ANSWER THESE QUESTIONS ABOUT YOUR HEARING-IMPAIRED SON/DAUGHTER

(If you have more than one hearing-impaired child, please describe the oldest)

1. Date of Birth _____   2. Sex: _____ Boy _____ Girl
3. When did you *think* your child might not hear well?   Age _____
4. When did a doctor *tell* you this was true?   Age _____
5. When did your child begin special training?   Age _____
6. Do you know or suspect the cause of your child's deafness?   _____ No
     _____ Yes

     If yes: What was (or might be) the cause?

---

7. What is the extent of your child's hearing loss?
     _____ Profound (hears only loud noises, even with a hearing aid: 91 dB +)
     _____ Severe (can tell different kinds of noises: 71–90 dB)
     _____ Moderately severe (can hear speech in a quiet room with an aid: 56–70 dB)
     _____ Moderate (can hear in most situations with an aid: 41–55 dB)
     _____ Mild (responds like a hearing child when aid is worn: 27–40 dB)
8. Does your child *like* the hearing aid and *want* to wear it?
     _____ NO-doesn't like it, won't wear it
     _____ No-doesn't really like it, but will wear it
     _____ Yes-likes it okay, but not enthusiastic
     _____ YES-always wants to wear it
9. Does your child have any handicaps in addition to deafness?
     _____ No _____ Yes
     (If yes, what? _____)
10. What kind(s) of communication is used at home? (check all that are used)
     _____ speech; _____ signs; _____ fingerspelling; _____ cued speech
11. What kind(s) of communication is used at school? (check all used by child's teachers)
     _____ speech; _____ signs; _____ fingerspelling; _____ cued speech
12. What kind of school program does your child attend? _____ residential;
     _____ classes with deaf students only; _____ partially mainstreamed;
     _____ mainstreamed

PLEASE ANSWER THESE QUESTIONS ABOUT YOUR FAMILY

1. Number and ages of other children: _____ brothers   (ages: _____)
                                           _____ sisters   (ages: _____)

2. Are any other family members or relatives deaf or hard-of-hearing?
   _____ no;   _____ yes   (What is their relationship to your hearing-impaired child?)

3. With whom does your hearing-impaired child live now?   _____ both natural parents;   _____ mother only;   _____ father only;   _____ mother and stepfather;   _____ father and stepmother;   _____ other (who?_____)
   _____ adoptive parents (at what age was child adopted?   _____)

4. Check services that   Check services that parents have *used*
   have been *available* for
   you as a parent:

		Mother	*Father*
parent education	____	_____	_____
parent counseling	____	_____	_____
sign language class	____	_____	_____

5. Do parents use any manual communication with child?
   Mother: _____ no   _____ yes   (What kind? _____)
                                        (poor skills: 1 2 3 4 5 6 good skills)
   Father: _____ no   _____ yes   (What kind? _____)
                                        (poor skills: 1 2 3 4 5 6 good skills)

6. Mother's education: _____ years of schooling.
   Mother's occupation: _____

7. Father's education: _____ years of schooling.
   Father's occupation: _____

8. Primary language used at home: _____

9. Race/Ethnic Identity: _____

10. Residence: City or town _____   State _____

IMPACT OF CHILDHOOD HEARING LOSS ON THE FAMILY:
A Questionnaire for Parents

Please answer ALL questions as honestly as you can. Circle SA if you STRONGLY AGREE. Circle "a" if you "agree". Circle "d" if you "disagree." Circle SD if you STRONGLY DISAGREE.

1. I often regret the extra time our family must devote to the
   problems of hearing impairment.   SA   a   d   SD

2. I can feel proud of the way I have responded to the special needs of my hearing-impaired child.   SD   d   a   SA

3. Differing opinions from professionals have made it hard for me to make decisions about schooling for my hearing-impaired child.   SA   a   d   SD

4. We have more family arguments about our hearing-impaired child than we have about other things.   SA   a   d   SD

5. My communication skills are quite adequate for my child's needs.   SD   d   a   SA

6. I feel satisfied with the educational progress of my hearing-impaired child.   SD   d   a   SA

7. Much of the stress in my family is (was) related to deafness (hearing impairment).   SA   a   d   SD

8. I wish I could communicate as well with my hearing-impaired child as I do with (my) hearing child(ren).   SA   a   d   SD

9. I've had a lot of good professional advice about education for my hearing-impaired child.   SD   d   a   SA

10. My hearing-impaired child's behavior has often been a source of worry to me.   SA   a   d   SD

11. I wish some of the other members of my family could communicate more easily with my hearing-impaired child.   SA   a   d   SD

12. Sometimes my friends/neighbors have been thoughtless or cruel about my child's hearing loss.   SA   a   d   SD

13. Family and friends usually treat my hearing-impaired child the same as they would treat a hearing child of the same age.   SD   d   a   SA

14. I tend to treat my hearing-impaired child like a child who is a good deal younger.   SA   a   d   SD

15. Many times I have been angry because of the way professionals treated me as the parent of a hearing-impaired child.   SA   a   d   SD

16. Because of hearing loss, it was (is) necessary for me to forget many hopes and dreams that I had for my child.   SA   a   d   SD

17. My hearing-impaired child is often left out of family conversations because of communication problems.   SA   a   d   SD

18. I have no regrets about the educational opportunities that have been available to my hearing-impaired child.   SD   d   a   SA

19. In the preschool years, my child's hearing loss created so many demands that I never had time for myself.   SA   a   d   SD

20. I feel confident that my hearing-impaired child can handle most situations as well as a hearing child.   SD   d   a   SA

21. It was really hard to find a doctor who could tell us that our child has a hearing loss.   SA   a   d   SD

22. Parents of hearing-impaired children are expected to do too many things for them. This has been a burden for me. SA a d SD
23. There are many things I can't seem to communicate to my hearing-impaired child. SA a d SD
24. It is frustrating for me as a parent to have so many different opinions among professionals who work with hearing-impaired children. SA a d SD

REFERENCES

Barsch, R. H. 1968. *The parent of the handicapped child: The study of child-rearing practices.* Springfield, IL: Charles C. Thomas.

Erting, C. 1982. Deafness, communication, and social identity: An anthropological analysis of interaction among parents, teachers and deaf children in a preschool. Ph.D. diss., American University, Washington, DC.

Erting, C., and K. P. Meadow. 1978. Mother-child interaction project, interview schedule. Washington, DC: Kendall Demonstration Elementary School, Gallaudet University. Mimeographed.

Freeman, R. D., C. F. Carbin, and R. J. Boese. 1981. *Can't your child hear? A guide for those who care about deaf children.* Baltimore: University Park Press.

Freeman, R. D., S. F. Malkin, and J. O. Hastings. 1975. Psychosocial problems of deaf children and their families: A comparative study. *American Annals of the Deaf* 120: 391–405.

Friedrich, W. N., M. T. Greenberg, and K. A. Crnic. 1983. A short form of the questionnaire on resources and stress. *American Journal of Mental Deficiency* 88: 41–48.

Greenberg, M. T. 1983. Family stress and child competence: The effects of early intervention for families with deaf infants. *American Annals of the Deaf* 128: 407–417.

Gregory, S. 1976. *The deaf child and his family.* New York: John Wiley and Sons.

Holroyd, J. 1973. *Manual for the questionnaire on resources and stress.* Los Angeles: UCLA Neuropsychiatric Institute.

Lytle, R. R., C. Feinstein, and B. Jonas. 1987. Social and emotional adjustment in deaf adolescents following transfer to a residential school for the deaf. *Journal of the American Academy of Child Psychiatry* 26: 237–241.

Lytle, R. R., and B. S. Jonas. 1984. Predictors of social and emotional adjustment in deaf adolescents at a residential school. In *The habilitation and rehabilitation of deaf adolescents,* ed. G. B. Anderson and D. Watson, 62–80. Proceedings of the National Conference on the Habilitation and Rehabilitation of Deaf Adolescents, April, Wagoner, Oklahoma.

Meadow, K. P. 1967. The effect of early manual communication and family climate on the deaf child's development. Ph.D. diss. University of California, Berkeley.

———. 1968. Parental responses to the medical ambiguities of deafness. *Journal of Health and Social Behavior* 9: 299–309.

Mendelsohn, J. Z., and B. Fairchild. 1984. Years of challenge: Parents, adolescence and deafness. In *The habilitation and rehabilitation of deaf adolescents,* ed. G. B. Anderson and D. Watson, 110–122. Proceedings of the National Conference on the Habilitation and Rehabilitation of Deaf Adolescents, April, Wagoner, Oklahoma.

Mindel, E. D., and M. Vernon. 1971. *They grow in silence—the deaf child and his family.* Silver Spring, MD: National Association of the Deaf.

Moses, K. L. 1985. Infant deafness and parental grief: Psychosocial early intervention. In *Education of the hearing impaired child,* ed. F. Powell, T. Finitzo-Hieber, S. Friel-Patti, and D. Henderson, 86–102. San Diego: College-Hill Press.

Schwartz, S. 1987. *Choices in deafness: A parents' guide.* Washington, DC: Woodbine House.

Schlesinger, H. S. 1985. Deafness, mental health, and language. In *Education of the hearing impaired child,* ed. F. Powell, T. Finitzo-Hieber, S. Friel-Patti, and D. Henderson, 103–116. San Diego: College-Hill Press.

Schlesinger, H. S., and K. P. Meadow. 1972. *Sound and sign: Childhood deafness and mental health.* Berkeley: University of California Press.

Stein, R. E. K., and C. K. Reissman. 1980. The development of an impact-on-family scale: Preliminary findings. *Medical Care* 18: 465–472.

Thompson, R. E., A. Thompson, and A. T. Murphy. 1979. Sounds of sorrow, sounds of joy: The hearing-impaired parents of hearing-impaired children—A conversation. In *The families of hearing-impaired children,* ed. A. T. Murphy, 337–351. Washington, DC: The Alexander Graham Bell Association for the Deaf.

14

Expression of Affect by Deaf and Hearing Infants

ROBERT H. MacTURK

The purpose of this report is to examine the patterns of facial expressions in two groups of nine-month-old infants engaged in face-to-face interaction: deaf infants with deaf mothers and hearing infants with hearing mothers. Previous investigations have demonstrated that infants are capable of regulating social and affective interaction. They can respond positively or negatively to environmental stimuli and thereby affect the environment. Much research has focused on reciprocity in early interaction (e.g., Ainsworth, Bell, and Stayton 1974; Brazelton, Koslowski, and Main 1974; Anderson, Vietze, and Dokecki 1977). These interactions are also referred to as the "dance" of dialogue (Bakeman and Brown 1977; Stern 1977); or turn-taking and mutual regulation between mothers and infants (Brazelton 1982; Chappell and Sander 1979; Gianino and Tronick 1987).

Recent investigations of deaf infants and their mothers have helped us understand how mothers and infants seek a mutually satisfying interaction when one or both members of the dyad are deaf. Meadow-Orlans (Meadow-Orlans et al. 1987) observed the patterns of interaction between deaf and hearing mothers and their deaf or hearing infants when the babies were three- and six-months-old. The mothers were asked to play normally with their baby for three minutes, then, for one minute, keep an expressionless "still-face." This was followed by a return to normal play for two minutes. Meadow-Orlans' analysis of the first three minutes of normal interaction revealed remarkable similarities between the deaf infants and hearing infants. At three months of age, both groups spent most of the three minutes attending to their mother's face while at six months of age, the infants shifted their major focus of attention to objects. These results suggest that auditory contact with the environment is a relatively minor factor in development

This research was supported by the Division of Maternal and Child Health, Bureau of Health Care Delivery and Assistance (Grant #MCJ-110563), the Beltone Institute for Hearing Research, and the Center for Studies in Education and Human Development, Gallaudet Research Institute. An abbreviated version of this paper was presented at The Annual Meeting of the Developmental Psychology Section of the British Psychological Society, Cardiff, Wales, Great Britain, September 1988.

of interactive skills. Moreover, it suggests that the dyadic interaction system is very flexible, and that mothers and infants can accommodate a wide range of resources or circumstances.

However, since these data were drawn from episodes of normal mother–infant interaction, infants' interpersonal resources were not greatly challenged. Sroufe and Waters (1977) have argued that the detection of individual differences in interactive competence requires a challenge of considerable magnitude if the infant is to mobilize available interpersonal resources. A common stressor for infants in studies of early interaction is the mother's expressionless ("still-face") presentation to her infant. This method serves to test infants' self-regulatory abilities through contradictory messages: the mother is available for social interaction, as shown by her proximity and eye contact, but she denies interaction by being unresponsive.

Gianino (1988) examined infants' stress and coping strategies during a still-face episode using a coding protocol derived from the Monadic Phase coding system (Tronick, Als, and Brazelton 1980). He found evidence for systematic differences when he compared infants' stress levels in dyads comprised of deaf infants/deaf mothers, hearing infants/deaf mothers, and hearing infants/hearing mothers. Furthermore, these differences appeared to be related to the hearing status of members of the dyad, with deaf infants of deaf mothers displaying the greatest amount of stress and hearing infants of hearing mothers the least. These conclusions are limited, however, because normal dyadic interactions were not assessed. Thus the observed differences may reflect fundamental differences in infants' interactive patterns rather than their reactions to a stressful situation.

One conclusion that may be drawn from Meadow-Orlans' and Gianino's work is that, during episodes of normal interaction, deafness per se does not seriously affect the course of interaction but, during the maternal still-face episode, greater stress was experienced by the deaf infants with deaf mothers. The strength of this conclusion must be tempered by the fact that (1) not all interaction episodes were coded with the same coding system and (2) the coding systems employed by Meadow-Orlans and Gianino may not be sensitive enough to detect the full range of the infant's emotional responses during the different episodes.

For example, Tronick's Monadic Phase coding system (1978), though designed to represent the continuum of affective expressions from most negative to most positive, includes expressive categories that mask important differences. One code illustrates this problem. The definition for the infant code "neutral attend-mother's face" includes the negative expressions of grimace, pout, wary, and frown in addition to a neutral expression. Thus the increased neutral affect reported for the deaf infants is confounded by the inclusion of negative affective expressions. Gianino's Infant Regulatory Scoring System is also limited in that it only assesses three categories of affect: positive, neutral, and negative. Although these were measured as discrete entities, the full range of an infant's facial expressions is severely restricted.

STUDY DESIGN AND PROCEDURES

The primary goal in this investigation of the patterns of facial expressions in deaf and hearing infants was to move toward an examination of the role of auditory input in relation to infants' emotional appraisal of normal and discrepant events. An underlying theme in research on mother–infant interaction concerns the importance of parents' verbal and vocal behavior as indicators of responsivity and sensitivity to the infant's facial expressive communication. Despite the presumed importance of auditory contact with the environment, this assumption has not been examined directly. If the picture emerging from the work of Meadow-Orlans and Gianino holds (that is, deaf and hearing infants are similar during periods of normal interaction but display different reactions during a stress-inducing episode), then their patterns of emotional expression should be similar. Specifically, both groups of infants should show a similar range of facial expressions during the baseline condition of normal mother–infant interaction but the deaf infants would react more negatively during a period of maternal still-face.

A secondary goal was to examine the feasibility of employing a coding system developed for hearing infants with a group of deaf infants. The facial expressive environment experienced by deaf infants of deaf parents is very different from that of their hearing peers. For example, American Sign Language contains many facial components that change or modify communicative intent and may substitute for vocal intonations in spoken language (Baker and Padden 1978). Therefore, it was unclear whether a coding system designed for hearing subjects would be appropriate for assessing facial expressions in deaf subjects whose primary mode of communication requires that both linguistic and emotional information be carried on the face.

Subjects

Subjects included two groups of infants and their mothers. Group 1 consisted of three deaf infants with deaf mothers. Group 2 had three normally hearing infants with normally hearing mothers. Dyads were seen when the infants were nine months old. These deaf parents communicate with each other primarily through sign language; on the interaction videotapes, all the deaf mothers used their voices in addition to sign language. All subjects were recruited from the Gallaudet University faculty and staff and were from predominantly middle-income backgrounds with both parents present in the home. All the infants were healthy and developing appropriately.

Procedures

This study employed the standard face-to-face interaction methodology in which the mother and the infant were seated across from each other and videotaped using two cameras and a split screen generator. The mother was asked to play with her infant (three minutes), turn away (thirty seconds), turn back with a still face (sixty seconds), and play again with her infant (three minutes).

The infants' facial expressions were coded using Izard and his colleagues' (Izard, Dougherty, and Hembree 1983) system for identifying affect expressions by holistic judgments (AFFEX). This system employs ten anatomically based facial expressive categories: interest, joy, surprise, sadness, anger, contempt, shame (if gaze direction and posture are included), disgust, fear, and (physical) distress. The expressions of fear, disgust, and distress are typically elicited by external stimuli (i.e., inoculations, bitter-tasting substances, etc.) and would not be expected to occur during face-to-face interactions. The contempt and shame expressions occur rarely in infants under one year. Therefore, Table 14.1 lists the categories and definitions of only those facial expressions observed during the study. The coder was trained in the criteria established by Izard et al. (1983) using the training manual and videotapes created for that purpose.

The videotapes were coded using a remote-controlled Panasonic AG-6300 videocassette recorder connected to an IBM-compatible personal computer running a program for data acquisition and recording. The onset of each change in facial expression was keyed into the PC's keyboard, while the time (in videoframes or $1/30^{th}$ of a second intervals) was obtained from the videotape control pulse. The resulting data set is a time-based sequential record of the infant's affect during the three interaction episodes.

The data for this report were obtained from the first two minutes of both play episodes and the one minute of maternal still-face. The two play episodes are thought to reflect a dyad's typical interactive pattern, while the maternal still-face is considered a moderately stressful situation for the infant.

ANALYSIS AND RESULTS

The data were processed through a series of data reduction programs to yield a count of onset frequencies for each discrete facial expression for each group of infants. The data were analyzed using the loglinear modeling procedure suggested by Bakeman and colleagues (Bakeman, Adamson, and Strisik in press). The basic analytic procedure consists of constructing a conceptual model of the relationships among the variables and testing the fit between the model and the observed data. To the extent that the conceptual model is consistent with the observed data, the result is a nonsignificant X^2 value.

Previous investigations of interactions of deaf and hearing infants suggested that the two groups would vary according to episode. Specifically, we expected to find that differences between the deaf and hearing infants would be minimal during the first episode and more pronounced during the still-face episode. This prediction was based on the finding by Meadow-Orlans et al. (1987) of nonsignificant group differences between hearing and deaf infants and a heightened level of

Table 14.1
AFFEX Categories and Descriptions

Anger: The brows are drawn down sharply together, the eyes are squinted, and the mouth can either be wide open and tense or rectangular or squarish in appearance.

Sadness: The inner corners of the brows are raised, the eyes are squinted, and the mouth is drawn into a frown or straight back, and may be opened or closed.

Interest: The brows are raised, there is an enlarged, widened appearance of the eye region, and the mouth may be open and relaxed or the lips may be pursed together.

Joy: The forehead is smooth, the cheeks are raised, and the mouth is drawn up into a smile.

Facial Expression Blends: Blends are characterized by combination of any of the above expressions. When an infant simultaneously signals two different emotions (e.g., anger and sadness), a blend occurs. A blend of anger and sadness, for example, may look like this: the baby's eyebrows are sharply drawn together, yet the mouth may be formed into a frown.

distress experienced by the deaf infants during the still-face episode (Gianino 1988).

The formal loglinear model tested the hypotheses that (1) there is an association between the two groups of infants and the interaction episodes; and (2) there is an association between the groups and the facial expressions displayed.

The results of the analysis, shown in Table 14.2, revealed an adequate fit between the model and the observed data ($X^2 = 14.67$, $df = 7$, $p = .04$). The data obtained during the still-face episode were weighted (i.e., the frequencies were doubled) in order to correct for the differences in time between the episodes. In an effort to determine the nature of the association between the groups and episodes, a separate series of X^2 analyses was conducted. These analyses revealed the following:

1. During the initial period of normal mother–infant interaction (Table 14.2, Play 1), there was a marginally significant association between hearing status and facial expression category ($X^2 = 12.03$, $df = 5$, $p = .03$).
2. During the maternal still-face and second interaction (Play 2) episodes, the association between the infants' hearing status and the category of facial expression becomes dramatically stronger (still-face: $X^2 = 70.31$, $df = 5$, $p < .001$; second interaction: $X^2 = 17.67$, $df = 5$, $p < .01$).

The range of facial expressions and the magnitude of difference of the expressive displays were only marginally significant for the two groups of infants (see Figure 14.1). The deaf infants never showed any negative emotions during the first interaction episode. It is notable that the proportions of a blended positive facial expression were lower for the deaf infants. When they displayed a facial expression, it tended to be a pure exemplar and not a mixture of features. The most frequent expression for both groups was interest and the least frequent was negative affect. The most significant difference was in the proportion of positive

Table 14.2
Frequencies of Expressions of Affect, by Group and Episode

Category	Deaf	Hearing	Total
First Interaction Episode[a]			
Anger	0	1	1
Negative Blends	0	2	2
Sadness	0	4	4
Interest	24	31	55
Positive Blends	2	18	20
Joy	9	11	20
Total	35	67	102
Maternal Still-Face Episode[b]			
Anger	6	41	47
Negative Blends	2	20	22
Sadness	6	6	12
Interest	118	60	178
Positive Blends	4	68	10
Joy	6	24	30
Total	142	157	299
Second Interaction Episode[c]			
Anger	17	10	27
Negative Blends	4	9	13
Sadness	5	0	5
Interest	23	31	54
Positive Blends	2	14	16
Joy	16	19	35
Total	67	83	150

Note. Overall, $X^2 = 14.67$, $df = 7$, $p < .05$.
[a] $X^2 = 12.03$, $df = 5$, $p < .05$.
[b] $X^2 = 70.31$, $df = 5$, $p < .001$.
[c] $X^2 = 17.67$, $df = 5$, $p < .01$.

blends. The hearing infants were almost five times as likely to show a blended positive emotion (i.e., interest combined with joy). This contrasts with the deaf infants, who displayed purer examples of the positive emotional states.

Not until the infants were confronted with the ambiguity of the maternal still-face episode did the two groups begin to differ (Figure 14.2). For the deaf infants, there was a minor increase in the proportion of negative affect. This change, combined with an increase in interest (from 69% to 83%), suggests a general broadening of the range of emotions and, at the same time, a flattening of the magnitude of emotional expression. The increase in interest implies that the deaf infants were more likely to respond to a socially ambiguous situation by attempting actively to process or to understand the nature of the ambiguous situation. In comparison, the hearing infants changed their patterns of facial expressions dramatically. The proportion of positive blends decreased sharply, while

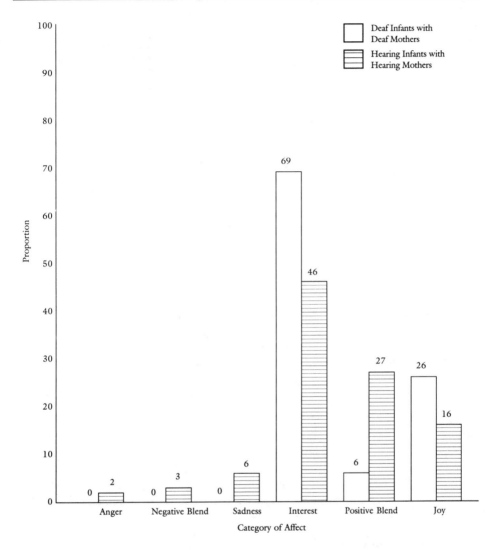

Figure 14.1. Proportion of facial expression, by group, for interaction episode 1.

anger and negative blends increased. Instead of the emotional damping observed with the deaf infants during still-face, the hearing infants displayed a wider range and magnitude of expression.

The resumption of normal interaction (Figure 14.3) resulted in a significant increase in the magnitude of facial expressive behavior for the deaf infants. Pure exemplars of anger displayed a six-fold increase, as did expressions of joy. In terms of overall expressivity, negative emotions increased from 9 percent to 39 percent, and positive emotions (positive blends plus joy) increased from 7 percent to 27 percent. In contrast, the hearing infants displayed what might be an emotional carryover from the previous episode. This is reflected in the proportions of anger (26% vs. 12%) and in the small reduction in negative blends (13% vs. 11%).

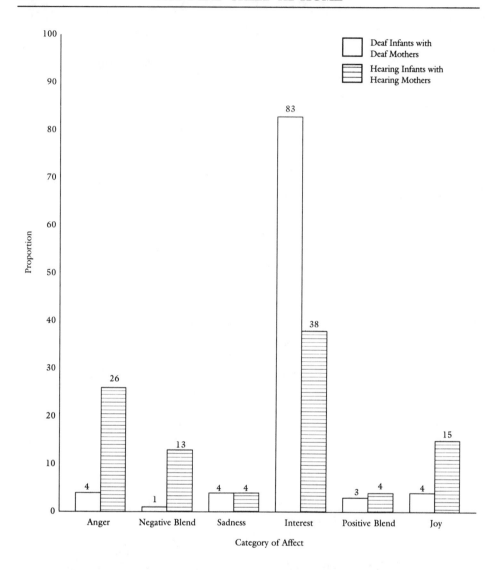

Figure 14.2. Proportion of facial expression, by group, for the still-face episode.

Both groups of infants displayed a negative emotional carryover from the still-face to the second interaction episode. The deaf infants increased their nega-tive *and* positive emotional displays once the mother resumed normal interaction, while the hearing infants decreased their negative displays and increased their pos-itive displays. This suggests that, as Gianino (1988) reported, the deaf infants were more stressed during the period of still-face. There was a sharp increase in the expression of interest during maternal still-face, an expression that is consid-ered to be a powerful marker of the infant's cognitive processing (Lewis and Bal-dini 1979). This implies that the deaf infants (compared to the hearing infants) devoted more energy to understanding the change in the mother's expression, and

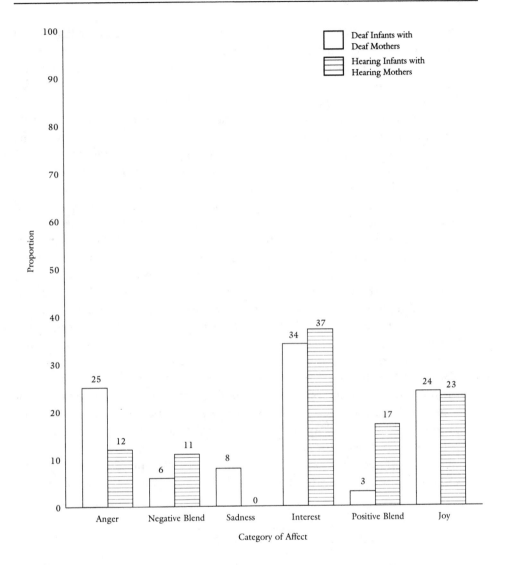

Figure 14.3.   **Proportion of facial expression, by group, for interaction episode 2.**

the increase in negative emotional displays observed during the second interaction episode may represent an emotional release.

CONCLUSIONS

The data obtained from the two groups of infants suggest several conclusions.

1. Infants, regardless of their hearing status, displayed similar patterns of facial expressions during the first period of normal social interaction. This implies

that auditory contact is not a salient dimension in infants' emotional appraisal of events occurring during episodes of playful interaction.

2. The differential changes observed during the still-face episode suggest that a moderately stressful situation is required to assess an infant's ability to modulate his or her emotions. To the extent that the mother is able to read and respond appropriately to her infant's signals in an effort to maintain a mutually satisfying interaction, we would expect to see little emotional variability. The data presented in Table 14.2 support this conjecture; no significant group differences were observed during the first period of normal interaction.

3. Maternal still-face may represent a more complex perturbation of social interaction than is suggested by the original conceptualization. It has been argued that maternal still-face is disruptive because of the contradictory messages of invitation (gaze contact) and denial (nonresponsiveness) of social interaction (Bloom, 1977; Tronick, Als, et al. 1978; Fogel, et al. 1983). However, in our data there is a sharp increase in negative emotional expressions and a decrease in interest for the hearing infants during the still-face episode. While the deaf infants showed some increase in negative emotions, their expressions of interest increased considerably. This suggests that the deaf infants' reactions to the disruptive and contradictory elements of maternal still-face are not solely emotional but also contain aspects of cognitive processing.

4. The AFFEX coding system appears to be an appropriate tool for use with deaf infants with deaf mothers despite the differences in the facial expressive environment. This conclusion must be tempered by the small size of the two groups and by the lack of similar data for the mothers. Since the mother's facial expressive behavior is unknown at this time, it is impossible to tell if the differences observed between the two groups reflect only the infants' contribution or if they are attempting to match their expressions to their mothers'.

REFERENCES

Ainsworth, M. D. S., S. Bell, and D. Stayton. 1974. Infant–mother attachment and social development: Socialization as a product of reciprocal responsiveness to signals. In *The integration of a child into a social world*, ed. M. P. M. Richards, 99–135. London: Cambridge University Press.

Anderson, B. J., P. Vietze, and P. R. Dokecki. 1977. Reciprocity in vocal interaction of mothers and infants. *Child Development* 48: 1676–1681.

Bakeman, R., L. B. Adamson, and P. Strisik. In press. Lags and logs: Statistical approaches to interaction. In *Interaction in human development*, ed. M. H. Bornstein and J. Bruner. Hillsdale, NJ: Lawrence Erlbaum and Associates.

Bakeman, R., and J. V. Brown. 1977. Behavioral dialogues: An approach to the assessment of mother–infant interaction. *Child Development* 48: 195–203.

Baker, C., and C. Padden. 1978. Focusing on the nonmanual components of American Sign Language. In *Understanding language through sign language research*, ed. P. Siple, 59–90. New York: Academic Press.

Bloom, K. 1977. Operant baseline procedures suppress infant social behavior. *Journal of Experimental Child Psychology* 23: 128–132.

Brazelton, T. B. 1982. Joint regulation of neonate–parent behavior. In *Social interchange in infancy: Affect, cognition, and communication,* ed. E. Z. Tronick, 7–22. Baltimore: University Park Press.

Brazelton, T. B., B. Koslowski, and M. Main. 1974. The origins of reciprocity: The early mother–infant interaction. In *The effect of the infant on its caregiver,* ed. M. Lewis and L. Rosenblum, 49–77. New York: John Wiley and Sons.

Chappell, P. F., and L. W. Sander. 1979. Mutual regulation of the neonatal–maternal interactive process: Context for the origins of communication. In *Before speech: The beginnings of interpersonal communication* ed. M. Bullowa, 89–109. Cambridge: Cambridge University Press.

Fogel, A., G. Diamond, B. Langhorst, and V. Demos. 1983. Affective and cognitive aspects of the two-month-old's participation in face-to-face interaction with its mother. In *Social interchange in infancy: Affect, cognition, and communication* ed. E. Z. Tronick, 47–58. Baltimore: University Park Press.

Gianino, A. F. 1988. *Stress and self-regulation in six-month-old deaf and hearing infants with deaf mothers.* Report prepared for the Beltone Foundation (Available from the Gallaudet Research Institute, 800 Florida Avenue, NE, Washington, DC 20002).

Gianino, A. F., and E. Z. Tronick. 1987. The mutual regulation model: Infant self and interactive regulation, coping and defense. In *Stress and coping.* ed. T. Field, P. McCabe, and N. Schneiderman, 47–68. Hillsdale, NJ: Lawrence Erlbaum and Associates.

Izard, C. E., L. M. Dougherty, and E. A. Hembree. 1983. *A system for identifying affect expressions by holistic judgments* (AFFEX). Newark, DE: Instructional Resources Center, University of Delaware.

Lewis, M., and N. Baldini. 1979. Attentional processes as an individual difference. In *Attention and cognitive development,* ed. G. A. Hale and M. Lewis, 135–172. New York: Plenum Press.

Meadow-Orlans, K. P., R. H. MacTurk, C. T. Prezioso, C. J. Erting, and P. S. Day. 1987. Interactions of deaf and hearing mothers with three- and six-month-old infants. Paper presented at the Biennial Meeting of the Society for Research in Child Development, April, Baltimore, Maryland.

Sroufe, L. A., and E. Waters. 1977. Attachment as an organizational construct. *Child Development* 48: 1184–1199.

Stern, D. 1977. *The first relationship.* Cambridge, MA: Harvard University Press.

Tronick, E. Z., H. Als, and T. B. Brazelton. 1980. Monadic phases: A structural descriptive analysis of infant–mother face-to-face interaction. *Merrill-Palmer Quarterly* 26: 3–24.

Tronick, E. Z., H. Als, L. Adamson, S. Wise, and T. B. Brazelton. 1978. The infant's response to entrapment between two contradictory messages in face-to-face interaction. *Journal of the American Academy of Child Psychiatry* 27: 74–77.

15

Directiveness in Mother–Infant Interactions

Patricia E. Spencer, Mary K. Gutfreund

Maternal directiveness has been reported as characteristic of interactions between hearing mothers and their deaf children. Studies of hearing children have shown that maternal directiveness, especially in the choice of communicative topics, is negatively associated with child language development. These findings have led to concern that excessive directiveness of hearing mothers with deaf children contributes to their difficulties in acquiring language. This chapter provides a review of selected studies of maternal directiveness and presents data from four groups of mothers and infants: (1) hearing mothers with hearing infants, (2) hearing mothers with deaf infants; (3) deaf mothers with deaf infants; (4) deaf mothers with hearing infants. Infants' hearing losses ranged from moderate-severe to profound; although the term *hearing impaired* might be audiologically more appropriate in describing some of the children, the term *deaf* is used to describe them all. Analyses are directed toward determining the causes of maternal directiveness in dyads of hearing mothers and deaf infants. Finally, the implications of the findings will be discussed as they relate to early intervention programs for hearing families and their deaf infants.

DEFINITIONS OF DIRECTIVENESS

Determining the effect of mothers' directiveness on their children's language progress is complicated by the fact that the term *directiveness* has a variety of meanings. Tannock (1988, p. 154) categorized these meanings as generally falling into one of three groups.

1. Response control—the mothers' use of syntactic forms (imperatives, questions) intended to elicit a response from the child;

The authors wish to thank Dr. Barbara Bodner-Johnson and Dr. Mary June Moseley for contributing to the conceptualization and interpretation of the studies reported. In addition, we appreciate the work of Natalie Grindstaff and Anne Marie Baer in preparing transcripts of the language of the deaf mothers.

2. Turn-taking control—the mothers' tendency to provide many utterances and take lengthy turns in the interaction;
3. Topic control—the mothers' tendency to initiate and establish interaction topics that are unrelated to the child's activity or expressed interest.

Adding to the definitional confusion is the fact that directiveness and responsiveness are often inaccurately treated as though they are mutually exclusive categories of behavior. In fact, a mother may be very responsive to her child's interests in the establishing of interactive topics but produce response control utterances when responding to the child's lead. That is, the mother may allow her child to control the setting of topics but may respond to the child's topic by asking related questions or by giving suggestions for further activities related to the topic in order to extend the time on it. This type of response control, which would include turnabouts (Kaye and Charney 1981) and the scaffolding behaviors described by Bruner and his colleagues (Ratner and Bruner 1978) seems to support child language development. Investigations attempting to define effects of maternal directiveness, therefore, need to consider response control separately from turn-taking control and topic control.

In contrast to response control behaviors, topic control directiveness, in which the mother may override signals of the child's interest in a particular object or event in order to redirect attention and communication to a topic of her own choosing, does not appear to support language development. A number of studies have reported positive associations between children's language developmental levels and the degree to which mothers relate their communicative behaviors to the child's focus of attention (Barnes et al. 1983; Harding 1983; Harris et al. 1986; Masur 1982; Petersen and Sherrod 1982; Rocissano and Yatchmink 1983; Tomasello and Todd 1983). By extension, maternal topic control should be negatively correlated with child language development. However, these studies emphasizing associations between the two variables have generally failed to demonstrate a causal link between mothers' behavior and the rate of the child's development. For the most part, the studies leave unanswered the question whether maternal topic control directiveness *causes* delayed language development or is instead an adaptive response to a child's delayed language development. However, Tomasello and Farrar (1986) have presented data that do suggest such a causal link. Their study showed that infants learned to comprehend modeled words efficiently when those words represented objects on which the infants had spontaneously fixed their attention, but learning was much less efficient for words that were modeled after the adult directed the infant's attention to the object.

The general conclusion in the literature on maternal directiveness therefore suggests a positive, causal relationship between maternal behaviors that allow the child's attention focus to guide the interactive topics and the child's rate of language development. Maternal overcontrol of topics, failing to take the child's attention focus into account, is considered to affect development negatively.

Rocissano and Yatchmink (1983, p. 1230) offered an explanation for the positive effects on child language development of providing input matching a child's current attention focus. This explanation assumes that an individual has a finite amount of cognitive capacity available at any one time with which to process information. They argue that engaging in social interaction is itself a formidable task for a young child and that attending to the conversation partner's focus of attention requires considerable expenditure of the available cognitive capacity. If the conversation partner takes the responsibility for monitoring the focus of the child's attention, basing conversation topics on that focus, more of the child's cognitive energy will be available for other tasks. The task at issue here, of course, is that of processing the language input provided and making a cognitive match between the words seen or heard and the objects or activities to which they refer.

DIRECTIVENESS AND MOTHERS OF DEAF CHILDREN

Like studies of hearing children, studies of deaf children have defined directiveness in different ways, although hearing mothers of deaf children have been consistently characterized as overly directive. Early studies approached the issue by making judgments about the affective tone of mother–child interactions, with hearing mothers of deaf children rated as showing more "tension" and "antagonism" than those of hearing children (Goss 1970) or judged to be more didactic, inflexible, and intrusive during interactions with their children (Schlesinger and Meadow 1972). The latter study, like some to be reported here, also suggested that these characteristics were ameliorated in dyads in which the deaf child's language ability was relatively high.

Interactive behaviors of hearing mothers with their deaf children have often been found to show high levels of imperative syntactic structures and other response control strategies. Goss (1970), using Bales Interactional Analysis procedures, showed that hearing mothers of deaf children were likely to give more suggestions to their children than were mothers of hearing children. Hyde, Elias, and Power (1981) reported greater maternal use of imperative and directive syntactic structures with deaf children than with hearing children. White and White (1984) also reported high rates of production of imperatives by mothers of deaf children; however, imperative production was less for mothers whose deaf children had higher language levels than for those whose children had lower language levels. As suggested above, maternal response control directiveness can be supportive of child language development and therefore may be appropriately used with deaf children. It is of concern, however, that only the imperative syntactic forms occur in greater numbers with these children. Mothers' use of questions, another response control syntactic device, has been reported to occur *less* often with deaf children than with hearing children (Goss 1970).

Topic control, which has been posited to have negative consequences for child language development, has been addressed by another group of studies of deaf children and their mothers. Hearing mothers of deaf two-year-olds were reported to make more references to their own behaviors and fewer to the behaviors or attention focus of their children than did mothers of hearing infants or toddlers (Cross, Johnson-Morris, and Nienhuys 1980). In addition, Gregory (1988) observed that behaviors of hearing mothers with deaf infants were less contingent upon the infants' behaviors than was the case for deaf mother–deaf infant dyads. Such a lack of contingency indicated that infant behaviors did not typically serve as initiators of joint focus on a topic. Similarly, Wedell-Monnig and Lumley (1980) reported a greater number of spontaneous attempts to interact, that is, behaviors not contingent on the infants' behaviors, by hearing mothers of deaf toddlers compared to mothers of hearing toddlers. Meadow et al. (1981) reported more initiating behaviors unrelated to the child's current activity or attention focus from hearing mothers of deaf children compared to deaf mothers with deaf children and hearing mothers with hearing children. In none of these studies, however, were the language development levels of the deaf and hearing children matched.

Nienhuys, Horsborough, and Cross (1985) reported that levels of maternal topic control did not differ significantly for dyads with deaf and hearing children when those children were matched for language development level. In another report, however, Cross, Nienhuys, and Kirkman (1985) found that mothers' speech to deaf children was less often semantically contingent on child activity than was mothers' speech to hearing children, regardless of child language level. The authors suggested that the behaviors of the mothers of deaf children reflected "maternal *beliefs* about the conversational competence of deaf children rather than direct feedback from the child's . . . conversation" (p. 269). In addition, the authors reported that their deaf subjects were less active contributors to the interactions than were their hearing subjects. This finding concurs with that of Wedell-Monnig and Lumley (1980).

The studies of hearing mothers and deaf children reviewed above suggest several factors that may explain the high incidence of maternal topic control directiveness in those dyads. The phenomenon has been variously attributed to

1. The delayed language development of the children, necessitating more directive maternal behaviors in order to ensure that interaction continues;
2. Maternal beliefs and/or fears about communicative failure, leading them to believe they must exert more control in order for interaction to proceed;
3. Communicative passivity or inactivity on the part of the children, making it necessary for the mother to do more to "fill in the spaces" in the interaction.

Although these potential explanations are not mutually exclusive, they suggest different intervention approaches if topic control is to be more equitably shared between mother and infant. It seems important, therefore, to investigate further the origins of maternal topic control directiveness in dyads of hearing mothers with deaf children. The two analyses presented in the following sections represent an attempt to clarify the factors influencing maternal topic control in dyads of hearing mothers and deaf children.

TWO ANALYSES OF MATERNAL TOPIC CONTROL DIRECTIVENESS

Procedures

The data for both analyses were obtained from three-minute segments of mother–infant interaction videotaped when the infants were twelve months old. During the interaction, mother and infant were seated face to face. The infant was seated in a standard high chair. No toys were provided during the interaction. Several objects (i.e., microphone, lights, and cameras) were visible to both the infant and the mother.

These interactive samples were part of a lengthier videotaping session. All the mother-infant dyads were participating in a longitudinal study and had been videotaped at least twice before under the same conditions. Each dyad was videotaped in color by two cameras, one focused on the mother and the other on the infant. The output of the two cameras was fed into a special effects generator to produce a split-screen image. Time (in minutes, seconds, and video frame number) was superimposed on the image and allowed for detailed, time-specific coding of mother and infant behaviors.

Subjects

Nineteen mother–infant dyads participated in the study. They included

1. Seven hearing mothers and hearing infants (Group HH);
2. Three hearing mothers and deaf infants (Group HD);
3. Four deaf mothers and deaf infants (Group DD);
4. Five deaf mothers and hearing infants (Group DH).

All the mothers except one in group HH and one in group HD had attended college. Because educational levels are generally lower for deaf persons than for hearing persons in the U.S. (Schein 1987), these deaf mothers form a somewhat unusual group of deaf adults. Their high educational level suggests, however, that any differences found between the groups can be attributed more readily to hearing status than to education or social class.

Except for hearing loss, none of the infants had any known or suspected handicapping condition. The infants in Group HD had less severe losses than did those in Group DD. In addition, HD infants wore hearing aids on a consistent

Table 15.1
Characteristics of Subject Dyads

Group	Infants' Sex	Infants' Hearing Status	Mothers' Hearing Status	Mothers' Education
HH	F	Hearing	Hearing	M.A.
HH	M	Hearing	Hearing	M.A.
HH	F	Hearing	Hearing	H.S. +
HH	M	Hearing	Hearing	M.A.
HH	F	Hearing	Hearing	M.A.
HH	M	Hearing	Hearing	M.A.
HH	M	Hearing	Hearing	M.A.
HD	M	Moderate-Severe	Hearing	H.S.
		Mild-Moderate (r)	Hearing	B.A. +
		Severe (l)		
HD	F	Moderate-Severe	Hearing	B.A. +
DD	M	Profound	Deaf	M.A.
DD	F	Severe-Profound	Deaf	B.A. +
DD	F	Severe-Profound	Deaf	M.A.
DD	F	Severe	Deaf	M.A.
DH	F	Hearing	Deaf	M.A.
DH	M	Hearing	Deaf	M.A.
DH	F	Hearing	Deaf	B.A.
DH	M	Hearing	Deaf	B.A.
DH	M	Hearing	Deaf	M.A.

Note. HH and HD infants included in Analysis 1; DD and DH infants added for Analysis 2

basis, and two of the three HD subjects were in programs focusing on oral language without signing support. None of the DD infants were yet using hearing aids. They were acquiring a visual/manual language as they interacted with their signing families. DH infants had variable sign/speech input. Four of the five mothers frequently vocalized while signing to their infants, but only two of those mothers consistently produced intelligible speech. Both groups of deaf infants were participating with their families in parent–infant intervention programs. The hearing infants were not in educational or day care programs. Table 15.1 provides a summary of information about the participating mothers and infants.

Judgments about the similarity of infants' language levels were based on observations of the taping sessions in which the families had participated and on information from interviews with the mothers. At the time the data were gathered, the infants in all four groups demonstrated similar levels of expressive communication behaviors: All had been observed to use pointing and other gestures to express communicative intentions; and vocal and/or manual language had not yet developed to the point of producing several consistent, conventional words, although spoken proto-words and babysigns were observed. All of the infants were observed to comprehend and to respond to simple messages directed to them by their mothers, with mothers reporting their infants' language comprehension as more advanced than their language production.

Analysis 1: A Discourse Analysis of the Interaction between Two Groups of Mothers and Infants

A discourse-level analysis, focusing on contributions of new topics by mothers and infants during the interaction, was performed on the videotaped interaction samples of dyads in Groups HD and HH. A transcript of the communicative behaviors of each dyad was made and reviewed in order to identify (1) the sequence of topics in which the dyad engaged; (2) the initiating and responsive behaviors in each topic engagement; (3) the occurrence of additional potential initiating behaviors (i.e., behaviors that could have served to change the activity or focus of attention of the dyad but that failed to elicit a response from the partner).

For mothers, behaviors considered as potential topic initiations and responses included spoken and/or signed formal language, conventional gestures, and physical contact or manipulation of the infant. Potential topic-initiating and responding behaviors by the infant included gesturing, establishing physical contact with the mother, vocalizing, and producing large body movements, such as twisting around in the chair or arching the back to look at an object. In some dyads, the mother treated an infant's prolonged gaze at an object as a topic initiation and responded contingently. When such an episode was identified for a specific dyad, all subsequent gazes toward that object by the infant were categorized as potential topic initiations.

As would be expected from earlier studies of interactions between hearing mothers and deaf infants compared to those of hearing mothers and hearing infants, the mothers in Group HD produced greater proportions of their dyads' topic initiations (median 41.7%) than did the Group HH mothers (median 20.0%) (Mann-Whitney $U = 2.5$; $p < .058$). It is important to note that a topic initiated by the mother represented a maternal communicative behavior that was not contingent on the infant's prior behavior. Any language input provided to the infant, therefore, was not predicated upon the infant's pre-existing focus of visual attention or expression of interest. Thus, the infants in Group HD received significantly less input contingent on their own focus of attention than did the infants in Group HH. In addition, HD mothers produced more utterances per minute than did the mothers of the hearing infants. The mothers in Group HD displayed both more topic control and more turn-taking control directiveness than did the mothers in Group HH.

This finding is more complex than it first appears. Additional investigation revealed that when the infants produced a potential initiating behavior, both groups of mothers were equally likely to provide a contingent response. While HD mothers were more directive, they were not less responsive than were HH mothers when given a clear opportunity to respond contingently. Furthermore, both groups of infants were equally likely to respond contingently to their mothers' potential initiations. (Overall, the infants were less responsive than were the mothers.)

The groups did differ in the number of behaviors produced by the infants that served as potential initiations. The HD infants produced fewer potential initiation behaviors (median = 8) than did the HH infants (median = 14) (Mann-Whitney $U = 3.0; p = .058$). The increased turn-taking control of the HD mothers may simply have prevented their infants from having sufficient time and opportunity to contribute as many potential initiating behaviors as the other infants did. Alternatively, it is possible that HD mothers' directiveness in initiating topics was a natural reaction to their infants' low rates of communicative activity. Such a compensatory process has been reported in dyads of hearing mothers with relatively passive hearing infants (Hoff-Ginsburg 1987).

In summary, this analysis replicated others' findings of increased topic control directiveness by hearing mothers of deaf infants compared to mothers of hearing infants. This occurred despite the lack of any significant difference in language functioning levels between the two groups of infants and in spite of equivalent rates of responsiveness from the two groups of infants to their mother's communicative behaviors. The production of fewer potential topic-initiating behaviors by HD infants, however, raised a question whether that factor, rather than differences in maternal expectations, might be responsible for the pattern of excess maternal topic control observed in Group HD.

This finding was disturbing to us because of reported passivity in older deaf children (Meadow 1980) and earlier reports of lessened interactive participation by deaf infants (Cross, Nienhuys, and Kirkman 1985; Wedell-Monnig and Lumley 1980). We wondered if there could be something intrinsic to deafness that tends to decrease the activity level of the deaf infants. Or, could a lack of maternal responsiveness to earlier communicative behaviors, such as changes in the infant's gaze direction, teach the infant that his or her role is that of responder rather than initiator? Our second analysis addressed these possibilities.

Analysis 2: A Special Case of Topic Control—Mother's Responses to Infant Object-Focused Visual Attention Episodes

This analysis used the same videotaped interaction sequences as in the first analysis. In this case, however, tapes from two additional mother-infant groups were used. Group DD (deaf mothers with deaf infants) was included to determine whether the fact of infant deafness and the demands of visual communication necessitated more topic control directiveness from mothers. If this were so, and if it were necessary to be more directive when communicating with deaf infants, then

Group DD would show topic control patterns similar to those of Group HD. If, on the other hand, maternal anxieties about their infants' language development produce directiveness, Group DH (deaf mothers with hearing infants) would be more like Group HD.

The latter two groups differ in that Group DH infants can clearly receive communicative signals carried through their mothers' preferred language modality (vision) while Group HD infants are unable to perceive fully their mothers' auditory language. In addition, deaf mothers can be confident that their hearing infants will acquire sign language with time and that they will be able to communicate fully with them; hearing mothers face the possibility that their deaf infants may not be able to communicate fluently using their parents' auditory language system. Despite these differences, both groups of mothers come to interactions with their infants knowing that the infants' processing abilities and needs are different from their own. We posited that the behaviors of both groups of mothers would therefore reflect some additional anxiety or concern about the conduct of the interaction when compared with those of mothers who know that their infants' communicative needs and modalities match their own. If such concerns result in mothers' increased control of topic initiation, groups HD and DH should show more directive patterns compared to groups DD and HH even when infant language level and rate of infant initiating behaviors are similar across the groups.

The infant behavior that served as a basis against which mothers' responses were measured was that of directing gaze away from the mother to look at a new object or event during an ongoing interaction. When an infant turns away to establish a new focus of attention, the mother can usually determine the new gaze focus. If she chooses to treat that change in focus as a topic initiation and gives a contingent response, a new dyadic topic will be established. Before the age at which infants begin to produce gestures and vocalizations in an intentional manner, changes in their focus of visual attention often provide the most salient opportunity for mothers to assume that the infant wants to change topics and to respond in a contingent manner.

The numbers of changes in gaze to look away from the mother were similar for the four groups of infants in the study, and thus the changes provided an opportunity to measure the mothers' responses to a potential topic-initiating behavior produced at a similar rate by deaf and hearing infants. No statistically significant differences occurred between the groups of infants on the total time looking away from mother, the proportion of look-away time attending to objects compared to looking away without a specific focus, or the mean duration of episodes of looking away.

Before coding mothers' responses to their infants' episodes of looking away, transcriptions of the language of all the deaf mothers were prepared by two deaf native signers. These transcripts were consulted during coding when there was any doubt as to the relevance of the mother's behavior to the infant's new attention focus. Coding was done by the two authors. Percentage of agreement, calculated for four of the tapes was 86 percent.

The system for coding mothers' responses was exhaustive and mutually exclusive. It included the following categories:

1. Respond: The mother produced a verbal or nonverbal behavior that was directly related to (contingent on) the infant's new focus of visual attention (e.g., the infant looks at a light; the mother says or signs, "That's a light").
2. Wait: The mother waited quietly while the infant looked away.
3. Redirect: The mother attempted to redirect infant's attention to a focus of mother's choice. This category included two types of behaviors.
   a. a simple attention-getting behavior used to redirect visual attention to the mother herself (e.g., snapping fingers, tapping on the child's leg, saying or signing "Look at me!");
   b. the direct initiation of a new topic or activity not related to the current focus of the infant's visual attention (e.g., the infant looks at a light; the mother takes the infant's hands, pats them together, and says, "Pat-a-cake, pat-a-cake").
4. Continue: The mother continued the behavior in which she was engaged before the infant looked away from her.

Mothers frequently produced a sequence of responses during an extended infant look-away episode. *Wait* and *continue* responses were coded only if they lasted for one second or longer. *Respond* and *redirect* behaviors were coded regardless of duration.

Analysis

The duration of time spent in each type of response was determined for each mother and converted to a proportion of the time her infant looked away from her. Group differences were first tested using the Kruskal-Wallis one-way rank analysis of variance (Siegel 1956). Where this test revealed a significant difference among the groups, the Mann-Whitney U test was employed to compare pairs of groups and thus identify the source(s) of the difference.

Results

As shown in Table 15.2, no statistical differences emerged among the four groups of mothers in their responses coded *redirect* or *continue*. However, mothers whose hearing status does not match that of their infants (HD and DH) made these responses to infant look-aways more frequently than did mothers in matched status dyads (DD and HH).

A comparison of the proportion of time that mothers waited after the infant looked away did show significant differences among groups. Deaf mothers with deaf infants (DD) used this response more than did mothers in any of the other

Table 15.2
Mothers' Responses During Infants' Object-Focused Episodes
(Mean Percentage Duration: Range in Brackets)

Mother's Responses	Dyads				Kruskal-Wallis H values	Mann-Whitney U Test
	Hearing Mother Deaf Infant	Hearing Mother Hearing Infant	Deaf Mother Deaf Infant	Deaf Mother Hearing Infant		
	($N=3$)	($N=7$)	($N=4$)	($N=5$)		
Redirect	38.7 (25–47)	8.7 (0–23)	14.7 (6–22)	21.9 (9–32)	4.78	
Continue	22.3 (12–29)	11.1 (2–26)	8.9 (0–23)	18.4 (10–24)	4.14	
Wait	16.0 (8–31)	34.7 (0–37)	70.4 (60–90)	41.8 (16–59)	9.29*	HD < DH, DD DH, HH < DD
Respond	23.3 (16–36)	45.7 (22–67)	6.0 (0–11)	18.6 (0–58)	11.24*	DD < HH, HD HD, DH < HH
Wait + Respond	39.3 (24–49)	80.4 (63–97)	76.4 (67–90)	60.5 (51–74)	12.43**	HD < HH, DD, DH DH < HH, DD

*$p \leq .05$
**$p \leq .01$

three groups. Indeed, this was the Group DD mothers' most characteristic response mode, comprising 70 percent of their coded time. Deaf mothers with hearing infants (DH) were second in proportion of the time they waited, significantly higher than Group HD mothers.

Differences among groups also were found for the respond code. DD mothers had less time in this code than did HH and HD mothers; HD and DH mothers had significantly less time than HH mothers did.

Wait and respond behaviors were defined as the most positive or contingent responses to infant look-aways because both allowed the infant to set the attention focus without interruption by the mother. Therefore, these categories were combined with results shown as the last row in Table 15.2. There it can be seen that HD mothers rank last, with the least time in the combined wait + respond category (39%). This is significantly below that of mothers in the three other groups. Deaf mothers with hearing infants (DH) show significantly less time in the wait + respond category than do the two groups whose hearing status matches that of their infants (HH and DD).

Several conclusions can be drawn from these findings.

1. HD mothers had less time in the combined wait + respond category than any other group of mothers. Therefore, they less often allowed their infants to

establish a new focus of attention than was the case for any of the other groups of infants.

2. The DH group performed in an intermediate way. Those mothers had more time than Group HD in the wait or combined wait + respond categories. DH mothers had less time than HH or DD mothers, however, in the wait + respond category.

3. HH and DD mothers, while both allowing their infants high levels of autonomy in establishing a new attention focus, showed distinctly different ways of doing so. HH mothers most often provided a response during their infant's looking away. In contrast, DD mothers were overwhelmingly likely to wait during the look-away episode.

The difference in preferred response type between DD and HH mothers led to an additional consideration. Earlier in this chapter we pointed out the importance of mothers' providing their infants with language input contingent on their current interest, as shown by their focus of visual attention. Since DD mothers tended to wait while their infants looked at objects, how was contingent input provided? Further examination of the tapes of dyads in which the infants were deaf disclosed that DD mothers provided contingent responses *after* 45 percent of infant look-away episodes. That is, while HH mothers responded *during* their infants' episodes of turning away to look at an object, DD mothers often responded immediately *after* their infants looked back at them. The timing of contingent input was different between the two groups.

The hearing mothers of deaf babies (HD) did not follow the pattern shown by DD mothers, however. HD mothers responded only 9 percent of the time after their infants looked back at them. HD mothers generally failed to provide contingent input either during or after their infants looked away to focus on an object.

DISCUSSION

In combination, the two analyses summarized above indicate that hearing mothers of deaf infants (HD) were less likely to follow their infants' lead and thus less likely to provide them with contingent language input than were the other three groups of mothers. This difference occurred despite similarities across the groups in the developmental level of infant communicative behaviors, the rate of infant responsivity to mothers' behaviors, and the frequency of infants' gazes toward objects. Therefore, differences in level and rate of infant interactive behaviors cannot be said to account for the differences found between the topic control behaviors of HD mothers and mothers in the other groups. Other factors must be considered.

The fact that there appeared to be some increased maternal control of topic setting in the other group in which mother and infant hearing status differed (Group DH) suggests that this factor influenced maternal topic control behaviors.

Mothers in mismatched dyads may carry emotional burdens related to their concerns about being able to effectively influence their infant's language development—burdens that are not shared by the mothers in the matched dyads. Schlesinger (1987) suggested that mothers facing a situation in which they feel powerless, or fearful of being unable to contribute to their infants' development, may increase their attempts to control elements that they *can* control—such as the choice of communicative topics. As discussed earlier, such anxieties would be less powerful for deaf mothers of hearing infants (DH) than for hearing mothers of deaf infants (HD) and might explain the lesser degree of topic control found for DH mothers compared to the HD mothers.

In addition to emotional factors, we believe that cognitive factors influence the pattern of maternal topic control directiveness found for HD dyads and, to a lesser degree, DH dyads. The "finite cognitive capacity" concept applied earlier to explain why contingent input enhances infant language acquisition may also be helpful in explaining patterns of maternal topic directiveness. Mother–infant interaction generally proceeds at an automatic or intuitive level. This automaticity can be disrupted, however, when mothers must use cognitive energy constantly to remain alert to differences between their own habitual communication modalities and those of their infants. Hearing mothers of hearing infants assume that the infant receives their spoken messages regardless of the infant's direction of gaze. Similarly, deaf mothers whose habitual communication is through the visual mode and who have thoroughly incorporated rules for visual communicative turn-taking have no need to remain consciously aware of those rules during an interaction with their deaf infants. Hearing mothers with deaf infants, however, have the added task of keeping their infants' needs for visual input uppermost in their minds during interaction. This task complicates the interactive process for the HD mother and necessitates that she consciously remain aware of aspects of her own and her infant's behavior that do not require attention or the expenditure of cognitive processing energy by the HH or DD mothers. Awareness of HD infants' visual needs, coupled with a lack of understanding of the rules for turn-taking in visual communication, may cause the HD mothers to try constantly to maintain their infants' visual attention. In that case, the mothers could hope to avoid anticipated difficulties in regaining their infants' attention once it had been directed to something else.

To a lesser degree than for hearing mothers with deaf infants, the interactive task for deaf mothers with hearing infants is also complicated by the difference between their hearing status and that of their infants. If these mothers are to respond to their infants' vocal communicative behaviors, they must remain consciously alert for visual evidence of those behaviors. However, our findings for dyads of deaf mothers and hearing infants remain somewhat ambiguous and serve only as a first report on this group. We suggest that additional research on these dyads is merited. Future findings may help to clarify the origins of maternal topic control directiveness in all mismatched mother-infant dyads.

Our findings of increased maternal directiveness in dyads of hearing mothers and deaf infants, however, concur with a number of earlier reports. The end results of a history of excessive maternal control of interactive topics merit serious consideration. The HD infants in this study, who were at greater risk for language delays than any of the other groups, were experiencing interactions *less* supportive, rather than more supportive, of language acquisition than were the other infants. This raises concerns that even during the prelinguistic period, the language-learning needs of deaf infants with hearing parents are not being met. This is the case regardless of the language approach being used (speech plus speechreading, signing plus speech, or cued speech), if the infant's hearing loss necessitates some reliance on visual language input.

Excessive maternal topic control also raises concerns about the degree to which the deaf infants of hearing mothers are being provided opportunities to develop a sense of "efficacy" and positive self-esteem. Patterns of early maternal overcontrol or disregard of infant indications of interest in a topic change may lead to the infants' developing patterns of passivity or learned helplessness. White and White (1984) reported disturbing relationships between features of early maternal nonresponsiveness and later social-emotional problems in children.

We suspect that the lower number of attempts to use gestures and vocalizations to initiate new topics by the HD infants compared to HH infants was due to their having different histories of maternal responsiveness to their changes in gaze direction to indicate a new interest. By failing to respond contingently to HD infants' changes in direction of gaze, their mothers may have inadvertently reinforced passive rather than active communicative behaviors and may have given the infants the impression that their own interests were not as important as those of their mothers.

Because of the importance of children's social-emotional and language development, we propose that parent-infant programs focus on modifying patterns of excessive maternal dominance when they are found. Intervention programs should continue to provide counseling and support for the emotional needs of hearing parents who are facing the diagnosis of their infant's hearing loss and its potential effects on the child's development. In addition, the parents' cognitive needs should be addressed. Parents (as well as teachers) should be assured that it is not the amount of language they produce but the amount of *contingent* language received by the infant that critically affects development. In order more readily to provide contingent input, hearing parents of deaf infants need to have access to the model of sequential timing of input that we have reported for deaf mothers with deaf infants. That model can best be demonstrated by deaf adults, either parents or teachers, who are used to interacting with deaf infants. Parent-infant programs will benefit hearing parents, therefore, by including more deaf teachers and encouraging more interaction between deaf parents and hearing parents participating in the program.

REFERENCES

Barnes, S., M. Gutfreund, D. Satterly, and G. Wells. 1983. Characteristics of adult speech which predict children's language development. *Journal of Child Language* 10: 65–84.

Cross, T. G., J. E. Johnson-Morris, and T. G. Nienhuys. 1980. Linguistic feedback and maternal speech: Comparisons of mothers addressing hearing and hearing-impaired children. *First Language* 1: 163–189.

Cross, T., T. Nienhuys, and M. Kirkman. 1985. Parent-child interaction with receptively disabled children: Some determinants of maternal style. In *Children's language,* Vol. 5, ed. K. Nelson, 247–290. Hillsdale, NJ: Lawrence Erlbaum and Associates.

Goss, R. 1970. Language used by mothers of deaf children and mothers of hearing children. *American Annals of the Deaf* 115: 93–96.

Gregory, S. 1988. Parent-child communication: The implications of deafness. Paper presented at Conference of the Developmental Section of the British Psychological Society, Cardiff, U.K.

Harding, C. 1983. Setting the stage for language acquisition: Communication development in the first year. In *The transition from prelinguistic to linguistic communication,* ed. R. Golinkoff, 93–113. Hillsdale, NJ: Lawrence Erlbaum and Associates.

Harris, M., D. Jones, S. Brooks, and J. Grant. 1986. Relations between the nonverbal context of maternal speech and the rate of language development. *British Journal of Developmental Psychology* 4: 261–268.

Hoff-Ginsberg, E. 1987. Topic relations in mother-child conversation. *First Language* 7: 145–158.

Hyde, M. B., G. C. Elias, and D. J. Power. 1981. Use of verbal and nonverbal control techniques by mothers of hearing impaired infants. In *Early intervention with young hearing impaired children,* ed. D. Power, G. Elias, and H. Hyde, 75–106. Mt. Gravatt, Australia: Mt. Gravatt College of Advanced Education, Centre for Human Development Studies.

Kaye, K., and R. Charney. 1981. Conversational asymmetry between mothers and children. *Journal of Child Language:* 8: 35–49.

Masur, E. E. 1982. Mothers' responses to infants' object-related gestures: Influences on lexical development. *Journal of Child Language* 9: 23–30.

Meadow, K. 1980. *Deafness and child development.* Berkeley: University of California Press.

Meadow, K., M. Greenberg, C. Erting, and H. Carmichael. 1981. Interactions of deaf mothers and deaf preschool children: Comparisons with three other groups of deaf and hearing dyads. *American Annals of the Deaf* 126: 454–468.

Nienhuys, T. G., K. M. Horsborough, and T. G. Cross. 1985. Interaction between mothers and deaf or hearing children. *Applied Psycholinguistics* 6: 121–139.

Petersen, G., and K. Sherrod. 1982. Relationship of maternal language to language development and language delay in children. *American Journal of Mental Deficiency* 86: 391–398.

Ratner, N., and J. Bruner. 1978. Games, social exchange and the acquisition of language. *Journal of Child Language* 5: 391–401.

Rocissano, L., and Y. Yatchmink. 1983. Language skill and interactive patterns in prematurely born toddlers. *Child Development* 54: 1229–1241.

Schein, J. 1987. The demography of deafness. In *Understanding deafness socially,* ed. P. Higgins and J. Nash, 3–28. Springfield, IL: Charles C. Thomas.

Schlesinger, H. 1987. Effects of powerlessness on dialogue and development: Disability, poverty, and the human condition. In *Psychological interventions with sensorially disabled persons,* ed. B. Heller, L. Flohr, and L. Zegans, 1–27. Orlando, FL: Grune and Stratton.

Schlesinger, H., and K. Meadow. 1972. *Sound and sign: Childhood deafness and mental health.* Berkeley: University of California Press.

Siegel, S. 1956. *Nonparametric statistics for the behavioral sciences.* New York: McGraw-Hill.

Tannock, R. 1988. Mothers' directiveness in their interactions with their children with and without Down syndrome. *American Journal on Mental Retardation* 93: 154–165.

Tomasello, M., and J. Farrar. 1986. Joint attention and early language. *Child Development* 57: 1454–1463.

Tomasello, M., and J. Todd. 1983. Joint attention and lexical acquisition style. *First Language* 4: 197–212.

Wedell-Monnig, J., and J. Lumley. 1980. Child deafness and mother-child interaction. *Child Development* 51: 766–774.

White, S. J., and R. E. C. White. 1984. The deaf imperative: Characteristics of maternal input to hearing-impaired children. *Topics in Language Disorders* 4: 38–49.

16

Mastery Motivation in Deaf and Hearing Infants

Robert H. MacTurk

The idea that infants are motivated to engage their environment has a long history in psychology, going back at least to the work of McDougall (1915). Only recently, however, has the concept of motivated behavior in infants received empirical attention. In his influential papers, White (1959, 1963) provided the conceptual basis for subsequent investigations of behaviors referred to as effectance, competence, or mastery motivation.

The term *mastery motivation* denotes an underlying motivational system that serves to instigate and maintain behaviors that promote learning. The overt expression of this motivational system is seen as a state-dependent phenomenon in which the stimulus (task attractiveness, difficulty, incongruity, etc.) introduces some degree of measurement error.

Some preliminary studies of effectance motivation in school-age children were conducted in the early 1970s by Susan Harter and her colleagues (Harter and Zigler 1974; Harter 1975), but it was not until the late 1970s that a concerted effort was made to operationalize the concept and to develop a methodology appropriate for the study of the motivational characteristics of infants (Jennings et al. 1979; Morgan et al. 1977).

The results of these early studies with both normally developing hearing infants and developmentally delayed hearing infants served to validate the methodology in terms of its relationships to standardized measures of competence (Yarrow, McQuiston et al. 1983; Messer et al. 1986), and parental influences on infants' motivation to master the environment (Jennings et al. 1979; McCarthy

This research was supported by the Division of Maternal and Child Health, Bureau of Health Care Delivery and Assistance (Grant #MCJ-110563), the Beltone Institute for Hearing Research, and the Center for Studies in Education and Human Development, Gallaudet Research Institute. An abbreviated version of this paper was presented at The Second International Symposium on Cognition, Education, and Deafness, July 1989. The efforts of Ms. Victoria M. Trimm for her assistance in modifying the original coding system for this project and for the reliability coding are gratefully acknowledged.

and McQuiston 1983; Yarrow et al. 1982; Yarrow, MacTurk et al. 1984). These studies focused on infants' motivation to explore the inanimate environment. Little emphasis was placed on efforts directed toward the animate environment (e.g., social motivation) or on socially mediated expressions of motivated behavior. More recent papers have addressed the social aspects of motivated behavior (MacTurk, Hunter et al. 1985; MacTurk, Vietze et al. 1985; Wachs 1987). These latter investigations established the importance of the social domain and provided a key to further understanding of the interface of cognition and personality (Yarrow, McQuiston et al. 1983).

Since the subjects of previous investigations of mastery motivation were all normally hearing infants, there are no data to indicate the possible influence of audition on this domain. Indeed, there is very little data of any kind relating to the early development of deaf infants.

The purpose of this report is to examine the motivational characteristics of a small group of deaf twelve-month-old infants using the methodology developed by Leon Yarrow and his colleagues (Yarrow, Klein et al. 1975; Jennings et al. 1979; Yarrow, McQuiston et al. 1983). Even though this report is exploratory in nature, we did have some expectations, which were based on anecdotal reports and on the results of an earlier pilot study of mother–infant interaction (Meadow-Orlans et al. 1987).

The deaf infants were expected to display an increased level of behaviors directed toward the experimenter or the mother. This expectation is partly based on some hearing mothers' reports that they felt their (as yet undiagnosed deaf) baby was especially alert or vigilant in his or her attention to people and that this vigilance was one of the factors that led them to suspect a hearing impairment.

Empirical support is contained in a report by Meadow-Orlans (Meadow-Orlans et al. 1987) which found that deaf infants spent more time looking at their mothers in a face-to-face interaction situation than did hearing infants. Because deaf infants evidently rely on the visual channel to a greater degree than hearing infants, we expected to find that this reliance on visual attention to people would interfere with their engagement with the toy and result in a reduction of more sophisticated, motivated behaviors, compared to the hearing infants.

METHODS

Subjects

The subjects on which this report is based consist of seven deaf infants (four girls and three boys) and three normally hearing infants (one girl and two boys) who were seen in a laboratory setting when they were twelve months old. All the infants came from middle-income families with both parents present in the home. For the deaf infants, mothers' mean age was 31.3 years and education level was 15.3 years. The fathers' mean age was 33.7 years and education level was 16.5

Table 16.1
Tasks for Assessing Mastery Motivation

Object	Description
Farm Door	A plastic barn with double doors on the front that are latched. A small plastic animal is hidden inside and can be obtained by unlocking the latch and opening the doors.
Surprise Box	A yellow rectangular box with five pop-up doors that may be opened by operating the buttons, dials, levers.
Discovery Cottage	A brightly colored house with a small front door and a hinged roof. Two dolls are hidden in slots located behind the door and under the roof that may be obtained by opening the door or raising the roof.
Shapes & Slides	A brightly colored box with three holes on the top where dolls of different shapes are placed. Levers are provided which, when pressed, release the doll down a slide.

Note. In order to equalize the stimulus value of the objects for both groups of infants, all noise making components have been silenced.

years. For the hearing infants, mothers' mean age and education level were 34.5 years and 18 years, respectively; the fathers' mean age and education level were 36 years and 19 years. Two of the deaf infants have deaf parents, as does one of the hearing infants.

Procedures

Four mastery motivation tasks were presented to the infants in a fixed order for three minutes each. During the administration of the tasks, the infant sat on the mother's lap at a feeding table, and the examiner sat across from the mother and infant. At the start of each session, the infant was given a warm-up toy for approximately one minute. Following the warm-up period, the infant was given each toy in a standard order for three minutes. In presenting the toy to the infant, the examiner first demonstrated it to the infant, and if no interest was shown within the first minute, it was demonstrated again. Unlike standard procedures for administering developmental tests in which encouragement is provided to the child to secure optimal performance, both the mother and the examiner refrained from interacting with or encouraging the child while he or she had the toy. After the initial demonstration, the examiner sat quietly while the child played with the toy, except to reposition the toy or to prevent it from being pulled off the table. Table 16.1 lists a description of the toys.

Each mastery motivation assessment session was videotaped from behind a one-way mirror. These videotapes were coded using a remote-controlled Panasonic AG-6300 videocassette recorder connected to an IBM-compatible personal computer running a program for data acquisition and recording. The onset of each behavior change was keyed into the PC's keyboard while the time (in video-frames or 1/30th of a second intervals) was obtained from the videotape control

Table 16.2
Laboratory Behavior Codes

Measure	Level	Code	Behavior
Look	0	00	Only look at apparatus
Explore	1	11	Only touch apparatus
		12	Only mouth apparatus
		13	Only passively hold apparatus
Manipulate	2	21	Manipulate
		22	Examine
		23	Bang
		24	Shake
		25	Hit or bat
		26	Drop object
Task-directed	3	31	Task-related activity
		32	Grasp or hold
		33	Reach for apparatus
Goal-directed	4	41	Goal-directed activity
		42	Reset/replace toy
Success	5	51	Obtain toy
Social	8	80	Look at experimenter
		81	Vocalize to experimenter
		82	Look at mirror
		83	Look at mother
		84	Vocalize to mother
		85	Lean back on mother
		86	Reject object
		87	Offer, give object
Off-task	9	95	Engage with nontask object
		99	Other
Facial Expressions			
Negative (cry, fuss)		15	
Obscured		16	
Neutral		17	
Interest/Excitement		18	
Positive (smile, laugh)		19	

pulse. The resulting data set is a time-based, sequential record of the infant's actions during the mastery motivation assessment session.

The coding scheme (Table 16.2) was designed to capture the range of an infant's behavior in three categories: behaviors directed toward the objects; behaviors directed toward the mother or experimenter; and facial expressions of affect (crying/fussing, neutral, interest/excitement, and smiling/laughing).

The object-related behavior codes were derived in part from studies of exploratory behavior (Switzky, Haywood, and Isett 1974; Belsky, Garduque, and Hrncir 1984) and served as the basis for the first three levels of object-associated activities (Look, Explore, and Manipulate). The next two levels (task-directed and goal-directed) were derived from general theories of motivation (Piaget 1952; Atkinson 1957; Hunt 1965) and from observations of infant behavior during the administration of standardized developmental assessments (Yarrow, Rubenstein, and Pedersen 1975). The levels were conceived of as characterizing a hierarchy with the categories of look, explore, manipulate, task-directed, and goal-directed activities, ordered in terms of the skill required from the infant.

The behaviors directed toward the examiner and/or the mother were considered to be a form of social referencing in which infants employed the emotional responses of adults as a guide to continued interaction with the objects (Wenar 1972; Feinman 1982; Clyman et al. 1986). Facial expressions of affect are considered to be a window through which the infant's emotional appraisal of events may be assessed. Such expressions represent, from birth onward, a primary motivational system (Izard 1971; Izard and Malatesta 1987). White (1959) also connected the two domains when he wrote that it is the "[positive] feeling of efficacy" (p. 322) that reinforces motivated behavior.

Empirical evidence supporting the relationship between affective displays and motivational constructs has been reported by Harter (Harter, Shultz, and Blum 1971; Harter 1974) and Lutkenhaus (1984) for older children and by Demetre and Vietze (1984) and Hunter, Kosisky, and McQuiston (1984) during early infancy.

Behaviors in the three categories were mutually exclusive and were exhaustive within a category but not between categories. Since the categories represent three relatively independent behavioral patterns that can logically coincide, it was possible to record and tally the number of changes and the durations of the infant's socially oriented behaviors while he or she was actively engaged with the toy, and simultaneously to record changes in facial expression.

The actual coding was performed at the individual behavior level, and codes were combined during the initial data processing phase by adding the frequencies and durations to yield six primary measures of mastery motivation (look, explore, persist, social, off-task, and positive affect).

Measures of Mastery Motivation

Based on previous investigations of mastery motivation (Jennings et al. 1979; Yarrow, McQuiston et al. 1983), we chose to focus on the six measures of mastery motivation and three latency measures that were derived from a separate series of analyses of the raw sequential data set.

1. Visual attention to the toys (Look),
2. Exploratory behavior (Explore);
3. Persistence on task-related activities (Persist);

4. Off-task behavior;
5. Social behavior (Social);
6. Positive Affect;
7. Latency to task involvement;
8. Latency to social behavior; and
9. Latency to positive affect.

Visual attention and exploratory behaviors are common measures of infants' behavior with objects. When infants look at objects, it reflects their awareness of the objects and is generally considered to represent an initial exploration of the objects' properties. Exploratory behavior has often been employed as a measure of an infant's interest in learning about the characteristics of objects and the environment (McCall, Eichorn, and Hogarty 1977; Ruff 1984).

Persistence in goal-directed behavior was the primary measure of mastery motivation. Task persistence has long been considered an index of motivation. (McDougall 1915; Tolman 1932). More recently, Atkinson (1957), Feather (1962), and Weiner, Kun, and Benesh-Weiner (1980) have pointed to persistence as the defining characteristic of motivated behavior. Thus we assumed that the length of time an infant spent in attempting to master a task would serve as a valid index of mastery motivation.

The coding scheme enabled us to assess individual behaviors (dropping, mouthing, looking at mother, etc.), which were determined, on an *a priori* basis, to constitute the subordinate categories of look, explore, manipulate, task-directed, goal-directed, success, social, and off-task. We formed the superordinate categories by summing explore and manipulate into Explore, and task- and goal-directed into Persist. The rationale for this pooling was based on the similarities between the behaviors in explore and manipulate and task- and goal-directed, and is analogous to the distinction that Weisler and McCall (1976) drew between motor-aided perceptual examination and active physical interaction. Explore and manipulate were considered similar because of the general nature of the actions involved. Mouthing, touching, banging, and shaking were all behaviors that could be done with any toy and did not relate to particular toy properties. The task- and goal-directed categories, on the other hand, involved actions that were specific to an individual toy. The social codes 85 (lean back), 86 (reject object), and 87 (offer, give object) represent a broader conceptualization of social behaviors than is typical. Leaning back on mother was considered to represent proximity seeking behavior; since the infant could engage with the toys and lean back against mother at the same time, this code was not included in the computations of Social. Codes 86 and 87 represent object-mediated social activity (Bronson, 1966), and, though they were rare occurrences, we felt these behaviors were important enough to include as examples of the infants' attempts to engage the examiner with the toys.

Off-task behaviors included actions directed toward non-task objects, such as the edge of the table or the mother's jewelry, and were considered to be examples of low motivation or distractibility. In previous reports (Yarrow, Mc-

Quiston et al. 1983; Yarrow, MacTurk et al. 1984), off-task was combined with socially directed activities and was believed to represent inattention and/or low mastery motivation. Subsequent reports (MacTurk, Hunter et al. 1985; MacTurk, Vietze et al. 1985; MacTurk, McCarthy et al. 1987) examined social and off-task behaviors separately and found that the ability to integrate socially oriented behaviors into the ongoing stream of object-related activities represents an important dimension of motivated behavior. This separation of categories was maintained in this report.

The measures of latency to task involvement, social behavior, and positive affect were selected as indicators of eagerness to engage with the objects and people in the near environment. The latency measures represented the time from the presentation of the toy to the first instance of a task-related act, a social behavior, or an overt positive affective display.

Reliability

Inter-rater reliability was assessed by having two trained observers independently code seven (out of a total of forty) toys. Each entry for each pair of records was counted an agreement if (1) the two codes were recorded within a one-second window and (2) the observed behaviors were coded in the same category (look, explore, persist, etc.). Inter-rater agreement was computed for the object-related activities, social, and facial expressions separately by dividing the total number of agreements by the number of agreements plus disagreements and multiplying by 100 to yield a percent index of rater agreement. The percent of agreement for the object-related behaviors was 86 percent, for social, 92 percent, and for facial expressions, 78 percent.

RESULTS

Table 16.3 shows the means and standard deviations for the primary measures of mastery motivation. Contrary to our expectations, no dramatic group differences were found for the measures of task engagement (Look, Explore, Persist, or Off-task). Both the deaf infants and hearing infants displayed equal durations of persistent, task-related activities. Not only were the groups equally motivated to engage with the toys, but they also displayed a similar distribution of other toy-related behaviors. This finding suggests that hearing status is not an important dimension with regard to an infant's motivation to explore and to learn about objects in the environment.

Given the absence of group differences for the measures of task-related activities, we were surprised to find that our initial prediction regarding social behavior was supported by the data. The major group differences appeared in the measures

Table 16.3
**Means and Standard Deviations for the Measures of Mastery Motivation for Deaf
and Hearing Infants**

Category	Deaf Infants		Hearing Infants	
	Mean	SD	Mean	SD
Look	31.5	14.5	27.0	17.0
Explore	62.4	23.9	62.3	25.0
Persist	57.9	23.6	68.8	37.3
Social	30.4	25.8	12.8	12.6
Off-task	6.4	10.6	10.1	11.7
Positive Affect	30.8	39.0	3.8	5.2
Latency to Task Engagement	8.5	15.8	3.5	4.7
Latency to Social	13.4	14.6	52.5	49.4
Latency to Positive Affect	96.1	61.3	151.5	44.6

Note. Means are measured in seconds.

that tap the social/affective component of motivated behavior. The deaf infants spent close to 2.5 times longer engaged in socially directed behaviors, that is, looking at the examiner and/or mother (both directly or in the mirror) than did their hearing peers. The deaf infants also spent eight times longer laughing and smiling compared to the hearing infants.

Not only did the deaf infants display longer durations in social and positive affect measures, but they also did so with dramatically shorter latencies. The hearing infants spent 52 seconds engaged with the toy before attempting to involve the mother or examiner in their activities, compared to only 13 seconds for the deaf infants. A similar picture emerges for latency to positive affect: the hearing infants spent approximately 2.5 minutes manipulating the object before smiling or laughing, while the deaf infants waited only 1.5 minutes. It appears that the deaf infants are more adept at integrating socially oriented activities into their attempts to master the objects in their near environment. Even though they spent more time engaging in social behaviors and were quicker to do so, social behavior did not occur at the expense of their task-directed activities.

The differences in the measures of social behaviors and positive affect prompted a series of additional analyses designed to examine the specific behaviors that preceded instances of social/positive affect (e.g., lag sequential analysis). For this analysis, the probability of one behavior following another (the conditional probability) was computed. Then, by comparing the conditional probability with that expected by chance alone (the unconditional probability), a z-score was derived. This establishes both the significance level and the direction of the observed transition. For example, a z-score of -1.96 for the transition from criterion behavior A to target behavior B indicates that the transition occurred significantly ($p < .05$) fewer times than would be expected by chance alone.

The results of this analysis are contained in Table 16.4. For the social category, we found that both Look and Persist had significant negative z-scores, suggesting an inhibitory effect on the infants' social behavior regardless of their hearing status. When the infants were engaged with the object, either visually or in active exploration, they were unlikely to proceed to a social behavior. This finding was not unexpected, since both Look and Persist typify a high degree of involvement with the toy. This focused attention to objects has been shown to be a powerful marker of the infant's cognitive processes and has also been shown to represent a salient dimension of infants' interactions with objects during the last half of their first year of life (McCall et al. 1977; Lewis and Baldini 1979; Ruff 1984, 1986). A similar pattern held for the transitions to Positive Affect, though the z-scores were attenuated, probably due to the comparatively low frequency of these transitions.

Turning to the behaviors associated with an increased likelihood of Social, we found that Explore, Off-task, and Positive Affect tended to be precursors of socially oriented behaviors. This was particularly true for the deaf infants. For Off-task, both groups were about equally likely to follow with a Social, while the probability for the transition to Positive Affect was significant only for the deaf The off-task behaviors imply boredom with the task at hand and the infants are therefore more likely to display an increased openness to engage with the animate environment. The deaf infants were more likely to follow Positive Affect with a Social than were the hearing infants. (In fact, that transition never occurred for the hearing infants.) Although part of this likelihood may be due to the small number of infants in the hearing group, the finding remains unusual, primarily because one would expect socially oriented behaviors to be associated with laugh-

Table 16.4
Conditional Probabilities and z-Scores for the Transitions from a
Mastery Behavior to a Social Behavior for Deaf and Hearing Infants

Behaviors	Deaf Infants		Hearing Infants	
	Conditional Probability	z-Score	Conditional Probability	z-Score
Look	13.9	−2.31**	4.5	−2.67**
Explore	22.9	1.98*	15.3	1.78
Persist	12.4	−6.36***	6.1	−4.28***
Off-task	30.2	3.08**	31.3	4.50***
Positive Affect	28.2	3.60***	0.0	0.0

*$z > 1.96, p < .05$.
**$z > 2.26, p < .01$.
***$z > 3.30, p < .001$.

ing and/or smiling. This finding raises the possibility that the positive affect/social axis may have a different psychological function for the deaf infants.

The Explore to Social transition was significant for the deaf infants and approached significance for the hearing group. This finding is particularly interesting both in terms of (1) when, in the course of object-related activities, social behaviors would be expected to appear; and (2) the infants' management of their apparent need to maintain contact with the animate environment while simultaneously mastering inanimate objects.

DISCUSSION

These results support the following conclusions:

1. Both deaf and hearing infants exhibit similar amounts of motivated behavior toward objects. This offers additional support to White's (1959) notion that there is an underlying motive to engage in and benefit from interactions with the environment. It also indicates that auditory contact with their surroundings is not a determining factor in infants' attempts to master objects.
2. The deaf infants spent a longer period of time engaged in behaviors directed toward the experimenter and the mother than did the hearing infants. They were able to do so without any apparent sacrifice to the deployment of their task- and goal-directed activities. This finding implies that the deaf infants were more skillful at integrating the competing demands of social- and object-oriented endeavors than were hearing peers.
3. The deaf infants engaged with the social environment and displayed a positive emotional response to the situation more quickly than the hearing infants. In addition, positive affect was more likely to be followed by a social behavior for the deaf infants. This finding indicates that the integration of social behaviors and object-oriented activities serves either a different function or a more potent one in the early development of deaf infants.

All the group differences were in the measures dealing with the infants' contact with the social environment. The deaf infants were more social, were faster to engage in a social behavior, and, when not actively engaged with the object, were more likely to move to a social behavior than their hearing peers. This conclusion suggests that, as early as the first year of life, deaf infants have developed an important set of compensatory behaviors in an effort to obtain (presumably) the same amount of information from their environment through two sensory channels (visual and tactile) as the hearing infants obtain through three (auditory, visual, and tactile).

It is important to note, however, that the integration of social behaviors into the stream of object-related activities is not solely a function of hearing status.

From the data contained in Table 16.4, we see that both groups of infants were almost equally likely to follow an explore with a social behavior. This finding suggests that, at some level, all infants need to monitor their social environment. Furthermore, this monitoring (or social referencing [Feinman 1982; Feinman and Lewis 1983]) followed a predictable sequence of actions. It is interesting to note that the transition associated with an increase in Social was from Explore—a set of behaviors considered in the current context to represent a more elementary level of mastery motivation. Clyman et al. (1986) typified this as "post-action referencing," which implies that the infants felt secure enough to explore the objects in the first place but still required some external affirmation with regard to their attempts to acquire more information about the toys (Feinman 1982; Klinnert et al. 1983).

This finding raises the possibility that the link between the infant's attachment/affiliative and exploratory/motivational systems may be elucidated via this particular transition. Indirect evidence for this contention is provided by some preliminary data reported by Wachs (1987). He found that infants who displayed less differentiation between social- and object-directed motivation also appeared to display difficulties in establishing a secure attachment relationship with the mother. We might expect that variations in the infant's pattern of early social referencing may serve as an index of the later attachment relationship—a hypothesis we intend to examine more closely in the future.

In a more speculative vein, we believe that these results extend our understanding of some of the factors that contribute to the expression of motivated behavior during early infancy. One of the central influences on the development of later intellectual competence and its precursors (exploratory behavior) has been the notion of an appropriately responsive environment, one that enables the infant to create effects and receive feedback. White (1959) stated that "motivation must be conceived to involve . . . transactions in which behavior has an exploratory, varying, experimental character and *produces changes in the stimulus field* [emphasis added]" (p. 329).

The effect of a responsive environment on the infant's development has received much attention and has been shown repeatedly to constitute an important factor in both contemporaneous and subsequent development in social-emotional and cognitive areas. Virtually all the studies have examined responsiveness in hearing infants and have employed measures that explicitly require auditory contact—for example, parental vocal responsiveness (McCarthy and McQuiston 1983), or measures that confound physical responsiveness and vocal responsiveness (Bell and Ainsworth 1972; Riksen-Walraven 1978).

The existing literature, however, has never addressed the possible effects of deafness as a way to investigate the influence of audition on the patterns of parent–infant interaction. Our data indicate that auditory contact with the environment is not a necessary condition for the infants' expressions of motivated behavior. There were no consistent differences either in the infants' persistence with objects or in the other measures of object interaction. The deaf infants may have developed a set of behaviors that offset the lack of auditory contact with the environment and also enable them to engage in and benefit from their interactions with their surroundings on an equal footing with their hearing peers.

What needs to be addressed in future studies is the nature of the hypothesized compensatory mechanism and its developmental trajectory. It is perhaps obvious that its manifestations would not spring *de novo* at the onset of increased interest in objects but, rather, would have its precursors in the patterns of early parent–infant interaction. These data, which are currently being collected, offer the opportunity to understand the adaptations required of deaf infants to operate effectively in a world that presumes auditory contact. The data may also shed light on the question of what constitutes an appropriately responsive environment.

REFERENCES

Atkinson, J. W. 1957. Motivational determinants of risk-taking behavior. *Psychological Review* 64: 359–372.

Bell, S., and M. Ainsworth. 1972. Infant crying and maternal responsiveness. *Child Development* 43: 1171–1190.

Belsky, J., L. Garduque, and E. Hrncir. 1984. Assessing performance, competence, and executive capacity in infant play: Relations to home environment and security of attachment. *Developmental Psychology* 20: 406–417.

Bronson, W. C. 1966. Early antecedents of emotional expressiveness and reactivity control. *Child Development* 37: 793–810.

Clyman, R. B., R. N. Emde, J. E. Kempe, and R. J. Harmon. 1986. Social referencing and social looking·among twelve-month-old infants. In *Affective development in infancy,* ed. T. B. Brazelton and M. W. Yogman, 75–94. Norwood, NJ: Ablex Publishing Company.

Demetre, J., and P. M. Vietze. 1984. Affective expression in relation to problem-solving. Paper presented at the Annual Meeting of the American Psychological Association, April, Toronto, Canada.

Feather, N. T. 1962. The study of persistence. *Psychological Bulletin* 59: 94–115.

Feinman, S. 1982. Social referencing in infancy. *Merrill-Palmer Quarterly* 28: 445–470.

Feinman, S., and M. Lewis. 1983. Social referencing at 10 months: A second order effect on infants' responses to strangers. *Child Development* 54: 878–887.

Harter, S. 1974. Pleasure derived by children from cognitive challenge and mastery. *Child Development* 45: 661–669.

———. 1975. Developmental differences in the manifestation of mastery motivation on problem solving tasks. *Child Development* 46: 370–378.

Harter, S., T. R. Schultz, and B. Blum. 1971. Smiling in children as a function of their sense of mastery. *Journal of Experimental Child Psychology* 12: 396–404.

Harter, S., and E. Zigler. 1974. The assessment of effectance motivation in normal and retarded children. *Developmental Psychology* 10: 169–180.

Hunt, J. McV. 1965. Intrinsic motivation and its role in psychological development. In *Nebraska symposium on motivation* Vol. 13, ed. D. Levine, 189–282. Lincoln: University of Nebraska Press.

Hunter, F. T., S. A. Kosisky, and S. McQuiston. 1984. Positive affect during object manipulation. Paper presented at the Annual Meeting of the American Psychological Association, April, Toronto, Canada.

Izard, C. E. 1971. *The face of emotion.* New York: Appleton-Century-Crofts.

Izard, C. E., and C. Z. Malatesta. 1987. Perspectives in emotional development I: Differential emotions theory of early emotional development. In *Handbook of infant development,* 2d ed., ed. J. D. Osofsky, 494–555. New York: John Wiley and Sons.

Jennings, K. D., R. J. Harmon, G. A. Morgan, J. L. Gaiter, and L. J. Yarrow, 1979. Exploratory play as an index of mastery motivation: Relationships to persistence, cognitive functioning and environmental measures. *Developmental Psychology* 15: 386–394.

Klinnert, M. D., J. J. Campos, J. F. Sorce, R. N. Emde, and M. Svejda. 1983. The development of social referencing in infancy. In *Emotion: Theory, research, and experience: Vol. 2. Emotion in early development,* ed. R. Plutchik and H. Kellerman, 242–261. New York: Academic Press.

Lewis, M., and N. Baldini. 1979. Attentional processes as an individual difference. In *Attention and cognitive development,* ed. G. A. Hale and M. Lewis, 135–172. New York: Plenum Press.

Lutkenhaus, P. 1984. Pleasure derived from mastery in three-year-olds: Its function for persistence and the influence of maternal behavior. *International Journal of Behavioral Development* 7: 343–358.

MacTurk, R. H., F. T. Hunter, M. E. McCarthy, P. M. Vietze, and S. McQuiston. 1985. Social mastery motivation in Down syndrome and nondelayed infants. *Topics in Early Childhood Special Education* 4: 93–109.

MacTurk, R. H., M. E. McCarthy, P. M. Vietze, and L. J. Yarrow. 1987. Sequential analysis of mastery behavior in 6- and 12-month-old infants. *Developmental Psychology* 23: 199–203.

MacTurk, R. H., P. M. Vietze, M. E. McCarthy, S. McQuiston, and L. J. Yarrow. 1985. The organization of exploratory behavior in Down syndrome and nondelayed infants. *Child Development* 56: 573–581.

McCall, R. B., D. H. Eichorn, and P. S. Hogarty. 1977. Transitions in early mental development. *Monographs of the Society for Research in Child Development* 420 (3, Serial No. 171).

McCarthy, M. E., and S. McQuiston. 1983. The relationship of contingent parental behaviors to infant motivation and competence. Paper presented at the Biennial Meeting of the Society for Research in Child Development, April, Detroit.

McDougall, W. 1915. *An introduction to social psychology.* 9th ed. London: Methuen.

Meadow-Orlans, K. P., R. H. MacTurk, C. T. Prezioso, C. J. Erting, and P. S. Day. 1987. Interactions of deaf and hearing mothers with three- and six-month-old infants. Paper presented at the Biennial Meeting of the Society for Research in Child Development, April, Baltimore.

Messer, D. J., M. E. McCarthy, S. McQuiston, R. H. MacTurk, L. J. Yarrow, and P. M. Vietze. 1986. The relationship between mastery behavior in infancy and competence in early childhood. *Developmental Psychology* 22: 366–372.

Morgan, G. A., R. J. Harmon, J. L. Gaiter, K. D. Jennings, N. F. Gist, and L. J. Yarrow. 1977. A method for assessing mastery motivation in one-year-old infants. *JSAS Catalog of Selected Documents in Psychology* 7: 68. (Ms. No. 1517)

Piaget, J. 1952. *The origins of intelligence in children.* New York: International Universities Press.

Riksen-Walraven, J. M. 1978. Effects of caregiver behavior on habituation rate and self-efficacy in infants. *International Journal of Behavioral Development* 1: 105–130.

Ruff, H. A. 1984. Infants' manipulative exploration of objects: Effects of age and object characteristics. *Developmental Psychology* 20: 9–20.

———. 1986. Components of attention during infants' manipulative exploration. *Child Development* 57: 105–114.

Switzky, H. N., H. C. Haywood, and R. Isett. 1974. Exploration, curiosity, and play in young children: Effects of stimulus complexity. *Developmental Psychology* 10: 321–329.

Tolman, E. C. 1932. *Purposive behavior in animals and man.* New York: Appleton-Century.

Wachs, T. D. 1987. Specificity of environmental action as manifest in environmental correlates on infant's mastery motivation. *Developmental Psychology* 23: 782–790.

Weiner, B., A. Kun, and M. Benesh-Weiner. 1980. The development of mastery, emotions and morality from an attributional perspective. In *Minnesota symposium on child psychology* (Vol. 14), ed. A. Collings, 376–402. Hillsdale, NJ: Lawrence Erlbaum and Associates.

Weisler, A., and R. B. McCall. 1976. Exploration and play: Resume and redirection. *American Psychologist* 31: 492–508.

Wenar, C. 1972. Executive competence and spontaneous social behavior in one-year-old infants. *Child Development* 43: 256–260.

White, R. W. 1959. Motivation reconsidered: The concept of competence. *Psychological Review* 66: 297–333.

White, R. W. 1963. Ego and reality in psychoanalytic theory. *Psychological Issues* 3: 1–40.

Yarrow, L. J., R. P. Klein, S. Lomonaco, and G. A. Morgan. 1975. Cognitive and motivational development in early childhood. In *Exceptional infant 3: Assessment and intervention,* ed. B. Z. Friedlander, G. M. Sterritt, and G. E. Kirk, 175–187. New York: Brunner/Mazel.

Yarrow, L. J., R. H. MacTurk, P. M. Vietze, M. E. McCarthy, R. P. Klein, and S. McQuiston. 1984. Developmental course of parental stimulation and its relationship to mastery motivation during infancy. *Developmental Psychology* 20: 492–503.

Yarrow, L. J., S. McQuiston, R. H. MacTurk, M. E. McCarthy, R. P. Klein, and P. M. Vietze. 1983. Assessment of mastery motivation in the first year of life: Contemporaneous and cross-age relationships. *Developmental Psychology* 19: 159–171.

Yarrow, L. J., G. A. Morgan, K. D. Jennings, R. J. Harmon, and J. L. Gaiter. 1982. Infants' persistence at tasks: Relationships to cognitive functioning and early experience. *Infant Behavior and Development* 5: 131–142.

Yarrow, L. J., J. Rubenstein, and F. A. Pedersen. 1975. *Infant and environment: Early cognitive and motivational development.* Washington, DC: Hemisphere Publishing Corp.

17

Attachment Behavior of Deaf Children with Deaf Parents

KATHRYN P. MEADOW-ORLANS, MARK T. GREENBERG, CAROL ERTING

Following the seminal work of Bowlby (1969) and of Ainsworth and her colleagues (1973, 1978), a great deal of research has accumulated describing the development of attachment in children to their mothers.

This has been, in fact, a primary interest of psychiatrists and psychologists for the past 15–20 years. Similarly, there has been an increasing, although much less extensive, interest in the personality development and characteristics of deaf persons. Beginning with the Heiders (1941) and Levine (1956), important series of studies have been conducted by groups at the New York Psychiatric Institute (Altshuler, 1974; Altshuler et al., 1976; Rainer et al., 1969), Michael Reese Hospital (Grinker, 1969; Mindel and Vernon, 1971), and the University of California, San Francisco (Schlesinger, 1978, 1979a; Schlesinger and Meadow, 1972). These studies have contributed a great deal to our knowledge of the influence of profound childhood deafness on personality development. However, until the publication of Greenberg's data (Greenberg and Marvin, 1979), no research report has appeared in the literature linking deafenss to attachment theory. Greenberg reported attachment/separation data on twenty-three profoundly deaf pre-school children, all of whom had hearing mothers and fathers.

The purpose of this paper is to report similar research data collected from seventeen profoundly deaf preschool children, all of whom have deaf mothers and fathers. Hearing status of the parents of deaf children is a critical factor in determining the paths their development will take. Many studies have demonstrated the higher educational achievement levels of deaf children of deaf parents in comparison with deaf children of hearing parents (Brasel and Quigley 1977; Meadow 1968a; Stuckless and Birch 1966; Vernon and Koh 1970), and their more positive social and behavioral adjustment (Harris 1978; Meadow 1969; Meadow et al.

This paper was published originally in the *Journal of the American Academy of Child Psychiatry*, 22 (1983): 23–28, and reprinted in S. Chess and A. Thomas (Eds.), *Annual Progress in Child Psychiatry and Child Development, 1984*. (New York: Brunner/Mazel, 1985), 176–188. Reprinted by permission of the *Journal of the American Academy of Child Psychiatry*.

1981; Stokoe and Battison 1981). These findings have been replicated with numerous populations despite the consistently lower educational and occupational status of deaf parents compared with the hearing population, and their more limited access to parent education and to mental health facilities (Schein 1979).

The Office of Demographic Studies at Gallaudet University has reported that 3 percent of deaf children participating in their Annual Survey of Hearing Impaired Children and Youth have two deaf parents. An additional 6 percent of these children have one deaf parent (Rawlings and Jensema 1977). So, despite the rarity of deaf child/deaf parent families, they comprise a theoretically interesting and important group because deaf families are capable of communication (in sign language) with their deaf children from infancy onward, and because deaf parents find the diagnosis of deafness less traumatic than do hearing parents (Meadow 1967). Even those hearing families who are willing to learn sign language face delays related to the diagnosis of deafness (Meadow 1968b; Spradley and Spradley 1978), to the acquisition of a new language mode, and to internal and external conflicts about the acceptability of signed communication (Moores 1978; Winefield 1981).

SUMMARY OF ATTACHMENT THEORY

Four phases or stages of attachment have been delineated during the child's first four years of life. The first two phases occur in early infancy and are marked by differential responsiveness to one or to a few caregivers on the part of an infant (Bowlby 1969). During phase III, which begins at approximately eight months of age, young children actively seek proximity to specific caregivers and often show distress at separation from these significant others. Three general types of behavior have been enumerated as characteristic of phase III: secure, avoidant and ambivalent (Ainsworth et al. 1978). During the later part of phase III, after the age of two, most children do not show acute distress when they are separated from their mothers for brief periods of time (Maccoby and Feldman 1972). Until some time after their third birthday, however, they usually seek proximity to the significant caregiver upon reunion (Marvin 1977). Bowlby (1969) has characterized phase IV as showing the ability of the child and the mother to come to an agreement (or partnership) about the mother's plan to separate from the child and to return. As this development progresses, the child becomes less dependent on the mother for constant presence and support. Marvin (1972, 1977) found that by the age of four most children were capable of achieving the phase IV partnership with their mothers in a laboratory situation. However, he found all two-year-olds and 75 percent of children at the third birthday demonstrating phase III attachment patterns.

Because of the delay in language acquisition among most deaf children, and the supposed lessened abilities of these children to reach verbal agreement with their mothers or to understand the mother's explanation for her leave-taking,

Table 17.1
Demographic Information—Seventeen Deaf Children by Age

| | Age | |
	Younger than 3 Years (N = 10)	3 Years or Older (N = 7)
Characteristic		
Mean age (in months)	21.7	44.7
Age range (in months)	12–33	36–40
Mean hearing loss (dB, speech range, unaided)[1]	97 dB	100 dB
Sex		
Male	5	2
Female	5	5
Mothers' education		
High school graduate	—	1
Some college	10	6
Fathers' education		
High school graduate	1	2
Some college	9	5
Hearing status of grandparents: One or both sets of grandparents deaf	8	6
Fathers' occupation:		
Student or unemployed	1	1
Blue collar	1	3
White collar	7	3
Not available	1	—

[1]Hearing loss information was not available for one child in each age grouping.

Greenberg and Marvin (1979) hypothesized that their deaf subjects would be delayed in their achievement of the phase IV (partnership) attachment pattern. However, they found that deafness per se did not lead to such a delay; instead, a strong relationship was found between the deaf child's communicative competence and attainment of the phase IV pattern.

METHOD

Subjects

The research group consisted of seventeen deaf children, all of whom had two deaf or hard-of-hearing parents. The children came from fourteen different families (that is, three families had two children who each participated in the study). Table 17.1 presents demographic information separately for the children, divided into younger (twelve to thirty-five months) and older (thirty-six to sixty months) groups. All parents routinely utilized either simultaneous communication (voice plus manual signing) or manual communication without voice (American Sign Language or Sign English) in everyday interaction with their children. In thirteen of the fourteen families, the mother was the primary caregiver. In one family the father filled this role, and he participated in the videotaping of his two children. All the families were intact at the time the videotaping was carried out. All children were enrolled in the preschool program of the Kendall Demonstration Elementary School, Pre-College Programs, Gallaudet University. None had been identified as having handicaps in addition to deafness.

Procedure

Each parent-child dyad was videotaped in a thirty-minute sequence consisting of three segments (see Meadow et al. 1981). During the first eight minutes, parents and children engaged in free play and shared simple refreshments. The room was approximately 3.5 by 4.5 meters and contained two chairs, two tables, and a large variety of toys. Fruit juice and cups were placed on one of the tables; cookies were "hidden" in a coffee can placed with the toys. During the free-play segment, parents read a letter telling the child where the cookies were hidden. The separation segment began after eight minutes when the parent was given a signal to leave the room. The parents were told that they could explain as much as they wished regarding their departure. The reunion segment began when the parent returned after the child had been alone for three minutes.

Coding

Attachment behavior was classified by means of a two-step data reduction process following Greenberg and Marvin (1979). First, the children were classified into categories describing the outcome of preseparation planning, separation behavior, and reunion behavior.

Preseparation planning began at the point where the parent first communicated that he or she was leaving the room, and ended when he or she actually went out the door. The children's reactions were classified as follows:

1. Agrees with parent's departure—any verbal or nonverbal indication that the child was willing for the parent to leave.
2. Disagrees with parent's departure—any verbal or nonverbal indication that the child was not willing for the parent to leave, or that the child expects/insists on accompanying the parent.
3. No response to parent's departure—the child may or may not watch the parent during the explanation or leave-taking, but neither agrees nor disagrees with the parent's action. In cases where parents gave no explanation, no planning was possible and the child was also scored as "no response."

Separation activities of the children were also categorized in three ways.

1. Play/manipulatory toy exploration without any search or distress.
2. Play and search—toy play accompanied by occasional search behaviors such as calling parent, looking at, or approaching the door.
3. Distress and search—active attempts to reach parent by crying; angry, aggressive behavior or pounding on the door; unaccompanied by sustained play.

Reunion activities were coded during the first thirty seconds after the parent returned to the room.

1. Approach—the child moves within arm's reach of the parent within fifteen seconds after she or he returns. Parent's approaching the child was not coded even though it resulted in proximity.
2. Sociable—although child did not approach the parent, he or she either greeted the parent with a smile or engaged in pleasant communication or interaction with him or her in the context of play within thirty seconds.
3. Avoidance—the child ignores the parent after reunion, that is, fails to acknowledge the parent's return by greeting, smiling, or responding to the parent's communications.
4. Resistance—the child shows angry/aggressive behavior, communicates negative affect, or resists contact with the parent; avoidance and resistance may both be accompanied by gaze aversion.

The second step of data reduction was classification of each child in phase III or phase IV of Bowlby's attachment model (Marvin 1977). Children were classified in phase III if they displayed the proximity-based patterns characteristic of younger children (Ainsworth 1973; Waters 1978). Variations of phase III patterns included approaching, avoiding, or resisting the parent upon reunion regardless of preseparation agreement or disagreement. Children were classified in a phase IV partnership if they (1) agreed to the departure-reunion plan, (2) played during separation with no distress (with or without search), and (3) responded with social behavior without approach upon reunion.

Coder Agreement

All videotapes were coded independently by two raters. Estimates of agreement were computed as the number of agreements divided by the number of agreements plus the number of disagreements. Coder agreement equaled 94 percent for the preseparation categories, 100 percent for separation categories, 94 percent for reunion categories, and 88 percent for the attachment phase classification.

Table 17.2
Classifications of Attachment Pattern/Phase by Age

	Age	
Sequence	Younger than 3 Years (N = 10)	3 Years or Older (N = 7)
Preseparation planning		
Agree	1	5
Disagree	0	0
No response	9	2
Behavior while alone		
Play	0	3
Play and search	5	3
Distress	5	1
Reunion		
Sociable without proximity-seeking	2	6
Sociable with proximity-seeking	6	1
Avoidance or resistant behavior	2	0
Attachment phase		
Phase III		
Secure	8	2
Avoidance or resistant	2	0
Phase IV		
Goal-corrected partnership	0	5

RESULTS

Table 17.2 shows the distribution of attachment behaviors for the two age groups (younger and older than three years). Similar to findings of young hearing children (Weinraub and Lewis 1977), only one child under the age of three years gave a verbal or nonverbal consent to the parent's plan for departure. While these younger children were alone, they were affected noticeably by the separation, with 50 percent becoming distressed (crying and calling for mother). Separations of four of the five distressed children were terminated early (i.e., before the prescribed three minutes had expired). Upon reunion, the majority of the younger children sought proximity to their caregivers and were sociable, while 2 (20%) showed avoidant or resistant patterns. These findings for both separation and reunion are comparable to those of hearing children (Ainsworth et al. 1978; Maccoby and Feldman 1972). As Table 2 indicates, all of the children under the age of three displayed phase III patterns, which is in precise agreement with Marvin's (1977) data on hearing children. Of these children, 20 percent showed anxious or insecure attachments, which is a similar but somewhat lower percentage than that reported for hearing children (Ainsworth et al. 1978; Waters 1978).

Of the children ages three and older, five (71%) reached agreement with their parents regarding the plan for separation and reunion, only one showed distress while alone, and all were sociable upon reunion with only one child seeking proximity. Once again, findings are almost identical with those of Maccoby and Feldman (1972) and Marvin (1977) in documenting both the increased communication regarding separation, the absence of distress while alone, and the presence of sociable behavior without proximity-seeking upon reunion in children who had reached their third birthday. As Table 17.2 indicates, five (71%) of the older deaf children were classified in the more advanced phase IV partnership pattern which is an almost identical finding with Marvin's data on hearing four-year-olds (75% of children in that age group had achieved the partnership phase).

DISCUSSION

The findings reported above indicate that the deaf children of deaf parents who participated in our study are comparable to children with normal hearing who have participated in research projects in the past. They are neither precocious nor delayed in their development of secure attachment with and independence from their caregivers. These findings are similar to data on the social interaction of deaf children and deaf parents that we have reported previously (Meadow et al. 1981). That earlier report compared three groups of deaf children with hearing children. That is, deaf children and deaf mothers performed in a similar manner to that of hearing children and hearing mothers; both of these groups exhibited interaction that was more complex and more mature than that of deaf children with hearing parents. In terms of attachment behavior, deaf children of deaf parents in this study performed in a manner that was similar to that of deaf children of hearing parents when the children had high communicative ability (Greenberg and Marvin 1979).

These three sets of findings are in vivid and startling contrast to those reported by Galenson and her colleagues (1979). Based on clinical observations of four deaf children and their deaf mothers, they concluded

> All the deaf mothers had introduced early self-bottle feeding by two or three months, with the bottle first propped and later held by the baby . . . any . . . attempts at self-feeding solids were firmly discouraged, even well into the second year of life [p. 132] . . . during the second year . . . severe separation anxiety appeared and persisted. The clinging to the mother was of course aggravated by the deaf child's need to keep his mother in view in order to maintain contact with her . . . The severe separation anxiety suggested that there was considerable difficulty in the establishment of a stable maternal mental representation . . . The phase of autonomy in these deaf infants lagged well behind that of the hearing child, and its form and shape were unusually distorted [p. 135] . . . [there was] delay in developing the usual type of transitional object attachment to blankets or teddy bears during the first 16 months . . . [the deaf mothers'] emotional attachment failed to provide the requisite dependability for the child's optimal development. (p. 136)

In a previous paper (Meadow et al. 1981), we speculated about possible reasons for the discrepancies between our conclusions and those of the Galenson group. These may be summarized in the context of the attachment data as well.

The Galenson data were collected in New York at a school that has long been known as a center for oral-only education, whereas data on deaf mothers and deaf children reported in this paper were collected at a preschool on the campus of Gallaudet University, which is associated with the support of American Sign Language and Sign English. Since sign language was forbidden in the New York preschool, it is difficult to know how the deaf parents communicated either with their children or with the hearing researchers, and this might well have influenced both the kinds of observations that were made and the comfort that the deaf mothers displayed toward their deaf children. A second and probably more cogent explanation of differences in the two sets of observations could be that the deaf parents who enrolled themselves and their deaf children in an educational program where their preferred communicative mode was unwelcome are a self-selected unrepresentative group. Most deaf families prefer to send their deaf children to schools where sign language is used; those who follow a different pathway may comprise a subgroup that "identifies with the oppressors" (Schlesinger 1979b).

The influence of the sociolinguistic environment is becoming recognized as a major factor in deaf education (Erting 1978; Meadow 1980). The notion that the deaf parents in the New York group and those in the Gallaudet group may come from two distinct populations is supported by the following information: (1) one of four Lexington children had deaf grandparents compared to fourteen of seventeen Gallaudet children who had either one or two sets of deaf grandparents; (2) one of four New York children had college-educated parents, while sixteen of seventeen Gallaudet mothers and fourteen of seventeen Gallaudet fathers had some college; (3) none of the New York mothers breast-fed their children, while four of seven Gallaudet mothers for whom we have data breast-fed their children. (New York data are found in Galenson et al. 1979, pp. 131–133.)

SUMMARY AND CONCLUSIONS

In summary, we can say that the seventeen profoundly deaf children of two deaf parents included in this study exhibited attachment patterns following almost exactly those reported for hearing children of similar ages. Half of the children younger than age three showed signs of distress when separated from their parent in the laboratory setting; the majority sought proximity and were sociable with the parent upon reunion while two exhibited avoidance or resistance to the parent's overtures. Five of the seven children age three or older had achieved the more advanced attachment pattern ("goal-corrected partnership" with the parent); the remaining two were classified as "secure" in their attachment while not yet achieving the more mature pattern.

These data were compared with other data reported from clinical observations in different settings, and some reasons for differences in the results were suggested.

We conclude that deaf children of deaf parents may follow a variety of developmental patterns. These may depend even more heavily on parental characteristics, history, and environment than the developmental course of non-hearing-impaired children. The developmental complexities created by deafness should be of great interest to behavioral scientists and clinicians alike, and it is clear that many issues remain to be resolved.

REFERENCES

Ainsworth, M. D. S. 1973. The development of infant-mother attachment. In *Review of child development research, Vol. 3,* ed. B. M. Caldwell and H. N. Ricciuti. Chicago: University of Chicago Press.

Ainsworth, M. D. S., M. C. Blehar, E. Waters, and S. Wall. 1978. *Patterns of attachment.* Hillsdale, NJ: Lawrence Erlbaum and Associates.

Altshuler, K. Z. 1974. The social and psychological development of the deaf child: Problems and their treatment and prevention. *American Annals of the Deaf* 119: 365–376.

Altshuler, K. Z., W. E. Deming, J. Vollenweider, J. D. Rainer, and R. Tendler. 1976. Impulsivity and profound early deafness: A cross cultural inquiry. *American Annals of the Deaf* 121: 331–345.

Bowlby, J. 1969. *Attachment and loss; Vol. 1, Attachment.* New York: Basic Books.

Brasel, K. E., and S. P. Quigley. 1977. Influence of certain language and communication environments in early childhood on the development of language in deaf individuals. *Journal of Speech and Hearing Research* 20: 81–94.

Erting, C. 1978. Language policy and deaf ethnicity in the United States. *Sign Language Studies* 19: 139–152.

Galenson, E., R. Miller, E. Kaplan, and A. Rothstein. 1979. Assessment of development in the deaf child. *Journal of the American Academy of Child Psychiatry* 18: 128–142.

Greenberg, M. T., and R. S. Marvin. 1979. Patterns of attachment in profoundly deaf preschool children. *Merrill-Palmer Quarterly* 25: 265–279.

Grinker, R. R. 1969. *Psychiatric diagnosis, therapy and research on the psychotic deaf.* Washington DC: Social Rehabilitation Service, U.S. Department of Health, Education and Welfare.

Harris, R. I. 1978. Impulse control in deaf children; research and clinical issues. In *Deaf children: Developmental perspectives,* ed. L. Liben, 137–156. New York: Academic Press.

Heider, F., and G. M. Heider. 1941. Studies in psychology of the deaf. *Psychological Monographs* 53: 242.

Levine, E. S. 1956. *Youth in a soundless world: A search for personality.* New York: New York University Press.

Maccoby, E. E., and S. S. Feldman. 1972. Mother-attachment and stranger-reactions in the third year of life. *Monographs of the Society for Research in Child Development* 37 (3 Serial No. 148).

Marvin, R. S. 1972. Attachment-, exploratory- and communicative behavior in 2-, 3-, and 4-year-old children. Ph.D. diss., University of Chicago.

————. (1977). An ethological-cognitive model of the attenuation of mother-child attachment. In *Advances in the study of communication; Vol. 3. Development of social attachments,* ed. T. M. Alloway and L. Krames. New York: Plenum Press.

Meadow, K. P. 1967. The effect of early manual communication and family climate on the deaf child's development. Ph.D. diss., University of California, Berkeley.

————. 1968a. Early manual communication in relation to the deaf child's intellectual, social, and communicative functioning. *American Annals of the Deaf* 113: 29–41.

————. 1968b. Parental responses to the medical ambiguities of deafness. *Journal of Health and Social Behavior* 9: 299–309.

————. 1969. Self-image, family climate, and deafness. *Social Forces* 47: 428–438.

————. 1980. *Deafness and child development.* Berkeley: University of California Press.

Meadow, K. P., M. T. Greenberg, C. Erting, and H. Carmichael. 1981. Interactions of deaf mothers and deaf preschool children; comparisons with three other groups of deaf and hearing dyads. *American Annals of the Deaf* 126: 454–468.

Mindel, E. D., and M. Vernon. 1971. *They grow in silence—The deaf child and his family.* Silver Spring, MD: National Association of the Deaf.

Moores, D. F. 1978. *Educating the deaf: Psychology, principles, and practices.* Boston: Houghton Mifflin.

Rainer, J. D., K. Z. Altshuler, and F. J. Kallmann. 1969. *Family and mental health problems in a deaf population,* 2d ed. Springfield, IL: Charles C. Thomas.

Rawlings, B. W., and C. J. Jensema. 1977. *Two studies of the families of hearing impaired children.* Washington, DC: Office of Demographic Studies, Gallaudet University.

Schein, J. D. 1979. Society and culture of hearing-impaired people. In *Hearing and hearing impairment,* ed. L. J. Bradford and W. G. Hardy, 479–487. New York: Grune and Stratton.

Schlesinger, H. S. 1978. The acquisition of bimodal language. In *Sign language for the deaf,* ed. I. M. Schlesinger and L. Namir. New York: Academic Press.

———— 1979a. The deaf child. In *Basic handbook of child psychiatry, Vol. 1,* ed. J. D. Call, J. D. Noshpitz, R. L. Cohen, and I. N. Berlin, 421–426. New York: Basic Books.

———— 1979b. From object to subject. *Journal of Rehabilitation of the Deaf* 12: viii–xii.

Schlesinger, H. S., and K. P. Meadow. 1972. *Sound and sign: Childhood deafness and mental health.* Berkeley: University of California Press.

Spradley, T. S., and J. P. Spradley. 1978. *Deaf like me.* New York: Random House.

Stokoe, W. C., and R. Battison. 1981. Sign language, mental health, and satisfactory interaction. In *Deafness and mental health,* ed. L. K. Stein, E. D. Mindel, and T. Jabaley, 179–194. New York: Grune and Stratton.

Stuckless, E. R., and J. W. Birch. 1966. The influence of early manual communication on the linguistic development of deaf children. *American Annals of the Deaf* 111: 452–460; 499–504.

Vernon, M., and S. D. Koh. 1970. Early manual communication and deaf children's achievement. *American Annals of the Deaf* 115: 527–536.

Waters, E. 1978. The reliability and stability of individual differences in infant-mother attachment. *Child Development* 49: 483–494.

Weinraub, M., and M. Lewis. 1977. The determinants of children's responses to separation. *Monographs of the Society for Research in Child Development* 42 (4 Serial No. 172).

Winefield, R. M. 1981. Bell, Gallaudet, and the sign language debate: A historical analysis of the communication controversy in education of the deaf. Ph.D. diss., Graduate School of Education, Harvard University.

18

Symbolic Play Behavior of Deaf and Hearing Toddlers

PATRICIA E. SPENCER, DAVID DEYO, NATALIE GRINDSTAFF

Symbolic cognitive abilities typically emerge from their sensory and motor bases in a child's second year. Such abilities are increasingly represented in both language and play during this time. In this study, we investigated symbolic play behaviors of deaf toddlers to determine whether the lack of input in one sensory modality (audition) affects the acquisition of early symbolic abilities. Previous studies of the play behaviors of deaf children have dealt with older children and, we believe, have produced contradictory findings because effects of deafness were confused with effects of language delay experienced by many deaf children.

Symbolic play, sometimes called pretend or pretense play, was hypothesized by Piaget (1962) to be one aspect of the semiotic function, a general cognitive capacity for symbolic processes that also includes language and mental imagery. As such, symbolic play has been referred to as a "window on the cognitive, social and language development of the child" (DiPane et al. 1987, p. 2), an index of emerging representational capacity (Bretherton 1984), and an index of cognitive development or maturity (Bruner, Oliver, and Greenfield 1966; Lowe 1975; McCune-Nicolich 1981; Nicolich 1977). Observation and assessment of play behaviors have been recommended for use in assessing cognitive functioning of young children, especially those with some form of language delay (Ungerer et al. 1979). Longitudinal studies using both Piagetian and psychometric scales of development have provided evidence of qualitative changes in cognitive functioning at approximately the same ages (one year and twenty-one to twenty-two months) that qualitative changes in play behaviors have been noted (McCall, Eichorn, and Hogarty 1977; Uzgiris 1983). In addition, a number of studies have shown relationships between the acquisition of language and the demonstration of symbolic play behaviors (Bates 1976; McCune-Nicolich 1981; McCune-Nicolich and Carroll 1981).

The authors gratefully acknowledge the assistance of Dr. Lorraine McCune, who gave us permission to use the coding manual for her coding system and helped train us in the use of that system. We also thank Dr. Mary Gutfreund for assisting with the coding and analysis of data.

Infants usually exhibit simple symbolic play around the time of their first birthday. Gestures showing recognition of object function, such as bringing an empty cup to the lips, soon become associated with "play" affect as the action becomes progressively distanced from the original sensorimotor action performed in using the object (Werner and Kaplan 1963). Stages in the progressive distancing of symbolic play behaviors from their functional origins have been described by Belsky and Most (1981), by McCune (McCune-Nicolich 1981; Nicolich 1977), by Ungerer and Sigman (1984), and by others. According to Nicolich (1978), symbolic play includes one of the following:

1. Treating an inanimate object as though it were animate (i.e., pretending to feed a doll);
2. Performing an everyday action in the absence of the necessary materials (i.e., pretending to drink from an empty cup);
3. Knowingly substituting one object for another (i.e., using a seashell as though it were a doll's hat);
4. Performing actions usually done by someone else (i.e., pretending to fix something using toy tools);
5. Performing an action that is not carried out to its usual outcome (i.e., picking up a purse, and waving good-bye, but not actually leaving).

In addition to providing evidence of a child's level of symbolic functioning, symbolic play is a mechanism and a supportive context for further development of symbolic functioning. Children are more able to take the lead in selecting activities and in manipulating and combining actions and their symbols during play than when they participate in feeding, dressing, and other daily routines that more closely follow the caregiver's agenda (DiPane et al. 1987). Thus, play provides a context in which the child has the freedom to practice creating and using symbols. Participation in symbolic play activities builds flexibility and fluency in symbolic functioning, just as participation in linguistic activities results in increased linguistic functioning. As with linguistic functioning, children's symbolic play tends to reach higher levels when the mother is actively engaged and participating in the play activity than when she is not involved (Slade 1987a). Joint mother-child engagement in play therefore represents the "proximal zone of development" (Vygotsky 1978) in which the child functions, because of environmental support, at a higher-than-usual level and has the opportunity to integrate that level of behavior into his or her repertoire.

Because symbolic play is presumed to influence development, play is an important research area for those interested in facilitating the development of deaf children. A description of the developmental sequence of their play behaviors would provide important information about the role of audition in symbolic development and the degree to which visual input can compensate for auditory input. A description of the acquisition of symbolic play behaviors by deaf children is necessary if those behaviors are to be used to assess deaf children's cognitive-symbolic development. Few studies are now available that describe or analyze the symbolic play behaviors of deaf children; few are available that describe play during the infant-toddler period when symbolic play emerges. In fact, there are no data to indicate whether the coding systems that assess levels of symbolic play in hearing children are valid and reliable for deaf children.

Available studies present an incomplete, contradictory picture of the play behaviors of deaf children, raising doubts about the quality and quantity of their play compared to that of hearing children. Darbyshire (1977) reported that his forty-five deaf subjects (mean age six years, two months) engaged in less "make believe" play than did a comparison group of hearing children. Furthermore, Darbyshire reported that the deaf children exhibited fewer substitutions in their play and had more difficulties with rule-governed games than did hearing children. It should be noted that this study relied heavily on teachers' responses to questionnaires and one therapist's observations as data sources. In a second analysis, Darbyshire concluded that four- and five-year-old deaf children were considerably less mature in their behaviors than were hearing children of the same age. This is reminiscent of a report by Singer and Lenahan (1976) that deaf children's play was similar to that of hearing children who were several years younger. In both of Darbyshire's studies, the findings were confounded by the fact that the deaf children were of lower socioeconomic status than the hearing children. Social class previously had been reported by Smilansky (1968) to affect play.

Higginbotham and Baker (1981) measured levels of social participation and cognitive play in a group of seven orally trained deaf children, ages forty-seven to sixty-six months. Data were obtained by time-sampling observations of free-play activities with peers at preschool. The researchers found that the deaf children engaged in more solitary play, fewer cooperative activities, more "constructive" play, and less dramatic play compared to hearing children of the same age. ("Dramatic play" would be analagous to the "symbolic play" discussed here.) Higginbotham and Baker concluded from their study that "communicative handicaps" due to hearing loss interfere with the development of both cognitive play and social play.

Mann (1985) analyzed fifteen-minute samples of the free play of five orally trained deaf children, ages thirty-six months to seventy-two months. In order to minimize the influence of the children's language level on the results of the study, the observations were made while the investigator wore a noise-masking device. Unlike other investigators, Mann found that the deaf children demonstrated levels of play equal to those of hearing children of the same age. The deaf children spent less total time engaged in play than did the other children, however.

Casby and McCormack (1985) studied the relationship between symbolic play and language performance (measured by the number of different "language units" the children were reported to produce) in twenty deaf students, ages thirty-eight to sixty-nine months. The aspect of symbolic play measured was the ability to substitute blocks for functional objects in an activity that had been demonstrated using the functional objects. The deaf subjects had hearing parents and were enrolled in educational programs that used a total communication approach. The investigators used both oral language and signed language to communicate instructions to the children. A relationship was found between the language levels and the levels of play demonstrated by the children; that is, those with higher language functioning showed significantly more ability to make the play substitutions than did those with lower language skills. The investigators concluded that deaf children do engage in symbolic play and that their communication performance and symbolic play levels are associated. This conclusion agrees with that of Vygotsky (1978), who reported that deaf children with good oral language could make substitutions in play more readily than could deaf children with less speech fluency. Given the context in which Vygotsky's studies were done, it is probable that speech was the only formal language system to which his subjects had been exposed.

Gregory (1985) also reported a study of play behaviors of deaf children in oral programs. Her five subjects were videotaped at two years and again at two-and-one-half years of age during play sessions in their homes with their hearing mothers. Compared to a group of hearing children, the deaf children engaged in less symbolic play and more "inappropriate" play. Also, the mothers of the deaf children more often prompted their children's play behaviors than did the mothers of the hearing children. All these differences were more pronounced for older children. This variation suggests that the differences in play behaviors between the two groups of children may have been related to lower language abilities in the deaf children. The difference in language abilities of the two groups can be expected to have increased with age.

Another study (Pien 1985), which analyzed communication behaviors of deaf toddlers using total communication, serendipitously reported a play-language relationship. While analyzing language samples from five deaf children three years of age and younger, Pien noted that the child who engaged in the most pretend play was also the most linguistically advanced child in the group. Due to the focus on communication, the children's play behaviors were not documented in detail. Pien's primarily anecdotal account, however, lends support to the previous reports of an association between language skill and the symbolic play behaviors of deaf children.

Due to the hypothesized relationship between language and symbolic play development in hearing children, the findings summarized above from studies of deaf children may not reflect the effect of deafness itself on symbolic development. All these studies either employed deaf children with hearing parents or failed to differentiate between the performances of those children and of deaf children with deaf parents. It has been well documented that deaf children with signing deaf parents develop language skills in Sign at a rate and in a pattern similar to that of the oral language of hearing children (Bellugi and Klima 1975), while deaf children with hearing parents typically have significant language delays (Meadow-Orlans 1987; Schlesinger and Meadow 1972). Previous reports of deviant or delayed play behaviors of deaf children may well be due, not to deafness, but instead to accompanying, but not inevitable, delays in communication and language skills.

In order to identify effects of auditory deprivation on the development of early symbolic play, we compared the play behaviors of a group of young hearing children with those of a group of young deaf children who have deaf parents. These deaf children would have progressed through the sensorimotor period without having input from one of the major sensory systems integrated with their other sensory and motor experiences. They would not have experienced the massive amount of sequential input that is received by hearing children through auditory processing of language. However, deaf children with deaf parents participate in early reciprocal communicative interactions with their parents, as do hearing children (Meadow et al. 1981), and deaf children with deaf parents show the same distribution of attachment behaviors as do hearing children (Meadow, Greenberg, and Erting, see chap. 17). Furthermore, it has been shown that the sign language used by most deaf parents, American Sign Language (ASL), represents levels of abstraction and complexity equivalent to those of spoken languages (Bellugi and Klima 1975; Klima and Bellugi 1979; Stokoe, Casterline, and Croneberg 1976; Wilbur 1976). Based on this information, we predicted that the interactive and communicative experiences of deaf children with deaf parents would provide a basis for the acquisition of symbolic behaviors equivalent to those of hearing children, and that deaf and hearing toddlers would not differ in the levels or the amounts of symbolic play they demonstrated.

METHODS AND PROCEDURES

Subjects

Four deaf toddlers with deaf mothers and four hearing toddlers with hearing mothers participated in this study. As Table 18.1 shows, all the children were between twenty-four and twenty-eight months of age. All the mothers had college degrees. Because of their high educational levels, these deaf mothers are an atypical group in the deaf population, which generally attains lower educational levels than does the hearing population. However, their high education levels make this group of deaf mothers more equivalent educationally to the hearing mothers who typically participate in normative studies of infant and child development.

The deaf children had hearing losses in the severe-profound to profound range and were enrolled in parent-infant educational programs. The deaf mothers used either ASL or forms of Sign English as their primary language. The hearing children were from English-speaking homes. All the children were evaluated using either the Alpern-Boll Developmental Profile II (Alpern, Boll, and Shearer 1980) or the Bayley Scales of Mental Development (Bayley 1969) and were found to be functioning developmentally within normal ranges for age.

Table 18.1
Characteristics of Subjects

	Sex	Age (months)	Hearing Status	Mother's Education
Steven	M	28	Severe to Profound	B.A.
Lisa	F	24	Severe to Profound	B.A.
Ann	F	28	Severe to Profound	B.A.
Sally	F	27	Profound	M.A.
Tony	M	25	Hearing	M.A.
Jennifer	F	25	Hearing	M.A.
Eva	F	27	Hearing	B.A.
Sue	F	25	Hearing	M.A.

Procedures

Play sessions of approximately twenty minutes were videotaped in the participating family's homes. This amount of time appeared to be the minimum necessary to obtain representative play samples from the children. Although some children sat down with the toys and immediately began to engage in high-level play, others appeared to "warm up" over a period of time. After their initial adjustment to the situation, these children also showed elaborated play. However, shorter sessions would have resulted in their "highest level of play" being misjudged.

For these analyses, only the first twenty minutes of play were used in those cases in which the session ran longer. If a symbolic play (SP) episode was in progress at the end of the twenty minutes, however, the time until the completion of that episode was included in the analyses.

During the play session, mother and child were seated on the floor and were given a box of toys containing most of those found by Nicolich (1977) to facilitate symbolic play. The toy set included several dolls, plastic tools and a tool box, a set of dishes and utensils, toy vehicles and people figures to ride in them, popbeads, two books, a sponge, sunglasses, a plastic headband, stuffed animals, a comb and brush, finger puppets, a toy iron, doll clothes and a blanket, a telephone, a puzzle with animal figures, and a small purse. In addition, a large seashell and some popsicle sticks were included to provide items that could be readily used in object substitution activities. At the start of the session, each mother was asked to play with her child as she normally would when time was available and was told that the focus of the analysis would be on the child's level and type of play behaviors.

Coding System

The coding system used was based on one developed by McCune-Nicolich (1980, revised 1983). The system shown in Figure 18.1 defines five levels of symbolic play, of which levels 2 through 5 were coded and used in our analysis. (Level 1

Level 1 Pre-symbolic
   Child demonstrates correct function of object. No evidence of pretending.
Level 2 Auto-symbolic
   Child pretends with an object. Play involves the child's own body and behaviors.
Level 3 Single Scheme Symbolic
   Child extends play beyond self by (a) including other participants (mother, doll), or (b) pretending at activities normally performed by another person.
Level 4 Combinations
   Child combines several play behaviors that focus on an object or a theme.
   4.0 Single action repeated in different locations or on different objects.
   4.1 Single action repeated with different participants.
   4.2 More than one action is used with the same or related objects.
   4.3 More than one action is used with the same or related objects, and actions occur in a logical sequence.
Level 5 Planned Symbolic
   Child shows evidence of preplanning play behaviors, or demonstrates object substitutions.
   Categories modified for this study:
     5.1 Preplanning or object substitution (nonverbal evidence).
     5.2 Preplanning or object substitution (verbal evidence).
     5.3 Preplanning 4.3 sequence.

Adapted from L. McCune-Nicolich, "A Manual for Analyzing Free Play," (1980, revised 1983).

Figure 18.1   Play behaviors can be categorized at five levels in an ordinal scale.

play develops long before age two and was not considered to be important for this analysis.) Figure 18.1 lists the coding categories, which included most of those developed by McCune plus several modified categories developed by the authors. Our modifications were not necessary in order to use the system with deaf subjects. We modified the categories to allow for differentiation between verbal and nonverbal evidence for level 5 behaviors so that any differences between the two groups of children on that variable could be explored.

There is considerable evidence that the levels in McCune's coding system form an ordinal scale (1982). McCune has reported wide variation in the age at which stages are reached, however, and level 5 behaviors have occurred at eighteen months for some subjects but not until twenty-six months for others. Due to the ages of our subjects, levels 4 and 5 were of the most interest to us.

Level 4 play consists of combinations of play behaviors focused on an object or a theme. Level 4.0 and 4.1 combinations involve a single action that is repeated with variations. For example, at level 4.0 the child repeats the same action but involves different objects (hammering to "fix" a table, a chair, and a toy car). At level 4.1 the child repeats the same action but involves more than one participant (feeding a doll, feeding self, feeding mother).

Level 4.2 and 4.3 combinations involve a series of related actions that form a theme. For example, at level 4.2 the child may execute several play behaviors that combine to form a doll theme (feeding the doll, combing the doll's hair, giving the doll a hug.) If the related behaviors occur in a logical order (bathing the doll, drying with a cloth, dressing the doll), the combination is coded at level 4.3.

Level 5 play shows evidence of preplanning or object substitution. This is considered to be evidence of abstract thought (Slade 1987b) in that the child must be thinking of an object or activity that is not currently in sight. McCune has included nonverbal evidence of preplanning (i.e., searching for a specific object before engaging in an activity with it) as well as verbal evidence (i.e., saying "doll" and then beginning to play with the doll) at this level.

We modified McCune's coding system for level 5 behaviors in order to separate nonverbal evidence of preplanning from verbal evidence of preplanning. In our modification, level 5.1 behaviors show nonverbal evidence of preplanning (searching for a specific object or performing an intervening act before beginning play). Examples of these behaviors from our data include searching through the toy box to find the baby bottle in order to feed the doll, and turning the doll's head to the correct position before feeding her. In our coding system, level 5.2 behaviors include verbal evidence of preplanning (announcing an activity by using either speech or signs before the activity occurs), and object substitutions (e.g., using a seashell for a doll's hat and laughing to show that the substitution is recognized).

Acceptable evidence of this level of symbolic representation often has been limited to object substitution in studies of play. However, object substitution occurs relatively rarely in free-play situations. One of McCune's contributions to the study of play in infants and toddlers was her realization that mental preplanning shows the same level of representation as does object substitution. For this reason, our level 5.1 category should not be thought to be less advanced than level 5.2. We combined these two categories rather than treating them as ordinal when comparisons of play levels were made.

In McCune's system, level 5.2 behaviors are combinations (level 4 behaviors) that also show evidence of preplanning. Because of our differentiation of verbal and nonverbal planning, we had to use 5.3 as the code label for preplanned combinations. In addition, we determined that in order to be coded as level 5.3, play sequences must be in logical order and must show evidence of preplanning before the first behavior in the combination occurs.

Procedures for Coding

Before behaviors were coded, the language of the deaf mothers and children was transcribed by one of the authors (Grindstaff), a Deaf native signer. Some coding decisions (particularly those related to preplanning and maternal prompting) required full understanding of the language produced by the children and mothers. The preparation of language transcripts by a native signer, therefore, was a necessary first step for accurate and reliable coding in those instances. Transcripts of the language of two of the hearing dyads were also available. The other two hearing children had readily intelligible language, and their tapes were coded by the two hearing authors (Spencer and Deyo) without reference to transcripts.

All tapes were then reviewed to note onset and termination time of each discrete play behavior and of each episode. An episode consists of one or more behaviors during which the child's attention is focused on a specific object. Each single-behavior episode representing at least the "auto-symbolic" level was coded as level 2 or 3. (A 5.1 or 5.2 code for combination and preplanning can be given to single play behaviors when appropriate). After each discrete behavior in the episode had been coded, multi-behavior episodes, or combinations, were coded with a 4-level code (and a 5.3 code when the behaviors indicated logical order and preplanning).

Inter-rater reliability

Three of the eight tapes were coded independently by two people. Inter-rater reliability was computed for those three tapes. The levels of agreement were 88.7 percent for identification of play behaviors, 96.7 percent for assignment of play levels 2 and 3, and 77.8 percent for agreement on level assignment for sequences at levels 4 and 5. These levels of agreement suggest that the coding system, which was originally developed to measure play behaviors of hearing children using oral language, can also be used reliably with children who are learning a visual-manual language.

Timing of episodes was performed independently by two people for two of the tapes. A level of agreement of 78.5 percent was obtained for onset and termination times when measurements were made to the exact second. Level of agreement was 93 percent when an allowance of one second was made. All tapes that were not used for the calculation of inter-rater reliability were coded and timed by one of the coders, and then the coding and timing were reviewed by a second coder. Disagreements were resolved by consensus.

Analytic Procedures

Statistical analyses of group differences were performed using the Mann-Whitney *U* test. This test determines the significance of group differences based on the degree of separation between the values (in rank order) for individuals in each group. For ease of presentation, group means and the groups' ranges of individual values, instead of individual or group rank values, are provided in the data tables in this chapter. Because the time recorded varied among dyads, values for most measures were converted to proportions to allow for meaningful comparison across groups and across subjects.

Correlations between the proportion of time in symbolic play and other play measures were calculated using the Spearman Rank Correlation Coefficient. The groups were combined for these analyses. Relationships between symbolic play and other characteristics of the subjects (amount of language produced, maternal play styles) were informally evaluated. Because of the use of informal analyses, the small number of subjects in each group, and the fact that this is a first look at symbolic play behaviors of deaf children with deaf parents, our findings must be considered preliminary.

RESULTS

Group Differences in Symbolic Play

Table 18.2 displays individual data and group means for a variety of measures of the subjects' symbolic play performance. Neither the total proportion of available time in symbolic-level play nor the mean duration of symbolic play episodes differed significantly between the groups. These data, therefore, do not indicate the existence of any group difference in the amount, or quantity, of symbolic play. The two measures were significantly correlated, however ($r_s = .738, p < .05$).

The groups are also similar on the quality of play produced as measured by the highest productive level (HPL). HPL is defined as the highest level at which at least two nonimitated, nonprompted play behaviors are demonstrated (Mc-Cune-Nicolich 1980, revised 1983). Only one child, from the hearing group, failed to demonstrate level 5 as the highest productive level.

Table 18.2 also provides data on the proportion of symbolic play episodes prompted or initiated by the mother. The groups were similar on this measure, although considerable within-group differences were evident. Considering the two groups together, the proportion of play episodes prompted by the mother was negatively correlated with the proportion of time in which symbolic play occurred ($r_s = -.625$). This correlation failed to reach the .05 confidence level, however.

A final measure reported in Table 18.2 is the number of themes (or play "topics") engaged in by the two groups per minute of symbolic play. Although the two groups did not differ significantly on this measure, there was a trend toward higher numbers of themes per minute in the hearing group compared to the deaf group. We initially considered themes/minute as a potential measure of "flexibility" in symbolic functioning, and thus expected it to be associated with higher symbolic play performance. However, there was no consistently positive relationship between this measure and either the proportion of available time spent in symbolic play ($r_s = -.270$) or the HPL. The quality of play and the number of themes exhibited may be related in a curvilinear manner rather than a linear one. Although severe restriction in theme changes may indicate inflexibility, progression through themes too quickly may indicate attentional problems or an inability to elaborate activities successfully.

Table 18.3 shows the group means and the range of scores within each group on measures related to levels 4 and 5 of symbolic play. No significant group differences were found on measures of the length of play combinations or on the frequency of occurrence of play combinations (level 4). The occurrence of level 5 symbolic play was also similar for the two groups. No significant differences were

Table 18.2
Characteristics of Symbolic Play Behaviors, Deaf and Hearing Subjects (Individual and Group Data)

Characteristics Measured	Deaf Toddlers					Hearing Toddlers				
	Lisa	Ann	Steve	Sally	Mean	Eva	Jen	Sue	Tony	Mean
I. Percentage of Time in Symbolic Play	63	37	27	25	38.0	44	39	38	15	34.0
II. Mean Duration of Symbolic Play Episodes	55.1	20.0	21.9	33.2	32.6	37.9	46.2	62.1	12.9	39.78
III. Highest Productive Levels	5.3	5.3	5.1/5.2	5.1/5.2	(NA)	5.1/5.2	5.1/5.2	5.1/5.2	4.2	(NA)
IV. Maternal Prompts (in %)	16	11	23	30	20.0	12	14	34	35	23.8
V. Themes per Minute of Play	0.55	0.87	0.72	0.80	0.74	0.90	0.90	0.24	2.25	1.07

Table 18.3
Descriptions of Higher Levels of Symbolic Play, Deaf and Hearing Groups

	Deaf Toddlers		Hearing Toddlers	
	Mean	Range	Mean	Range
I. Level 4 (combinations)				
1. Percentage of SP time	71.3	59–78	80.0	53–90
2. Number of level 4 episodes	7	4–10	6	3–10
3. Longest combination (number of behaviors)	9	7–13	8	3–11
4. Longest duration of combination (seconds)	188	78–384	204	23–378
II. Level 5 (preplanned)				
1. Percentage of SP time	37.5	15–59	24.8	0–44
2. Number of level 5 episodes	6	2–10	6	0–9
3. Percentage of level 5 episodes with verbal preplanning	59	25–80	89	67–100

found in the proportion of symbolic play time in which level 5 behaviors occurred, the frequency of occurrence of level 5 episodes, or the production of verbal evidence compared to nonverbal evidence of preplanning of level 5 behaviors. There was a trend, however, toward greater production of verbal announcements of preplanning in the hearing group than in the deaf group. Less between-group overlap in scores occurred for this measure than for most others.

The proportion of available time spent in symbolic play was significantly correlated with the proportion of that time in which Level 4 play ($r_s = .643$; $p \leq .05$) and Level 5 play ($r_s = .774$; $p \leq .05$) occurred. These correlations indicate that children who showed more symbolic play were more likely to engage in higher levels of symbolic play than the other children were.

In summary, the hearing and deaf groups did not differ significantly on any of the measures of either quantity or quality of symbolic play. We were unable to identify any systematic effects of deafness on early symbolic play. Individual deaf children matched, indeed sometimes exceeded, hearing toddlers in the proportion of time engaged in symbolic play as well as in the level of play produced.

In contrast to the absence of between-group differences, wide ranges of differences among individuals within groups were evident. Those differences are discussed below.

Individual Differences

We did not try to characterize the language levels of the subjects beyond their identification as "within the normal range" on developmental scales, due to the difficulty of assigning developmental levels to deaf children who are signing ASL or ASL-like forms. No measure equivalent to the "mean length of utterance"

(MLU) which can be used for spoken English is currently available for categorizing signed language. It was obvious, however, that the quantity and complexity of language produced varied among the children within each group. It was also apparent that the child in each group who produced the most time in SP also produced more vocal or signed utterances with more complex content than did the child with the lowest time in SP.

Intrigued by the individual differences observed, we reviewed tapes of the "high" and "low" exemplars from each group to look for previously uncoded evidence of differences in dyadic behaviors because these differences might help to explain differences in the amounts and levels of play demonstrated. Within the deaf group, Lisa and Sally demonstrated the highest and lowest amounts of symbolic play respectively. Several contrasts were evident between the behaviors of these two mother-child dyads. Lisa's mother engaged in pretend play herself, accepting and elaborating on the roles that Lisa assigned to her. Her mother never tried to redirect Lisa's attention to a new toy while she was already engaged with a toy, and the mother rarely tried to start new play activities, even when Lisa was seemingly at "loose ends." When the mother did attempt to direct Lisa's behavior by repositioning her or by suggesting a new activity, Lisa strongly and firmly rejected the attempt. Lisa was quite happy, however, to attend visually to her mother's sometimes extended explanations about the toys and their use. When told that the session could end at any time and that enough activity had been taped, Lisa's mother allowed the play to continue until a natural break occurred. Overall, this mother-child pair seemed to be relaxed and to be enjoying the playtime together.

In contrast, Sally's mother rarely participated fully in her daughter's pretend play, except for one fairly brief "tea party" sequence. This mother frequently interrupted her child's play to suggest play with another object. The mother did not become engaged with the toys, looking through them several times as though unable to find anything of interest. She finally decided upon a toy that could be used in an educational activity and told Sally to put away all the other toys in order to work with the new one. By the time Sally and her mother finished putting away all the other toys, Sally had lost interest in playing with the new, more educationally oriented toy. The mother persisted in trying to attract Sally's interest, however, and the pair engaged in separate activities as Mother manipulated the educational toy while Sally surreptitiously played with the one other toy she had been allowed to keep out of the box. Although Sally intermittently joined her mother in the educational play, Mother never joined in Sally's play. Sally complied with most of her mother's suggestions for play activities, resisting only passively, by giving intermittent visual attention to the activity or by seeming to fade into an inactive, quiescent state. Unlike Lisa, Sally frequently looked away when her mother was signing to her, although she reliably turned and attended after being tapped on the shoulder. When told that enough play had been taped, Sally's mother interrupted the play immediately and began to put away the toys. The general impression we have from watching the tape is that Sally has a rather tentative, slow approach to beginning play with an object and that her mother's pace is somewhat quicker, resulting in her distracting Sally frequently just as she was beginning to become comfortable with a play activity. In addition, Sally's mother does not seem comfortable "just playing." The total experience of the play session seems to have been less enjoyable for this mother-daughter pair than for Lisa and her mother.

Similar kinds of differences were seen on the tapes of Eva and Tony, the two hearing children who showed the most and least SP respectively. Eva's mother appeared almost passive on the tape at first, sitting quietly and merely supporting Eva's play. This mother did not interrupt play in progress. She cleared away toys after Eva stopped using them but never told Eva to interrupt her play to do so. In later parts of the tape, Eva's mother herself began to truly participate in the play, taking roles that Eva had assigned to her and "talking for" dolls and animals. Like Lisa, Eva seemed never to be at a loss for something to do and moved smoothly from one play activity to the next. She attended to and participated in her mother's discussions about the objects and their use. Like Lisa's mother, Eva's mother extended the play beyond the time when she was told that play could stop, allowing a play sequence to continue until its natural termination.

Tony and his mother apparently had a less enjoyable play session than did Eva and her mother. Although Tony's mother attempted to join him in play activities—and she did succeed in participating in two symbolic sequences—Tony usually stopped a play episode when his mother joined in it. Like Sally's mother, Tony's mother attempted to start a more educationally oriented construction game with Tony, but she was unable to obtain his participation. Tony's mother frequently asked him to label objects by asking, "What's that?" and holding the objects in front of him. While reading a book together, it appeared that the mother usually turned to a new page just a bit before Tony was ready to be finished with the previous one. Like Sally and her mother, Tony and his mother failed to engage in play in which they were both active participants. This tape ended just as the mother was told that enough time had been taped, so it is not possible to know her reaction.

The dyads that differed in the amount of SP displayed by the child also differed in the degree to which mother and child were able to engage mutually in play activities. Dyadic success in mutual engagement and the children's successful demonstration of SP seemed to be related to the degree to which mother and child were matched in the pacing of their behaviors and perhaps to the value that the mother placed on playing as opposed to more overtly educational activities. Neither the levels of play nor the degree of dyadic engagement was associated with the hearing status of mother and child, however.

DISCUSSION

In contrast to a number of earlier reports, we did not find differences between amount or level of symbolic play in deaf and hearing children. We conclude that lack of auditory input does not necessarily result in delays in symbolic functioning as shown by play behaviors. Deaf children who do show delays in symbolic play should, therefore, receive additional assessment to determine whether those delays are associated with organic or environmental difficulties that are interfering with development.

Before firm conclusions can be reached about relationships between hearing status and play behaviors, our findings need to be confirmed by further research with larger numbers of subjects. We believe, however, that our results differ from earlier ones primarily because our deaf subjects have deaf parents. These deaf children, unlike many deaf children whose parents are hearing, experience interactions with their parents much like those experienced by hearing children with hearing parents (Spencer and Gutfreund, chap. 15, this volume; Meadow et al. 1981). Therefore, research about the effects of auditory deprivation on development should use deaf children with deaf parents as subjects in order to avoid confounding the effects of deafness with those of the aberrant interactive and language experiences of many deaf children with hearing parents.

Deaf children with hearing parents provide an interesting group to study in regard to questions about the relationship between language development and early symbolic play behaviors. Because these children experience varying degrees of language delay, they should be studied to determine whether play is necessarily delayed when language acquisition is delayed due to environmental causes. If play behaviors develop normally even when language is delayed, assessment of play behaviors can provide a useful window for assessing cognitive-symbolic development and cognitive readiness for language acquisition. On the other hand, if symbolic play development is delayed in children with language delays, assessment of play behaviors will not provide an unbiased measure of those children's cognitive abilities.

Another area needing further study is that of the relationship between children's development of play and mothers' interactive behaviors. Our informal observations suggested that maternal interactive styles were related to the quality and quantity of children's symbolic play. More formal study of dyadic tempo, maternal responsiveness, and mothers' degree of participation in play sequences can provide information that can be used to enhance individual children's play development.

The findings of this study and other available reports on play behaviors of hearing and deaf infants and toddlers point out that investigators hoping to understand the development of symbolic functioning must not approach play as though it represents purely cognitive functioning. Indeed, a complex interaction between cognitive, linguistic, and social factors appears to influence the amount and level of symbolic play in which a particular child engages. Steps toward understanding that interaction will help us encourage deaf children's symbolic play in order to provide a rich and enjoyable context for the development of complex symbolic functioning.

REFERENCES

Alpern, G., T. Boll, and M. Shearer. 1980. *Manual: Developmental profile II*. Aspen: Psychological Development Publications.

Bates, E. 1976. *Language and context: The acquisition of pragmatics*. New York: Academic Press.

Bayley, N. 1969. *Bayley scales of infant development*. New York: Psychological Corp.

Bellugi, U., and E. Klima. 1975. Aspects of sign language and its structure. In *The role of speech in language,* ed. J. Kavanagh and J. Cutting, 171–205. Cambridge, MA: MIT Press.

Belsky, J., and R. Most. 1981. From exploration to play: A cross-sectional study of infant free play behavior. *Developmental Psychology* 17: 630–639.

Bretherton, I. 1984. *Symbolic play*. New York: Academic Press.

Bruner, J., R. Oliver, and P. Greenfield. 1966. *Studies in cognition*. Cambridge, MA: MIT Press.

Casby, M., and S. McCormack. 1985. Symbolic play and early communication development in hearing-impaired children. *Journal of Communication Disorders* 18: 67–78.

Darbyshire, J. 1977. Play patterns in young children with impaired hearing. *Volta Review* 79: 19–26.

DiPane, D., R. Fireoved, M. Fleck, and L. McCune. 1987. Play: A context for mutual regulation within mother-child interaction. Unpublished manuscript.

Gregory, S. 1985. The relationship between language development and symbolic play in deaf children. Paper presented at IRSA Conference, Brussels, Belgium.

Higginbotham, D., and B. Baker. 1981. Social participation and cognitive play differences in hearing-impaired and normally hearing preschoolers. *Volta Review* 83: 135–149.

Klima, E., and U. Bellugi. 1979. *The signs of language*. Cambridge, MA: Harvard University Press.

Lowe, M. 1975. Trends in the development of representational play in infants from one to three years—an observational study. *Journal of Child Psychology and Psychiatry* 16: 33–47.

Mann, L. 1985. Play behaviors of deaf and hearing children. In *Cognition, education, and deafness,* ed. D. Martin, 27–29. Washington, DC: Gallaudet University Press.

McCall, R., D. Eichorn, and P. Hogarty. 1977. Transitions in early mental development. *Monographs of the Society for Research in Child Development* 42(3).

McCune-Nicolich, L. 1980, rev. 1983. *A manual for analyzing free play*. Unpublished manuscript.

———. 1981. Toward symbolic functioning: Structure of early pretend games and potential parallels with language. *Child Development* 52: 785–797.

———. 1982. Play as prelinguistic behavior: Theory, evidence and applications. In *Infant communication: Development, assessment, and intervention,* ed. D. McClowry, A. Guilford, and S. Richardson, 55–80. New York: Grune and Stratton.

McCune-Nicolich, L., and S. Carroll. 1981. Development of symbolic play: Implications for the language specialist. *Topics in Language Disorders* 1: 1–15.

Meadow, K., M. Greenberg, C. Erting, and H. Carmichael. 1981. Interactions of deaf mothers and deaf preschool children: Comparisons with three other groups of deaf and hearing dyads. *American Annals of the Deaf* 126: 454–468.

Meadow-Orlans, K. 1987. Understanding deafness. Socialization of children and youth. In *Understanding deafness socially,* ed. P. Higgins and J. Nash, 29–57. Springfield, IL: Charles C. Thomas.

Nicolich, L. 1977. Beyond sensorimotor intelligence: Assessment of symbolic maturity through analysis of play. *Merrill-Palmer Quarterly* 23: 89–101.

———. 1978. Methodological issues in studying symbolic play. Paper presented at the Biennial Meeting of the Southeastern Conference on Human Development, Atlanta, Georgia.

Piaget, J. 1962. *Play, dreams and imitation.* New York: W. W. Norton.

Pien, D. 1985. The development of communication functions in deaf infants and hearing parents. In *Cognition, education, and deafness,* ed. D. Martin, 30–33. Washington, DC: Gallaudet University Press.

Schlesinger, H., and K. Meadow. 1972. *Sound and sign: Childhood deafness and mental health.* Berkeley: University of California Press.

Singer, D., and M. Lenahan. 1976. Imagination content in dreams of deaf children. *American Annals of the Deaf* 121: 44–48.

Slade, A. 1987a. A longitudinal study of maternal involvement and symbolic play during the toddler period. *Child Development* 58: 367–375.

———. 1987b. Quality of attachment and early symbolic play. *Developmental Psychology* 23: 78–85.

Smilansky, S. 1968. *The effects of socio-dramatic play on disadvantaged children.* New York: John Wiley and Sons.

Stokoe, W., D. Casterline, and C. Croneberg. 1976. *A dictionary of American Sign Language on linguistic principles.* 2d ed. Silver Spring, MD: Linstok Press.

Ungerer, J., and M. Sigman. 1984. The relation of play and sensorimotor behavior to language in the second year. *Child Development* 55: 1448–1455.

Ungerer, J., P. Zelazo, R. Kearsley, and K. Kurowski. 1979. Play as a cognitive assessment tool. Paper presented at Ninth Annual Interdisciplinary Conference on Piagetian Theory and its Implications for the Helping Professions, Los Angeles, California.

Uzgiris, I. 1983. Organization of sensorimotor intelligence. In *Origins of intelligence,* ed. M. Lewis, 123–163. New York: Plenum Press.

Vygotsky, L. 1978. *Mind in society: The development of higher psychological processes.* Cambridge, MA: Harvard University Press.

Werner, H., and B. Kaplan. 1963. *Symbol formation.* New York: John Wiley and Sons.

Wilbur, R. 1976. The linguistics of manual language and manual systems. In *Communication assessment and intervention strategies,* ed. L. Lloyd, 423–500. Baltimore, MD: University Park Press.

19

A Comparison of Deaf Students in Israel, Denmark, and the United States

ABRAHAM ZWIEBEL, KATHRYN P. MEADOW-ORLANS, BIRGIT DYSSEGAARD

Cross-national comparisons are difficult and problematic at best. When the comparison involves children with a sensory impairment, many additional problems arise. There may well be differences in national or cultural attitudes about the disability (or about disability in general) that are reflected in the family and educational treatment of a particular group of children. There may be differences in economic conditions or resources that influence educational opportunities of special groups. There may be differences in social or political philosophy influencing provision of medical or technical services and early diagnoses. Each of these areas of difference can be found in surveying the social/economic/political climates of the three countries with which we are concerned here: Israel, Denmark, and the United States. To review these differences is beyond the scope of this paper. However, we do believe that cross-national comparisons may contribute to broader understanding of some of the major influences on the development of children with disabilities—in this case hearing impairments—within specific cultural contexts.

METHOD

Subjects

During the 1984 school year, survey data were collected on 531 deaf students in Israel—virtually the total population of students receiving special education services related to a hearing loss. These students were in three kinds of settings: spe-

This chapter was published originally in the *International Journal of Rehabilitation* 1986, 9: 109–118. Reprinted by permission of Chapman and Hall, Publishers.

Table 19.1
Characteristics of Deaf Students Surveyed in Israel, the United States, and
Denmark

	Israeli		American		Danish	
Characteristic	Percent	Number	Percent	Number	Percent	Number
Sex						
Male	57.3	129	52.5	95	59.1	104
Female	42.7	96	47.5	86	40.9	72
	$X^2 = 1.72$; $df = 2$; $p = .42$					
Age						
6 to 9 years	41.8	94	30.4	55	51.1	91
10 to 12 years	58.2	131	69.6	126	48.9	87
	$X^2 = 16.0$; $df = 2$; $p < .01$					
Hearing Loss						
71 dB	8.6	19	44.6	79	17.6	29
71–90 db	17.2	38	16.4	29	19.4	32
91+ dB	74.2	164	39.0	69	63.0	164
	$X^2 = 80.38$; $df = 4$; $p < .001$					

cial day schools attended by deaf students only; self-contained classes of deaf students in schools for children without impairments; mainstream classes in schools with hearing children. For the purposes of this paper, 224 students were selected for comparison with groups of American and Danish students for whom data had previously been collected. These 224 students are all those between the ages of six and twelve who are not in mainstream placements.

Similar data had been collected by Dyssegaard in 1981–1982 for 398 deaf Danish students, ages six to eighteen, attending day schools or day classes. For this paper, the students six to twelve years old ($N = 177$) were selected.

Data on the American students resulted from a 1977–1978 study of 2,365 deaf students, conducted for the purpose of norming the inventory designed for this population. A random sample had been drawn for a comparison with Danish students previously reported. From that computer file, day students six to twelve years old ($N = 180$) were selected.

Table 19.1 shows characteristics of American, Danish, and Israeli students for age, sex, and hearing loss. There are no significant differences in the sex distribution of the three groups. Between 53 percent and 59 percent of each group are males. There are significant differences among the groups in distribution by age: 70 percent of the American students are between the ages of ten and thirteen, compared to 49 percent of the Danish students and 58 percent of the Israeli students. Significant differences in hearing loss are also found: 39 percent of the American students are profoundly deaf, compared to 63 percent of the Danish students, and 74 percent of the Israeli students.

Instrument

The Meadow/Kendall Social-Emotional Assessment Inventory (SEAI) for Deaf and Hearing-Impaired Students (Meadow 1983) was collected for all subjects. The SEAI consists of fifty-nine items which comprise three scales: social adjustment, self-image, and emotional adjustment. Teachers are asked to evaluate the behaviors of students in their classes on a four-point scale. The SEAI was translated into Danish by Dyssegaard and into Hebrew by Zwiebel. Both translations were retranslated into English by bilingual specialists without knowledge of the original, then evaluated and modified in consultation with educators and psychologists from Denmark and Israel. Factor analyses of the Danish and Israeli data revealed structures differing slightly from each other and from the American version. These were used to construct inventories for use by Danish and Israeli teachers. The three scales emerging from the original American study have been utilized for the present comparison.

Statistical Analysis

One-way analysis of variance was used for comparison of overall differences in mean ratings of the three groups of students. Duncan's multiple range test was used to evaluate differences between each pair. In addition, analysis of covariance was conducted to ensure that cross-national differences remain significant despite group differences in age and hearing loss.

RESULTS

Overall Level of Social-Emotional Adjustment: Students in Three Countries

The three groups of students were compared in terms of their scores on the three inventory scales: social adjustment (23 items), self-image (23 items), and emotional adjustment (13 items). Scores for the American, Israeli, and Danish students did not differ for scale 1 (social adjustment) or for scale 2 (self-image) (Table 19.2). Danish students received significantly more positive scores on items reflecting emotional adjustment (scale 3) compared to both the American students and the Israeli students. The previous analysis comparing additional numbers of Danish and American students showed no differences on this scale among older students, whether they were in day or residential settings (Meadow and Dyssegaard 1983; Dyssegaard and Meadow-Orlans 1987).

This similarity of scoring across the three national groups is also reflected in Figure 19.1, which presents the twenty-four inventory items that show no significant between-group differences. These twenty-four include five items on which

Table 19.2
Scale Scores in Social Adjustment, Self-Image, Emotional Adjustment for Israeli, American and Danish Students

Scale	Israeli		American		Danish		F	p
	Mean	SD	Mean	SD	Mean	SD		
Scale 1								
Social Adjustment	2.97	.49	2.94	.47	2.93	.60	.39	—
(N)	(220)		(169)		(167)			
Scale 2								
Self-Image	2.98	.43	3.03	.44	3.03	.45	.91	—
(N)	(220)		(140)		(165)			
Scale 3								
Emotional Adjustment	3.16	143	3.17	.43	3.37	.46	13.39	<.01
(N)	(224)		(169)		(171)			

students in all three countries were given consistently "high" ratings by their teachers (mean scores 3.2 or higher), eleven items on which students were rated "low" (below 3.0), and eight items with ratings in the intermediate range.

Part A of Figure 19.1 shows items indicating an absence of bizarre behavior, destructive behavior, accident-prone behavior, or rude mannerisms, plus the demonstration of a willingness to attempt communication with others. Part C of Figure 1 shows instances in which students were seen negatively by teachers in all three countries. These include several items that reflect immaturity (e.g., proneness to tantrums, dependence on others, inability to accept criticism or failure, demanding attention from teachers and peers). Others reflect difficulties in cooperative activities in the classroom or on the playground and an inability to demonstrate leadership.

All three groups of students were perceived by their teachers as being within the normal range for items describing somewhat pathological behavior, although some students were seen as having mild behavioral and disciplinary problems. All groups of students were seen as being somewhat immature and as having problems in social and school relationships. On the positive side, they were seen as motivated in their schoolwork and to have communicative skills in addition to being motivated to communicate with others.

In the earlier analysis of Danish/American differences (Meadow and Dyssegaard 1983), ratings of the Danish students were summarized as reflecting characteristics of modesty, reserve, introspective and individually focused attitudes and behaviors, compared to American characteristics of assertiveness, creativity, extroverted and group-focused behaviors. In this chapter we will focus on the ratings of Israeli students by reviewing two sets of item comparisons reflecting possible cross-national differences: (1) eighteen items on which Israeli students received significantly more positive ratings than the American and/or Danish students (Table 19.3) and (2) seventeen items on which Israeli students received signifi-

A. Consistently high ratings: +3.20

    8. Engages in behavior considered by most teachers and students to be bizarre or strange (talking or signing to self, rocking, staring at lights for long periods, twirling).   (3.39)

  16. Tries to communicate with others (both deaf and hearing) by any means necessary: signs, speech, writing, pantomime.   (3.29)

  27. Engages in destructive behavior (breaking objects, defacing walls or furniture, scattering things in disarray).   (3.44)

  39. Has many accidents or mishaps resulting in breakage of objects or injuries requiring first aid.   (3.32)

  46. Has habits, mannerisms or traits considered to be rude or socially unacceptable (e.g. picks nose, makes obscene/sexual references).   (3.23)

B. Intermediate ratings: 3.01 to 3.19

    1. Obeys the rules; follows instructions or requests from adults in authority.   (3.19)

    2. Is kind and considerate.   (3.12)

    3. Relates well to peers and is accepted by them.   (3.11)

    5. Displays aggressive behavior, including fighting, scratching, biting other students and/or kicking or hitting animals.   (3.09)

  12. Isolated. Has few or no friends. May be considered withdrawn.   (3.10)

  18. Insists on repetition of usual routines. Changes in schedules, habits, route arrangements elicit extreme negative responses.   (3.01)

  29. Is trustworthy, dependable, reliable.   (3.05)

  34. Acts lethargic; lacks energy; is always tired.   (3.15)

C. Consistently low ratings: 3.00 and below

    9. Has generally acceptable emotional responses. Rages (tantrums) or violent outbursts occur only after extreme provocation if at all.   (2.95)

  19. Is self-reliant. Not overly dependent on others for help.   (2.88)

  20. Performs cooperatively in group of peers. Contributes to cohesion rather than to conflict.   (2.88)

  24. Gives up quickly. Expects to fail.   (2.80)

  35. Fails to accept criticism, especially if it is expressed as discipline or restriction.   (2.76)

  37. Demands attention. Must be center of everything. May insist on being first in line, or leader, or captain.   (2.71)

  43. Responds poorly to losing in games or failing to achieve in class.   (2.70)

  47. Participates in classroom or group activities; volunteers answers, offers opinions in discussions.   (2.98)

  49. Other students look to this student as a leader.   (2.10)

  52. Demands attention and help constantly. Takes disproportionate share of teacher's time.   (2.72)

  53. Participates well in organized play or games (takes role of leader or follower; plays to completion; follows rules).   (2.95)

Figure 19.1   Inventory items with no significant difference among Israeli, American, and Danish Students (*N* = 24 items).

cantly more negative ratings than the American and/or the Danish students (Table 19.4).

Part A of Table 3 presents four items on which Israeli students received higher ratings from their teachers than did either the American or the Danish students. Israeli students are seen as less likely to: (1) tease other students, (2) respond positively to a stranger using sign language, (3) behave impulsively, or

Table 19.3
Items on which Israeli Students Received Higher Ratings than American and/or Danish Students

Item No.	Item	Israeli ($\bar{X}$)	American ($\bar{X}$)	Danish ($\bar{X}$)	F
Part A—*Israelis Rated Higher Than Both American and Danish Students*					
14.	Teases, annoys, or pesters other students.	3.09	2.56	2.89	16.95**
38.	Shows excited, positive responses to stranger who is using signs.	3.10	2.85	2.83	6.02**
55.	Acts without thinking; implusive; doesn't consider or doesn't care about consequences.	2.93	2.64	2.48	14.53**
59.	Denies own misbehavior; may also blame others for own misdeeds.	2.70	2.40	2.48	5.39**
Part B—*Israelis Rated Higher Than Danish Students Only*					
13.	Lacks competence with tools, utensils, or equipment even when there is no apparent physical basis for lack of skill.	3.34	3.18	3.09	4.66**
15.	Shows initiative in completion of assignments; motivated to finish work.	3.20	2.87	2.82	3.20*
17.	Takes responsibility for fair share of tasks; helps to clean up after a project is finished.	3.19	3.09	2.77	14.41**
26.	Identifies with (shows excited recognition of) a stranger or visitor who wears a hearing aid.	3.13	2.96	2.51	26.21**
40.	Seems to understand the feelings of others; demonstrates empathy.	2.76	2.83	2.52	4.98**
41.	Tries to understand the communication of others by any means offered: listening, lipreading, signing, writing, gestures.	3.26	3.19	2.95	8.91**
45.	Accepts differences in other people; doesn't tease or exclude peers on basis of racial differences or physical handicap.	3.08	3.00	2.82	5.13**
Part C—*Israelis Rated Higher Than Americans Only*					
4.	Distinguishes between fact and fiction, real and imaginary				

Table 19.3   (*continued*)

Item No.	Item	Israeli ($\bar{X}$)	American ($\bar{X}$)	Danish ($\bar{X}$)	F
	events and/or people (understands that Superman does not really exist).	3.20	3.03	3.21	2.91*
25.	Complains of physical ailments that have no apparent medical basis (headaches, stomachaches, etc.)	3.29	3.05	3.42	9.57**
32.	Misbehavior not deterred by restrictions or by threat of punishment.	3.15	2.90	3.16	5.61**
44.	Daydreams; tunes out events in immediate environment.	3.01	2.62	3.06	14.99**
48.	Doesn't try to copy classmates' work nor take things belonging to others.	3.08	2.82	2.92	4.49*
58.	Displays twitches, mannerisms, tics of face or body.	3.36	3.21	3.53	6.75**

*$p \leq .05$
**$p \leq .01$

(4) deny misbehavior. Part B of Table 3 shows seven items on which Israeli ratings are significantly more positive than Danish ratings. (On six of these items, Israeli scores are higher than American scores, but the differences are not significant.) These seven items include those reflecting competence with tools, completion of schoolwork, acceptance of responsibility, identification with strangers wearing hearing aids, empathy for others and acceptance of others' differences, and broad efforts at communication. Part C of Table 3 shows six items on which Israeli students are rated significantly higher than American students but not Danish students. These include the ability to distinguish fact from fiction, physical complaints, recalcitrant behavior, daydreaming, copying from other students, and facial or body tics.

Table 19.4 shows the seventeen items on which the Israeli students are rated more negatively than one or both of the other groups. In part A of Table 19.4, there are nine items on which the Israeli students received lower ratings than either the American or the Danish students. These items include those related to pride in appearance and in group membership, concern with (fear of) danger, concern with cleanliness and with small details, acceptance of delay of gratification, cheerfulness and sense of humor, and willingness to interact with hearing people. In part B of Table 19.4, there are six items on which Israeli students received teacher ratings significantly below those of the Danish students, but not different from those of the U. S. students. These include items relating to negative feelings about their own physical size or strength and about their own motor

Table 19.4
Items on which Israeli Students Received Lower Ratings than American and/or Danish Students

Item No.	Item	Israeli ($\bar{X}$)	American ($\bar{X}$)	Danish ($\bar{X}$)	F
Part A—*Israelis Rated Lower Than Both American and Danish Students*					
7.	Takes pride in physical appearance/personal attractiveness; feels at least moderately pretty or handsome.	2.63	3.12	3.13	23.97**
10.	Has many fears; is overly and unrealistically concerned with danger, storms, injury, death.	3.01	3.28	3.24	7.37**
11.	Accepts some delay of gratification; does not expect instant satisfaction of every need, whim, or desire.	2.82	3.14	2.98	8.63**
21.	Is overly concerned with cleanliness; may wash hands constantly or be unable to tolerate specks of dust or dirt.	2.89	3.28	3.58	48.36**
22.	Shows great concern or preoccupation with minute details (may insist on perfection in writing or drawing).	2.79	2.99	3.24	13.66**
23.	Is happy, cheerful, pleasant, easygoing.	2.76	3.20	3.09	20.58**
50.	Demonstrates a sense of humor or wit (can appreciate funny situations or jokes at own expense).	2.56	3.08	3.02	24.83**
54.	Is willing to interact with hearing people; does not refuse to interact with peers or adults who have normal hearing.	3.07	3.28	3.46	15.96**
56.	Demonstrates acceptance/pride in own social group membership (racial, ethnic, linguistic, religious identity).	2.86	3.30	3.26	17.89**
Part B—*Israelis Rated Lower Than Danish Only*					
6.	Demonstrates negative feelings about physical size and/or strength.	3.23	3.23	3.45	5.73**
28.	Relates well to adults (both men and women).	3.10	3.19	3.40	9.10**
30.	Is anxious; nervous; worries about many commonplace events.	2.94	3.02	3.19	5.06**
31.	Demonstrates negative attitudes toward sign language (refuses to sign, pretends not to understand others' signing).	3.42	3.36	3.64	7.16**
36.	Demonstrates negative feelings about own motor skills, dexterity, or visible handicaps.	3.26	3.10	3.40	6.70**
57.	Avoids communicating through speech. Seems embarrassed to use voice.	3.03	3.18	3.34	6.56**
Part C—*Israelis Rated Lower Than Americans Only*					
42.	Curious; eager to learn new things; likes new experiences.	3.04	3.24	3.07	8.91**
51.	Generous. Shares with others.	2.92	3.10	2.90	3.71*

*p ≤ .05
**p ≤ .01

skills, negative attitudes toward sign language and toward spoken communication, ability to relate to adults, and high levels of anxiety. In part C of Table 19.4, there are two items on which the Israeli students received ratings significantly below those of the American students (but no different from Danish students). The Israeli students were seen as less curious and less generous than American children.

DISCUSSION

There was a high degree of similarity on the three summary scales among students in the three countries. Only one significant difference emerged in the nine comparisons for the overall scales: the Danish students were rated more positively on items reflecting emotional adjustment. Ratings on twenty-four of the fifty-nine inventory items (40%) did not differ significantly. The similarity of ratings for children living in countries so different in history, political philosophy, and educational/social resources for the handicapped is surprising. Examination of the content of the twenty-four items with no differences supports some of the generalizations about deaf children made by behavioral scientists in the past. It could be said that most deaf children (in any of the three countries surveyed) do *not* exhibit symptoms of extreme emotional disturbance. However, they do exhibit behaviors that might be called "immature" (e.g., dependence on teachers and peers and difficulty in appropriate social participation and cooperative activity) (Meadow 1980; Schlesinger and Meadow 1972).

Although Israeli students are not seen more positively on these general characteristics, some items where they have higher ratings lead us to suspect that they may be given more responsibility earlier and are therefore somewhat more mature than deaf students in Denmark and the U.S. The Israeli students are less impulsive than the U.S. and Danish students. However, despite the fact that Israeli students score significantly higher than groups from the other two countries, the item reflecting impulsivity is rated quite low—only two other items were given lower scores for the Israeli group as a whole. This is of particular interest, since both clinicians and researchers familiar with deaf children have frequently reported a high level of impulsivity (Altshuler 1974; Harris 1978). The only previous cross-national study of deaf children focused specifically on this characteristic and found that both American and Yugoslav populations tended toward heightened impulsiveness compared to hearing groups (Altshuler et al. 1976). The same general picture is true for the item related to empathy for others. Although Israeli students are rated significantly above the two other groups, all three groups received very low scores on empathy compared to most other items.

Several items on which Israeli students scored below Danish and/or American students might reflect the fact that their environment is more dangerous: They are more anxious and demonstrate more fears than do students in the two other groups. They also are seen as less happy and as having a lesser degree of humor. Possibly all children in Israel are expected to be serious and to grow up quickly, compared to expectations for children in Denmark and the United States. It would seem that at some level, cultural differences among deaf children emerge, despite the large numbers of cross-national similarities.

REFERENCES

Altshuler, K. Z. 1974. The social and psychological development of the deaf child: Problems, their treatment and prevention. *American Annals of the Deaf* 119: 365–376.

Altshuler, K. Z., W. E. Deming, J. Vollenweider, J. D. Rainer, and R. Tendler. 1976. Impulsivity and profound early deafness: A cross cultural inquiry. *American Annals of the Deaf* 121: 331–345.

Dyssegaard, B., and K. P. Meadow-Orlans. 1987. *Hørehandicappede Skoleelevers Sociale og Emotionelle Funktion.* Den Røde Serie, Nr. 18. København: Forlaget Skolepsykologi. Monograph series of the Danish Psychological Association.

Harris, R. I. 1978. Impulse control in deaf children: Research and clinical issues. In *Deaf children: Developmental perspectives,* ed. L. S. Liben, 137–156. New York: Academic Press.

Meadow, K. P. 1980. *Deafness and child development.* Berkeley: University of California Press.

———. 1983. *The revised SEAI manual (forms for school age and preschool students).* Washington, DC: Gallaudet University.

Meadow, K. P., and B. Dyssegaard. 1983. Teachers' ratings of deaf children: An American-Danish comparison. *American Annals of the Deaf* 128: 900–908.

Schlesinger, H. S., and K. P. Meadow. 1972. *Sound and sign: Childhood deafness and mental health.* Berkeley: University of California Press.

20

Responses to Loss of Hearing in Later Life

KATHRYN P. MEADOW-ORLANS, HAROLD ORLANS

Despite the large numbers of persons deafened late in life, relatively little empirical research has been conducted with this population. Kyle and his colleagues observed that "acquired hearing loss has been something of a Cinderella in social research on deafness" (Kyle, Jones, and Wood 1985, p. 119). Definitions of hearing loss and methods for determining estimates create wide ranges in the numbers of hearing-impaired persons that are given in different surveys. One estimate, computed on the basis of 1980 Health Interview Survey data, shows a total of 18.7 million persons with hearing impairments, with rates ranging from 18 per 1,000 population for those younger than age 17, to 284 per 1,000 population for those older than age 64 (Ries 1985, p. 5). Acquired deafness occurs at the rate of about 8 per 1,000, while prelingual deafness has an estimated rate of 1 per 1,000 (Schein 1987, p. 12).

The population of those with a hearing loss that occurred after age 24 (the focus of this chapter) is composed of important subgroups based on the age at onset of the loss, its sudden or progressive character, its severity, and the nature of any residual hearing. Differences between those who lost their hearing before and after age 19 are illustrated dramatically by the estimate that 86 percent of the former group use manual communication, compared to 10 percent of those who lost their hearing later in life (Schein 1987, p. 17).

THE PSYCHOLOGICAL EFFECTS OF ACQUIRED HEARING LOSS

Despite a persistent myth that deafened persons are likely to develop symptoms of paranoia, the research evidence is equivocal at best. Nett (1960) indicated that deafened persons are more likely to be paranoid, but her research is seriously flawed, with problems of definition and diagnosis of severity of loss foremost.

Some of the material in this chapter was published previously in *Adjustment to Adult Hearing Loss,* ed. H. Orlans (Ed.), (San Diego: College-Hill Press, 1985); in SHHH, 5(6) (1984) and 6(1) (1985); and in *Society,* 25 (1988): 32–39.

Myklebust (1964) and Thomas and Gilhome-Herbst (1980) found the prevalence of paranoia no higher in the groups they studied, while Cooper et al. (1974) found it higher in deafened individuals. "Suspiciousness" is not, of course, the same as the clinical condition of "paranoia," as illustrated by this report of response to progressive deafness: "When I saw two of my friends with their heads together, talking, I grew tense with suspicion. They must be talking about me because they seemed to be taking care that I should not hear what was said" (Heiner 1949, p. 47). It is easy to imagine how a tendency to be "suspicious" of others' conversations could be labeled "paranoia" or could expand to full-blown pathology.

Many clinicians agree that depression and withdrawal, and the resulting isolation, are the most prevalent psychological responses to severe hearing loss. Research findings as well as personal accounts support these observations. Beethoven's account of his deafness reflects profound depression (Solomon 1977), and Ellen Glasgow wrote that her deafness made her feel as though she "were waiting for an impenetrable wall to close round me" (1954, p. 181). Of 96 English subjects referred by physicians to hearing consultants, 20 percent "dreaded" meeting new people, 14 percent avoided meeting new people, and another 8 percent would meet someone new only if accompanied by a hearing person (Beattie 1981, p. 6). A series of interviews conducted with members of the Dutch Hard of Hearing Association were summarized thus: "The image that tentatively emerges . . . is one of suffering, fear and loneliness" (Breed, van den Horst, and Mous 1981, p. 316). "In the case of both the person who thinks of himself as hearing impaired and the one who does not, the greatest problem confronting him is his isolation . . . from social interaction. . . . [T]his type of isolation is a vicious circle, permitting the individual fewer and fewer opportunities for contact" (Miller 1975, pp. 58–59). (See also Kyle 1987.)

Reports of nervousness, anxiety, heightened fearfulness, and irritability are common in accounts by deafened persons themselves, by professionals who work with them, and by hearing persons with simulated deafness. Embarrassment also is reported frequently. These reactions may be more fleeting or situation-specific than paranoid or depressive symptoms.

Fatigue arises from trying to hear or speechread (lipread) and to make oneself understood (Oyer and Oyer 1979, p. 129). Fatigue, nervousness, and irritability are among the most noticeable effects of simulated deafness (von der Lieth 1972; Reichstein and von der Lieth 1981).

Deafened persons often report that they feel marginal; that they belong neither to the deaf nor to the hearing community. These feelings have been compared to those of members of racial or religious minority groups (Barker and Wright 1952). There is agreement that the redefinition of self is a dramatic necessity and that many hearing-impaired persons continue to have a sense of marginality for many years. This social loss is also a part of work adjustment. Kyle and Wood (1983) found that acquired hearing loss affects the quality of working life more than it affects the level of earnings, and that anxiety about the future was high among their deafened respondents. However, the effects of hearing loss on employment are quite varied. The degree of loss and the nature of the job, particularly whether contact with the public and use of the phone are required, obviously affect the ability to perform the same job. Reduced interaction with colleagues is a common cause of dissatisfaction.

Several studies have documented the family disruption that is linked with hearing loss. Deafened persons have special difficulty with children, who are particularly impatient with them. Husbands accustomed to a dominant role in their families may face an extremely difficult situation when their hearing loss forces them to be more dependent on their wives (Beattie 1981). Kyle and Wood (1983) reported that of their 105 respondents, 86 percent agreed that "deafness places a strain on hearing members of their families" and 43 percent agreed that they had much less contact with relatives.

The stigma attached to deafness by hearing persons has been reported often. The following reactions were reported by Heider and Heider (1941), as expressed by deaf people:

> They [hearing people] are impatient with deaf persons' slowness to understand; they whisper about private matters in front of deaf people; they believe that since deaf people can't hear speech they can't understand and are therefore inferior; they pity the deaf; the deaf are overprotected by, and lose their freedom to, hearing people; hearing people slight and take advantage of the deaf; hearing people tease and make fun of the deaf; and hearing people misunderstand the deaf. (pp. 81–96)

THE SURVEY: DESIGN AND PROCEDURES

The January-February 1984 issue of *Shhh* (the membership magazine for Self Help for Hard of Hearing People) contained a four-page questionnaire that readers were asked to complete and return. Questions were designed to collect demographic information on the organization's members, on the history of their hearing loss and its severity, and on their use of hearing aids and other assistive devices among other items. In addition, questions were included to tap the effects of hearing loss on respondents' work lives, their social lives, and their relationships with friends and family members. Most questions were close-ended, with multiple choices that were precoded for direct entry to a computer. However, five open-ended questions were devised inviting narrative replies for qualitative analysis. The questionnaire was prepared by the authors, with contributions from Howard (Rocky) Stone, president of SHHH and editor of *Shhh;* Patricia Clickener, vice president of the organization, and Michael Karchmer and Susan King of the Gallaudet Research Institute.

Responses were received from 1,670 persons, 28 percent of the 6,000 SHHH members. Seventy respondents (audiologists, teachers, counselors, and

Table 20.1
Personal and Household Income of Respondents

Annual Income	Personal Income (N = 1294)	Household Income (N = 925)
Under $5,000	16%	2%
$5,000–9,999	18	6
10,000–19,999	27	18
20,000–29,999	19	25
30,000–39,999	9	18
40,000–49,999	4	11
50,000 or more	7	20
	100	100

other professionals working with hearing-impaired persons or family members of hearing-impaired persons) had normal hearing. The number and quality of responses to specific questions varied: 1,518 persons replied to the question about the effects of hearing loss on their personal life; 1,415 answered the question about its effects on their work; and 1,069 offered suggestions about SHHH activities.

Characteristics of Respondents and Their Use of Assistive Aids

The mean age of respondents was 62; 30 percent were age 70 or older, only 11 percent were younger than 40. Women accounted for 62 percent of the questionnaire respondents (although only 52% of the organization's membership in December 1983 were women). Of the men, 73 percent were married and living with a spouse, compared to 45 percent of the women. Only 2.5 percent were non-Caucasian and only 9 percent had not completed high school. Table 20.1 shows the respondents' annual personal and household incomes. Their median personal income was $16,000 annually; median family income was $29,700, reflecting that only 24 percent of respondents were working full-time while 46 percent were retired.

Table 20.2 shows present age of respondents, by decades, together with their age at onset of deafness; Table 20.3 shows hearing levels. Median age at which members began to lose their hearing was 35. Although they reported frequent hearing tests (half had been tested within the past year) very few knew their precise decibel loss. One set of questions was drawn from the Gallaudet Hearing Scale (see Table 20.4), which some respondents found confusing or inapplicable to their cases (for example, they might understand normal speech but not shouting). The degree of hearing loss, especially of the sensorineural kind that most members have, is often complicated, idiosyncratic, fluctuating, and not easily assessed by a few written questions. Nonetheless, the answers clearly show a deterioration of

Table 20.2
Age of Members and Age at Onset of Hearing Loss, By Decade (Percent)

Decade	Respondents' Present Age (N = 1531)	Respondents' Age at Onset (N = 1531)
Under 10	0%	19%
10–19	a	11
20–29	3	12
30–39	8	12
40–49	8	14
50–59	19	14
60–69	29	13
70–79	25	5
80+	9	1
	100	100

ªLess than 0.5%.

Table 20.3
Decibel Level, Better Ear

Degree of Hearing Loss and Decibel Range	(N = 355)
Normal (under 27 dB)	3%
Mild (27–40 dB)	11
Moderate (41–55 dB)	19
Moderately severe (56–70 dB)	31
Severe (71–90 dB)	27
Profound (91 dB or more)	9
	100

hearing since the onset of loss and a substantial improvement achieved with a hearing aid.

Only 11 percent of respondents do not own a hearing aid. In most cases, it is because they are too deaf to benefit from one. More than half owned two aids, and 15 percent owned three or more. Seventy percent reported using their aid(s) "all the time," despite complaints about noise, static, and distortion. Their satisfaction with the hearing aids ranged from 26 percent who checked "excellent" to 60 percent "satisfactory" and 14 percent "poor." The most common complaints are about feedback and unwanted sound and noise, especially in a crowd; tinny sound, poor volume, distortion, and difficulty with discrimination; the aid may be uncomfortable, bulky, or tiring; it may irritate the ear; it may need repair too often, have battery problems or volume control problems, and not work on the phone; and it may be too expensive.

Table 20.4
Degree of Hearing Loss in Better Ear: At Onset and Now Without, and With
Hearing Aid

Hearing Ability and Estimated Decibel Range	At Onset (N = 1287)	Now without Aid (N = 1260)	Now with Aid (N = 1267)
Without seeing a person's face, respondent can:			
a. understand whisper across a room (under 27 dB)	40%	1%	13%
b. understand normal voice across a room (27–40 dB)	35	11	39
c. understand shout across a room (41–55 dB)	13	34	23
d. understand loud speech in ear (56–70 dB)	5	22	10
e. tell speech from other sounds (71–90 dB)	3	7	9
f. tell one kind of noise from another, hear loud noise, or hear nothing useful (over 90 dB)	4	24	6
	100	100	100

CONFRONTING DEAFNESS: ADJUSTMENT AND RESPONSE

A major part of the survey analysis was the qualitative review of responses to the five open-ended questions:

1. How has your hearing loss affected your personal life (e.g., family, social life, leisure activities)?
2. How has your hearing loss affected your working life?
3. Who and what has best helped you adjust to your hearing loss (e.g., spouse, friend, hearing aid)?
4. What could be done to help you now?
5. [What] other comments [do] you wish to make about your hearing loss and [what] suggestions [do] you have for SHHH activities or articles?

Varieties of the Experience of Deafness

There are many ways in which deafness descends upon individuals and a large range of responses to that experience. We are familiar with the characterization of deafness as an invisible condition. However, our respondents made it clear that in some cases, deafness is undetected by the hearing-impaired person as well as by others. One respondent wrote:

> If hearing impairment is the most prevalent disease, I wonder why I meet so few who have it. I go to a spa, to classes, to clubs. Occasionally someone says he or she is hard of hearing, but there is either no hearing aid or a dainty behind-the-

ear model and you don't even have to raise your voice. Where are all those people. In hiding?

Another person, a twenty-two-year-old woman who apparently had some hearing loss since infancy, wrote: "I couldn't figure out how the other kids heard what they did. After high school graduation, it 'clicked' in my mind." Another respondent said that for many years she "didn't realize how much I was missing." How can you know what you do not hear? The lack of realization can create problems in itself: "During school years, before I *knew* I had a hearing loss, my friends always complained that I was stuck up and thought I was better than anyone. They said I never answered them when they spoke to me!"

This condition that is not anticipated, that can go undetected, and if detected, cannot be quickly, precisely, and fully known, invites further disguise.

1. [I've] become an excellent bluffer.
2. I used every cover-up known! The only ones who suspected were my children.
3. I'm apt to laugh in response to [the movie] audience rather than what I've heard and comprehended.
4. I am one of the greatest hypocrites in pretending that I can hear or understand.
5. In most social situations I resided in my glass coffin, putting up an appearance. . . .I appeared pretty, neat, and smiling.
6. I wear two "faces"—one usually has a smile and has been described as vibrant—the other is bewildered.
7. Grin and act pleasant.
8. Smile a lot! Look pleasant!
9. I. . .often resisted even to attempt conversation because of the awful result when I lost the topic, and said something irrelevant because I misunderstood. When, worse yet, the group realized I wasn't hearing and several people at once attempted to tell me what was said, resulting in a loud jumble, and me still not understanding. At this point I would "freeze," pretend [to understand], and retreat as unobtrusively as possible, figuratively licking my wounds.
10. I try not to moan about my hearing loss. . .If someone isn't speaking loud enough, I say "Please speak up—I'm hearing impaired!" No apologies for me!. . . .I am not going to withdraw from life because of feelings of embarrassment.

Feelings of Isolation and Loneliness

As deafness grows, socializing may be reduced to one-on-one encounters, to life within the home and family, to dependence on the spouse, or, ultimately, to utter solitude. Some may seek the company of other deafened people, which is more easily done in urban areas than it is in rural areas. Some want to learn speechreading, fingerspelling, and/or signing, partly as a means of communication and partly to meet other people with similar problems.

At each stage in a gradual removal from hearing society, the prospect of solitude emerges, either as a desolate state or as a condition which is at least relaxing and for some, preferable to the constant pain of contending with people who believe that you hear:

1. When I had my hearing I was an outgoing person. I don't care to be with people any more.
2. I have become more isolated, personality changes from a fun-loving type to a more skeptical person, less willing to confront rejection.
3. I avoid socializing and going out. It's too painful to sit there and be left out. . . . I'd rather stay home—alone!
4. It's a *lonely* disease. My love of people, and being with them, diminishes daily.
5. I tend to enjoy being with myself, because it is easier.
6. I am least alone when I am alone. Most alone at a dinner or cocktail party.

Some of the most poignant responses came from very deafened elderly persons, usually but not always living alone. They desperately want some human contact but no longer know how to obtain it. A seventy-three-year-old-woman, a former public school teacher, widowed twice, now lives by herself in a city apartment. Her hearing loss began at age sixty-three; one ear is now "useless"; she wears an aid in the other but cannot make out words:

I cannot communicate with people—it takes so long—trying to comprehend their point. . . . Learning *anything* is not easy at my age. I'm alone—no one to try to talk to, no one to say *"you are too loud!"* etc. I can't understand TV, so I kept it on to feel that someone is with me.

A man of sixty-five, recently retired from work as a draftsman, lives with a wife who is apparently considerate and understanding. His hearing loss began at twenty-eight; despite two aids, he now can barely hear loud noises.

I am very despondent and wonder if life is worth living. . . .I don't feel even a psychiatrist can help me. . . .I am ready and waiting for God to take me out of my miseries and know that when I get up to heaven I'll be able to hear.

An eighty-nine-year-old woman, whose long, gradual loss started at eighteen, is now so profoundly deaf that she does not use her aid—"Too noisy. Sounds like an iron foundry." Never married, she lives alone.

My greatest need is more companionship. There is an *awfulness* about silence. If someone would just drop in once in a while—smile—say Hi! and hand me a note "I'm on my way to the store—do you need anything? Postage stamps? Could I make a phone call for you?" etc. My only female neighbor said "I could visit you oftener but I haven't time to sit down and write." Understandable, isn't it? I am days at a time without speaking a word. It is affecting my voice and I fear for my mind. I can't hear the alarm clock, telephone ring, door bell, radio, television—or the human voice.... HAVE SOMEONE CROSS THE THRESHOLD OF THE SHUT-IN...EVERYDAY.

Impact on Family Relationships

As the case of the despondent husband may suggest, even a good marriage and a loving family give no immunity from the pains of deafness. Deafened people can find refuge and comfort at home, where family members are sympathetic, familiar with the condition—here, at least, they do not have to announce it—and can cater to special needs. Some adults whose families have an established history of hearing loss (with either an early or late onset) seem to be among our better adjusted respondents. Living with hearing loss and expecting it themselves, members of such families may take it for granted, like poor eyesight, obesity, or other conditions that "run in the family." "My hearing loss never affected my personal life because my mother taught me just what a hearing loss meant," a woman of sixty-seven, with an 80-decibel hearing level in her better ear, wrote: "She was developing her hearing loss when I was born so I had no fear when I was hearing less at age twenty-five." A librarian with a moderate hearing loss, who hears fairly well with an aid, says, "five of my children have hearing loss so we all understand each other."

While some feel that family experiences have prepared them for deafness, and that family members are sympathetic and helpful, others have feelings of frustration, impatience, and anger.

1. My own husband talks to me from another room or with his back to me. My own mother forgets that I am deaf.
2. With my family it's a constant conflict between their desire to have background music and my desire to join in conversation.
3. I felt he [her husband] mumbled and he felt I didn't pay attention when he was talking.
4. After twenty years, my wife cannot make allowance for my inability to hear her from another room.
5. My husband gets mad because I can't hear, and I get angry because he can't remember to look at me when talking to me.

Even a spouse who is usually patient and considerate, "an in-house saint," can at times be curt and impatient. Hearing as well as deafened persons can get weary of conversation that requires close attention and careful enunciation. When family members talk to one another, deafened people can feel as left out as if they were at someone else's party. In the family as in society, good conversation with them must be one-on-one or, at least, one at a time.

1. If only my family . . . would try a little harder to make me feel more comfortable—sitting one to one for instance, but they'd all rather sit around the living room and converse among themselves.
2. My worst problem is my husband's family—they all have very tiny soft voices—a nightmare! They don't seem to speak up no matter how often I remind them, so the past year I've been practicing "not caring" what they say unless they make a point to speak clearly and directly to me.
3. My family and long time friends are supportive, but it is inconvenient to include me in most communication. My pad and pencil slow them down.
4. My large family has a reunion at Thanksgiving. I feel like an outcast. They try so hard to include me but the quick repartee is impossible.

Reflective respondents recognize that adjustment in the family is an intricate, interactive process requiring accommodations on both sides of the sound barrier. "There has been more adjustment needed for my family than me," observed a man who hears well with an aid, "they are the ones who must speak up to be heard." One woman complained that "my family always wanted me to wear my hearing aid for THEIR convenience" and another that "my parents treated me normal. I think *too* normal." It is apparent that excessive sensitivity and moodiness—defining expected conduct too strictly and changing that definition too often—can be obstacles to successful adjustment in the family.

Adjustments in the Work Place

Hearing loss in the middle years usually requires numerous adjustments at work or a change of job. At age fifty or sixty, fewer adjustments are needed if early retirement can be taken. Those whose hearing loss begins early in childhood or adolescence (and 30% of respondents began to lose their hearing before they were twenty) have prepared for work at which hearing is not vital, such as printing or proofreading, the graphic arts, computer programming or data processing, or work as a librarian, clerk, statistician, or bookkeeper. Housewives may have trouble with a phone and a doorbell, but not with their other responsibilities. ("I can still cook, scrub, dust, balance the checkbook, etc. I'm lucky!") It is those who work in professions and occupations that take good hearing for granted, depend on the phone, and must talk with people in crowded or noisy places who face the most problems.

Those who make a good adjustment tend to have moderate losses, get adequate hearing with aids, or can make suitable changes in their tasks or working conditions. This is more feasible if they have been working at the same job for a long time, know it well, are well regarded and on good terms with their colleagues, if their hearing loss is known and their workmates are helpful.

A teacher may "walk nearer to the pupil to hear his response" or may ask students to talk louder or repeat. A therapist may shift from working with young children with high-pitched voices to working with adults, meeting them in a quiet room. A physician may use a stethoscope with a built-in hearing aid. A paralegal aide may shift from interviewing and phoning to library research and writing; a writer, from interview stories to stories based on other kinds of research; a postal employee, from office work involving use of the phone to mail delivery.

Many speak of the help they have received from co-workers. A secretary "worked at the same place . . . forty years and had wonderful supportive people;" a management analyst "was successful in my Civil Service job because of understanding on the part of many fellow workers and supervisors;" a bank clerk's boss "helps me when I receive or make phone calls to make sure I understand;" help with the phone is widespread.

In exchange for such help and consideration, a deafened person is likely to work hard and reliably at the same task for many years, at relatively low pay and with little or no advancement. The real compensation is job security and the comfort and relaxation that comes from working where the hearing problem is known and accepted.

Many do not find that compensation. Trying and failing to hear, misunderstanding what is said, and making embarrassing, annoying, or serious mistakes, they work under constant physical and emotional strain. Thus an electronic technician who wore no aid mistook instructions and was labeled stupid and inattentive. She "took to writing down all instructions and met with much impatience and annoyance;" after additional mistakes, she was fired. The owner of a large farm machinery business had a nervous breakdown trying to operate it with a severe hearing loss. A typist was tense concentrating, so as not to misunderstand the tapes she transcribed. A collection agent sometimes missed important questions that the judge asked in a small claims court; a teacher missed students' questions and was concerned that he might not hear the fire alarm.

CONCLUSION

The patterns of adjustment to work, to social life, and within the family are similar. Some deafened persons manage remarkably well; some suffer painfully, are anxious, tense, or embittered; and some simply withdraw from the arena. The first response may come from a mild loss; a determined, astute, or cheerful outlook that overrides, negotiates, or dismisses obstacles; or a placid or kindly disposition that evokes kindness in others and accepts the lot that has been offered. The second response, a striving to retain what has been lost, to remain what one no longer is, must produce strain and discontent, if not desperation. The third response, withdrawal from society, may be regrettable, but if it is deliberately chosen as a realistic accommodation by a self-sufficient person, it should not be faulted. If, however, the individual feels lonely, fearful, shunned, and abandoned, this is surely one of the saddest responses to the experience of deafness.

REFERENCES

Barker, R. G., and B. A. Wright, 1952. The social psychology of adjustment to physical disability. In *Psychological aspects of physical disability,* ed. J. F. Garrett, 18–32. Rehabilitation Service Series No. 210. Washington, DC: Office of Vocational Rehabilitation.

Beattie, J. A. 1981. *Social aspects of acquired hearing loss in adults.* A report on a research project funded by the Department of Health and Social Security and carried out in the Postgraduate School of Applied Social Studies, University of Bradford (England), 1978–1981: contents and findings.

Breed, P. C. M., A. P. J. M. van den Horst, and T. J. M. Mous. 1981. Psychosocial problems in suddenly deafened adolescents and adults. In *Congress Report: Proceedings of the First International Congress of the Hard of Hearing,* ed. H. Hartmann, 313–320. Deutscher Schwerhorigenbund, Hamburg.

Cooper, A. F., D. W. K. Kay, A. R. Curry, R. F. Garside, and M. Roth. 1974. Hearing loss in paranoid and affective psychosis of the elderly, *Lancet* 2: 851–854.

Glasgow, E. 1954. *The woman within.* New York: Harcourt, Brace.

Hartmann, H. 1981. *Congress Report: Proceedings of the First International Congress of the Hard of Hearing.* Deutscher Schwerhorigenbund, Hamburg.

Heider, F., and G. M. Heider. 1941. *Studies in the psychology of the deaf:* No. 2. *Psychological Monographs* 53 (Whole No. 242).

Heiner, M. H. 1949. *Hearing is believing.* Cleveland: World Publishing.

Kyle, J. G., ed. 1987. *Adjustment to acquired hearing loss: Analysis, change, and learning.* Bristol, England: The Centre for Deaf Studies.

Kyle, J. G., L. G. Jones, and P. L. Wood. 1985. Adjustment of acquired hearing loss: A working model. In *Adjustment to adult hearing loss,* ed. H. Orlans, 119–138. San Diego: College-Hill Press.

Kyle, J. G., and P. L. Wood. 1983. *Social and vocational aspects of acquired hearing loss,* Final Report to MSC, School of Education Research Unit, University of Bristol, England.

Meadow-Orlans, K. P. 1985. Social and psychological effects of hearing loss in adulthood: A literature review. In *Adjustment to adult hearing loss,* ed. H. Orlans, 35–58. San Diego: College-Hill Press.

Miller, L. V. 1975. The adult and the elderly: Health care and hearing loss. *Volta Review* 77: 57–63.

Milne, J. S. 1977. A longitudinal study of hearing loss in older people. *British Journal of Audiology* 11: 7–14.

Myklebust, H. R. 1964. *The psychology of deafness.* New York: Grune and Stratton.

Nett, E. M. 1960. *The relationships between audiological measures and handicap.* A project of the University of Pittsburgh School of Medicine and the Office of Vocational Rehabilitation, U. S. Department of Health, Education, and Welfare.

Orlans, H. 1988. Confronting deafness in an unstilled world. *Society* 25: 32–39.

Orlans, H., and K. P. Meadow-Orlans. 1984. Who are the members of SHHH? A report on the *Shhh* questionnaire. *Shhh* 5: 3–5.

———. 1985. Responses to hearing loss: Effects on social life, leisure, and work. *Shhh* 6: 4–7.

Oyer, H. J., and E. J. Oyer. 1979. Social consequences of hearing loss for the elderly. *Allied Health and Behavioral Sciences* 2: 123–137.

Reichstein, J., and L. von der Leith. 1981. Learning from the experiences of student teachers with simulated hearing loss. In *Congress Report: Proceedings of the First International Congress of the Hard of Hearing,* ed. H. Hartmann, 302–307. Deutscher Schwerhorigenbund, Hamburg.

Ries, P. W. 1985. The demography of hearing loss. In *Adjustment to adult hearing loss,* ed. H. Orlans, 3–22. San Diego: College-Hill Press.

Schein, J. D. 1987. The demography of deafness. In *Understanding deafness socially,* ed. P. C. Higgins and J. E. Nash, 3–28. Springfield, IL: Charles C. Thomas.

Solomon, M. 1977. *Beethoven.* New York: Schirmer Books.

Thomas A., and K. Gilhome-Herbst. 1980. Social and psychological implications of acquired deafness for adults of employment age. *British Journal of Audiology* 14: 76–85.

von der Lieth, L. 1972. Experimental social deafness. *Scandinavian Audiology* 1: 81–87.

Author Index

Subject Index

An *f* following a page number indicates a figure; a *t* following a page number indicates tabular material.